Handbook of Education, Training, and Supervision of School Psychologists in School and Community, Volume II

Handbook of Education, Training, and Supervision of School Psychologists in School and Community, Volume II

Bridging the Training and Practice Gap: Building Collaborative University/Field Practices

Edited by **Judith Kaufman,**
Tammy L. Hughes, and Cynthia A. Riccio

Routledge
Taylor & Francis Group
New York   London

Routledge
Taylor & Francis Group
270 Madison Avenue
New York, NY 10016

Routledge
Taylor & Francis Group
27 Church Road
Hove, East Sussex BN3 2FA

© 2010 by Taylor and Francis Group, LLC
Routledge is an imprint of Taylor & Francis Group, an Informa business

Printed in the United States of America on acid-free paper
10 9 8 7 6 5 4 3 2 1

International Standard Book Number: 978-0-415-96279-7 (Hardback)

Library of Congress Cataloging-in-Publication Data

García-Vázquez, Enedina.
    Handbook of education, training, and supervision of school psychologists in school and community / Enedina García-Vázquez, Tony D. Crespi, and Cynthia A. Riccio.
        p. cm.
    Includes bibliographical references and index.
    Contents: v. 1. Foundations of professional practice -- v. 2. Bridging the training and practice gap : building collaborative university/field practices.
        ISBN 978-0-415-96260-5 (v. 1. : alk. paper) -- ISBN 978-0-415-96279-7 (v. 2. : alk. paper)
    1. School psychologists--In-service training--Handbooks, manuals, etc. 2. School psychology--Study and teaching. I. Crespi, Tony D. II. Riccio, Cynthia A. III. Title.

LB3013.6.G37 2009
371.7'130683--dc22   2009017882

Visit the Taylor & Francis Web site at
http://www.taylorandfrancis.com

and the Routledge Web site at
http://www.routledgementalhealth.com

Contents

Volume I Contents   ix
Editors   xiii
Contributors   xv
Introduction   xxvii

PART I
Contemporary school psychology training:
University/field collaboration   1

1 Is everything old new again? School psychology training past,
  present, and future   3
  TAMMY L. HUGHES, JUDITH KAUFMAN, AND JEFFREY A. MILLER

PART II
What about supervision anyway? Trainers as supervisors   17

2 Contemporary issues in supervision   19
  JUDITH KAUFMAN

3 Competency-based school psychology practica: A collaborative
  training model   37
  J. STEVEN WELSH, SARAH MECHE, AND CARMEN BROUSSARD

4 Collaborative supervision of internship experiences   55
  GEORGE W. HEBERT AND CONSTANCE PATTERSON

5 Supervision of school psychology interns in a pediatric hospital   71
  ROBERT M. GORDON AND MICHELE ZACCARIO

6 Promoting university and schools partnership: Transnational
   considerations and future directions   89
   CHRYSE HATZICHRISTOU, AIKATERINI LAMPROPOULOU, KONSTANTINA
   LYKITSAKOU, AND PANAYIOTA DIMITROPOULOU

PART III
Difficult dialogues   109

7 Multicultural competence and diversity: University and
   field collaboration   111
   EMILIA C. LOPEZ AND MARGARET R. ROGERS

8 Problematic behaviors: Mediating differences and
   negotiating change   129
   TRACY K. CRUISE AND MARK E. SWERDLIK

9 Ethical and legal challenges: Negotiating change   153
   A. NICHOLE DAILOR AND SUSAN JACOB

10 Discrimination, harassment, and other challenging topics   169
   JUDITH KAUFMAN AND TAMMY L. HUGHES

11 Developing professional identity: Values, behaviors,
   and reputation   185
   LEA A. THEODORE, TAMMY L. HUGHES, AND JUDITH KAUFMAN

12 Preparing school psychologists to address the needs of gay,
   lesbian, bisexual, transgender, and questioning youth   205
   SUSAN JACOB, DANIEL D. DREVON, CHRISTINE M. ABBUHL, AND
   JONNIE L. TATON

PART IV
Professional issues   227

13 Certification and licensure for school psychologists:
   Considerations and implications for education, training,
   and practice   229
   TONY D. CRESPI

14 Continuing education: Fostering lifelong learning   245
   JULIE SNYDER, RALPH E. CASH, SARAH VALLEY-GRAY, AND
   KRISTEN CUNNINGHAM

15 Collaboration in school-based crisis intervention 263
STEPHEN E. BROCK, ELISE L. MARTINEZ, LLECENIA NAVARRO, AND
EVELYN TERAN

16 Community collaboration and university-based clinics in
school psychology 291
EDWARD M. LEVINSON, LYNANNE BLACK, MARY ANN RAFOTH,
AND JAIME E. SLONIM

PART V
Into the future 307

17 Creating congruent change: Linking research to practice 309
TAMMY L. HUGHES, JUDITH KAUFMAN, AND SALLY A. HOOVER

18 Envisioning the future: Looking into the crystal ball 321
TAMMY L. HUGHES, JUDITH KAUFMAN, TONY D. CRESPI, CYNTHIA A.
RICCIO, AND ENEDINA GARCÍA-VÁZQUEZ

Index 329

Volume I Contents

PART I
Contemporary school psychology training: The university

1 School psychology as a profession: Introduction and overview
CYNTHIA A. RICCIO, ENEDINA GARCÍA-VÁZQUEZ, AND TONY D. CRESPI

2 Putting school psychology training into historical perspective:
What's new? What's old?
THOMAS K. FAGAN

3 Creating a school psychology training program: The horse that
became a camel, or what tail wags the dog?
JUDITH KAUFMAN

4 What is so special about the specialist degree?
DANIEL C. MILLER, KATHY DEORNELLAS, AND DENISE MARICLE

5 Combined–integrated training: An alternative to traditional
school psychology training models
ABRAHAM GIVNER

PART II
Foundations of training

6 How much theory do we teach?
BONNIE KAUL NASTASI

7 Teaching ethical and legal issues
BARBARA BOLE WILLIAMS, AMANDA SINKO, AND FRANK J. EPIFANIO

8 Multiculturalism and diversity: Implications for the training of
   school psychologists
   ELSA ARROYOS-JURADO, IVELISSE TORRES FERNÁNDEZ, AND
   RACHEL L. NAVARRO

9 Preparing students for leadership roles
   CLARE N. LOWELL, ROBERT J. RIMMER, AND ROGER D. ZEEMAN

PART III
Training for assessment and evidence-based practice

10 Culture and psychoeducational assessment: Cognition and
    achievement
    YUMA I. TOMES

11 The importance of personality assessment in school psychology
    training programs
    TAMMY L. HUGHES, KARA E. MCGOEY, AND PATRICK OWEN

12 Neuropsychology in school psychology
    CATHERINE A. FIORELLO, JAMES B. HALE, SCOTT L. DECKER, AND
    SCHEHERA COLEMAN

PART IV
Training for intervention: Systems, settings, and
special populations

13 School-based mental health: Training school psychologists for
    comprehensive service delivery
    ROSEMARY B. MENNUTI AND RAY W. CHRISTNER

14 Educating consultants for practice in the schools
    SYLVIA ROSENFIELD, MARY LEVINSOHN-KLYAP, AND KATURAH CRAMER

15 Adolescent incarceration and children's psychiatric
    hospitalization: Training school psychologists for
    nontraditional settings
    TONY D. CRESPI AND JEFFREY R. LOVELACE

16 A framework for working with emotional and behavioral
    disorders: Considerations for trainers
    ANITA SOHN MCCORMICK AND CONSTANCE J. FOURNIER

17 Training for work with special populations: Children with
chronic illness
LEADELLE PHELPS

PART V
School psychology training: Rooted in the past, practicing
in the present, and contemplating the future: Summary
and conclusions

18 Into the future: New directions for education and training
ENEDINA GARCÍA-VÁZQUEZ, TONY D. CRESPI, CYNTHIA A. RICCIO,
TAMMY L. HUGHES, AND JUDITH KAUFMAN

Index

Editors

Tony D. Crespi, EdD, ABPP, is presently a professor of psychology at the University of Hartford in Connecticut. A licensed psychologist, licensed marriage and family therapist, certified school counselor, and certified school psychologist, he holds board certification in school psychology from the American Board of Professional Psychology. A past president of Trainers of School Psychologists, he has published several books and approximately 100 professional articles, focusing on such areas as professional credentialing and clinical supervision, ethics and legal issues, and psychopathology in adolescents.

Tammy L. Hughes, PhD, is an associate professor at Duquesne University and the 2009–2010 president of the Division of School Psychology (16) of the American Psychological Association (APA). She is also the cochair of the School Psychology Leadership Roundtable and a past president of Trainers of School Psychologists, and serves on the APA Presidential Task Force planning the summit on the Future of Psychology Practice: Collaborating for Change. She is committed to solving the social issues that children face at school by bridging the gap between university teaching and field-based training. Dr. Hughes is an associate editor for *Psychology in the Schools* and serves on the editorial board of *The Journal of School Violence* and the *International Journal of Offender Therapy and Comparative Criminology.* She is the author and coauthor of numerous books, journal articles, chapters, and other publications on child violence, differentiating emotional disturbance and social maladjustment, and understanding the relationship between emotional dysregulation and conduct problems in children.

Judith Kaufman, PhD, ABPP, is a professor at Fairleigh Dickinson University (FDU). She holds a diploma in school psychology and currently serves as secretary of the American Academy of School Psychology and chair of the Advisory Board of Trainers of School Psychologists. Dr. Kaufman has held leadership positions in several national and regional organizations and has chaired several APA site visit teams. Prior to coming to FDU, Dr. Kaufman was director of school psychology training at Ferkauf Graduate School and also served as visiting faculty at the University of Wisconsin, Madison, and the Institute of Education, London, United Kingdom. Her research interests include supervision, cultural and individual differences, and risk and resiliency factors in emerging adulthood.

Cynthia A. Riccio is a professor, director of training for the School Psychology program, and a member of the neuroscience faculty at Texas A&M University. Her research interests include attention deficit/hyperactivity disorder, pediatric neuropsychology, and learning/language disorders. She also is involved in research related to autism spectrum disorders. Her current research has direct implications for the practice and science of school psychology across disability areas, with an emphasis on the developmental trajectory from middle school to high school and beyond.

Enedina García-Vázquez, PhD, associate dean/deputy director, leads the Information Sciences and Security Systems department of the Physical Science Laboratory at New Mexico State University. She holds tenure and full professor rank in the Counseling and Educational Psychology department. Dr. Vázquez serves as the editor of the *Trainers' Forum*, the journal of the Trainers of School Psychologists, a national organization concerned with the graduate preparation of future school psychologists. Dr. Vázquez is also the chair of the National Association of School Psychologists (NASP) Program Approval Board. In this capacity, she leads the process for school psychology programs seeking NASP approval.

Contributors

Christine M. Abbuhl, BA, is a school psychology doctoral student at Central Michigan University. Her primary research interest is deliberate self-harm in adolescents. Her writing in this book developed through working with a diverse group of professionals in creating a program to address the needs of local gay, lesbian, bisexual, transgender, and questioning (GLBTQ) youth.

Elsa Arroyos-Jurado, PhD, is an associate professor and director of training in school psychology at New Mexico State University. She earned her PhD in school psychology from the University of Iowa. Her interests include multicultural competencies in practice and training, neuropsychology, and mentoring of students and early career faculty.

Lynanne Black, PhD, is a certified school psychologist and assistant professor at Indiana University of Pennsylvania. She has taught numerous courses at the undergraduate and graduate levels in the areas of educational psychology, learning, behavior, assessment and intervention, and family–school relations. Her specialties include preschool assessment, parental involvement, and emergent and early literacy.

Stephen E. Brock, PhD, is a professor at California State University, Sacramento (CSUS). He worked for 18 years as a school psychologist before joining the CSUS faculty. Dr. Brock is the California representative to the National Association of School Psychologists (NASP) Delegate Assembly. In addition, he is a member of the National Emergency Assistance Team and cochair of the PREPaRE Crisis Prevention and Intervention Training Curriculum.

Carmen Broussard, PhD, is an associate professor of school psychology at Nicholls State University, where she also serves as program director for the Specialist in School Psychology program. Her research interests include assessment and intervention with early reading and mathematics, functional behavior assessment and intervention with disruptive behaviors in young children, and program evaluation of graduate training programs.

Ralph E. Cash, PhD, NCSP, is an associate professor of psychology at Nova Southeastern University (NSU), director of The NSU School Psychology Assessment and Consultation Center, a past president of the Florida Association of School Psychologists (FASP), and president of the National Association of School Psychologists. Dr. Cash recently received FASP's Lifetime Achievement Award for his service to the profession.

Ray W. Christner, PsyD, NCSP, is a school psychologist with South Middleton School District, Boiling Springs, Pennsylvania, and is on the faculty at the Philadelphia College of Osteopathic Medicine. He is coeditor of *School-Based Mental Health: A Practitioner's Guide to Comparative Practices* (Routledge, 2008) and *Cognitive-Behavioral Intervention in Educational Settings: A Handbook for Practice* (Routledge, 2005).

Schehera Coleman, MEd, is pursuing her PhD in school psychology at Temple University. Ms. Coleman is also a certified school psychologist currently working for the School District of Philadelphia.

Katurah Cramer, PhD, received her doctoral degree in school psychology at the University of Maryland. Her publications are on consultation supervision and instructional assessment. She currently provides on-line coaching for new instructional consultation team facilitators. She is on family leave until 2011 from the Howard County Public Schools, where she has been a school psychologist.

Tracy K. Cruise, PhD, is a professor of psychology at Western Illinois University (WIU). She is a certified school psychologist and licensed clinical psychologist who teaches and supervises Child Psychotherapy for the School Psychology and Clinical/Community Mental Health graduate programs at WIU. Dr. Cruise publishes and presents workshops in the area of child abuse (e.g., Child Abuse & Neglect: The School's Response) and internship supervision.

Kristen Cunningham, PsyD, is a clinical and adjunct faculty member at the Center for Psychological Studies at NSU. She is the acting director of the School Psychology Assessment and Consultation Center at the Psychology Services Center at NSU. Dr. Cunningham also serves as the chief psychologist at the Autism Spectrum Disorders Assessment and Diagnostic Clinic at the Unicorn Children's Foundation Clinic of NSU's Mailman Segal Institute for Early Childhood Studies.

A. Nichole Dailor, MS, is a doctoral student at Central Michigan University finishing her dissertation on the use of an e-mail discussion list to facilitate peer consultation for resolving ethical concerns. She completed her APA pre-doctoral internship in August 2008 through the Menta Group and currently is a school psychologist for the Bourbonnais Elementary School District in Bourbonnais, IL.

Scott L. Decker, PhD, specializes in neuropsychology and research methodology. He was a coauthor of the Bender-Gestalt II and taught neuropsychology and research methodology. He also served in a joint appointment at the University of Illinois at Chicago Neuropsychiatric Institute as a pediatric neuropsychologist. Currently, he is an assistant professor at Georgia State University.

Kathy DeOrnellas, PhD, LSSP, is an assistant professor in the School psychology graduate program and the director of the Specialist in School psychology graduate program at Texas Woman's University. She is a licensed psychologist. She also contracts with area school districts to provide psychological services and maintains a private practice where she provides assessment and therapy for children and families.

Panayiota Dimitropoulou, PhD, is a school psychologist working in a primary school setting. She is a member of the scientific team of the Centre for Research and Practice in School Psychology. Her research interests include mental health promotion, school-based prevention and intervention programs, and learning difficulties.

Daniel D. Drevon, BS, is a doctoral student at Central Michigan University. He conducts his research through the Center for Research, Training, and Consultation on GLBTQ Youth Issues at Central Michigan University. His research interests include GLBTQ youth issues and applied behavior analysis.

Frank J. Epifanio, PhD, NCSP, was a former associate professor in the School Psychology program at Rowan University, Glassboro, New Jersey. He was past president of the New Jersey Association of School Psychologists. He was also a school psychologist and director of special services. He died in November 2008 after a brief illness.

Thomas K. Fagan, PhD, is a 1969 graduate in school psychology at Kent State University and is professor of psychology and coordinator of the School Psychology program at the University of Memphis. He serves as historian to the National Association of School Psychologists and to the Division of School Psychology in the American Psychological Association. Dr. Fagan is a professor of psychology at the University of Memphis and has twice served as president of the NASP.

Ivelisse Torres Fernández, PhD, is an assistant professor in the Department of Counseling and Educational Psychology at New Mexico State University.

She earned her PhD in school psychology from the University of Iowa. Her research interests include social–emotional development in children and adolescents, resiliency, child and adolescent psychopathology, and multiculturalism and diversity.

Catherine A. Fiorello, PhD, received her doctoral degree in school psychology from the University of Kentucky in December 1992. She is an associate professor and director of the School Psychology program at Temple University. She specializes in assessment, especially developmental assessment in early childhood, assessment of children with disabilities, and cognitive and neuropsychological assessment.

Constance J. Fournier, PhD, is a clinical professor in the Department of Educational Psychology at Texas A&M University and is a licensed psychologist. She has appointments in the Special Education and School Psychology programs. She has numerous presentations and publications, and is active in the American Psychological Association (APA), NASP, and Council for Exceptional Children.

Abraham Givner, PhD, NCSP, is a professor of psychology and director of the Combined School-Clinical Child Psychology program, Yeshiva University, Bronx, New York, where he holds the Ferkauf-Silverstein Chair in School Psychology. Dr. Givner is a licensed psychologist in New York and New Jersey. He received his PhD in educational psychology from Yeshiva University in 1972. He is one of the founding members and the treasurer of the Consortium of Combined-Integrated Doctoral Programs in Psychology.

Robert M. Gordon, PsyD, has been working at the Rusk Institute of Rehabilitation Medicine at New York University Langone Medical Center since completing his doctoral degree at Yeshiva University's Child Clinical/School Psychology program in 1986. At the Rusk Institute, Dr. Gordon is the director of intern and postdoctoral fellow training and a clinical associate professor. He received a certificate in psychoanalysis and psychotherapy from Adelphi University in 1999. He has specialties in neuropsychological and forensic testing and psychotherapy with children and adults with physical and learning disabilities and chronic illnesses. He has published in the areas of ethics, supervision, relational psychoanalysis, dream interpretation, group therapy, and parental coping styles.

James B. Hale, PhD, MEd, ABSNP, is a licensed psychologist, certified school psychologist, and certified special education teacher. He is an associate professor and associate director of Clinical Training in the Department of Psychology at the Philadelphia College of Osteopathic Medicine.

Dr. Hale has pursued multiple lines of research, including studies that differentiate reading and math disability subtypes, challenge assumptions about the validity of global IQ interpretation, examine language and psychosocial functions associated with right hemisphere learning disabilities, and explore neuropsychological aspects of ADHD and medication response. Dr. Hale is an active researcher, practitioner, presenter, and author, including his coauthorship of the critically acclaimed, bestselling book *School Neuropsychology: A Practitioner's Handbook* (Psychology Press/Taylor & Francis, 2003).

Chryse Hatzichristou, PhD, is a professor of school psychology and director of the Center for Research and Practice in School Psychology at the Department of Psychology, University of Athens, Athens, Greece. She received her master's degree from Harvard and her PhD from the University of California, Berkeley. She chairs the Division of School Psychology of the Hellenic Psychological Society, and she has served as secretary of the Executive Committee of the International School Psychology Association. Her primary research interests include service delivery models, primary and secondary prevention programs in schools, school-based consultation, and cross-cultural and cross-national issues in school psychology.

George W. Hebert, PhD, is currently an assistant professor at the Louisiana State University Health Sciences Center in New Orleans, where he coordinates the APA-accredited Louisiana School Psychology Internship Consortium. Dr. Hebert is a licensed psychologist who has served in both urban and rural school settings. In addition, he served many years as the director of a public child/adolescent mental health clinic. His current research interests are focused on measurement issues surrounding various responses to intervention models. Dr. Hebert has always been active in the field of school psychology in both state and national professional organizations.

Sally A. Hoover, PhD, is currently director of pupil services at Quaker Valley School District, Sewickley, Pennsylvania. She is responsible for supervising psychology, guidance, and health service providers, including school psychology practicum students, and interns in a K-12 environment. Her responsibilities include providing universal screening in reading and math, coordinating direct services to general and special education students, and running special education programs.

Susan Jacob, PhD, is a professor of psychology at Central Michigan University (CMU). She is the author of numerous books and articles on ethical–legal issues in school psychology and also serves as the director of CMU's Center for Research, Training, and Consultation on GLBTQ Youth.

Aikaterini Lampropoulou, PhD, is a school psychologist working in a clinical setting. She is a member of the scientific team of the Centre for Research and Practice in School Psychology. Her research interests include mental health promotion, school-based prevention and intervention programs, and family–school partnership.

Mary Levinsohn-Klyap, PhD, who received her doctoral degree in school psychology from the University of Maryland, is the Howard County (Maryland) Public Schools district facilitator for problem-solving teams. Her work includes providing professional development in consultation and teaming with staff and interns. She has taught consultation courses at the University of Maryland.

Edward M. Levinson, EdD, NCSP, is the chair of the Educational and School Psychology Department and a professor of educational and school psychology at Indiana University of Pennsylvania. He has authored three books and more than 70 journal articles. His chapters on vocational assessment and/or transition appear in all five editions of the NASP's *Best Practices in School Psychology,* and his chapters on career development appear in both editions of the NASP's *Children's Needs.*

Emilia C. Lopez, PhD, is a professor and the director of the bilingual and multicultural specializations in the School Psychology program at Queens College, City University of New York. Her areas of interest are multicultural consultation, providing services via interpreters, bilingual School Psychology, and cross-cultural competencies.

Jeffrey R. Lovelace, MS, is a certified school psychologist with the West Hartford (Connecticut) Public Schools. He received his master's degree and specialist training in the School Psychology program at the University of Hartford. He has also completed course requirements for credentialing as a licensed professional counselor.

Clare N. Lowell, EdD, is an assistant professor of education at Marymount Manhattan College, New York City. She was a teacher and administrator in public education on Long Island for over 30 years. She earned her doctoral degree at Hofstra University, her master's in journalism at Columbia, and her master's in English literature at Adelphi.

Konstantina Lykitsakou, PhD, is a school psychologist working in a preschool setting. She is a member of the scientific team of the Centre for Research and Practice in School Psychology. Her research interests include mental health promotion, school-based prevention and intervention programs, systemic family therapy, statistics, and research methodology.

Denise Maricle, PhD, is an associate professor in the School Psychology graduate programs and the director of the Doctoral School Psychology graduate program at Texas Woman's University. Her research interests include school neuropsychology, neuropsychological assessment with children, role and function of school psychologists, and others. She teaches graduate level courses in school psychology and psychological tests and measurements for undergraduates.

Elise L. Martinez, MA, is a school psychologist in the Western Placer Unified School District in Lincoln, California. She is also a graduate student at CSUS. Ellie's research interests are in the area of crisis intervention with a specific interest in youth suicide postvention.

Anita Sohn McCormick, PhD, is a clinical assistant professor in the School Psychology program in the Department of Educational Psychology at Texas A&M University. She holds a PhD and a master's degree in school psychology. Her research interests include bilingual and cultural issues in assessment and evidence-based interventions for English language learner students.

Kara E. McGoey, PhD, is an associate professor and the director of the School Psychology Training program at Duquesne University in Pittsburgh, Pennsylvania. She is also a consultant to the Early Childhood Program at Children's Hospital of Pittsburgh and the University, Community, Leaders and Individuals with Disabilities Center at the University of Pittsburgh. Dr. McGoey's research interests and recent publications include topics on the assessment of and intervention with young children with behavior problems.

Sarah Meche, BA, has her bachelor's degree in psychology and is currently a graduate student in the School Psychology program at Nicholls State University. Sarah's research interests include autism spectrum disorders and the functional behavioral assessment and intervention with children with low-incidence disabilities.

Rosemary B. Mennuti, EdD, NCSP, is a professor and the director of School Psychology programs in the Department of Psychology at the Philadelphia College of Osteopathic Medicine. She is coeditor of *Cognitive Behavioral Interventions in Educational Settings: A Handbook for Practice* (Routledge, 2005) and *School-Based Mental Health: A Practitioner's Guide to Comparative Practices* (Routledge, 2008).

Daniel C. Miller, PhD, ABPP, ABSNP, NCSP, LSSP, is a professor in the School Psychology programs and chair of the Department of Psychology and Philosophy at Texas Woman's University, Denton. Dr. Miller is a licensed psychologist and a past president of the National Association of School Psychologists.

Jeffrey A. Miller, PhD, ABPP, is a diplomate in school psychology and the associate dean for graduate studies and research at Duquesne University. He is a past president of the American Academy of School Psychology and the current chair of the School Psychology Specialty Council. Dr. Miller's scholarship is in the areas of school psychology training and neuropsychology for teaching and learning.

Bonnie Kaul Nastasi, PhD, is an associate professor in the Department of Psychology at Tulane University. Dr. Nastasi's research focuses on the use of mixed methods research to develop culturally specific theories and evidence-based interventions. She is president-elect of Division 16 of the American Psychological Association.

LLecenia Navarro, PhD, is a practicing school psychologist in Sacramento, California. Her current interests include bilingual assessments, academic and behavioral interventions, and crisis intervention and response. She holds a BA degree in liberal studies and an MA in education from the California State University, Sacramento.

Rachel L. Navarro, PhD, is an assistant professor in the Department of Counseling and Educational Psychology at New Mexico State University. She earned her PhD in counseling psychology from the University of Missouri. Dr. Navarro specializes in multicultural vocational psychology. She teaches research methodology, career development, assessment, and counseling practicum courses.

Patrick Owen, PsyD, is a licensed psychologist and certified school psychologist working full time as a practitioner at Kershaw County School District in Camden, South Carolina. He is interested in how results from personality assessment measures inform the implementation of individualized education program goals. His previous publications address the usefulness of performance-based measures in the applied setting.

Constance Patterson, PhD, is a faculty member and field placement coordinator at Walden University. Dr. Patterson is interested in the range of issues involved in training school psychologists, especially as they enter the field during internship experiences. She lives in New Orleans, Louisiana.

LeAdelle Phelps, PhD, is a professor at the University at Buffalo, State University of New York, and has published three books and more than 75 journal articles and book chapters on adolescent health-related issues. She has been identified as one of the top 20 researchers in school psychology and received the 2006 Division 16 Jack Bardon Award.

Mary Ann Rafoth, PhD, is dean of the College of Education and Educational Technology at Indiana University of Pennsylvania. Her research interests involve learning skills, alternatives to retention, school readiness issues, and program and student learning outcomes evaluation. Dr. Rafoth has more than 30 publications and 50 presentations, including several chapters in the NASP's *Best Practices in School Psychology* series.

Robert J. Rimmer, EdD, is an assistant professor of educational leadership at William Paterson University, Wayne, New Jersey. He served for 32 years in public education as a teacher, counselor, principal, and superintendent of schools. He earned master's degrees from William Paterson in student personnel services and educational administration and his doctorate from Rutgers.

Margaret R. Rogers, PhD, is a faculty member of the School Psychology program at the University of Rhode Island. Her research interests include cross-cultural competencies of school psychologists, recruitment and retention of underrepresented students in psychology, and social justice.

Sylvia Rosenfield, PhD, is a professor at the University of Maryland and teaches the two-semester consultation course sequence to school psychology students. Her research and publications focus on instructional consultation and other forms of consultee-centered consultation. Her publications include *Implementing Evidence-Based Academic Interventions in Schools* (Oxford University Press, 2009), and *Instructional Consultation, Instructional Consultation Teams: Collaborating for Change* (Guilford Press, 1996).

Amanda Sinko, MA, is a school psychology graduate student and graduate assistant at Rowan University. She is currently completing her practicum in the Southampton Township School District in New Jersey and with the New Jersey Department of Education's Developing Safe and Civil Schools Project.

Jaime E. Slonim, MEd, is a graduate student completing her internship with the Seneca Valley School District in Harmony, Pennsylvania. She earned her master's degree in educational psychology from Indiana University of Pennsylvania in 2007. Her professional interests include neuropsychological assessment, executive dysfunction, trauma and resilience, and minority issues.

Julie Snyder, MS, is a doctoral student at the Center for Psychological Studies (CPS) at NSU. During her formal academic training she served as coordinator of continuing education at CPS. She is currently completing her predoctoral internship at the University of Miami/Mailman Center for Child Development.

Mark E. Swerdlik, PhD, ABPP, is a professor of psychology and coordinator of the School Psychology graduate programs at Illinois State University. He is a diplomate in school psychology and assessment psychology and a fellow of Division 16 (School Psychology) of the American Psychological Association. Dr. Swerdlik has more than 30 years of experience as a university educator. His scholarship is in the area of clinical supervision.

Jonnie L. Taton, MS, Ed, is a school psychologist with the Mt. Pleasant Public Schools, Mt. Pleasant, Michigan. She completed research on an instructional unit to foster more positive attitudes toward GLBTQ youth as part of her specialist degree studies at Central Michigan University.

Evelyn Teran, MA, completed her master's degree in school psychology at the California State University, Sacramento, after completing a double major in psychology and Spanish at the University of California, Davis. She currently works as a school psychologist with the Woodland Joint Unified School District.

Lea A. Theodore, PhD, is an associate professor in the School Psychology program at the College of William and Mary. Her research interests include developing classroom-based interventions for children with academic and behavior problems. Dr. Theodore is the vice president of professional affairs for the Division of School Psychology of the American Psychological Association and an associate editor for *School Psychology Quarterly*.

Yuma I. Tomes, PhD, is an associate professor and the director of the Master of Science School Psychology program at the Philadelphia College of Osteopathic Medicine. His research and teaching interests are multicultural/cross-cultural psychology, cognitive styles, and GLBTQ/diversity issues. Dr. Tomes is the author of several publications, book chapters, and reviews focusing on learning in diverse populations. Currently he is working on a cross-cultural text for mental health practitioners.

Sarah Valley-Gray, PsyD, is an associate professor and the director of continuing education at the Center for Psychological Studies at NSU. Dr. Valley-Gray spearheaded the development of the School Psychology programs at NSU and has served in a variety of leadership roles within the areas of training and credentialing.

J. Steven Welsh, PhD, is a professor of school psychology and the department head of psychology at Nicholls State University. He has presented and published articles on the topic of supervision in school psychology. He is a NASP program reviewer, has served as the chair of the NASP Special Interest Group in Supervision, and has consulted with school psychology training programs preparing for the accreditation process.

Barbara Bole Williams, PhD, NCSP, is a professor and the coordinator of the School Psychology program at Rowan University, Glassboro, New Jersey; the author of *Professional Ethics for School Psychologists: A Problem-Solving Casebook* (NASP Publications, 2008); a former member of the NASP Ethics Committee; a current member of the NASP's Ethics Advisory Panel; and the current national chair for revisions of NASP standards.

Michele Zaccario, PhD, is a licensed clinical psychologist employed as an assistant professor of graduate psychology at Pace University in New York City and as a pediatric psychologist at New York University Langone Medical Center's Rusk Institute of Rehabilitation Medicine and Neonatal Intensive Care Unit. She is a clinical supervisor of psychology doctoral students and leads multidisciplinary seminars on behavioral issues associated with medically fragile infants and children.

Roger D. Zeeman, PhD, NCSP, is the chair of education at Marymount Manhattan College, New York City. Previously, he was an associate professor and chair of special education at William Paterson University. Other professional experiences in New Jersey include school administrator, principal, and school and licensed psychologist. His degrees are from Harvard and Yeshiva.

Introduction

The field of school psychology is in a constant state of change. Demographics, definitions, disabilities, techniques, and strategies together with legislation and federal mandates are continuously shifting and creating new challenges for both education and training. At the same time, there are a core set of values shared by university and field-based trainers and practitioners that serve as the foundation of the profession. University training programs shape the future of the profession and simultaneously respond to the pragmatic needs of the populations we serve and the demands of the education system. While there have been several quality handbooks focusing on the history of school psychology, ethics, and professional practice and techniques, few, if any, focus on education and training issues and their translation to field-based practice. There is an explicit need to examine the essential tenets of the profession, critically review training and practice issues, and evaluate how the traditional and changing skills and issues translate into meeting the needs of children and the systems that serve them.

This two-volume handbook addresses the challenges of the training enterprise and its application. Volume I particularly examines contemporary issues of school psychology training at the university level. The topics explored range from broad considerations around the challenges of program development, considering various levels and models of training to the more specific issues of teaching of specialty skills and training for unique areas and special populations. Volume I serves as the template for the second volume of the handbook by way of raising questions and issues that ultimately play out in the field. Volume II is dedicated to bridging the training and practice gap.

Volume II examines issues critical to the practice of school psychology. Authors explore the nature of supervision at different stages of training (e.g., practicum and internship) and in a variety of settings. Each chapter raises issues, reflectively, for university training in a manner that facilitates the dialogue between university and field trainers. Problematic graduate student behaviors and the difficult dialogues that both university and field-based trainers encounter are responded to with an evidenced-based and direct approach. Volume II also considers issues of professional development, credentialing, and developing a professional identity, topics that predominate in practice settings yet are typically not addressed in any school psychology text.

Trainers of School Psychologists (TSP) are particularly proud to sponsor these two volumes. As an organization of university and field-based trainers representing school psychology programs at both the MA/specialist and doctoral levels of training across the country and internationally, we intend this handbook to serve our mutual goals in training the next generation of school psychologists. Specifically, the goal of this two-volume handbook is to support the TSP mission, which states:

> *TSP is committed to innovation and excellence in graduate training programs for specialist and doctoral school psychologists.... This is achieved by examining current trends in graduate education, providing professional growth opportunities to school psychology faculty, facilitating communication with field-based trainers and supervisors and initiating and supporting legislative efforts that promote excellence in training and practice.*

The contents of these volumes clearly support and further the mission of TSP and of the field itself. Each volume, while standing alone as an important resource, mirrors the other and enables issues and concepts to be translated from theory to practice. We invite all of our training colleagues to bridge the gaps.

Part I

Contemporary school psychology training

University/field collaboration

1 Is everything old new again?

School psychology training past, present, and future

Tammy L. Hughes, Judith Kaufman, and Jeffrey A. Miller

Volume I of *Handbook of Education, Training, and Supervision of School Psychologists in School and Community* focuses on the preparation of professionals within the university setting and examines in depth the best practices of teaching and training. Volume II centers on bridging the gap between university education and training with the pragmatics of field-based practice. Critical to this relationship is the collaboration between university and field-based trainers.

Clearly, the foundational skills acquired at the university level are the building blocks for future practice, whereas field-based experiences provide the application and expansion of skills through practicum training. Integration, refinement, and reinforcement of those skills are accomplished through internship and lifelong education. The university is the vehicle for collaboration and communication within the field. Field-based practitioners and trainers can inform university education with detailed feedback regarding professional preparation that students demonstrate, and the university's training program can provide consultation and continuing education through workshops and information sessions. Most importantly, the university can and should serve as a mechanism to bridge the gap between research and practice. The chapters in Volume II provide a contemporary review of literature, together with strategies and techniques that can enrich the collaborative enterprise, providing knowledge and opportunities to strengthen both training and practice and educate, in the best possible way, the next generation of school psychologists.

Although the history of school psychology as a profession has been well documented (Fagan & Wise, 2000; Chapter 2, Volume I, among others), the evolution and development of school psychology training programs is less well known. The assumption is that training practices have developed in parallel with the growth and recognition of the profession of school psychology. Certainly, with the establishment of the Division of School Psychology (Division 16) of the American Psychological Association (APA) in 1944–1945 and the development of the National Association of School Psychologists (NASP) in 1968, when there was an enormous growth of membership in the profession, there has been an increasing relative conformity in training and credentialing requirements across states to practice as a school psychologist. Typically, as a profession becomes well defined, and particularly as a specialty becomes recognized within a profession, professional organizations evolve to protect and further the interests of that enterprise. Within school psychology, NASP has affiliate state associations in every state, along with an informal but strong connection with the International School Psychology Association. The APA has a direct relationship with state psychological associations, many of which have a school psychology division. Although both APA and NASP, along with their affiliates, represent the interests of school psychologists, these groups frequently approach problems from a variety of angles that may or may not conflict. In fact, these groups often become deeply involved with important legislative issues that can result in changes in the provision of services to children and role and function of school psychologists. Ultimately, changes in practice expectations and requirements become important university training considerations.

Although the promulgation of professional standards has been ongoing, training program adjustments have been less uniform. Training programs have been asked to adapt from a master's-only profession to a master's plus certification (e.g., EdS, CAGS) to address the requirements of a national credential in addition to state requirements (i.e., Nationally Certified School Psychologist). They have also had to consider practices for emergency certification (Crespi & Hughes, 2006) and respecialization for psychologists who are not credentialed to practice (e.g., developmental psychologist), as well as for other professional practice psychologists hired to help address the shortages of mental health providers in the school system (Tharinger & Palomares, 2004). The responsiveness and changes of training programs to these types of challenges are not as clearly delineated as the type of changes that follow from credentialing standards.

The reality that national and state credentialing agencies were impacting the definition and practice of the school psychologists created the need for discussions among academics in training programs about training issues independent of the politics of any professional organization. Trainers of School Psychologists evolved in the early 1970s in order to represent all levels of school psychology training. In 1977, the Council of Directors of School Psychology Programs was developed, focusing on doctoral training programs. Other organizations have emerged either formally or informally to address training needs. School Psychology Synarchy, now called School Psychology Specialty Council, was developed as an interorganizational group to examine, advocate, and ensure quality for education, training, credentialing, and professional practice in school psychology. The Interorganizational Committee (IOC) was initially developed in 1978 to collaborate between APA and NASP on issues surrounding the accreditation, titling, and credentialing of school psychologists and address differences in requirements when necessary. The IOC was disbanded in

December 2002 after the APA Board of Directors concluded that the IOC was not an effective mechanism to deal with issues that have arisen between the two associations. The multimember IOC team was replaced by establishing direct lines of communications between NASP and the APA's Practice Directorate's Office of Policy and Advocacy in the Schools to continue exchanges between organizations, which remains in place at the time of this writing. In addition, many states have either a formal or informal trainers' network that meet regularly (e. g., School Psychology Educators Council of New York State) or on an as-needed basis to respond to legislative and training changes. Although each organization serves a slightly different audience, they are similar in their provision of peer support networks, providing a venue for active collegial interaction within states and across training programs throughout the United States and internationally.

It is obvious that the ongoing conversation among training programs is the best way to prepare future school psychologists while responding to the developing needs of the field, faculty shortages, limited diversity among both faculty and student training populations, and fulfilling the requirements of national, regional, and state credentialing bodies. In the history of our profession, there have been multiple forces that have impacted the evolution and direction of our training models.

FOCUS, FACTORS, AND FORCES

Professional psychologist training is highly regulated in general. Professional school psychology practice has even more regulation because of the bifurcated nature of our professional organizations (e.g., NASP and APA) and because state boards of education (SBE) regulate graduate programs that certify personnel to work in public schools. Thus, field supervisors may be flummoxed by the operation of graduate training programs that may be Byzantine by the very nature of the ivory tower but also seem to frequently change the expectations of the students we train and the nature of the relationship with field-based trainers.

The gap between research and practice is perpetuated, in part, by the disconnect between university faculty and field supervisors. The university supervisor may assume that since an article has been published in a top tier journal with a high impact factor rating, its findings are being implemented in the schools by practicing school psychologists. Similarly, field-based trainers may assume that university faculty are aware of the political realities of their school system and the nature of the barriers to implementing research findings. Also, because faculty are faced with the challenges of keeping up with practice and staying current on the issues impacting the delivery of services, it can be the case that a university faculty member perpetuates a dated practice or approach because the university faculty member was confident of the practice when originally trained. Of course, the changing landscape of education and psychology can render previous approaches and practices ineffective.

These issues have existed for a long time, and the typical solutions employed include annual field supervisor meetings with the university faculty or e-mail blasts updating supervisors on the latest change in internship logs. Although these approaches are helpful, they fail to work because they lack practice and repetition. University faculty are very good at creating curricula and conducting research. Field supervisors are very good at dealing with changing regulations around special education laws, supporting the school environment in a crisis situation, or knowing the newest fad illicit drugs or social practices in which youth are engaged. However, because each group is not routinely involved in the other's context, the annual supervisor meeting or one-way communication of e-mail does little to effectively share each other's knowledge bases.

From an analysis of this gap, it will be clear that there are several pragmatic barriers. A primary barrier is time. Ask any university faculty member and he or she will say there is not enough time to do the research, teaching, and service to earn tenure and promotion and also try to be involved in schools in an in-depth manner. In a similar way, field supervisors are often so busy that they have to write reports at home and find themselves with caseloads so big that they cannot really keep track of what is happening on the university side of their supervisee's training experience.

Given this gap, how does the field begin to find bridges and pull down barriers? The first step is for university faculty *and* field supervisors to all consider themselves trainers of school psychologists. Reframing the field supervisor as a trainer with the same goals and responsibilities for the training of future school psychologists removes the class system between faculty and practitioners. To some extent, the APA approval system for internships does equalize the commitment and responsibilities for student training, but certainly not to the extent that is seen in medical education. Furthermore, the culture of an APA internship is not widely adopted by local school systems, and thus the model is not well promulgated. What is required is that all of these trainers work collaboratively. University faculty meet frequently to change the curriculum in response to changes in accreditation requirements. Teams of practitioners, similarly, meet to change their procedures in response to changes in federal and state laws. What would it look like if faculty members were engaged with school districts as they retool their policies and site supervisors were involved in curriculum revisions? Certainly, time is an issue, and attending extra meetings is never pleasant; however, there are many technologies that can facilitate such collaboration. For example, imagine having both faculty and practitioners in local communities on mailing lists that allowed for bidirectional communication about local issues or policy drafts in both settings posted to secure internet sites that allowed for each group to comment on the other's local issues. Advances in teleconferencing make the possibility of a 1-hour meeting a real option where drive time is eliminated.

Why is this so important now? In higher education, there are trends toward preparing graduates to hit the ground running. In the sciences, we are seeing the emergence of training programs that teach not just chemistry, for example, but communication skills, finance, logistics, and business administration as well. Furthermore, students expect internships to be mentored by scientists working in business. The idea is that the graduate with a professional science master's degree in chemistry can walk into a major corporation and produce the reports and provide the essential information on his or her area of science that decision makers need immediately. In the same way, for different reasons, we are seeing a move to reduce the time to degree in professional psychology with the provision to get all supervision for licensure in predoctoral experiences. What this portends is also seen in other fields: that is, there is an expectation for more field experiences to be incorporated into the training program. In postsecondary education, we are seeing strong trends toward "service learning." In nursing education, for example, the majority of time is spent in practice mentored by faculty and field-based trainers. More and more students are demanding practical experiences as part of their training and grow increasingly impatient with "stand and deliver" education modalities. Students of the next generation ("net geners") want to collaborate, customize, and innovate. They want to have fun and make a difference in their educational experiences. Furthermore, they are increasingly technologically savvy and want to leverage what technology can offer to an educational experience. This will push for more hybrid or blended instructional settings in which the didactic instruction can happen in the computer lab of the local school where the student is taking a field experience. In the interest of improving preparation for professional practice, the lines between the university and the field practice are going to continue to blur. Therefore, it follows that school psychology training will need to move in this direction. These factors increase the importance of ongoing meaningful interaction between the university and field-based trainers.

This collaboration between trainers transcends delivering information to a student and moves into the area of new knowledge generation. Increasingly, accrediting agencies and foundations that fund higher education researchers are looking for measurable impact on children (in the case of K–12 education). Similarly, if university researchers want to influence public policy research, findings must show broad impact and be translatable to the nonresearchers and public officials. These trends strongly suggest movements in research for practice. The first is a move toward translational research designed to examine the ways of taking our bench science findings and transport them to practice. This research has been going on in medicine for a long time, but it has only started to be discussed in the social sciences (e.g., Tashiro & Mortensen, 2006). One reason translational research has not been widely discussed is the idiosyncratic nature of our population's responsiveness to intervention. In medicine, the medical model has been highly effective and allows for treatments to be applied across vast numbers of people. In psychology, we are just getting to the point of suggesting that we have a largely universal treatment for depression, namely cognitive behavioral therapy. Otherwise, for school psychologists, treatment decisions have to take into account local conditions, including socioeconomic status, parent involvement, and the quality of the school, among a myriad of other issues. Thus, the university researcher considering translational research should really be collaborating with the local practitioner. These kinds of partnerships could encourage the adoption of different training models for school psychologist training programs. Specifically, the local clinical scientist model (Stricker & Trierweiler, 1995) argues that research findings that take into account local influences should be communicated and shared to develop a knowledge base of what works and under what conditions. Conducting research in collaboration with the field supervisor and expecting the research to have a high impact on children (as will inevitably be necessary to secure funding) would get faculty on the ground in the schools, engage field supervisors directly in the scholarly endeavors that would allow them to be better consumers of research, and provide value-added services to the children in the schools.

The publications of researchers in universities need to include outlets that are easily accessible to the practitioner. This is a major problem for university faculty because the reward system (e.g., tenure and promotion) tends to not consider such publications as necessarily scholarly. This is an issue that has to be solved within the universities themselves. Nevertheless, coauthoring local clinical scientist informed and translational studies *with* our field supervisors would likely result in the writing of manuscripts to be more accessible to practitioners and provide more human capital to publish findings in both top tier and consumer-oriented outlets.

Our impact on policy will be dependent on our field's ability to translate our findings not only for practitioners but for government officials. Regulation of higher education will continue to increase. Inklings of this inevitability could be seen in the debates over the recently passed Higher Education Act, as well as strong pushes from the U.S. Department of Education in the 2000s. Further evidence comes from international higher education regulatory bodies that are moving to set standards for graduate training. The accountability movement will have an impact on how universities do business. For example, in Pennsylvania, the state Department of Education has instituted regulations on the credentials of faculty members who can teach in teacher training programs. It may not be long before other professional training programs' faculty complements are indirectly selected based on federal or state mandate. Thus, the convergence of the traditional responsibilities of the university academic and the qualifications to prepare a practitioner will likely require a partnership with field supervisors serving as adjunct professors who have the required credentials to serve in such a capacity. There will be an increasing emphasis on bringing experienced practitioners to the university to teach because of the increased focus on a connection with field experiences.

How should the next generation of practitioners be trained to meet the demands of the evolution of school psychologist training described here? One approach that we are seeing in doctoral level education training is differentiated into the professional practice doctorate (PPD) and the traditional research doctorate. For several years there has been a movement in doctoral training to differentiate the research doctorate from the professional practice doctorate (Council of Graduate Schools, 2007). This is also not new to psychology because the impetus behind the endorsement of the PsyD at the Vail Conference was tension between psychological practitioners and scientists/researchers. As another example, the Carnegie Foundation on the Advancement of Teaching has sponsored a 3-year study of the doctor of education (EdD) degree—the PPD in education—called the Carnegie Project on the Education Doctorate (CPED). A primary reason for the CPED initiative is that the EdD and the PhD in education are often hard to differentiate because the EdD has become the "PhD-lite" (Shulman, Golde, Bueschel, & Garabedian, 2007, p. 27). Shulman et al. argue that that the EdD has been defined not by how it uniquely prepares one for the practice of education, but rather by having fewer requirements than the PhD. The CPED initiative strives to create a meaningful conception of the EdD that clearly differentiates it from the PhD as the highest practice doctorate in the field of education.

School psychology is in a unique position in terms of differentiating the practice doctorate from the research doctorate. That is, because of the Boulder model (scientist–practitioner), the PhD has been the degree to award for those who plan a career in practice and for those who plan a career in science. However, there have been concerns about training programs' ability to implement this comprehensive scientist–practitioner model (Overholser, 2007). Trainers of doctoral level psychologists are very aware of which students are inclined to be researchers and which will finish the dissertation to never run a statistic again. Indeed, the intention behind the Boulder model was that science and practice are necessary to inform each other, but the endorsement of the PsyD indicates that that ideal may not play out in application. Furthermore, it would not be fair to argue that individuals with a PPD do not embrace science or scholarship, rather they should be individuals uniquely prepared to *translate* science into practice and through that process *transform* practice. In this way, the next generation of school psychology practitioners would be uniquely prepared to partner with school psychology academics to collaborate, train, and generate new knowledge for the advancement of our field.

NEW MODELS, NEW ROLES, AND NEW FUNCTIONS

Formally and systematically advancing the future of the school psychology profession by bringing together interdisciplinary experts, practitioners, trainers, and graduate students was the focus of the landmark experiences in the 1980 Spring Hill and 1981 Olympia conferences (Brown, Cardon, Coulter, & Meyers, 1982; Ysseldyke & Weinberg, 1982). More recently, the Futures Conference, held in Indianapolis in 2002, reviewed the current trends in our profession and projected several major initiatives for future training and practice (cf. *School Psychology Review* by D'Amato et al., 2004). Although these high-profile professional practice events have brought considerable focus on training with a clear effort toward affecting the direction of field at the national level, implementation barriers at the state level predominate. More specifically, changes at the national level trickle down irregularly to the state and local levels. Information dissemination is unsystematic and at times inaccurate. Trainers are faced with the question of how to maintain standardized training when the local environment is slow to adapt or may reject the changes.

One clear example of the ongoing discussion at the national level that is yet to be realized in most local settings is the need for population-based prevention and intervention services (e.g., public health) to meet the overwhelming challenges of today's students. In May 2009, APA hosted the Summit on the Future of Psychology Practice. This meeting brought together psychologists, community partners, and policy makers to consider the role psychological services play in solving social issues. Integrated health care, community partnerships, and the role of psychological services in the business environment were primary foci. School systems are a central part of a child's academic and social development, as well as a centerpiece of communities. Schools are an ideal setting for integrated models. However, the training implications for interdisciplinary work are complex. First, it is difficult to include this type of training in a curriculum that is already packed with credentialing requirements. For example, adding credit hours for training dedicated to family–school partnerships has been challenged by the ambivalence in some school systems about embracing an increased level of parental involvement (Christenson & Sheridan, 2001). University trainers have to consider the overall impact on our students, trained to consider national models and emerging trends, as we send them into local venues for practicum and internship experiences: Have we trained students for negotiating these differences, succeeding in the real world, and being change agents in the political climates of their districts? Second, there are logistical considerations at the university for delivering a program that would be administered in a cross-disciplinary environment. When roles expand, training in one skill (e.g., prevention) may be in stark contrast, and at times in conflict with, the roles steeped in the history and legal needs (e.g., gatekeeper) of the school setting (Canter, 2006).

Third, field-based training expectations would likely have to expand as cross-discipline communities seek to establish competencies. Even as trainers examine how to serve the academic and social health needs of children in the context of public policy accountability, the field remains heavily influenced by the medical model reinforced by special education mandates (Curtis, Grier, & Hunley, 2004), a reality that is unlikely to change. Take, for example, states that opt out of serving children ages 3 to 9 who fall into only the delay, rather than a specific disability, category. These systems are likely not yet prepared to address the broad needs of all children.

Determining the viability of new models for school psychology practice is a touchstone to building university and field-based training alliances. Universities must determine which new initiatives (e.g., response to intervention, positive behavior support) warrant changes to training programs, how to identify fads versus emerging trends, and how to instill a value system in students that allows them to make these decisions in their own practices. As suggested previously, trainers would be better informed if they consider not only the literature base but also the likelihood of the schools/districts where we send our students supporting these initiatives. Furthermore, it is critical to determine what type of support will be needed for field-based trainers to implement new models and how the university can support these efforts.

In an age of increasing accountability, there is less clarity about how the school psychologist will function in the general education environment. For example, when educational initiatives are meant to be carried out by the teaching staff, it is important to determine the school psychologist's role. Does this type of consultation include only initial implementation and training? How are school psychologists connected to accountability for implementing evidence-based practices (EBPs)? Does the role include policing of general education? Is there a difference when the EBP centers on a mental health issue rather than an educational issue? When accountability is the focus, is consultation voluntary? Is this meaningfully different from the types of consultation already practiced? Accountability structures promise to only complicate the developing roles of the school psychologist and should be a consideration for the university and field.

NEW DIRECTIONS: CRISIS AND OPPORTUNITY

As we continue to reach in new directions, we also revisit the foundations on which our training was built. The initial agreements by the APA at the 1954 Thayer Conference that allowed for separate agencies to credential school-based practice (e.g., SBE) and non-school practice (e.g., state psychology boards) are being tested, as some states (e.g., Pennsylvania) allow for SBE credentials to practice outside of the school setting, and proposed changes to the APA Model Licensure Act would no longer allow a practitioner to use of the title "psychologist" unless appropriately credentialed at the doctoral level. These legislative efforts force us to revisit the assumptions of our training programs (Fagan, 1986). For example, is there general consensus that the first 2 years of training are specific to school psychology practice, affirming a nondoctoral level of entry to practice? Is training beyond the first 2 years best described as the type of broader-based information that would apply to a generic professional practice psychologist practicing outside of schools? How does entry-level training prepare school psychologists to assume broader roles in leadership, consultation, policy, and independent practice of psychology? The issue of the place for specialist and doctoral education remains an ongoing discussion, prompted by regulations and guild squabbles more often than by actual concerns within school systems, and school psychologists may wonder whether this is where we should spend our time. Regardless of the absurdity, it is clear that some groups will be lobbying to provide services to school-aged children, whether within psychology (e.g., clinical and counseling psychologists) or outside of professional practice psychology proper (e.g., behavior specialists, developmental specialists), and as such, university and field-based trainers need to be at the table when those discussions occur (Worrell, 2007).

As there is an increase in the NASP training standards, it is important to ask whether we are already training doctoral level practitioners when the average specialist program is 75 credits. Does the dissertation define doctoral education, or are there different/appropriate capstone experiences that demonstrate doctoral level competency? Since there are other professional practice areas (e.g., audiology, speech and language pathology, and nursing) that award doctoral degrees for this level of course work and the Association of State and Provincial Psychology Boards requires 3 years of training for a doctoral degree, should the field move toward doctoral education?

Recently, there has been a proliferation of PPDs such as the doctor of occupational therapy (OTD), doctor of physical therapy (DPT), and practice doctorate in nursing (DNP). The DNP is particularly prolific, with about 75 programs currently admitting students and about 140 other universities considering offering the degree (American Association of Colleges of Nursing, 2008). In contrast, there are currently 8 APA-approved PsyD programs in school psychology.

This issue of differentiating research and practice degrees has culminated most recently for universities in changes by the National Center for Educational Statistics to the Integrated Postsecondary Education Data System (IPEDS) Reporting Categories for Doctoral Programs that will be mandatory for the 2010–2011 data collection year. Specifically, IPEDS is moving away from the "first professional" category to a dichotomous reporting structure of (a) doctor's degree—research/scholarship and (b) doctor's degree—professional practice.

Although there is some discussion centered around acknowledging that current practices may already meet doctoral standards, the potential barriers to such a move have not been fully examined. For example, is the field interested in such a move? What are the costs and benefits to universities and practitioners? How would an increase in doctoral training translate into results for children? Although there are some reports that even non-doctoral-granting institutions would be eligible to give a PPD (Miller, 2009), the full extent of this possibility is currently unknown. Furthermore, even if there is some support for doctoral education, it is unclear whether such a move would positively impact training shortages, particularly when the need for documenting evidence-based practice may continue to reside with university trainers.

When these factors are taken together, it seems that we are at a time of reconceptualizing training programs and the development of a new generation of programs. Today, training programs are housed within traditional university settings, professional schools of psychology, and online-only environments (see Chapter 3, Volume I, for more details), yet new directions are certain to follow. At present, we recognize challenges to training to meet the needs of an increasingly diverse student population with a relatively homogeneous workforce, a condition that is certain to get worse if the projected personnel shortages of both university and field-based trainers are realized (NASP, 2007). This leaves us with the challenge of developing and supporting appropriate training sites, better articulating the shared responsibilities of supervision, so that we can attend to the business of developing the next generation of competent school psychologists. Discussions of supervision and negotiating conflict are expanded in Chapters 2 through 6 of this volume.

Will we travel full circle as we consider the challenges ahead? Do the core issues remain the same since the inception of school psychology as a profession with different emphases, different tools, and different readings, or has our profession fundamentally changed? The chapters in this volume will attempt to answer the challenging questions that are raised and provide both theoretical and pragmatic approaches to issues emerging in bridging the gap between university and field-based training. The volume is composed of five sections focusing on the contemporary issues that we face at both the university and the field, the importance of supervision and supervisors as trainers, preparing for difficult dialogues with our students and other professionals, embracing unique professional roles, and preparing for future practice. We invite you to expand your participation in the training of the next generation of school psychologists.

RESOURCES

Council of Graduate Schools. (2007). *Task force report on the professional doctorate.* Washington, DC: Author.

The Council of Graduate Schools provides a comprehensive review of the current status of the professional practice doctorate from a multidisciplinary perspective. Issues related to setting up a professional practice doctorate in a university are covered. These topics are of interest to those interested in setting up school psychology professional doctorates in their training programs.

Shulman, L. S., Golde, C. M., Bueschel, A. C., & Garabedian, K. J. (2006). Reclaiming education's doctorates: A critique and a proposal. *Educational Researcher, 35*(3), 25–32.

Shulman and colleagues examine the differences between the professional practice doctorate in education (EdD) and the research doctorate (PhD). Particular focus is given to the differences in terms of purpose of the degree, philosophy, and capstone experiences. This paper provides an analogy for school pscholology's consideration of the practice degree.

REFERENCES

American Association of Colleges of Nursing. (2008). *Doctor of nursing practice (DNP) programs*. Retrieved from http://www.aacn.nche.edu/dnp/DNPProgramList.htm

Brown, D. T., Cardon, B. W., Coulter, W. A., & Myers, J. (Eds.). (1982). The Olympia proceedings [Special issue]. *School Psychology Review, 11.*

Canter, A. (2006). *School psychology.* (COPSSE Document Number IB-4). Gainesville, FL: University of Florida, Center on Personnel Studies in Special Education.

Christenson, S. L., & Sheridan, S. M. (2001). *Schools and families: Creating essential connections for learning.* New York: Guilford.

Council of Graduate Schools. (2007). *Task force report on the professional doctorate.* Washington, DC: Author.

Crespi, T. D., & Hughes, T. L. (2006). Internship training in school psychology: Shortages and risks of emergency certification. *The School Psychologist, 20,* 163–164. (Reprinted in *Communiqué, 35,* p. 45, 2007.)

Curtis, M. J., Grier, J. E. C., & Hunley, S. A. (2004). The changing face of school psychology: Trends in data and projections for the future. *School Psychology Review, 33,* 49–66.

D'Amato, R. C., Sheridan S. M., Phelps, L., & Lopez, E.C. (2004). Psychology in the Schools, School Psychology Review School Psychology Quarterly, and Journal of Educational and Psychological Consultation Editors collaborate to chart school psychology's past, present, and "futures." *School Psychology Review, 33,* 233–238.

Fagan, T. K. (1986). School psychology's dilemma: Reappraising solutions and directing attention to the future. *American Psychologist, 4,* 851–861.

Fagan, T. K., & Wise, P. S. (2000). *School psychology: Past, present, and future* (2nd ed.). Bethesda, MD: NASP Publications.

Miller, J. A. (2009, February). *Examining the professional practice doctorate in school psychology.* Symposium conducted at the Trainers of School Psychologists convention held at the National Association of School Psychologists annual convention, Boston, MA.

National Association of School Psychologists. (2007). School psychology, 2004–2005: National and regional demographic characteristics, professional practices, employment conditions, & continuing professional development. Retrieved from http://sss.usf.edu/Resources/Presentations/2007/NASP/School_Psychology_2004_2005.ppt#326

Overholser, J. C. (2007). The boulder model in academia: Struggling to integrate the science and practice of psychology. *Journal of Contemporary Psychotherapy, 37*(4), 205–211.

Shulman, L. S., Golde, C. M., Bueschel, A. C., & Garabedian, K. J. (2006). Reclaiming education's doctorates: A critique and a proposal. *Educational Researcher, 35*(3), 25–32.

Stricker, G., & Trierweiler, S. J. (1995). The local clinical scientist: A bridge between science and practice. *American Psychologist, 50*, 995–1002.

Tashiro, T., & Mortensen, L. (2006). Translational research: How social psychology can improve psychotherapy. *American Psychologist, 61*(9), 959–966.

Tharinger, D. J. & Palomares, R. S. (2004). An APA-informed perspective on the shortage of school psychologists: Welcome licensed psychologists into the schools (and did we mention xeriscape gardening together?). *Psychology in the Schools, 41*, 461–472.

Worrell, F. (2007). Professional psychology, school psychology, and psychological science: Distinctiveness, deindividuation, or separation? President's message. *The School Psychologist, 61*, 96–101.

Ysseldyke, J. E., & Weinberg, R. J. (1982). The Spring Hill Symposium on the future of psychology in the schools. *American Psychologist, 37*, 547–552.

Part II

What about supervision anyway?

Trainers as supervisors

2 Contemporary issues in supervision

Judith Kaufman

Supervisors serve as the keepers of the faith and the mentors of the young. Theirs is a quiet profession that combines the discipline of science with the aesthetic creativity of art. . . . It is a curious paradox that at their best they are the least visible.

Alonso (1965)

The supervisory enterprise is critical to the educational process, not only for the expansion and reinforcement of skills and the transmission of the cultural practices of the profession but to support the development of mindfulness and self-reflection as they are exhibited in service delivery and in broader life contexts. Volume I comprehensively discusses the education and training of the prerequisite skills for effective practice of school psychology. The manner in which these skills are applied, the growth and development of those practice skills, and the reinforcement of the professional role and function evolve first through the collaboration between the university and field-based supervisors and ultimately through the practice setting. The nature of supervision changes as knowledge and skills are expanded, moving from early skill development and reinforcement to the integration of those skills in contextual settings as students move into the field for practicum and internship and, ultimately, as an independently practicing professional. Thus, far beyond the university's training program, supervision is an integral part of lifelong learning.

Supervision can be defined as "that process which improves and/or maintains the school psychologist's professional competence and functioning within an applied setting" (Strein, 1982, p. 4). The National Association of School Psychologists (NASP), in its position statement on supervision, defined supervision as "an ongoing, positive, systematic, collaborative process between a school psychologist and school psychology supervisor that focuses on promoting professional growth and exemplary professional practice leading to improved performance of all concerned" (National Association of School Psychologists, 2004, p. 1). Supervision can be viewed as an ongoing developmental process that models effective parenting and supports the solidification of professional identity (Kaufman & Schwartz, 2003). It is through supervision that the rituals and traditions of our field are transmitted and molded to meet the changing demographic and contextual needs of our education systems.

Much has been written about theoretical models of supervision (i.e., Harvey & Struzziero, 2000; Kaufman & Schwartz, 2003; Todd & Strom, 1997) and thus they will not be the primary focus of this chapter; however, it should be noted that there is limited evidence-based research to support a specific model or approach to be endorsed as a best practice for supervision (McIntosh & Phelps, 2000). Supervision in diverse settings with multicultural clients is clearly a critical consideration; Chapter 8 in Volume I and Chapter 7 in this volume focus directly on those issues and certainly remains an underlying consider=ation throughout this chapter. Subsequent chapters in this volume focus on the application of supervision to various levels of training and different settings and examine the process from an international perspective. Therefore, the goal of this chapter is to focus on generic issues, different conceptual approaches, and challenging negotiations, encompassing all levels of training. Specific issues of concern include the establishment of university–field connections, congruence of school-based learning and pragmatics of practice, the use of the supervisory enterprise as a critical aspect of continuing education and lifelong learning (see Chapter 14, Volume II), and examination of models of engaging in the process.

Practicum, internship, and early career school psychologists receive at least two types of supervision: administrative and skill/professional, and in all probability, these two forms of supervision come from different individuals. Administrative supervision focuses on the functioning of the service unit and the performance of job duties in accordance with conditions of employment and assigned responsibilities, and it may be carried out by individuals who are not necessarily credentialed in school psychology (NASP, 2004). Professional supervision encompasses the oversight of specific professional practice in school psychology and supporting practices consistent with the highest level of professional standards and must be carried out by licensed or certified school psychologists (NASP, 2004). In some settings and at certain levels of professional development, supervision focusing on personal characteristics and style may encompass a third aspect of supervision. Although administrative supervision is critical to job performance and compliance with state and federal mandates, practice-based professional supervision and personal development are the primary focal points of this chapter.

TRANSTHEORETICAL AND DEVELOPMENTAL MODELS

In the supervision literature, particularly that literature that focuses on the supervision of therapy, much of the writing has been embedded in a specific theoretical orientation; the particular orientation provides the parameters of the didactic and process interaction of supervision. For example, Liese and Beck (1997) used a cognitive therapy orientation in supervision, incorporating agenda setting, homework assignments, and routine feedback. Others might use a behavioral, psychodynamic, feminist, or culturally embedded model.

Recently, there has been an effort to focus on broader based developmental and transtheoretical models to facilitate and maximize the professional growth process, emphasizing the emergence of skills and attitudes irrespective of theoretical perspective. The development of a conceptual framework remains the responsibility of the training program as it meets its stated goals and objectives. As students progress through their educational program, they may be exposed to different theoretical models that potentially could become incorporated into practice. Although supervisors may have different orientations, it is not their primary responsibility to foster a conceptual framework, but rather to facilitate the growth of clinical skills, behaviors, and attitudes and to provide didactics when appropriate.

After extensive research, Aten, Strain, and Gillespie (2008), along with others (e.g., Kaufman & Schwartz, 2003; Mahrer, 2005; Prochaska & Norcross, 2007), concluded that a single theoretical model of supervision could not encompass the complexities of the supervision process or the complexities of human behavior. Being wedded to a particular theoretical model may be delimiting in facilitating the supervisees' growth and may increase apprehension about the process of change. Aten et al. suggested that a transtheoretical approach permits supervisees to operate with varying levels of proficiency across skill sets, facilitates a holistic approach to professional growth and development, and provides a greater flexibility in learning and in practice. The transtheoretical model has proven effective in facilitating change in a wide range of disorders, from addictive behavior (Petry, 2005) to stuttering (Floyd, Zebrowski, & Flamme, 2007). Given the model's broad utility and empirical support, it was suggested that the model could also be applied to clinical supervision (Aten et al.).

The six stages of change developed within the transtheoretical model for change have been modified to conceptualize the general development of the supervisee and for the acquisition of specific skill sets. These stages are as follows:

1. The precontemplation stage, where the supervisee may not be aware of the possibility of change or may be resistant to change
2. The contemplation stage, where the supervisee is aware of the need for change but is not yet engaged in the process
3. The preparation stage, where areas are targeted for change and where collaborative goal setting between the supervisor and supervisee is negotiated

4. The action stage, where there is a genuine commitment and the beginning of action toward change
5. The maintenance stage, where the supervisee exerts a purposeful and conscious effort to sustain the change accomplished
6. The termination stage, where increased competency has been achieved in a particular area, a new skill set has been obtained and/or deficits repaired in a particular problematic area, or there has been progression to a new level of development, and where the change has become automatic and does not require conscious attention (Aten et al., 2008, pp. 2–3).

The transtheoretical model also provides guidance to the supervisor to facilitate the passage through the developmental stages and includes consciousness raising, dramatic relief, self-reevaluation, environmental re-evaluation, self-liberation, stimulus control, counterconditioning, contingency management, social liberation, and the establishment of helping relationships between the supervisor and supervisee. A comprehensive discussion of these techniques can be found in Aten et al. (2008).

The recognition that there is a developmental process in supervision independent of theoretical orientation is a critical one, and it is implicitly addressed in theoretically oriented models but not directly focused on. Integrating a developmental model assumes that supervision is an ongoing growth process and is integrated throughout the course of professional practice. In addition to the transtheoretical approach, Stoltenberg (2005) proposed an integrated developmental model (IDM) as a three-stage process, where as supervisees gain experience, supervision decreases. What is important to note within the IDM format is that a supervisee may be at Level 3 in assessment, but in fact at Level 1 in individual treatment. Similarly, context can also impact developmental level, where for example, a student may be at Level 3 in a homogeneous school district but at Level 1 with respect to issues of diversity. Research suggests that with such a "level" approach, specific competencies can be measured in order to determine an individual's progress (Stoltenberg). In his research, Stoltenberg has specified markers of development, where essentially the focus of beginners is primarily on their own behavior in the application of skills. As skills evolve and are reinforced, in Level 2, the focus is on the client, developing a better understanding of the client's cognitive and affective world. Level 3 integrates a self–other awareness, where the focus is on both the client and, simultaneously, self-awareness. True achievement of Level 3 occurs when the behavior is integrated across domains of practice.

Kaufman and Schwartz (2003) suggested that the supervisory process parallels Erickson's stages of development, successfully resulting in the integration of professional identity. They pointed out that the effective supervisor must be cognizant of both the growth process and the potential for regression when faced with new and unfamiliar situations. Mahrer (2005) applied a discovery-oriented approach to the supervision process, where he sees the supervisor as a discovery-oriented teacher. His approach is detailed in his book, *Supervision of Psychotherapists* (2005).

Approaching supervision from a developmental or transtheoretical perspective recognizes the fundamental nature of skill development and the integration of therapeutic skills along with self-awareness. As we view child development as an evolving process, with occasional regressions and deviations along the way, so too we should view the education of effective mental health professionals. Approaching supervision with such an understanding provides opportunities to facilitate and nurture the best possible professional development.

THE DYNAMICS OF GROUP VERSUS INDIVIDUAL SUPERVISION

While credentialing (NASP) and licensure (American Psychological Association [APA]) standards specify a minimum number of hours of individual supervision, many settings supplement that individual supervision with group experiences. School psychology literature provides definitions for individual supervision; however, very few definitions include group supervision (McIntosh & Phelps, 2000). Bernard and Goodyear (2004) described group supervision as supervision with more than one supervisee.

Group supervision is purported to have many advantages, including multiple perspectives, vicarious learning, feedback from peers, and exposure to multiple cases (Riva & Cornish, 1995). Factors have been identified that indicate that there are also potentially negative effects associated with group supervision. These include interpersonal issues among members, weak group leadership, weak group members, and anxiety about group exposure (Linton, 2003). Until recently, research supporting the efficacy of group supervision has been limited, and those studies that are available are primarily anecdotal. Since 2000, there has been an increase in research in this area across specific disciplines, including school psychology (Bernard & Goodyear, 2004). In a recent investigation (Riva & Cornish, 2008), group supervisors were surveyed at Association of Postdoctoral and Internship Centers sites. Findings indicated that group process within group supervision varies but is incorporated more widely than the sharing of didactic information. Although several group supervisors did receive some training, not all focused on group dynamics. It was suggested that supervision courses should include a module on group supervision. The most common topics discussed within the group supervisory process included ethics and multicultural practices. The most common format for group supervision is case presentation, with a distribution of 60% of the time spent on clinical information, 25% on sharing of didactic information, and, in general, 10% on processing the dynamics of the group's behavior (Riva & Erickson, 2008).

It is important to understand the dynamics, value, and efficacy of incorporating group supervision (Haboush, 2003). Haboush pointed out that the training facility needs to determine its model and what role supervision plays, whether to emphasize specific skill development or to support more independent functioning, contrasting "directing" or "enabling" competence (Eshel & Koriat, 2001). Although both models are essential in the development of quality school psychologists, the more effective model in group supervision is potentially the enabling approach, which fosters greater autonomous functioning and critical analysis and promotes an inner sense of competence (Habouch, 2003).

In order for supervision to be effective in a group setting, the facilitator needs to be aware of group theory and the developmental phases of group process. Groups typically pass through a stage of resistance before beginning to work together in a more in-depth manner. There are times when the behavior of the supervision group is more important to analyze then the issues being discussed (Heiman & Ettin, 2001). Much of school psychology functioning involves a team or group process; the ability to negotiate interpersonal relationships in sometimes emotionally charged situations is an important skill. Similarly, understanding individual contributions to a group process is also important and reflects on the efficacy of the inclusion of group supervision in training.

Ethical issues that are generated when considering group supervision include those issues of confidentiality and dual relationships where the supervisor may also be a professor or advisor. Guidelines and concerns need to be discussed prior to the beginning of supervision so that standards and boundaries remain clear (Harvey & Struzziero, 2000). APA ethical guidelines require supervisors to inform students at the outset of supervision what criteria for evaluation should be (APA, 2002), and these criteria should be clearly operationalized in all evaluation forms. Furthermore, should group supervision be a requirement, both the program and the field should have provisions for students who do feel uncomfortable within a particular group or with a dual relationship. APA guidelines (2002) also indicate that training programs are required to inform students if they will be required to divulge certain types of personal information within courses. Riva and Erickson (2008) found that a significant component of the group supervision process involved a discussion of ethics and the limits of confidentiality. Students may be discussing practica or internship cases from systems that other students are not affiliated with, and thus the boundaries of confidentiality become a critical concern and information sharing becomes a real challenge. Individual supervision is essential to the growth and development of knowledge, skills, and attitudes. Recent research suggests that group supervision, if conducted in a knowledgeable and mindful way, can add a significant dimension to the education of professional school psychologists not only in broadening the exposure to case material but in the understanding of group processes and the dynamics of interaction.

FOSTERING CULTURAL COMPETENCE

Although university training programs make a committed effort to provide exposure to diverse populations, it is not always possible given geographic location and sociocultural environments. Therefore, supervisors may encounter students with limited exposure to diversity. Furthermore, the supervisee and supervisor may be of different cultural/lifestyle backgrounds that may require open and frank discussion or negotiation. There is no question that with the changing nature of the population in the United States, the typical triad of student, school psychologist, and supervisor will contain someone of a differing racial or ethnic background, most typically, given the demographics of our profession, the child (Leong & Wagner, 1994).

On a recent site visit in the Midwest, I met a graduate student who was from an inner city neighborhood, African American, and gay. Although the faculty were sensitive to the "culture shock" of the young man, both the supervisor and the supervisee found their worldviews equally alien. Although the young man expressed attitudes and behaviors he considered to be normative when dealing with clients, the program faculty saw that same behavior as problematic. Extensive negotiation was necessary for acculturation of both the student and the faculty.

Bernard and Goodyear (2004), along with many others (see Chapter 7, this volume), advocated that supervisors have a particular responsibility for assuring that multicultural issues receive attention in supervision. There are multiple components of dealing with these issues, the first being the content of supervision in which the impact of race, ethnicity, and culture is evaluated in light of the presenting problem and manifested behavior.

A female practicum student was assigned to evaluate a 14-year-old Orthodox Jewish male in a bicultural day school. She introduced herself and appropriately closed the door to begin her evaluation. The young man, shortly thereafter, went to open the door slightly. Once again, the student shut the door, and again the young man opened it. The graduate student decided to continue the testing with the door slightly ajar. When reporting the situation to her supervisor, she begins her supervision with, "The boy I tested really is afraid of women, or he must have some kind of social phobia!" The supervisor then pointed out that within Orthodox Judaism, a young man is not permitted to be in a closed space with someone he is not immediately related to. This is an overt, behavioral example of where lack of cultural knowledge affected the case conceptualization. All too often, more subtle issues are present in the helping and supervisory relationships, or the process of supervision including the supervisee's feelings about race, ethnicity and culture, worldview, and expectations that may impact on both understanding and interacting with clients and their families. Discussing these issues becomes a vital aspect of supervision (Bernard & Goodyear, 2004).

Power issues associated with both multicultural aspects and the supervisory relationships also need to be considered, particularly when the supervisor and supervisee are of different racial, cultural, or economic backgrounds. Assumptions about power may be attributed to the individual from the perceived "majority" culture and may impact on the effectiveness of the supervision enterprise (Bernard & Goodyear, 2004). Early and ongoing discussion of supervisor and supervisee expectations of performance, orientation, and evaluative power is critical, along with considerations of the impact of cultural background and experiences of prejudice and possible oppression (Gloria, Hird, & Tan, 2008). As the majority of supervisors continue to be Caucasian and female, it is increasingly important to understand their level of competence in multicultural supervision, and there has been an initiation of research in this area (see Gloria et al.).

There is no question that there is little diversity and an underrepresentation of minorities in school psychology, in our graduate programs, on our faculties, and, most importantly, in the field (Zhou et al., 2004). With such a shortage, there is an increased need for faculty and supervisors to become culturally competent in order to facilitate the cultural growth of the next generation of professionals. Although both NASP and APA, in their accreditation standards, emphasize multiculutralism in the curriculum and in practice, beyond that, training programs have an ethical responsibility to provide such exposure to their students to deal with the realities of the world.

SUPERVISION AS LIFELONG LEARNING

Strein (1982) examined the self-managed professional development using a "supervisory pool" concept, emphasizing that supervision is not something that is necessarily done to an individual, but that supervision is a process. In a self-managed model, intended for individuals who are assumed to possess the basic competencies of the profession, the supervisee is at the center of the model and, although having a designated supervisor, may have a large interdisciplinary pool of individuals from whom to draw knowledge and support. This model has received limited attention in the literature (Keller & Protinsky, 2007; Morrissette, 2001) with virtually no reference to school psychology; however, many professional organizations (APA, NASP, National Register of Health Service Providers) employ self-managed continuing education modules for skill enhancement (see Chapter 14, in this volume), with no reference to a self-management model for supervision, an approach that warrants further investigation for its potential efficacy. Such a model may be particularly applicable where there are insufficient numbers of "qualified" professionals within a particular school district. Furthermore, practicing school psychologists surveyed indicated the importance of clinical supervision (Fischetti & Crespi, 1999) and overwhelmingly endorsed the need for such supervision to enhance the knowledge base and to provide peer support. Through considering self-managed supervision, universities, together with school districts, can provide collaborative relationships, thus promoting congruent knowledge, skills, and attitudes.

WHO SUPERVISES THE SUPERVISORS: QUANDARIES FOR UNIVERSITY-BASED TRAINERS?

Field-based supervisors play a vital role in the education and training of future school psychologists and indeed may be considered a "finishing school." Barnett, Erickson Cornish, Goodyear, and Lichtenberg (2007) discussed what qualities make for effective supervisors and, similarly, for effective supervision. These qualities include (a) the ability to provide constructive feedback in an unthreatening and supportive environment; (b) being nonjudgmental and validating; (c) normalizing the experiences that supervisees are having, creating a safe environment for discourse; and (d) being respectful and empathic and encouraging growth experiences in the supervisee. Undesirable or less desirable qualities include (a) telling students what to do as opposed to exploring options, (b) providing vague and diffuse feedback, and (c) supporting only approaches and techniques that the supervisor incorporates. Although it is expected that students will encounter challenges, differing philosophical and theoretical approaches, and multiple supervisory styles, it is also expected that skill-based supervision and practice approaches be congruent with the university training model. In urban and well-populated suburban areas, it often is possible to handpick field-based trainers; however, in more rural areas, there may be just a few individuals appropriately credentialed and sufficiently experienced to provide supervision.

NASP (2004) advocates for the availability of professional administration and professional supervision to all school psychologists regardless of level of experience and proficiency. Although the administrative supervision may be readily available, professional supervision may not be as available. Therefore, universities may assume additional responsibilities, and although not directly responsibly, faculty may need to negotiate supervisory conflict and take an active role in supervising supervisors, focusing on the conceptual, interpersonal, and technical skills required in supervision. It is interesting to note that although NASP advocates for professional supervision, supervision skills themselves are not among the domains of competence specified by NASP.

Little is known about the training practices or the significant events and issues that arise in supervisor training (Ellis, 2006). It has been suggested that supervisor training follows a hierarchical or developmental model similar to that of the trainee, evolving from novice to expert (Sansbury, 1982). In Ellis's recent study employing a critical incidents questionnaire

(Ellis, 2006), he found that similarities existed between the issues generated by training supervisors and trainees. These include emotional awareness, competence, and autonomy. Worthington (2006) has provided an extensive review focusing the changes that take place when both the supervisor and supervisee gain experience. A major consideration is whether supervision should be reactive or proactive and whether the supervisor should wait for critical incidents to occur. Most supervisors approach the process with younger trainees in a proactive fashion and, as each becomes more proficient, respond in a more reactive manner. After an extensive review of the literature, Worthington concluded that although the supervisee improves with "age" and training, the supervisor does not appear to change with age. "Supervisors appear to be neglected or given minimal attention by most professional environments, yet are expected to change with age and to age with quality" (Worthington, 2006, p. 158). Within the school psychology specialty, many training programs provide opportunities for their field-based supervisors to participate in continuing education programs, attend program meetings, and teach practica and content courses. However, these experiences are primarily educational and do not focus on supervisory issues. The primary interaction around supervision typically focuses on a problematic student or issue and not necessarily on any discussion of the process.

Silva and Dana (2001) provided an interesting approach to the possibility of "supervising supervisors" through collaborative supervision of field-based experiences. Typically, the student is assigned a field-supervisor, and the university provides group supervision or designates an individual to coordinate practicum experiences. Collaborative supervision goes beyond that as a dynamic, interactive, and relational process, where both supervisors are present in the session with either an individual student or groups of students. Although potentially more time intensive for the university faculty, the benefits may be considerable. Students obtain exposure to different viewpoints, supervisors may learn from each other, and most importantly, the university trainers can facilitate congruence between the education and field-based practices. University trainers have the potential of modeling best practices in potentially problematic situations (Silva & Dana, 2001).

Research in the training of supervisors and in their ongoing supervision remains sparse and inconclusive in the clinical and counseling fields. There is virtually no information focusing the supervisors of school psychologists. Who nurtures and trains supervisors, and what are the most effective strategies? These questions remain a challenge for our training programs, as well as for our profession.

SUPERVISION LAND MINES

In many fields, where a supervisor has a predominately administrative role, the primary focus of supervision is performance. In the field of school psychology, together with other human services professions, effective supervision may also focus on feelings in relation to performance, as well as to feelings about the psychological relationship to the client (U.S. Department of Labor, 2008). In addition, supervision may also focus on feelings generated in the interaction between supervisor and supervisee. Several potential problems may be generated by a "feelings" focus, although this focus is essential to the growth and development of individuals entering the profession. The supervisory relationship, while directly focusing on effective "job" performance, encompasses a wider sphere of learning. There are potentially four themes, if not more, beyond skill development: (a) coping and defensive style, (b) dealing with power and authority, (c) accountability and responsibility, and (d) ethical concerns, all of which contribute to a sense of mindfulness and self-reflection (Wiener, 2007).

The university may gloss over issues and not actually share issues surrounding problematic students in order that they may have a field placement. By the same token, field-based supervisors may not share issues with the university in order to appear competent and able to handle even the most difficult of situations. Conversely, each setting may be too quick to point to issues, the university telling the field supervisors that it is their responsibility to deal with issues, while the field supervisors hold the university accountable. Neither dynamic benefits the trainee, the setting, or the recipients of the service. Collaboration is critical, and the sharing of issues and problems both operationally and specifically is essential. Furthermore, responsive feedback mechanisms, along with a designated individual in each setting, are essential in order to avoid taking what might be a difficult situation and creating a serious problem.

Obviously, there is some feedback that is more difficult to provide than others. Observation of growth and positive interaction are relatively simple to reinforce; however, providing feedback that addresses a supervisee's personality, professional behavior issues, and interaction outside of the supervisory process, that is, with other trainees or school staff, can be anxiety producing and challenging for the supervisor. Many supervisors report withholding feedback from trainees when that feedback is negative or may be subjective, or that is reflective of the supervisor's feelings. In order to avoid miscommunication, it is recommended that feedback be directly communicated and be as specific as possible, with documented examples whenever possible (Wood, Miller, & Hargrove, 2005). In the APA's *Guidelines for Accreditation* (2005), it is clearly stated that evaluation to the student must be provided *in writing*. Although providing written feedback may seem daunting, it protects the faculty, the training program, and, most importantly, the student from legal and ethical issues. Chapter 8 in this volume provides excellent strategies on dealing with problem behaviors.

Sobell, Manor, Sobell, and Dum (2008) provided an alternative approach to providing feedback, finding that trainees often have a difficult time in integrating negative comments. Incorporating motivational interviewing techniques, trainees were required to provide regular self-evaluations of their own audio taped sessions. Although there can be several limitations using such an approach, including issues of social desirability and cognitive misperceptions, trainees found the approach quite helpful, did report negative components, and expressed greater motivation for change (Sobell et al., 2008). Self-evaluation should not be the sole method for providing feedback to trainees. Whether using audiotape, videotape, or analysis of process notes, the trainee's comments about performance could provide opportunities for the supervisor to engage in dialog about challenging issues and also provide insight as to the self-awareness and mindfulness of the supervisee.

Intervention is critical to the supervisee's development, although sometimes difficult to negotiate. Stoltenberg (2005) suggested that there are different interventions appropriate at different levels of development. At the beginner level, Level 1, prescriptive interventions are found to be particularly useful, providing specific input and direction. At Level 2, conceptual interventions help to link theory to practice and to broaden and solidify skills and ideas. The most difficult intervention is at Level 3, which is confrontive: supervisees are challenged to move beyond what is safe and to try new interventions, expand their view of the process, or embrace more difficult clients and situations. Throughout the process, Stoltenberg also recommended catalytic interventions that focus on self-awareness, mindfulness, and the overall processes of treatment. Although Stoltenberg's developmental approach is not yet empirically supported, there is general agreement in literature supporting this approach to intervention. If we "enable" problems, avoid constructive but negative feedback, or fail to provide interventions, serious consequences may result, including covering up issues, avoiding confrontation, blaming others, and generating threats and negative consequences. More importantly, problem behaviors may persist and ultimately damage the populations we wish to help.

Incorporating feelings into the supervisory process also generates both transference and countertransference. The impact of these processes has been closely examined in the psychoanalytic literature (Wiener, 2007; Zaskavsky, Nunes, & Eizirik, 2005) but has received limited attention in the supervision of school psychology trainees and school psychologists (Tharinger, 1998). Nonetheless, the relationship between the supervisee and the supervisor remains of critical importance both in professional functioning and in relation to the populations served. Obviously, the framework of supervision shapes the focus of the supervisor's response and the underlying dynamic process (Wiener, 2007). Some typical emotional encounters may involve sympathy, apology, creating diversions with irrelevant issues, and creative excuses, along with tears, "innocence," and sometimes anger. As individuals trained to be aware of feelings within an emotional landscape, we may be particularly susceptible to such encounters and to rationalize challenging, difficult, or unacceptable behavior on the part of the supervisee. Many of us are, as well, particularly sensitive to the challenges we faced as beginning professionals and therefore may overly identify with the plight of the student, which in the long run may be more damaging than dealing with the behavior directly. Ethical supervision involves a clearly articulated supervisor–supervisee relationship that is vigilant about the use and misuse of power and boundary crossings, while allowing for both learning and personal discourse (Bridges, 1999).

It is important that supervisors make themselves available (Tracey, 2006), and many supervisors provide personal contact information so that trainees can reach them in emergency situations. One supervisor was quoted as saying, "I want to be there for them when they are facing a very critical decision" (Tracey, 2006, p. 48). What is an emergency and what boundaries exist need to be established at the outset of supervision. There are those individuals who expect that their supervisors are on call 24/7 and assume that e-mail, text messages, and cell phone messages are responded to instantly. Gross (2005), in a study of doctoral students in practicum, reported that they did not receive adequate supervision and were undervalued as trainees, raising the question of "how much is enough?" Furthermore, the perception of what is "enough" supervision is an interaction between level of professional development and personal characteristics.

Many barriers can be overcome by offering a counseling session for supervisees before they begin seeing clients, in which models of supervision, expectations, and philosophy are discussed while the supervisor gauges the skill level of the supervisee. Expectations of supervision need to be made clear at the outset so that the process benefits both the supervisor and supervisee (Tracey, 2006). Although it is expected that trainees are able to negotiate a myriad of relationships, there may be instances when a supervisee/supervisor match may appear untenable or unworkable. Of course there may be clear-cut instances of harassment and/or discrimination, which is beyond the responsibility of the supervisee (see Chapter 10, this volume); however, many of the initial issues of "mismatch" may be overcome through a clear and open dialog between the supervisor and supervisee. A supervisor recently indicated that she was more successful with supervisees to whom she did not feel an emotional attachment. Without the "need to please" and feelings of protectiveness, it was possible for her to be more objective, directive, and challenging, resulting in a positive growth experience (Kaufman, 2008, personal communication).

A reflective supervisor, through the challenges in supervision, may recognize that a shift in style and approach may be necessary for particular trainees. A supervisor, in sharing his experience (personal communication), indicated that he was working with a very dependent, relatively new supervisee who was constantly seeking guidance and references, worrying about doing the "right thing," but not listening to her client. The supervisor became increasingly impatient, having primarily supervised more advanced students, and found that he was about to seriously criticize the student. He said he felt himself ready to shout at her and then remembered his first challenging case. At the next session, he began to alter his style and expectations and found that the trainee's behavior began to move in a positive direction.

Training programs need to evolve policies and procedures to handle situations when there is a genuine mismatch between student and supervisor or between trainee and setting and clearly articulate domains of responsibility. How much should the student be responsible for? When does the training director intervene? Under what circumstances can a student change supervisors or be removed from a setting? In order to protect the integrity of training, parameters need to be articulated and communicated early in the training and supervisory experience.

SUMMARY AND CONCLUSIONS

There is no doubt that although there are many theories and approaches to supervision, together with the expression of professional preferences, there are a limited number of evidence-based models to support the supervisory enterprise. There are several directions for critical research in the field, potentially examining the effectiveness of group versus individual supervision, effective models, what trainees require at different levels of development, and similarities and differences between university-based and field-based supervision. The clearest conclusion that can be drawn is that supervision is essential to the continuance of our profession.

RESOURCES

Bieschke, K. (Section Ed.). (2008). Special section: Systemic approaches to trainees with professional competence problems. *Training and Education in Professional Psychology, 2,* 4.
This special section provides creative and challenging approaches in evaluating and dealing with trainees' competence issues throughout the training enterprise and offers excellent insight into dealing with troubling issues.

Harvey, V. S., & Struzziero, J. A. (2008). *Professional development and supervision of school psychologists II.* New York: Corwin/National Association of School Psychologists.
This comprehensive volume presents contemporary issues in both professional development and supervision and is updated and modified from its earlier edition. Examples, vignettes, and evaluation forms are integrated throughout the book.

Worthington, E. L., Jr. (2006). Changes in supervision as counselors and supervisors gain experience: A review. *Training and Education in Professional Psychology,* 8, 2, 133–160.

Worthington provides an excellent review of literature, focusing on what goes on during the supervision process, and provides findings from a wide variety of studies on changes that take place depending on the level of competence of the trainee and the supervisor.

REFERENCES

Alonso, A. (1965). *The quiet profession.* New York: Basic Books.

American Psychological Association. (2002). Ethical principals of psychologists and code of conduct. *American Psychologist, 57,* 1060–1073.

Aten, J. D., Strain, J. D., & Gillespie, R. E. (2008). A transtheoretical model of clinical supervision. *Training and Education in Professional Psychology, 2*(1), 1–9.

Barnett, J. E., Erickson Cornish, J. A., Goodyear, R. K., & Lichtenberg, J. W. (2007). Commentaries on the ethical and effective practice of clinical supervision. *Professional Psychology: Research and Practice, 38,* 268–275.

Bernard, J., & Goodyear, R. (2004). *Fundamentals of clinical supervision* (3rd ed.). Boston: Allyn & Bacon.

Bridges, N. (1999). The role of supervision in managing intense affect and constructing boundaries in therapeutic relationships. *Journal of Sex Education and Therapy, 24*(4), 218–225.

Ellis, M. V. (2006). Critical incidents in clinical supervision and in supervisor supervision. *Training and Education in Professional Psychology, 8*(3), 122–132.

Eshel, Y., & Koriat, A. (2001). The informal curriculum: The latent aspect of psychological training. *School Psychology International, 22,* 387–400.

Fischetti, B. A., & Crespi, T. D. (1999). Clinical supervision for school psychologists: National practices, trends and future implications. *School Psychology International, 20*(3), 278–288.

Floyd, J., Zebrowski, P., & Flamme, G. (2007). Stages of change in stuttering: A preliminary view. *Journal of Fluency Disorders, 32,* 95–120.

Gloria, A. M., Hird, J. S., & Tan, K. W. (2008). Self-reported multicultural supervision competence of white predoctoral intern supervisors. *Training and Education in Professional Psychology, 2*(3), 129–136.

Gross, S. (2005). Students' perspectives on clinical and counseling practica. *Professional Psychology: Research and Practice, 36*(3), 299–306.

Harvey V., & Struzziero, J. (2000). *Effective supervision in school psychology.* Bethesda, MD: National Association of School Psychologists.

Heiman, M. L., & Ettin, M. F. (2001). Harnessing the power of the group for latency-aged sexual abuse victims. *International Journal of Group Psychotherapy, 51,* 265–282.

Kaufman, J., & Schwartz, T. (2003). Models of supervision: Shaping professional identity. *The Clinical Supervisor, 23*(1), 143–158.

Keller, J. F., & Protinsky, H. (2007). A self-management model for supervision. *Journal of Marital and Family Therapy, 10*(3), 281–288.

Leong, F. T., & Wagner, N. M. (1994). Cross-cultural supervision: What do we know? What do we need to know? *Counselor Education & Supervision, 34*(2), 117–131.

Liese, S. B., & Beck, J. S. (1997). Cognitive therapy supervision. In C. W. Watkins (Ed), *Handbook of psychotherapy supervision* (pp. 114–133). New York: Wiley.

Linton, J. M. (2003). A preliminary qualitative investigation of group processes in group supervision: Perspectives of master's level practicum students. *Journal for Specialists in Group Work, 28,* 215–226.

Mahrer, A. R. (2005). *Supervision of psychotherapists: The discovery-oriented approach.* London: Whurr Publishers.

McIntosh, D. E., & Phelps, L. (2000). Supervision in school psychology: Where will the future take us? *Psychology in the Schools, 37*(1), 33–38.

Morrissette, P. (2001). *Self supervision: A primer for counselors and the helping professions.* New York: Psychology Press.

National Association of School Psychologists. (2004, April). *Position statement on supervision in school psychology.* Position paper adopted by the NASP Delegate Assembly.

Petry, N. M. (2005). Stages of change in treatment seeking pathological gamblers. *Journal of Consulting and Clinical Psychology, 73,* 312–322.

Prochaska, J. O., & Norcross, J. C. (2007). *Systems of psychotherapy: A transtheoretical analysis* (6th ed.). Belmont, CA: Wadsworth.

Riva, M. T., & Cornish, J. A. (1995). Group supervision practices at psychology predoctoral internship programs: A national survey. *Professional Psychology: Research and Practice, 26,* 523–525.

Riva, M. T., & Cornish, J. A. (2008). Group supervision practices at psychology predoctoral internship programs: 15 years later. *Training and Education in Professional Psychology, 2*(1), 18–25.

Sansbury, D. L. (1982). Developmental supervision from a skills perspective. *The Counseling Psychologist, 10*(1), 53–57.

Silva, D. Y., & Dana, N. F. (2001). Collaborative supervision in the professional development school. *Journal of Curriculum and Supervision, 16,* 304–321.

Sobell, L. C., Manor, H. L., Sobell, M. B., & Dum, M. (2008). Self-critiques of audiotaped therapy sessions: A motivational procedure for facilitating feedback during supervision. *Training and Education in Professional Psychology, 2*(3), 151–155.

Strein, W. (1982, August). *Applying the supervisory pool concept to supervision in school psychology.* Paper presented at American Psychology Association (90), Washington, DC.

U.S. Department of Labor, Office of the Assistant Secretary for Policy. (2008). *Supervisor training: Working partners for an alcohol & drug free workplace.* Washington, DC: Author.

Stoltenberg, C. D. (2005). Enhancing professional competence through developmental approaches to supervision. *American Psychologist, 60* (8), 857–864.

Tharinger, D. J. (1998). School psychologists: Promoting secure and autonomous attachment: A focus on supervision. *The School Psychologist, 52,* 106–123

Todd, T. C., & Storm, C. L. (1997). *The complete systematic supervisor.* Boston: Allyn & Bacon.

Tracey, M. D. (2006). More effective supervision. *Monitor on Psychology, 37*(3), 48–49.

Wiener, J. (2007). The analyst's countertranference when supervising: Friend or foe? *Journal of Analytical Psychology, 52*(1), 51–69.

Wood, J., Miller, T. W., & Hargrove, D. S. (2005). Clinical supervision in rural settings. *Professional Psychology: Research and Practice, 36*(2), 173–179.

Worthington, W. L., Jr. (2006). Changes in supervision as counselors and supervisors gain experience: A review. *Training and Education in Professional Psychology,* 8(2), 133–160.

Zaskavsky, J., Nunes, M. L. T., & Eizirik, C. L. (2005). Approaching counter-transference in psychoanalytical supervision: A qualitative investigation. *The International Journal of Psychoanalysis, 86,* 1099–1131.

Zhou, Z., Bray, M. A., Kehle, T., Theodore, L. A., Clark, E., & Jensen, W. R. (2004). Achieving ethnic minority parity in school psychology. *Psychology in the Schools, 4,* 443–450.

3 Competency-based school psychology practica

A collaborative training model

J. Steven Welsh, Sarah Meche,
and Carmen Broussard

Preinternship practicum or externship training has long been a topic of discussion in the general psychology literature (Lewis, Hatcher, & Pate, 2005; Ko & Rodolfa, 2005; Hatcher & Lassiter, 2004) and specifically in the school psychology literature (Brown, 1981; Brown, & Minke, 1986; Clair, Osterman, Kiraly, Klausmeier, & Graff, 1971; Crespi & Lopez, 1998; Harrison & Prus, 2008; Kramer & Ryabik, 1981; Pryzwansky, 1971; Welsh, Wilmoth, & Hodnut, 1999). Both the American Psychological Association's (APA's) *Guidelines and Principles for Accreditation of Programs in Professional Psychology* (APA, 2000) and the National Association of School Psychologists' (NASP's) *Standards for Training and Field Placement Programs in School Psychology* (NASP, 2000) have established requirements for preinternship supervised practica as required components of preservice professional preparation. For example, in Section III of the NASP *Standards for Training*, "Field Experiences/Internship," Item 3.1 stipulates that "closely supervised practicum experiences that include the development and evaluation of specific skills are distinct from and precede culminating internship experiences that require the integration and application of the full range of school psychology competencies and domains." Although the NASP standards are explicit regarding the number of hours required for the internship (1,200 hr), the NASP standards do not offer such specificity regarding number of hours required or recommended at the practicum level.

Historically, doctoral and specialist programs have required extensive field-based training (Brown, 1981). However, there has been significant variability in field-based training curriculum components at the preinternship level (Brown & Minke, 1986). Doctoral candidates generally complete more field-based practica prior to the internship than specialist program students. Rodolfa, Owen, and Clark (2007) reported some variability in opportunity to participate in practica course work between PhD and PsyD training programs; these differences were likely due to the fewer number of years typically required to complete the PsyD program. Teglasi and Pumroy (1982) reported that there is little difference between doctoral and nondoctoral programs with regard to the early field-based practicum experiences. Common early field-based training experiences typically ranged from initial shadowing and observation to later participation in live assessment or consultation referrals under conditions of appropriate supervision. Interestingly, Tarquin and Truscott (2006) reported that students completing practica continue to report a high percentage of time engaged in assessment activities, even though faculty have focused attention on the expanded role function of school psychology practitioners. Considering that fewer hours of course work are required for program completion for specialist as compared with doctoral programs, it appears likely that students enrolled in specialist programs have fewer opportunities to participate in preinternship field-based practica.

Fagan (1977) offered an early description on practicum, internship, and externship course work that has remained applicable until the present day. In his article, Fagan described 10 essential elements that characterize the preinternship practicum training. Summarized, they are (a) experiences may occur in public or private agencies, (b) clinical supervision responsibility remains with university faculty, (c) academic credit is offered, (d) training is completed prior to the internship, (e) training is required for program completion, (f) training is generally limited to a specific academic term, (g) the range of professional activity is limited in scope, (h) campus-based instruction typically occurs concurrently, (i) the primary focus is on training rather than service, and (j) the placement is usually on a part-time basis. The focus of this chapter is to provide an overview of a competency-based model of professional preparation that incorporates the supervision of school psychology candidates completing field-based training practica training at the preinternship level. There has been increased discussion in the literature about establishing a competency-based approach to field-based practica (Harrison & Prus, 2008; Kaslow, 2004; Welsh, Stanley, & Wilmoth, 2003). The competency-based model for training and practice was further elucidated with the recent publication of *School Psychology: A Blueprint for Training and Practice III* (NASP, 2006). This chapter will review a competency-based model for externship training developed at Nicholls State University. In addition, references to supporting literature regarding competency-based training will be embedded throughout this chapter.

ILLUSTRATION OF TRAINING PROGRAM

The externship is intended to function as the initial application-based training students complete that occurs between introductory didactic and practicum training and the culminating internship placement. In order to provide the reader with a foundation for the structure of supervision in a competency-based training system, a brief description is given of the training model of a NASP-approved school psychology program that prepares candidates at the specialist level. The program incorporated a data-based problem solving model (Tilly, 2002), with curriculum objectives and outcomes matched to current NASP standards for training programs. The philosophical roots of the data-based decision maker as a practice model for school psychologists are found in Gray's (1963) concept of the role of the school psychologist as a data-oriented problem solver and later by Edwards (1987) with the "data-based problem solver" model. This practice model was derived from the scientist–practitioner model of graduate training in applied psychology developed at the Boulder Conference in 1949. The data-based problem-solver model is the recommended model for the training of school psychologists, endorsed in both the *Standards for Training* (NASP, 2000) and in *School Psychology: A Blueprint for Training and Practice II* (Ysseldyke et al., 1997). Externship competencies were developed from the more generally stated NASP (2000) practice standards.

A chief characteristic of a competency-based model of training is the incorporation of the data-based problem solver model (Edwards, 1987) that emphasizes an empirically based decision-making approach applied to all aspects of school psychology practice. Training emphasis is given to the development of a "single-case" scientist–practitioner approach to school psychology practice. This practice strategy may be applied to assessment, intervention, consultation, and counseling and appears particularly well suited to meet emerging practice initiatives such as multitiered response to intervention models and ongoing progress monitoring of children's acquisition of preacademic and academic skills. Working in collaboration with field-based supervisors employed in a nearby school district, specific practice competencies stated in behavioral terms were generated from the NASP (2000) *Standards for Training*. More recently, Harrison and Prus (2008) published a list of sample competencies linked to each general NASP practice standards, as well as suggested *Best Practices V* (Thomas & Grimes, 2008) chapters, with either primary or secondary content devoted to professional practice competencies. Three additional performance standards or general competency areas were created that addressed accurate work completion, dissemination of information, and professional conduct. The compilation of the competency-based performance became the foundation for the development of specific training objectives for school psychology students enrolled in preinternship practicum course work. This model also provided a structure for the supervision of students enrolled in school psychology practicum courses. Behaviorally stated training objectives provide the supervisor with a set of measurable performance competencies on which to (a) focus supervision on a broad array of practice skills, (b) provide specific performance feedback to candidates, and (c) develop remediation action plans when necessary.

A key component of the competency-based model of training is the development of a strong collaborative relationship between university faculty and school district clinical supervisors. This important step helps ensure that field-based personnel have ample input into the development of school psychology practice competencies. Field-based supervising school psychologists were instrumental participants in the development of specific competency indicators for the field-based components of the overall school psychology program curriculum. This close collaborative process is important to facilitate the identification and acquisition of a relevant skill-set match between the school psychological service needs of the district and the training program's curriculum. A second important component of the training model is that district supervising school psychologists are full participants in the progress monitoring and evaluation of school psychology students' completing practicum course work. Collaboration at the evaluation level has fostered the development of a cotrainer relationship between university faculty and field-based supervisors. Building a strong collaborative relationship between the university and school personnel in the preparation of school psychology students is essential in creating a successful bridge between university preparation and their initial introduction and completion of field-based training experiences.

One positive outcome of the cotrainer relationship between the university faculty and field-based clinical supervisors was the identification of three essential elements for the preparation of school psychologists. (Kaufman et al., 2000; Welsh et al., 1999, 2003). First, coplanning field-based practicum training objectives worked effectively to build a curriculum bridge between the university components of training and application-based learning objectives. One such objective is to establish a transparent curriculum connection between field-based and university-based training functions to enhance the benefits of the instructional components of the program. Theoretical constructs may be more intelligently discussed or challenged on the basis of knowledge gained in the school-based setting. Second, the school-based practicum provides a connection between the science of school psychology and the data-based practice of school psychology. As the field-based clinical supervisors collaborate effectively with the university instructional staff and supervisors, transfer of training issues may be minimized. Finally, collaborative competency-based training creates the opportunity for practicum students to develop professional maturity through the early application of a broad foundation of applied professional skills coupled to a broad array of presenting problems prior to the internship. In essence, the transition from the world of early graduate school training experiences to field-based application training (e.g., practica or externships), to the internship, to eventual entry into professional practice becomes organized around a seamless collaborative competency-based training model.

COLLABORATIVE COMPETENCY-BASED TRAINING

The collaborative competency-based training allows for the articulation of clearly defined expectations for students' skill-set acquisition that are communicated as well defined behavioral competency indicators (Welsh et al., 2003). This model closely approximates the behavioral model of supervision as discussed by Conoley and Sullivan (2002) and Knoff (1986). At the practicum stage of training, the supervision and performance evaluations of student progress are assessed via *skill present/skill not present* indicators. This dichotomous approach to candidate evaluation enhances the feedback from field-based supervisors and makes clear to the novice student the performance expectations for discrete learning experiences. Through this process, university supervisors, field-based clinical supervisors, and practicum students become keenly aware of progress toward the acquisition of the myriad professional competencies outlined in the curriculum. Ultimately, the model provides for the monitoring of performance consistency as students progress through the practicum training experience. In essence, supervisors ensure that students not only demonstrate the acquisition of professional competencies but perform these skills consistently as opportunities to engage professionally are presented.

The evaluation and supervision of the practicum students' professional skill acquisition is accomplished through the review of case presentations, intervention development, ethical practice, knowledge of assessment, special education law, case problem analysis, and teaming. Practicum students log their daily activities via an online log system. Data obtained from activity log are used to provide analysis of the scope of the practicum students' experiences and assist in the development of constructive feedback to the student and for planning for future practicum experiences. Students participate in self-evaluation of their progress in the attainment of applied practice competencies, followed by an evaluation by field-based supervisors. The outcome of ongoing supervision by field-based and university supervisors via the review of daily logged activities, keyed to practice competencies and supervisors' evaluations results in the development of an ecological inventory of practice competencies that may be reinforced or remediated as necessary. This feedback looping facilitates close correspondence between classroom knowledge and professional skill application.

SUPERVISION IN A COMPETENCY-BASED MODEL

Supervision of candidates during the externship placement occurs at multiple levels. Including supervision sessions, candidates complete approximately 255 hr of training each semester for a total of 560 hr across two semesters. Typically, for every 12 contact hours per week, candidates receive 4 hr of supervision. The intensive 3:1 (activity:supervision) supervision ratio is deemed essential in that novice candidates are participants in live cases.

Individual supervision occurs at the school placement site. The site-based supervisor models, observes, and evaluates candidate acquisition and performance of professional practice competencies. The modeling-imitative approach to supervision allows the candidate to progress from candidate observation of the supervisor, to coparticipation with the supervisor, to observation by the supervisor, and finally to limited supervised practice independence. The supervisor also monitors candidate performance via feedback from multidisciplinary team members and consultation with school staff.

School psychology candidates participate in additional group supervision at both the district and university settings. Candidates meet with the director of the psychological services unit for 1 hr of group supervision each week. The director of the unit is a certified school psychologist who is responsible for the clinical supervision of school psychologists in the district. Supervision at this level generally consists of case staffings and instruction in various skill areas that are related to professional practice. In addition, district policies and procedures are reviewed.

The university supervisor routinely makes site visits to observe candidates and to consult with field-based supervisors regarding candidate progress. Candidates submit weekly logs of field-based activities to the university supervisor. University-based supervision consists of 2 hr each week of group supervision. Additional individual supervision by university faculty is available on an as-needed basis. Candidates prepare case presentations that are critiqued by the supervisor and fellow school psychology candidates. Additional focus is given to professional, ethical, and legal practice issues by the university supervisor.

The competency-based training model provides several benefits to both the school psychology candidate and the supervisor. These include providing a well-defined and clearly articulated (written) set of training objectives, well-defined expectations (skill acquisition and performance consistency), highly specific feedback from supervisors, candidate self-monitoring and self-evaluation, and supervisor-selected training focus. The aforementioned are particularly beneficial when supervising the "problem student." Namely, specific skill deficiencies are easily identified and targeted for additional training focus. The development of specific remediation strategies is readily accomplished and allows for precise monitoring of candidate progress in skill weakness areas. Finally, a permanent product record is embedded in course evaluation documents and automatically generated as evidence of supervisor's remediation strategies. This is particularly valuable if remediation is not successful and the candidate is ultimately judged as not successful in completing the externship course and challenges his or her evaluation via university due process procedures.

PROFESSIONAL COMPETENCIES

The school district supervisors and school psychology program faculty collaborated to identify practice competencies and develop an instrument that outlines planned training competencies that school psychology candidates must complete during externship. This instrument is used to evaluate candidate progress toward acquiring professional practice competencies. The curriculum of professional competencies covers eight essential areas of practice. These areas will be outlined below, with examples of specific competencies linked to the practice standards articulated in the *Standards for Training* (NASP, 2000) that the candidates must acquire and consistently perform. Harrison and Prus (2008) provided additional examples of suggested competencies linked to the NASP training standards. Hatcher and Lassiter (2004) also provided a list of suggested practicum competencies promulgated by the Association of Directors of Psychology Training Clinics Practicum Competencies Workgroup.

Data-based decision making and accountability

School psychologists have knowledge of varied models and methods of assessment that yield information useful in identifying strengths and needs, in understanding problems, and in measuring progress and accomplishments. School psychologists use such models and methods as part of a systematic process to collect data and other information, translate assessment results into empirically based decisions about service delivery, and evaluate the outcomes of services. Data-based decision making permeates every aspect of professional practice.

Competency examples

1. Interprets referral concerns and writes referral questions specific to referral concerns
2. Administers test(s) appropriate for age of student and for referral concerns
3. Demonstrates understanding of adaptive behavior evaluation instruments and data
4. Can logically and accurately state the rationale for prereferral interventions prior to individual assessment
5. Identifies and measures the impact of knowledge of data-based decision making for a student or a targeted group of students

Consultation and collaboration

School psychologists have knowledge of behavioral, mental health, collaborative, and/or other consultation models and methods and of their application to particular situations. School psychologists collaborate effectively with others in planning and decision-making processes at the individual, group, and system levels.

Competency examples

1. Demonstrates solution-focused consultative efforts that reflect concrete (observable) outcomes
2. Solicits and analyzes feedback with regard to collaborative process and acts on feedback to modify own behavior
3. Models and promotes collaborative behaviors between and among parents and educators
4. Identifies and measures the curricular or behavioral impact of a teacher consultation (or series of consultations) on the performance of a specific student or a targeted group of students

Effective instruction and development of cognitive/academic skills

School psychologists have knowledge of human learning processes, techniques to assess these processes, and direct and indirect services applicable to the development of cognitive and academic skills. School psychologists, in collaboration with others, develop appropriate cognitive and academic goals for students with different abilities, disabilities, strengths, and needs; implement interventions to achieve those goals; and evaluate the effectiveness of interventions. Such interventions include, but are not limited to, instructional interventions and consultation.

Competency examples

1. States rationale of explanation of the results of behavioral intervention pursuant to the referral question
2. Communicates intervention strategy appropriate to teacher and/or parent
3. Demonstrates knowledge of and can apply, at a minimum, three individual behavioral interventions and three class-wide behavioral interventions
4. Identifies and measures the impact of an instructional intervention for a single student

Socialization and development of life skills

School psychologists have knowledge of human developmental processes, techniques to assess these processes, and direct and indirect services applicable to the development of behavioral, affective, adaptive, and social skills. School psychologists, in collaboration with others, develop appropriate behavioral, affective, adaptive, and social goals for students of varying abilities, disabilities, strengths, and needs; implement interventions to achieve those goals; and evaluate the effectiveness of interventions. Such interventions include, but are not limited to, consultation, behavioral assessment/intervention, and counseling.

Competency examples

1. Demonstrates ability to document student progress using SOAP (subjective, objective, assessment, plan) note format
2. Demonstrates the ability to identify when students reveal problems that are beyond the scope of the counseling session and are appropriately referred to the supervisor
3. Can state limits of confidentiality with minors
4. Identifies and measures the student impact of a counseling intervention(s) for a student or targeted group

Student diversity in development and learning

School psychologists have knowledge of individual differences, abilities, and disabilities and of the potential influence of biological, social, cultural, ethnic, experiential, socioeconomic, gender-related, and linguistic factors in development and learning. School psychologists demonstrate the sensitivity and skills needed to work with individuals of diverse characteristics and to implement strategies selected and/or adapted based on individual characteristics, strengths, and needs.

Competency examples

1. Demonstrates cultural sensitivity in written and verbal communication with student, parents, and peers
2. Demonstrates, through speech and posture, receptivity to ideas of others

School and systems organization, policy development, and climate

School psychologists have knowledge of general education, special education, and other educational and related services. They understand schools and other settings as systems. School psychologists work with individuals and groups to facilitate policies and practices that create and maintain safe, supportive, and effective learning environments for children and others.

Competency examples

1. Objectively defines the role of the school psychologist as a mental health provider and identifies areas in which school systems provide mental health services in active support of student health, adjustment, and personal growth and development

Prevention, crisis intervention, and mental health

School psychologists have knowledge of human development and psychopathology and of associated biological, cultural, and social influences on human behavior. School psychologists provide or contribute to prevention and intervention programs that promote the mental health and physical well-being of students.

Competency examples

1. Demonstrates knowledge of national organizations that foster awareness and provide training and direct assistance to schools in prevention, crisis intervention, and mental health
2. Demonstrates knowledge of human development and psychopathology as factors that influence student performance in the curricular and social aspects of their school experience
3. Identifies and applies effective prevention strategies for common school crisis situations
4. Demonstrates knowledge of the school system's crisis/safety plan and of the specific crisis/safety plan for the school

Home/school/community collaboration

School psychologists have knowledge of family systems, including family strengths and influences on student development, learning, and behavior, and of methods to involve families in education and service delivery. School psychologists work effectively with families, educators, and others in the community to promote and provide comprehensive services to children and families.

Competency examples

1. Does not by word or deed discredit a teacher/parent to another teacher/parent
2. Demonstrates empowerment skills in consultative strategies with parents
3. Models and promotes collaborative behaviors between and among parents and educators
4. Adequately prepares for questions to be asked by parents

Research and program evaluation

School psychologists have knowledge of research, statistics, and evaluation methods. School psychologists evaluate research, translate research into practice, and understand research design and statistics in sufficient depth to plan and conduct investigations and program evaluations for improvement of services.

Competency examples

1. Designs intervention appropriate to behavioral concerns
2. Demonstrates scientific method through application of intervention strategies and analysis of data
3. States rationale of explanation of the results of academic intervention pursuant to the referral question

School psychology practice and development

School psychologists have knowledge of the history and foundations of their profession; of various service models and methods; of public policy development applicable to services to children and families; and of ethical, professional, and legal standards. School psychologists practice in ways that are consistent with applicable standards, are involved in their profession, and have the knowledge and skills needed to acquire career-long professional development.

Competency examples

1. Demonstrates adherence to confidentiality standards as reflected in written and verbal communication about individual student case records
2. Interprets and applies the Family Educational Rights Privacy Act
3. Demonstrates understanding of the extent of his or her level of professional development and responsibly performs duties as an extern, by not exceeding or abdicating these responsibilities
4. Adheres to procedural sequence in dissemination of student specific information, i.e., supervisor of special education (first), parent (second), schools (third), and third parties (fourth)

Information technology

School psychologists have knowledge of information sources and technology relevant to their work. School psychologists access, evaluate, and utilize information sources and technology in ways that safeguard or enhance the quality of services.

Competency examples

1. Demonstrates ability to accurately use computer scoring systems

Additional competency area 1: completes work accurately

1. Test protocols are completed accurately
2. Data are interpreted and synthesized into a meaningful, informative, easy to read and understand report and recommendations

3. Completes appropriate sequence(s) of assessment tasks in a timely manner
4. Demonstrates understanding of corrective action procedures for "aborted" tests

Additional competency area 2: dissemination of information

1. Effectively and sensitively interprets evaluation results/data to parent and/or teachers
2. Interprets evaluation results without exceeding the limitations of the assessment tools used
3. Writes letters to parents without use of jargon, yet effectively communicates abstract assessment issues
4. Describes student behavior without attribution

Additional competency area 3: professional conduct

1. Demonstrates effective interpersonal communication and personal management style
2. Demonstrates, through speech and posture, receptivity to ideas of others
3. Does not by word or deed discredit a teacher/parent to another teacher/parent
4. Demonstrates observable change in professional behavior consistent with supervisor(s) suggestions
5. Offers suggestions and criticisms to appropriate supervisor in private

The preceding list is intended to provide the reader with a sample of professional practice competencies addressed during preinternship field-based practica. The complete list contains a total of 145 specific professional practice competencies. A complete copy of the Planned Experience Competencies Evaluation forms may be obtained from the following Web site: http://pac.lafourche.k12.la.us.

DISCUSSION

Preinternship practica represent a critical period in the development and acquisition of professional skill sets as the school psychology student transitions from the university classroom to applied school-based settings. This chapter reviewed a collaborative competency-based model of training and supervision of school psychology students completing field-based training at the preinternship level. The practicum functions as a bridge between university-based course work and the culminating internship. The collaborative competency-based model was structured around a training approach where emphasis was given to the development of single-case research designs applied to the broad spectrum of school psychology practices. The *Standards for Training* (NASP, 2000) provided the foundation for the development of a comprehensive collection of training objectives. From the NASP practice standard elements 2.1 through 2.11, a list of specific objectively stated practice competencies were generated. In addition, additional global practice elements of accurate work completion, dissemination of information, and professional conduct were created.

As reported by Welsh et al. (2003), preinternship practica serve three essential functions in the preparation of school psychologists. First, the field-based practicum functions as a link between the classroom component of training and application-based learning. Second, the practicum provides a connection between the science of school psychology and the data-based practice of school psychology. Finally, the practicum creates the opportunity for a school psychology student to develop professional maturity through the early application of a broad foundation of applied professional competencies and exposure to various presenting problems prior to the internship.

Supervision and evaluation of candidate progress are assessed via skill present/skill not present indicators. In addition, the model provides for the monitoring of performance consistency as candidates progress through externship training experiences. Supervision of candidates during the externship placement occurs at multiple levels. Including supervision sessions, candidates complete approximately 255 hr of training each semester for a total of 560 hr across two semesters. The site-based supervisor models, observes, and evaluates candidate acquisition and performance of professional practice competencies. The supervisor also monitors candidate performance via feedback from multidisciplinary team members and consultation with school staff. School psychology candidates participate in additional group supervision in both district and university settings. Candidates meet with the director of the psychological services unit for 1 hr of group supervision each week and the university supervisor for 2 hr each week. The university supervisor routinely makes site visits to observe candidates and to consult with field-based supervisors regarding candidate progress.

The key component to the development of this competency-based training model lies in the collaborative relationship between university faculty and district school psychologists. The school district supervisors and school psychology program faculty collaborated to identify practice competencies and develop the model that outlines planned training competencies that school psychology candidates must complete during externship. This model is used to evaluate candidate progress toward acquiring professional practice competencies. The relationship between the university and the district evolved over time and continues to evolve. District supervising school psychologists were instrumental participants in the development of specific competency indicators for the field-based component of the curriculum. They continue to be instrumental in the modification of these competencies as NASP standards for training and the field of school psychology evolves. School-based supervisors of candidates are full participants in the progress monitoring and evaluation of school psychology candidates. The data that are accumulated from these various evaluations are used to facilitate program evaluation and modification. Therefore, district supervising school psychologists are important collaborating participants in ongoing program development as the program trains the school psychologists that may soon work along side them. This collaborative relationship has led to the development of a cotrainer relationship between university faculty and field-based supervisors.

SUMMARY

The competency-based preinternship approach to training appears to be well supported in contemporary literature. Whether elements of a competency-based practicum curriculum are defined in very explicit behavioral terminology or in more broad-stroke general categories, it is important to note that a competency-based model does not guarantee that all students will have the exact same set of learning experiences. For example, students may employ skills associated with a behavioral consultation with a regular education or a special education teacher. One student may have the opportunity to teach social skills to a child with a child with high-incidence concern, whereas another student my assist a child with a low-incidence concern. Competency indicators may be addressed through a variety of different experience opportunities. One student may become familiar with effective crisis prevention through the review of a formal plan and "table-top" walk-through of procedures. Another student may be exposed to an actual crisis response activity. In some cases, specific competency performance opportunities cannot be predicted or may occur at very low rates, limiting the student's opportunity to acquire mastery with a specific competency. In some cases, learning opportunities may be serendipitous, and by just being in the right place at the right time, some students may be afforded excellent learning opportunities, while others are less fortunate.

Even within the context of a competence-based model, trainers should work collaboratively with field-site personnel to ensure to the greatest extent possible that appropriate learning opportunities are made available to all students. Student readiness and assertiveness may affect the extent to which they seek out learning opportunities. It is not uncommon for students who have completed testing courses prior to enrolling in field-based practica to feel more comfortable participating in psychoeducational evaluations. However, students may feel less confident engaging in behavioral or instructional consultation activities or referring a family to an outside mental health resource because of limited experience with assuming the role of consultant or case manager. It is critical that students develop their critical thinking and a data-based problem solving skills prior to beginning the culminating internship. Mitigating the variability in learning opportunities is the responsibility of the site and university-based supervisors. Ensuring a rotation of shadowing with several district professionals may ensure that students are exposure to a sufficiently broad range of learning opportunities. Shadowing professionals other than school psychologists may be advisable in order that students be exposed to a broad range of professional expertise in a multidisciplinary working environment.

The function of preinternship field-based practica is to introduce students to initial applied professional experiences. Naturally, supervision of these neophytes is critical in order to ensure that students develop a broad range of professional competencies prior to entering the culminating internship. This chapter has discussed a competency-based training model for the preinternship preparation of school psychologist. Implicit in this presentation is the development of a cotrainer relationship with field-based supervisors. The extent to which field-based supervisors and university faculty collaborate can have a profound impact on translating classroom-based content to the applied world of professional practice. Ultimately, the acquisition of well-established data-based decision making skills, developing the ability to engage successfully in a problem solving leadership role, building effective professional communication skills, and understand how to effectively utilize clinical supervision are critical competencies that should be acquired during the preinternship field-based practicum training.

RESOURCES

National Association of School Psychologists. (2000). *Standards for training and field placement programs in school psychology.* (Expanded descriptions of domains of school psychology training and practice, pp. 22–35). Retrieved October 15, 2008, from http://www.nasponline.org/standards/FinalStandards.pdf
This document describes the NASP-approved set of comprehensive standards for preparation, credentialing, and professional practice in school psychology. The expanded descriptions of the standards are helpful in developing training competencies.

Proceedings of the multisite conference on the future of school psychology [Special issue]. (2004). *School Psychology Review, 33*(1).
Included in this issue is an overview of the proceedings from the 2002 Futures Conference. Articles included discussions of the conference proceedings, comments, and themes addressed. Additional information can be found at http://www.indiana.edu/~futures

Ysseldyke, J. E., Burns, M. K., Dawson, M., Kelly, B., Morrison, D., Ortiz, S., Rosenfield, S., & Telzrow, C. (2006). *School psychology: A blueprint for the future of training and practice III.* Bethesda, MD: National Association of School Psychologists.

The *Blueprint* provides a guide to practice and training in school psychology. The authors offer a discussion of the foundation of training and practice, domains of competence, service delivery, and competencies of students.

REFERENCES

American Psychological Association. (2000). *Guidelines and principles for accreditation of programs in professional psychology* [Brochure]. Washington, DC: Author.

Brown, D. (1981). Graduate training in school psychology. *Journal of Learning Disabilities, 14,* 378–379.

Brown, D. T., & Minke, K. M. (1986). School psychology graduate training: A comprehensive analysis. *American Psychologist, 41,* 1328–1338.

Clair, T., Osterman, R., Kiraly, J., Klausmeier, R., & Graff, M. (1971). Practicum and internship experiences in school psychology: Recent trends in graduate training. *The American Psychologist, 26,* 566–574.

Conoley, J. C., & Sullivan, J. R. (2002). Best practices in the supervision of interns. In A. Thomas & Grimes, J. (Eds.). *Best practices in school psychology IV* (pp. 131–144). Washington, DC: National Association of School Psychologists.

Crespi, T. D., & Lopez, P. G. (1998). Practicum and internship supervision in the schools: Standards and considerations for school psychology supervisors. *Clinical Supervisor, 17,* 113–126.

Edwards, R. (1987). Implementing the scientist-practitioner model: The school psychologist as data-based problem solver. *Professional School Psychology, 2*(3), 155–161.

Fagan, T. K. (1977). Standards for field placements in school psychology. *School Psychology Digest, 6*(2), 34–50.

Gray, S. W. (1963). *The psychologist in the schools.* New York: Holt, Rinehart & Winston.

Hatcher, R., & Lassitter, K. (2004). *Report on practicum competencies.* The Association of Directors of Psychology Training Clinics Practicum Competencies Workgroup.

Harrison, P., & Prus, J. (2008). Best practices in integrating Best Practices V content with NASP standards. In A. Thomas & J. Grimes (Eds.), *Best practices in school psychology V* (pp. 77–99). Bethesda, MD: National Association of School Psychologists.

Kaslow, N. (2004). Competencies in professional psychology. *American Psychologist, 59,* 774–781.

Kaufman, J., Crespi, T., Rosenfield, S., Welsh, J. S., Wilmoth, C., & Hodnett, E. (2000, March–April). *Models and techniques for the supervision of school psychologists in training.* Mini-skills workshop presented at the annual meeting of the National Association of School Psychologists, New Orleans, LA.

Knoff, H. M. (1986). Supervision in school psychology: The forgotten or future path to effective services. *School Psychology Review, 15*(4), 529–545.

Ko, S., & Rodolfa, E. (2005). Psychology training directors' views of number of practicum hours necessary prior to internship application. *Professional Psychology: Research and Practice, 36*, 318–322.

Kramer, J., & Ryabik, J. (1981). The practicum in school psychology: Making use of a university-based psychological service center. *Psychology in the Schools, 18*, 197–200.

Lafourche Parish Public Schools. (2005). Lafourche Parish pupil appraisal center. Retrieved on July 2, 2009 from http://pac.lafourche.k12.la.us.

Lewis, B., Hatcher, R., & Pate II, W. (2005). The practicum experience: A survey of practicum site coordinators. *Professional Psychology: Research and Practice, 36*, 291–298.

National Association of School Psychologists. (2000). *Standards for training and field placement programs in school psychology* [Brochure]. Washington, DC: Author.

Pryzwansky, W. (1971). Practicum training in the school setting. *Psychology in the Schools, 8*, 307–313.

Rodolfa, E., Owen, J., & Clark, S. (2007). Practicum training hours: Fact and fantasy. *Training and Education in Professional Psychology, 3*, 64–73.

Tarquin, K., & Truscott, S. (2006). School psychology students' perceptions of their practicum experiences. *Psychology in the Schools, 43*(6), 727–736.

Teglasi, H., & Pumroy, D. (1982). Field experiences in school psychology programs. *Journal of School Psychology, 20*, 188–197.

Thomas, A., & Grimes, J. (Eds.). (2008). *Best practices in school psychology V.* Bethesda, MD: National Association of School Psychologists.

Tilly, W. D., III. (2002). Best practices in school psychology as a problem-solving enterprise. In A. Thomas & J. Grimes (Eds.), *Best practices in school psychology IV* (pp. 21–36). Bethesda, MD: National Association of School Psychologists.

Welsh, J. S., Stanley, J., & Wilmoth, C. (2003). Competency based pre-internship supervision of school psychologists: A collaborative training model. *The Clinical Supervisor, 22*(1), 177–189.

Welsh, J. S., Wilmoth, C., & Hodnut, E. (1999, April). *The benefit of early field based experiences in skills acquisition for pre-specialist students in school psychology: A competency based approach to professional preparation.* Paper presented at the annual meeting of the National Association of School Psychologists, Las Vegas, NV.

Ysseldyke, J., Dawson, P., Lehr, C., Reschley, D., Reynolds, M., & Telzrow, C. (1997). *School psychology: A blueprint for training and practice II* [Brochure]. Bethesda, MD: National Association of School Psychologists.

4 Collaborative supervision of internship experiences

George W. Hebert and
Constance Patterson

INTRODUCTION

As the role of the school psychologist continues to expand, so must the role of school psychology supervisors. School psychology has always been deeply rooted in both education and mental health. Therefore, it is of absolute importance that current school psychology trainers and supervisors support school psychology trainees to meet the challenges of these expanding roles from both perspectives. The literature on school psychology supervision is sparse compared with the published articles relating to counseling and clinical psychology supervision (McIntosh & Phelps, 2000). Ironically, school psychology interns probably receive attention from more "supervisors" than any other interns in all of the psychology specialties. The people overseeing the work of a school psychology intern (i.e., supervisors) could include the professional supervisor, the local educational agency (LEA) supervisor, the internship supervisor, and a university supervisor. With all of this supervision, one would expect this to be a lively area of research; however, this is not the case, and supervision in school psychology training needs to be investigated and documented in order to promote strong support to trainees and best practices in services from the beginning of the intern's professional career.

Although there have been many proposed definitions of supervision, the one developed by McIntosh and Phelps (2000) is perhaps the most comprehensive. These authors defined supervision as follows:

> an interpersonal interaction between two or more individuals for the purpose of sharing knowledge, assessing professional competencies, and providing objective feedback with the terminal goals of developing new competencies, facilitating effective delivery of psychological services, and maintaining professional competencies. (p. 33)

Most would agree that supervision of psychological services is a demanding set of professional challenges replete with liabilities. By necessity, the supervisor must maintain familiarity with emerging empirically supported practice, monitor multiple activities of the supervisee, understand and protect the many clients served by the supervisee, and participate in an ongoing relationship that fosters another's growth. Obviously, the complexities of supervision are both difficult to identify and difficult to explain. When supervising a trainee, the complexity of tasks is vastly expanded.

Supervision is designed to benefit both the intern and those receiving the services. Effective supervision therefore benefits the entire profession by increasing competency for practice and by protecting the public. The ultimate goal of supervision is the development of a competent, independently functioning practitioner. The primary subgoals may best be broken down into the functional competencies that would include assessment and case conceptualization, crisis assessment, individual and group intervention, consultation, research/evaluation, supervision-teaching, and management/administration. Related foundational competency areas that overlap with those previously mentioned include ethical and legal issues, relationships, effective interdisciplinary functioning, scientific knowledge, cultural diversity, and reflective practice as defined by the Competency Benchmarks Work Group (American Psychological Association [APA], 2007).

This chapter will address the complexities involved in the collaborative supervision that occurs during the school psychology internship, with particular reference to practice in the Louisiana School Psychology Internship Consortium, an internship in school psychology accredited by the APA. The notion of supervision as it relates to all involved parties and to the particular skill areas that would make one professionally competent will be explored. More specifically, the parties involved include the intern, the supervisors, and the people receiving services from the intern. The specific competency areas will be addressed as they relate to the role and function of the intern. As always, a review of the literature is appropriate place to begin in order to assess where the profession currently stands.

LITERATURE REVIEW

The internship has long been regarded as the capstone experience in school psychology; however, the literature regarding practicum and internship practices is lacking, especially when one considers the published research on other school psychology topics, such as assessment or treatment. Certainly, areas such as assessment and treatment lend themselves more easily to the rigors of scientific investigation. In addition, some trainers may believe that a student need only apply the skills that have been learned in the classroom to arrive at a level of successful competency for practice, and consequently undervalue the role of supervision. Some trainers probably believe that supervised practica bridge the gap between university training and the internship experience. However, empirical investigation of our training practices is necessary to perpetuate our science and to document successfully preparing effective practitioners. This section will chronologically review professional writings germane to supervision practice as it relates to the school psychology internship.

The Thayer Conference of 1954 appears to have developed the earliest definition of a school psychologist by consensus through a national conference (Fagan, 2005). The Thayer Conference also supported the need for supervised practica and internships as part of training for school psychologists (Murphy, 1981); however, it would be years before any specific descriptions of supervisory activities would appear in the professional literature. Like most evolved professions, the first school psychologists were not trained by school psychologists. Goh (1977) reported that early in our history, many school psychology students received their training from clinical and educational psychologists, guidance counselors, and special educators. Goh concluded that this was a result of the short history of school psychology as a highly specialized area of graduate education and that it would take years for the few doctoral programs to produce university trainers who themselves would be legitimate school psychologists.

As a means of skill delineation, Catterall (1973) documented a committee's attempts to define in behavioral terms a list of abilities that would represent the minimal level of competency to be performed by a person first entering the practice of school psychology. Although this article reports that every effort was made to envision the psychologist's role as much more than a psychometrician, it appeared that testing competencies were stressed significantly more than other skill areas, such as consultation. Historically, this is not surprising, since standardized testing was the primary form of assessment of children's needs.

It was not until Ross-Reynolds and Grimes (1981) edited a special issue of the *School Psychology Review* that supervision issues in the field of school psychology received major attention. In this special series of articles, competencies of both the practitioner and the supervisor were addressed, as were recommended strategies to facilitate successful supervision. Unfortunately, there have been few additional scientific investigations or writings regarding supervision practices. Some researchers have surmised that designing, implementing, conducting, and analyzing supervision research would be a monumental task and thus prohibitive (McIntosh & Phelps, 2000).

TRAINING FOR PROFESSIONAL ROLES AND FUNCTIONS

Internships provide a coherent, organized, and sequential series of training experiences designed to allow interns to acquire competencies across the breadth of roles and responsibilities in their area of specialty within the field. Given the diverse university training within school psychology, an internship that offers training to young professionals from multiple universities provides a rich learning environment as interns share from their varied perspectives, but this also poses additional challenges in meeting a wide variety of intern needs. Following the 2002 Competencies Conference: Future Directions in Education and Credentialing in Professional Psychology (Kaslow, 2004), there has been a growing awareness among trainers of school psychologists for the need to specify and measure outcomes based on a set of competencies for professional practice. In the past several years, an American Psychological Association Task Force on the Assessment of Competency in Professional Psychology (APA, 2007) had been working to identify the competencies necessary for best practice in the field of psychology and to begin to set standards for these for training and entry into the field. In early 2007, the task force produced a draft set of competencies to offer guidance for trainers. These competencies are based on the expectations of the APA ethical code and are consistent with standards of accreditation for training programs in professional psychology. Specific skill-based competencies include assessment and case conceptualization, crisis assessment, individual and group intervention, consultation, research/evaluation, supervision-teaching, and management/administration. A number of foundational competency areas apply across all the skills and include competencies with ethical and legal issues, relationships, effective interdisciplinary functioning, scientific knowledge, cultural diversity, and reflective practice as published in the final report of the Task Force (APA, 2007). The Competency Benchmarks Work Group suggested entry levels of competency in each area for trainees and for those about to enter the field as new professionals.

TYPES OF SUPERVISION

Supervision during internship comes in many forms. For the purpose of discussion, line supervision will be defined here as any type of supervision where there is a power differential between the intern and the supervisor. The various line supervisors include the LEA supervisor, the professional supervisor, the internship supervisor, and the university supervisor. Over the course of the internship, the power differential between the intern and supervisors will be diminished; the relationships will become more egalitarian, as the intern demonstrates increased competence and feels increased confidence in his or her capabilities. Other types of supervision that do not involve a power differential may include peer supervision and self-supervision. Each of these forms of supervision will be briefly discussed in the following sections.

Line supervision

Line supervision involves any type of supervision where there is an imbalance of power between the parties involved. In the work setting (i.e., the LEA), the supervisor may also be known as the boss and can be responsible for monitoring and supporting the functioning of many other professionals. The role of this person, also known as an administrative supervisor, largely involves facilitating successful entry into the system and mentoring the intern into the policies and practices in the LEA setting. The professional supervisor may serve as the surrogate university professor who monitors best practice and ethics. He or she is responsible for the day-to-day functioning of the professional-in-training and has ultimate responsibility for the clients under the intern's care. The internship supervisor ensures adherence to the mission and goals of the internship program and insists on high standards for all interns. Finally, the university supervisor monitors the internship experience to ensure that it provides appropriate integration of the elements of the university training program and verifies that the intern has consolidated the range of skills needed for official entry into the profession.

In some fashion, all of these supervisors interact with each other to ensure that the intern is receiving appropriate support and making sufficient progress. The responsibilities that each supervisor bears should be clarified, and the overlap between roles of the different supervisors should be discussed well in advance of working with interns. The methods and timing of communication need to be clear and designed to prevent problems and to facilitate problem solving as difficulties inevitably arise. Should there be conflict among the various supervisors, it is very important to protect the intern from being caught in the middle like children during marital discord. In each of the following sections, proper channels of communication will be suggested for the complex relationships.

LEA supervision

The LEA supervisor is primarily in charge of making sure the work is completed and is responsible for ensuring that professional personnel follow established policies and procedures. Traditionally, school psychologists serve as members of multidisciplinary teams, and in many school districts they report to a coordinator of pupil support and appraisal services. This coordinator usually reports to the director of special education. Even as the focus of services to school-aged children shifts to a more intervention orientation, the primary objective of most pupil appraisal coordinators continues to be to ensure that initial evaluations and re-evaluations of exceptional students occur within the appropriate time lines and conform to legal guidelines that define disability categories under Individuals with Disabilities Education Improvement Act and state statutes. Since this is usually a monumental task, in some settings little effort may be available to support broader professional roles or to improve the quality of the services. As a result, interns may see the LEA supervisor as perpetually drowning in the massive demands and work flow of the system and judge him or her as virtually ineffective in leadership roles and as not investing in any types of system change. This may undermine the intern's perception of the value of the supervision provided. Giving the intern and supervisor explicit opportunities to explore together the systemic demands and their impact on individual professional practice is an important tool for fostering a more functional supervisory relationship.

Professional supervision

The professional supervisor is the licensed psychologist who may work in a different setting than the intern, but who is ultimately responsible for the intern's clients. It is imperative that the professional supervisor impress upon the intern the need for ethical and empirically supported best practices, even if the school district appears to promote a factory conveyer-belt approach to service delivery. It is incumbent upon the professional supervisor to promote an ecological developmental perspective that allows the intern to conceptualize and assess a problem in its context, and to choose an empirically supported process that allows implementation of useful strategies and interventions and that allows the intern to both increase skills and learn more about himself or herself as a professional. It is the role of the professional supervisor to support the intern in having a genuine learning experience, and as part of that experience to question and challenge the various actions the intern may take. Posing questions and challenges in supervision promotes reflective practice. As developing professionals become more aware of areas of strength and needed growth, they can more readily understand the scope of their developing expertise and take on the responsibility for setting goals to expand and improve their competencies. This establishes the basis for lifelong learning, which is necessary for all practicing psychologists, as the field is constantly changing.

Importantly, raising challenges and questions is especially warranted when the intern performs or is asked to perform a service inconsistent with best practice. The complexities of negotiation and diplomacy appear to peak at this point. The professional supervisor may require the intern to inquire about the history or reasons for some type of practice in the respective LEA and report back during supervision. Once the reason for the practice is discovered, then alternative strategies can be explored. This challenge to established practices is a very important activity during supervision, for it teaches that psychologists as professionals must not perform duties like automated robots and allows the supervisor to model professional problem solving as it impacts needed social change. The professional supervisor should follow established protocol to address problem solving in collaboration with the LEA supervisor. As a learning exercise, the professional supervisor and intern should explore the rationale for not accepting anything less than best practice.

It may be customary practice in the LEA to deliver this less than best practice service, but the professional supervisor is responsible for ensuring that the intern is not forced to participate in inappropriate practices. Sometimes this can be a collaborative experience that models effective problem solving and helps the intern learn systems change skills. If the intern reports that some role must be performed according to the customary practice, it may be an appropriate time for the professional supervisor to engage the LEA supervisor in a conversation without the intern present. As noted earlier, if the intern is present during a disagreement between supervisors, it can place the intern in a compromising position. Therefore, it becomes imperative that the professional supervisor and LEA supervisor negotiate some type of agreement that will meet the need of the district and at the same time support the intern's training needs. The professional supervisor has the responsibility for gathering and coordinating the feedback about the intern's performance for quarterly evaluations. Working closely with the LEA supervisor and the internship supervisor, it is possible to compile a broad profile of the intern's competencies.

Internship supervision

Some school psychology internship programs are accredited by the American Psychological Association. These internships are generally the most sought after since they facilitate licensure eligibility in most states; however, internship programs must both maintain their integrity and follow appropriate empirically supported trends in training psychologists as these emerge. It generally falls upon the internship training director or coordinator to ensure that the internship experiences maintain the quality and integrity that APA has reviewed when accrediting the program. Therefore, this additional supervision is required in order to monitor and provide oversight in a programmatic fashion and to document that all interns demonstrate intermediate or advanced competencies by the end of the internship across all expected professional activities.

An organized internship generally has a curriculum, and the internship training director or coordinator usually has primary responsibility for managing and revising it. It is consistent with a best practice approach that the curriculum address training standards set by professional organizations (e.g., Ysseldyke, Morrison, Burns, Ortiz, Dawson, Rosenfield, et al., 2006). This ensures that all interns receive the same core instruction, regardless of their specific practice settings. Consequently, this helps guarantee that by the end of the year, all the interns can demonstrate similar levels of competence, despite the level of preparation provided by their sending universities.

The internship supervisor also bears the responsibility for ensuring that the varied personnel providing supervisory support to the intern are following procedures that address and promote the intern's learning needs first.

In addition, it is the internship supervisor's responsibility to ensure that all internship personnel collaborate to support interns and to facilitate good problem solving when difficulties arise.

University supervision

All graduate programs in school psychology designate a faculty member to serve as a contact person between the sending university and the internship site during their students' internship experiences. This person monitors the continuity of training from the university standpoint and, if the need arises, may advocate for the intern and serve as arbiter and ethical enforcer. Although there is a growing interest in closer collaboration between sending university and internship personnel, the university supervisor often plays a minor role during the internship year and may receive only quarterly or semiannual feedback on the student's internship performance.

The role of the university supervisor can be most vital when there are significant concerns that arise about the intern's performance. For small concerns, internship programs will generally engage in their own problem-solving process, in a collaborative effort among the intern, the supervisor, and the internship training director or coordinator; however, when more serious problems arise, the university supervisor, internship supervisor, and professional supervisor work closely together to support successful completion of the internship. Clear definitions of problem areas and open communication and documentation of the problems should be priorities in the collaboration. In this instance, the university supervisor may become actively involved in a remediation plan if significant problems have been identified. Problems may range from skill or performance deficits to personal illness that impacts practice. Skill or performance deficits may be resolved in a fashion that is analogous to an academic or behavioral intervention. More serious problems that are not responsive to intervention or remediation may require that the intern be counseled to consider other options, including resigning from the internship.

Peer supervision

Some internship sites set aside time during training to allow interns to engage in peer supervision without the presence of internship personnel. These sessions should be oriented toward allowing interns to ask questions, explore issues together, and offer assistance from their own areas of expertise. The format of peer supervision can range from interaction among the entire group of interns in a program to pairs or small groups, depending on issues or needs. The supervision sessions may be treatment oriented, but they may also be related to unusual cases or to ethical issues interns have encountered. Internships should provide some means for documentation of how the time was spent in order to monitor and ensure the integrity of this process.

Peer supervision opportunities can further facilitate the transition from intern to professional, and they are crucial to interns' professional development. Because peer supervision is often the primary mode of ongoing supervisory support in a school psychologist's career, it is important to model and encourage a rich peer supervision experience during internship. It is important to set expectations that interns will be engaged in providing support and peer supervision and to establish a schedule. Developing strategies for promoting effective interaction and problem solving should receive explicit attention throughout the period of internship. Asking interns to establish ground rules about how supportive peer supervisory interactions will occur and to decide how to structure this kind of support will give foster ownership of the process and encourage the expression of preferences about providing and receiving feedback. Training staff may choose to model a variety of ways to use peer supervision, including peer consultation, case presentation, skill observation and feedback, skill coaching, journal groups, and so on. Explicit guidelines for problem solving should also be part of the process of forming an effective peer supervision process.

PEDAGOGICAL ISSUES

The training standards that currently exist and those that have been proposed or are being developed (Ysseldyke et al., 2006; APA, 2007) have resulted in university programs producing some of the best prepared young professionals who have ever been trained to practice as school psychologists. Their content knowledge is increasingly tied to empirically supported practice and has both depth and breadth across key issues and roles; however, those working with these well-prepared young professionals-in-training at the internship level are challenged to address and support the complex translation of a rich knowledge base into competencies demonstrated through hands-on practice. Although many university training directors may believe their students have excellent skills and may quickly be ready for independent practice, internship training directors and supervisors who have repeatedly observed the struggle to integrate many discrete skills into a coherent professional identity may be somewhat more skeptical that this can be accomplished in a single year of internship. The following section describes training at the Louisiana School Psychology Internship Consortium. The internship is a consortium partnership among several school districts and coordinated under the auspices of the Louisiana State University Health Sciences Center. It offers a generalist internship in school psychology based in the schools for both doctoral and specialist students. Training focuses on using a planned and sequential set of professional practice and training experiences to allow students to develop, integrate, and hone a broad set of skills during internship. The ongoing collaboration among the training staff and various supervisors support intern professional development over the course of a 12-month year.

The application procedures of the Association of Psychology Postdoctoral and Internship Centers (APPIC) and National Matching Service are used to allow interns to be matched with specific school district sites on the basis of prior university training and desired internship experiences that are available in the setting. Within each of the sites, there is a 4-day-a-week practice, and interns are supervised by both a professional, licensed psychologist and an LEA administrative supervisor. The 5th day is spent in training and supervision activities.

Interns are provided with training activities and structured opportunities to engage in professional practice under the supervision of a licensed professional school psychologist. Supervision begins with intense support, and gradually this support becomes less intense and more collegial as the intern gains confidence and demonstrates growing levels of competence. The training curriculum supports translation of knowledge to skills as students practice in the school setting, and training personnel work with supervisors to ensure that interns demonstrate the application of their knowledge in a best practices model.

Even well-trained and knowledgeable interns may approach the beginning of their professional practice with minimal confidence and may benefit from considerable structure, support, and guidance. Internship trainers and supervisors need to meet the professionals-in-training at the level where they begin and be prepared to provide appropriate guidance, encouragement, and professional support. Asking students to disclose doubts or concerns may be a challenge, however. Graduate students are generally socialized to demonstrate their best skills and not to disclose their deficits or needs, since these may be perceived as weaknesses and result in poor performance evaluations and lower grades. In addition, they are likely to find the expectations for the new setting quite stressful, and in this state of heightened vulnerability, they may be even less willing to disclose what they perceive as weaknesses. Consequently, training personnel and supervisors should be prepared to normalize professional doubts and discomfort as part of the typical sequence of training activities.

The internship program invests a broad system of resources to support the developmental process that bridges the transition from university training toward independent professional practice. In order to best support and prepare new professionals, the internship provides regularly scheduled time set aside for didactic and experiential learning, and the training activities are geared for maximum engagement and participation from the interns. Interns will be asked to present on their areas of interest and expertise, incorporating empirical supported concepts. Each will be asked to participate in some training activity in their schools, and all will either present a poster or collaborate in a workshop presentation at the Louisiana School Psychological Association. These training activities allow interns to take more responsibility for their own professional development and have the added advantage of supporting earlier contributions to the field by allowing them to build stronger skills in presenting and training.

Psychologists generally enter the field with some notion of improving the functioning of others, and school psychologists are no exception. Interns will develop an understanding of the scope of practice in a given school or with a particular case, but interns should also be encouraged to develop an ecological perspective about their district. Interns can be supported in taking more systemic and ecologically valid perspectives if they are asked to gather data and build a profile of the district in which they are interning. Characteristics such as numbers of students, failing and successful schools, special education populations, range of family socioeconomic status (SES), student outcomes such as graduation rates, and the diversity of the student body can help interns understand the context in which they work, allow them to determine the value of their work to their constituent populations, and allow them the opportunity to understand the potential for social impact as they engage in their various roles. Understanding contextual issues also lays groundwork for recognizing and working more effectively with diversity and across roles and functions. Interns then discuss their district and school profiles with their supervisors in order to provide a context for their working together.

At a macro level, the internship should set the stage for professional development over the professional life span. Guided professional experiences should be appropriately matched to developing skill levels in order to support success, and supervisory feedback should allow both challenge and support as the intern takes on increased responsibility. Supportive reflection about practice experiences can foster accurate self-evaluation that permits students to build and demonstrate skills in determining their own strengths and needs, and to become able to identify and access resources to engage in ongoing professional development.

It is important to establish a collaborative learning environment, in which interns are involved in their own training and trainers model ongoing involvement in their own professional development. Some parts of the training are set aside to address issues that emerge from the interns' experiences, and there should be regular opportunities to share and discuss ethical challenges that arise; however, the domains of practice and competencies for effective practice should form a basis for a structured set of training experiences over the course of the internship. These should be anchored, specific and meaningful tasks, and whenever possible products are used to judge competency and document successful training experiences.

Effective internship training necessarily begins at the level of a student needs assessment. It is important to determine both the breadth of knowledge and the depth of training with which students enter their internship. Trainers must assess the nature of course work and practicum in the various domains of practice. A student who has had a single course in a given domain can be expected to have only rudimentary skill, whereas a student with several related courses and supervised practicum may have relatively well developed skills; however, assuming depth of training on the basis of extended exposure may not be accurate, and eliciting critical reflection on students' depth of understanding of practice in a given domain is advisable. Students may have had several courses in a given skill area but minimal supervision, meaning they may still be puzzled about how to effectively translate what they know into practice. Asking students to determine where they will need more support allows them to be increasingly self-directed and exert some control over their own learning goals.

In order to create an internship experience that supports integration of skills, internship trainers need to appreciate the range of roles typical for the school psychologist and address each. Central to these is the role of consultation, which provides many opportunities to exercise leadership and have multiple influences within the school community. Applying consulting skills provides a strong base for working effectively within multidisciplinary teams and provides a context for managing the other roles. For example, if an intern has established the role of consultant, they may be able to work with teachers in a number of ways that best serve students' and teachers' needs, and avoid the traditional referral to evaluation to eligibility decision process. Working in a consultation modality allows students to demonstrate their data-based decision making skills in defining problems, designing and implementing intervention, collecting data, and modifying individual and systemic problems. Overall, when using consultation, school psychologists-in-training may be able to demonstrate the range of their skills and avoid having a limited role.

Once a set of experiences has been chosen as the training experiences, training staff consider what kind of model will best support the interns in translating their knowledge about necessary skills into competencies for practice. One useful model would use assignments to review current literature to ensure similar exposure to the skill area across the internship group. A professional who has expertise in the skill area might provide a brief presentation or skill demonstration to interns. Interns would them be asked to become engaged in an application project, allowing sufficient time to implement the application and collect data (ideally using a pre–post design). Interns then come together to share their application experiences and are asked to judge their effectiveness and constructively critique each other's work. Interns would then be asked to go back to the literature to build on what they have already learned and go back to apply their enhanced learning to the problem they were addressing. At a later time, they would share the outcome of their redesigned or refined intervention. This model promotes active skill development, data-based decision making, and recursive reflection and allows young professionals to use the literature and support from one another and the training staff, to increase their professional effectiveness.

Internship trainers face many challenges in meeting the needs of a diverse group of trainees and must, like those who provide clinical supervision, be effective teachers, have expert clinical knowledge and skill, and demonstrate strong technical expertise (Harvey & Struzziero, 2000). In addition, training staff should have expertise in working with adult learners and be open to reciprocal learning from interns who bring unique perspectives and genuine expertise to their internship year.

SUPPORTING AN INTERN WITH A PROBLEM

The issues involved in working with interns who demonstrate performance deficits are complex, and the nature of the chapter allows only a brief discussion here; this is discussed in more detail in the Chapter 8 of this volume. Key to addressing any intern problem is to take a practical problem solving approach and to very carefully document the characteristics of the problem from the time it first becomes apparent. Having a competency-based evaluation tool is important to the process of correcting problems. This kind of form not only allows identification of the particular competencies that are not being adequately met but should form the basis of a remediation plan that identifies the deficits, which can be used to set specific objective goals and how they will be measured.

Case illustration

A very eager intern was approached in his school, but after school hours, by one of his coworkers who obviously thought much of him. This person revealed to the intern that he was feeling very depressed and somewhat hopeless. The intern, being a good person, offered some advice to his coworker, and they parted ways for the day.

A few weeks passed, with regular scheduled supervision, before the intern shared this incident with his professional supervisor. From the intern's perspective, this was a casual interaction, which occurred in the work setting as did so many interactions; however, when discussed, the professional supervisor pointed out many ethical concerns regarding that very interaction. First, although it was not the intern's intention, his behavior could be construed as practicing without a license. Because the intern did not tell or remind the coworker of his intern status and thus lack of a license, he may have unintentionally led the coworker to believe that he was an independently functional psychologist. In addition, this encounter not being discussed in a timely manner during supervision could further suggest that an intern was practicing independently. Second, the professional supervisor pointed out that the intern's behavior could easily be interpreted by others as falling outside the boundaries of competence for a school psychologist, since the usual nature of work in school psychology focuses on the academic and behavioral functioning of children in the school setting. Naturally, many school psychologists have received additional training to work with special populations; however, as in this present situation, the intern must always be careful not to operate outside of the competencies of his supervisor. Although they are two people, the intern–supervisor dyad functions as one unit under one license.

Third, the professional supervisor warned the intern that such practices can expose the school system to unwelcome liability. School psychologists hired by districts have a scope of services that they are to provide and for which the district assumes responsibility. Providing a service outside that purview can result in unnecessary litigation.

Finally, the supervisor pointed out the possible multiple relationship that such an encounter can create. All psychologists are advised to avoid multiple relationships that may impair their objectivity or effectiveness. The intern was advised that in future situations, the best ethical response would be to explain this part of the ethical code to the coworker as soon as he begins to reveal personal information. This response can preempt any movement toward what could be viewed as a multiple relationship.

In summary, this case example highlights the necessary breadth that professional supervision entails. Supervisors have a responsibility and may be answerable for every activity the intern performs on a school campus, whether it is related to the practice of psychology or not. Supervisors should point out and discuss the multifaceted ramifications that result from both the intern's actions and inactions. All trainees make mistakes; this serves as the reason for such structured supervision. It also further emphasizes the need for continued contact with other professionals in the field to help guide judgment.

SUMMARY

The internship has long been regarded as the capstone training experience for a psychologist. It has often been stated that the role of the intern is very different from that of a student. Internship supervision is a multifaceted part of training that is very difficult to describe. This may be the primary reason for the paucity of research regarding supervision; however, there is little disagreement on the vital role supervision plays in the professional development of a psychologist.

The internship experience brings with it various types of supervision. There is generally an LEA supervisor, a professional supervisor, an internship supervisor, and a university-based supervisor. There is never another time when one has to report to so many people. In addition, it often becomes necessary for these various supervisors to communicate with each other for the proper resolution of issues.

A successful internship year combines the learned competencies from graduate school with successful problem solving in new situations. Many systems have yet to appreciate the level of training that school psychologists receive, especially in their year of internship. The collaborative supervision during that year of internship is generally the richest learning experience of the budding professional. The successful future of school psychology requires an increased research focus on supervision. As a profession, there has been an imbalance in stating the importance of supervision when there has not been the research to support the efforts. Future efforts must explore the various complexities in supervision and generate a best practices approach based on the evidence.

RESOURCES

Kaslow, N. J. (2004). Competencies in professional psychology. *American Psychologist, 59*, 774–781.

This article provides the background for competency-based education and credentialing in professional psychology.

Kaslow, N. J., & Bell, K. D. (2008). A competency-based approach to supervision. In C. A. Falender & E. P. Shafranske (Eds.), *Casebook for clinical supervision: A competency-based approach* (pp. 17–38). Washington, DC: American Psychological Association.

This chapter focuses on the partnership that characterizes effective supervisory endeavors.

Kaslow, N. J., Dunn, S. E., & Smith, C. O. (2008). Competencies for psychologists in academic health centers (AHCs). *Journal of Clinical Psychology in Medical Settings, 15*, 18–27.

This paper provides information on the competency-based movement within professional psychology education, training, credentialing, and performance appraisal.

REFERENCES

American Psychological Association. (2007). *Assessment of competency benchmarks work group: A developmental model for the defining and measuring competence in professional psychology*. Washington, DC: Author.

Catterall, C. D. (1973). A competency based school psychology internship. *Journal of School Psychology, 11*(3), 269–275.

Fagan, T. (2005). The 50th anniversary of the Thayer conference: Historical perspectives and accomplishments. *School Psychology Quarterly, 20*(3), 224–251.

Goh, D. S. (1977). Graduate training in school psychology. *Journal of School Psychology, 15*(3), 207–218.

Harvey, V. S., & Struzziero, J. A. (2000). *Effective supervision in school psychology*. Bethesda, MD: National Association of School Psychologists.

Kaslow, N. J. (2004). Competencies in professional psychology. *American Psychologist,* *59*, 774–781.

McIntosh, D. E., & Phelps, L. (2000). Supervision in school psychology: Where will the future take us? *Psychology in the Schools, 37*(1), 33–38.

Murphy, J. P. (1981). Roles, functions and competencies of supervisors of school psychologists. *School Psychology Review, 10*(4), 417–424.

Ross-Reynolds, G., & Grimes, J. P. (Eds.). (1981). Supervision and continuing professional development [Special issue]. *School Psychology Review, 10*(4).

Ysseldyke, J. E., Morrison, D., Burns, M., Ortiz, S., Dawson, P., Rosenfield, S., et al. (2006). *School psychology: A blueprint for training and practice III.* Bethesda, MD: National Association of School Psychologists.

5 Supervision of school psychology interns in a pediatric hospital

Robert M. Gordon and
Michele Zaccario

INTRODUCTION

School psychology interns tend to have a strong foundation in psychological testing and consultation. There is a great deal of variability in their psychotherapy skills, depending on their program's emphasis and their specific externship and practicum experiences. When making the transition from a school setting to a pediatric rehabilitation hospital, interns are confronted with children and adolescents experiencing significant trauma, chronic illness, and issues of mourning and loss. Dealing with such issues potentially challenges their professional identity, cognitive schemas, and self-confidence.

Because of technological advances in the fields of neonatology and pediatrics, there has been a significant decrease in the mortality rate among medically fragile children (Deaton, 1996). These higher rates of survival have resulted in concomitant increases in the need for the provision of ongoing medical, psychological, and other intervention services. Thus, there is a greater demand for school and clinical psychology interns to be trained to work on acute pediatric units, as well as in pediatric rehabilitation settings.

Interns working in a pediatric rehabilitation hospital setting are presented with a comprehensive educational model of training that integrates aspects of child clinical psychology, neuropsychology, health psychology, and systems theory. The child clinical psychology component has a psychodynamic foundation and utilizes cognitive/behavioral strategies. The neuropsychology component emphasizes a process approach and a search for clients' strengths, whereas the health psychology perspective stresses the development and maintenance of flexible coping and problem-solving strategies. The systems approach highlights the importance of how the disability interacts with the client's family, culture, and value system.

SUPERVISION

Supervision is a critical component in influencing a school psychology intern's value and belief systems (Yerushalmi, 1999) and in increasing the depth and range of an intern's neuropsychological testing, psychotherapy, and consultation skills. The major aims of supervision include increasing awareness and exploration of client's relational patterns (Lesser, 1983), broadening and enriching constructions of therapeutic encounters (Yerushalmi, 1999), and being aware that the art of psychotherapy is a value-laden enterprise (Falender & Shafranske, 2004). Interns need to accept responsibility for the fact that their own personality, values, and beliefs infuse their theoretical convictions and form the foundation for their clinical decisions and interventions (Aron, 1999). Because one of the main aims of supervision is to integrate clinical practice and science, supervision facilitates the questioning attitude of the scientist, whereby skill in observation, interviewing, higher level thinking, and hypothesis testing are basic components of a more complex understanding of the client (Holloway & Walleat, 1994).

PSYCHOTHERAPY SUPERVISION

Within the relational model, supervision is viewed as unfolding within a dyadic relationship through which both participants are influenced and shaped by one another (Frawley-O'Dea, 1997). It is assumed that two distinct personalities exist, each with its own values, worldviews, vulnerabilities, biases, and blind spots (Rock, 1997). In effective supervision, the supervisor also needs to learn to change and admit not to knowing all the answers (Berman, 2000). Explicit acknowledgement that the supervisor is a participant–observer with vulnerabilities, anxieties, and needs, rather than an objective expert, creates a more flexible context for supervision (Sarnat, 1992).

The quality of supervision is facilitated when there is an atmosphere of trust and safety in which errors are expected and are viewed as a mutual opportunity to learn and improve (Feiner, 1994). Research studies have consistently indicated that highly rated supervisor qualities included empathy, support, a genuine interest, a sense of humor, understanding, validation, bidirectional trust and respect, and the encouragement to try new perspectives (Falender & Shafranske, 2004; Nelson, 1978). The amount of time and degree of commitment, as well as an emphasis on personal growth, are critical factors (Falender & Shafranske). Another significant issue is the importance of supervisors responding in a nondefensive manner to the supervisee's complaints, issues of conflict, or negative feedback (Falender & Shafranske; Gray, Ladany, Walker, & Ancis, 2001; Moskowitz & Rupert, 1983). Rock (1997) emphasized that supervisees need to be able to develop a therapeutic style that is compatible with their personality.

Supervision provides a forum for supervisors to model therapeutic skills, including self-disclosure, so that interns can generalize those skills to their own work (Gray et al., 2001). Good supervisors tend to self-disclose and allow for mistakes (Worthen & McNeill, 1996). Ladany and Walker (2003) suggested that supervisory disclosures had positive impact on the emotional bond of the supervisory relationship by communicating trust. In addition, disclosures by the supervisor models and encourages supervisee self-disclosure. Worthen and McNeil (1996) found that supervisor self-disclosure (e.g., sharing personal experiences with a similar challenging case) reduced the supervisees' negative attributions of their behavior and decreased anxiety by allowing them to "see" into the supervisor's behaviors and thoughts, thus normalizing and tacitly relabeling mistakes as learning experiences.

Supervisees are in a vulnerable position because of the dual nature of learning involved in becoming a clinician. As a developing therapist, the supervisee has to appear to know a great deal more than his or her client but is confronted in supervision as being less knowledgeable than the supervisor (Gill, 1999). These conflicting self-representations often trigger feelings of insecurity and shame, which often lead the supervisee to avoid discussing clinical mistakes and negative feelings about his or her clients (Buechler, 1992; Gill). Psychotherapy supervision often elicits feelings of shame, but it is rarely addressed in supervision (Buechler, 1992; Hahn, 2001). Instead, shame is usually hidden from oneself and others through avoidance, withdrawal, and self-criticism (Hahn, 2001).

School psychology trainees are also confronted with intense and challenging transference and countertransference reactions when working in a hospital setting with physically challenged children and adolescents. Transference is viewed as selectivity in awareness or inflexibility in perception (Fiscalini, 1995a, 1995b). Hoffman (1983), utilizing a social-constructivist perspective, stated that transference functions as a "Geiger counter," with past family patterns influencing clients to selectively notice specific personality traits, have specific relational expectations, and perceive meaning in situations that would be insignificant to someone else. Both the therapist and client are described as the initiators of transference–countertransference conflicts and treatment impasses (Aron, 1996). Countertransference combines issues arising from aspects of the therapist's personality that are particularly responsive to a client's characteristics (Berman, 2000). Children and adolescents elicit particular thoughts, memories, and feelings in the therapist, while the therapist's defenses, unconscious motivations, and vulnerabilities determine the unique countertransference response (Gabbard, 1995).

The transference reactions experienced by school psychology trainees working with children and adolescents who are physically challenged are intensified by several factors in a rehabilitation setting: the sudden and traumatic disruption of the child or adolescent's developmental process and defensive system, the expected psychological regression, and the prolonged and uncertain state of physical and psychological dependence (Gunther, 1987). Common countertransference reactions in school psychology interns include anger toward clients and their families who may frustrate the therapist's best efforts or not make significant progress; feelings of helplessness and hopelessness; fears of their own mortality; and anxieties regarding body integrity, loss of control, and the random nature of traumatic events (Gans, 1983; Gunther, 1987). These new and intense reactions often trigger rescue fantasies, overprotective responses, or avoidant reactions. Group and individual supervision provides an opportunity to normalize these reactions and view countertransference as a normal and expected reaction. Supervision also provides the trainee with critical information regarding the clients' emerging feelings, in trying to make sense of their traumatic experience and their struggle to integrate their disability into a new sense of identity, and how they impact on others.

As a result of working with children and adolescents with a diverse range of physical and/or cognitive traumas, school psychology interns often experience a disruption in their cognitive schemas (Cunningham, 2003). Schemas are complex cognitive structures that are utilized to interpret experience and organize and process sensory information in order to function effectively (Cunningham, 2003; McCann & Pearlman, 1990). Individuals develop schemas about the self and others based on emotional needs in five domains: safety, control, esteem, trust, and intimacy (Cunningham, 2003). The schemas that are most salient for an intern are those that are more susceptible to disruption in working with this population (Cunningham, 2003). Interns working with victims of random violence, terminal illness, and accidents will likely experience a heightened sense of vulnerability and an enhanced awareness of the fragility and unpredictable nature of life (McCann & Pearlman, 1990).

When conducting psychotherapy and neuropsychological testing with children and adolescents with physical disabilities in an inpatient rehabilitation setting, key attributes of an intern that promote psychotherapeutic work are flexibility, openness to learning and supervision, receptivity to feedback, and receptivity to viewing mistakes as opportunities for growth. Interns need to be comfortable with stepping out of the frame of traditional modes of psychological treatment, trusting their intuition and clinical instincts, and reacting in the moment. Trainees need to utilize all of the psychotherapeutic interventions that apply to various populations, while being aware of the variety of issues and dynamics that may arise, including the effects that recently acquired or longstanding physical disability may add.

NEUROPSYCHOLOGICAL TESTING SUPERVISION

In pediatric settings, especially on acute inpatient or rehabilitation units, psychological and neuropsychological assessments are hallmarked by medical and/or neurological referrals and diagnoses. The challenge presented to a school psychology intern is to appropriately extrapolate past intensive training and existent knowledge of psychological testing to medical patient populations. Interns are confronted—often for the first time—with pediatric diagnoses, including but not limited to cerebral palsy, traumatic and diffuse brain injuries, general bodily trauma, multiple sclerosis, cerebral vascular accidents, metabolic disorders, hematological disorders, orthopedic injuries, congenital conditions, spinal cord diseases/injuries, tumors, cancer (of various forms), seizure disorders/epilepsy, developmental disorders (e.g., autism), spina bifida, arthrogryposis, muscular dystrophies, sequelae of premature births or complicated deliveries, malnutrition, and/or failure to thrive, as well as exposure to toxins, drugs, or other noxious substances. These medical conditions are also often complicated by comorbid psychiatric diagnoses and/or result in secondary psychological sequelae, such as attention deficit/hyperactivity disorder, depression, anxiety, learning disabilities, and psychosis.

The school psychology intern must learn to choose and adapt testing batteries (a) to best serve the medically complex client; (b) to consider medical, neuropsychological, and psychiatric diagnoses when formulating cases and making recommendations; and (c) to write reports that will be informative to referring physicians, treating therapists, patient families, and school personnel. A school psychology intern needs to learn to expand or contrast a previously learned test battery in order to better meet the needs of patients, and to move fluidly among the different types of assessments required in a medical setting.

In supervision, the goal for both trainee and supervisor is to build upon the breadth and depth of an intern's existent assessment experience by facilitating the following: (a) knowledge of novel tests and measures, (b) establishment of rapport with challenging patients, (c) the formulation of nuanced behavioral observations apropos of presenting diagnoses, (d) the negotiation of challenging aspects of the testing session, and (e) the composition of an informed and well-written test report. The supervisor must meet the intern at his or her current experiential level, offering scaffolding when needed but autonomy where appropriate. The trainee, in turn, must be honest about his or her level of comfort and familiarity with regard to test batteries, scoring, interpretation, and report writing, as well as past exposure to various diagnoses and patient age ranges. Both supervisor and trainee should also be prepared and open to processing the inevitable discomfort, anxiety, and sadness that is naturally invoked during evaluation sessions of medically fragile children.

The evaluations conducted on pediatric inpatient, outpatient, and rehabilitation units range from mental status evaluations to psychoeducational or neurocognitive screenings to comprehensive neuropsychological assessments measuring neurocognition, preacademic or academic skills, adaptive skills, and emotional and personality functioning. These evaluations may occur at the onset of treatment to assess baseline functioning (presurgical assessments, prechemotherapy assessments), during a treatment protocol (such as chemotherapy or physical therapy) or hospital course to assess change in functioning and/or prior to discharge to assess current level of functioning and to make aftercare recommendations. Mental and coma status evaluations are conducted on a daily basis on an inpatient or rehabilitation unit in order to track more subtle progress or deterioration, and follow-up full neuropsychological evaluations are recommended at specified time intervals on an outpatient basis. A school psychology intern needs to learn to expand or contract a previously learned test battery in order to better meet the needs of clients, and to move fluidly between the different types of assessments required in a medical setting.

When a full neuropsychological assessment is indicated for either pediatric inpatients or outpatients, the following neurocognitive domains are surveyed: intellectual abilities; verbal and language skills; visual–spatial, sensorimotor, and visuomotor skills; attention, memory, and learning; executive functioning; adaptive skills; and preacademic and/or academic abilities. In addition, but just as essential for the comprehensive assessment of medically fragile, neurologically impaired, and/or developmentally challenged clients is an analysis of personality and social–emotional functioning. Specifically, an evaluator needs to consider the following domains: mood and affect, clarity of thinking and reality testing, self-perception and self-esteem, interpersonal relatedness and perception of others, and coping resources and stress tolerance. In addition, current symptoms and character structure need to be ascertained in order to delineate any potentially relevant Axis I or Axis II diagnoses that may be premorbid to, comorbid with, or exacerbating of the current medical presentation. Structured and unstructured clinical interviews, behavioral observations, and broad-band and/or narrow-band symptom measures (self, parent, and teacher reports and projective tests, such as the Rorschach [Comprehensive System], figure drawings, sentence completion, and apperception tests) are all useful in making clinical judgments regarding a client's emotional functioning. Most school psychology training programs do not include such a broad range of psychological testing, and thus targeted skills must be addressed in the supervisory process.

Supervision of the school psychology intern with regard to the completion of a full neuropsychological assessment includes building an appropriate and useful clinical battery, evaluating the validity and reliability of chosen tests, and interpreting the compiled data into a culminating report. For example, interns must learn to judge when an intelligence quotient score is actually an underestimate of overall cognitive potential, to appreciate what neurocognitive functioning is most negatively impacted by neurological trauma, and to decipher whether projective or objective measures will be more informative in assessing a particular client's emotional life. Biases and ambivalences that interns may harbor regarding the administration, scoring, and interpretation of various tests must also be determined and ameliorated in supervision. Specifically, interns are often uncomfortable conducting subtle mental status evaluations on comatose children and adolescents; they may not know how or when to abridge or amend a test battery on the basis of a presenting disability, or they may possess a bias for or against the utilization of projective measures with clients presenting with neurological diagnoses. These discomforts, lack of exposure, and biases may preclude the conduction of the most appropriate and meaningful test battery, thus, the guidance, support, and expertise of a supervising clinician are of paramount importance.

For the school psychology intern, another challenge is making appropriate and salient recommendations to parents, physicians, treating therapists, and school personnel in feedback sessions and in their comprehensive neuropsychological reports. The neuropsychological report is often the primary tool utilized in aftercare programs and schools to reintegrate the recovering child or adolescent in the home and school environment. Therefore, recommendations need to be relevant, clearly written, and feasible for implementation. They typically include (a) educational placement suggestions; (b) academic and classroom modifications; (c) assistive technology; (d) aftercare rehabilitative treatment (occupational, physical, and speech and language therapy); (e) psychotherapy, counseling, and group therapy; (f) behavior modification plans; (g) cognitive remediation; (h) medical or professional follow-up; and (i) suggestions for future assessments and re-evaluations. In addition, school psychology interns must be prepared, alongside their supervisors, to discuss these recommendations at length with parents, school personnel, physicians, and treating therapists, and explain and defend them if necessary at individualized educational planning meetings or potentially in litigation and/or arbitration.

CONSULTATION WITH STAFF, FAMILIES, AND SCHOOLS

Consultations with staff, families, and schools, as well as formal consultation liaison services, are regular responsibilities of psychologists working in a medical or rehabilitation setting. School psychology interns, in contrast to their clinical and counseling psychology counterparts, often do receive training and didactics focused on conducting consultative services. In the school setting, consultations often occur within a classroom or individual therapy setting at the request of a teacher or treating therapist (occupational therapist, physical therapist, or speech and language therapist), and often target behavioral issues that interfere with optimal academic performance. In the hospital setting, consultations are often initiated by treating physicians or other medical staff, and as patients approach discharge, consultations are conducted with school personnel in order to ensure proper classroom reintegration and aftercare treatment.

Within the hospital setting, pediatric psychologists and interns may assume a consultation liaison role for medical cases where there are concurrent neuropsychological, emotional, or behavioral issues. Commonly provided services include neuropsychological screenings, mental status evaluations, emotional screenings, family support and education, behavioral modification plans, and bedside individual play or psychotherapy. Referring physicians include general pediatricians, as well as specialists such as neonatologists, endocrinologists, gastrointestinal specialists, neurologists, hematologists, physiatrists, pediatric cancer specialists, geneticists, and pediatric surgeons. Nurses, therapists (occupational, physical, speech and language, respiratory, or swallowing), inpatient teachers, and social workers may also consult with pediatric psychologists for assistance with setting up behavioral or milieu management plans or cotreating patients in a therapy session. Consultations in the form of more formal didactic sessions also occur with residents and fellows, nurses and treating therapists, and referring physicians. Topics of interest may include, but are not limited to, patient management, child development, neuropsychological diagnosis and treatment, and parent support and education.

The following examples specifically illustrate the consultation liaison role that pediatric psychologists assume in a medical setting: (a) pediatric psychologists may be called into the neonatal intensive care unit to help new parents adjust to the long hospitalization and uncertain outcome of their newborn baby; (b) they may be called to a neurosurgical recovery floor to assess the mental status of a postsurgical brain tumor patient; (c) they may be asked by a physical therapist to cotreat a patient recovering from a motor vehicle accident because of resultant fears of crossing streets or riding in cars; (d) they may be brought in by gastrointestinal specialists or swallowing therapists to work behaviorally with the family of a toddler who has developed food aversions secondary to longstanding reflux; or (e) they may be approached by the rehabilitation nursing staff to formulate a milieu management plan to better meet the needs of adolescent inpatients.

With regard to discharge planning and re-integration of a pediatric patient into the school system, there is also a large consultative role for pediatric psychology. Neuropsychological assessment and reports, for example, are written with recommendations designed to ease the transition from the inpatient setting to the home environment. Often, written reports are followed by visits to the school to discuss reintegration of the returning pediatric patient; formal representation of student needs in an individualized educational planning (Committee on Preschool Special Education [CPSE] or Committee on Special Education [CSE]) meeting; and/or team meetings with parents, treating therapists, physicians, and school personnel to discuss treatment generalization and ongoing needs. The pediatric psychologist may be asked by school personnel to provide ongoing consultation services for students who present with rare or challenging medical and physical needs—for example, children recovering from traumatic brain injuries and children requiring ongoing cancer treatments.

School psychology interns are challenged to expand their knowledge of consultation to include the medical setting and pediatric medical diagnoses. In supervision, they will learn valuable techniques such as bedside neuropsychological screens, short-term psychotherapy skills, the documentation of information in a medical chart, and the facilitation of collaboration with physicians and other medical personnel. They will also learn how to report back to schools about clients' progress, how to reintegrate a patient back to the academic environment, and how to advocate for pediatric patients in formal academic planning meetings. Medical consultations within the hospital or school setting can be challenging, but they also represent a natural and appropriate progression for the school psychology trainee who already comes to the internship with appropriate child developmental knowledge, consultation experience, and a working understanding of the board of education and school system.

ETHICS TRAINING

Ethics training during graduate school training is often narrowly defined with a focus on correct or incorrect behavior and worst case scenarios, rather than emphasizing the underlying processes and values involved in ethically complex situations (Falender & Shafranske, 2007). Becoming an ethical professional requires maturity and the cognitive and emotional complexity to integrate the way one's actions affect others; the importance of moral values; and the character traits of honesty, personal responsibility, and integrity (Barrett & Barber, 2005; Falender & Shafranske, 2007). During the internship year, the school psychology trainee will begin to utilize a more nuanced application of rules and to consider multiple contextual factors when making ethical decisions (Falender & Shafranske, 2007).

Ethics are the values, principles, and norms assumed in a professional setting and are utilized in determining appropriate conduct (Caplan, Callahan, & Haas, 1987). A relational perspective of ethical decision making provides a more comprehensive model when school psychologist trainees are making the transition to working in a hospital setting. This model considers the importance of (a) values, (b) clients' and families' transference reactions, (c) staff countertransference reactions, (d) institutional context (including the impact of managed care), (e) cultural factors and the worldview of the client and their family, and (f) the importance of ongoing negotiation (Gordon, 1999).

Ethical challenges in a pediatric rehabilitation setting are complicated by the child's rapidly shifting cognitive and emotional development, degree of autonomy and separation/individuation, and family relationships (Deaton, 1996). Among the complex issues in pediatric rehabilitation are

(a) confidentiality (e.g., whether all client information needs to be communicated to the treatment team; Deaton, 1996), (b) assessment of decision making regarding consent and refusal of treatment (Deaton, 1996; Gordon, 1999), (c) dangerousness, and (d) conflicts among staff, family, and clients. From a legal perspective, a child or even an older adolescent does not have to play a role in decision making or consent to treatment (Deaton, 1996). Ethically, however, most health care professionals firmly advocate that children and adolescents should be allowed to express their choices and preferences in order to convey that their input is valued, to promote an atmosphere of trust and respect with the treatment team, and to increase their level of participation in their program (Deaton, 1996).

Decisions in pediatric rehabilitation involve considerations of the risk–benefit ratio (i.e., how much do the potential benefits of the decision outweigh the possible risks?). A lower level of reasoning and understanding is required when a client gives informed consent to a medical intervention with a beneficial risk–benefit ratio or refuses a treatment with an uncertain chance of success. On the other hand, a higher degree of reasoning, judgment, and awareness of the consequences is needed when a child or adolescent refuses a medical intervention with a highly beneficial risk–benefit ratio or if the decision poses a significant medical threat to the individual (Roth, Meisel, & Lidz, 1977. In determining the child's or adolescent's competence to make an informed decision, his or her preferences, level of cognitive functioning, and emotional maturity are critical factors (Fundidis, 2003). Children and adolescents need to appreciate the short- and long-term implications of decisions (Elliot, 1997).

DIVERSITY, CULTURE, AND WORLDVIEW

The quality and depth of supervision and training is enriched through utilizing a multifaceted and dynamic perspective of diversity, culture, sociopolitical issues, and worldview. Diversity includes all aspects of culture, as well as socioeconomic status, race, religion, disability or ableness, age, gender, and sexual orientation, which all interact (Falender & Shafranske, 2004). Competency in diversity requires self-awareness of one's attitudes, biases, assumptions, and knowledge of different components of diversity (Kaslow, 2004).

Individuals are influenced by different contexts, including the historical and sociopolitical. Sociopolitical factors include personal history of migration (e.g., where the family came from, why they came, what their respective journeys entailed, and aspirations); refugee flight or immigration status; fluency in standard English and other languages and dialects; extent of family support and resources; change in social status as a result of coming to this country; level of stress related to acculturation; history of oppression, prejudice, and discrimination; and the concept of health and healing (APA, 2003; Arrendondo, 2002; Falicov, 1995; Falender & Shafranske, 2004;

Hansen, Pepitone-Arreola-Rockwell, & Greene, 2000). It is critical to explore how individuals from different cultural groups perceive and experience the mental health delivery system; how clients assign meaning to time, body language, and eye contact; what psychotherapy represents; the meaning of visible and hidden illness, disability, and loss; and specific values (e.g., competition vs. cooperation, emotional restraint vs. expressiveness, independence vs. dependence; Brown & Landrum-Brown, 1995).

An individual's worldview includes assumptions, expectations, and beliefs a person holds about the self, others, and the world (Janoff-Bulman, 1989, 1992). Worldviews tend to be transmitted culturally and through abstraction from personal experience, and they represent an individual's and a culture's answers to fundamental questions (Koltko-Rivera, 2004). In the clinical realm, a client's worldview may influence how he or she presents symptoms and conflicts and his or her motivation to pursue and persevere in psychotherapy (Anderson, 1995). Specific aspects of a child's or adolescent's worldview that add depth and complexity to the clinical encounter include (a) time dimension (e.g., upholding past traditions, living in the present, and planning for the future); (b) locus of control (e.g., taking responsibility for one's actions, luck, chance, and fate); and (c) purpose and priorities in life (e.g., belonging, recognition, power, achievement, and self-transcendence; Koltko-Rivera, 2004).

Sue and Sue (2003) emphasized that culturally sensitive clinicians need to be aware of the underlying values inherent in the major schools of psychotherapy and how they interact with the values of different cultural groups. It is critical to take into consideration that the mainstream culture in this country values the traits of independence, achievement, and rational decision making (Fiske, Kitayama, Markus, & Nisbett, 1998). In contrast, individuals from Eastern cultures tend to prefer interdependence and harmony with others and subordination of individual to group goals (Fiske et al.).

Individuals with disabilities comprise 15% of the U.S. population (Olkin, 2002) and can be viewed as a distinct cultural group. In contrast to the medical model, which tends to depict disability as a deficit residing in the individual and carries within it a degree of stigma, Wright (1983) described disability as predominantly a social phenomenon. The social model locates the disablement in the environment and society, which fails to provide the necessary accommodations to include individuals with a disability. The model places a greater emphasis on issues of oppression, discrimination, and prejudice and their consequences. As a member of a cultural group, there is a focus on the identity dimension of disability, similar to race, gender, and social class. From the perspective of a culturally affirmative model (Serani, 2001), it is important for the school psychology intern to be aware of and avoid society's tendency to view disability in extremes—idealizing the heroic and superhuman qualities of the mountain climber with paraplegia or emphasizing incapacity as identity. Health care providers need to honor the individual and the collective experience of life in an ablist society (G. Payton, personal communication, October 31, 2007).

CASE ILLUSTRATIONS

The following case examples illustrate three aspects of pediatric psychological work, and each will demonstrate a unique supervisory challenge, specifically (a) consultation with families and medical personnel, (b) protection of client confidentiality during hospital stays, and (c) the resolution of conflicts that occur between patients, their families, and medical staff.

Case illustration 1: consultation with parents and medical personnel

D.H. is a 4-year-old female who presented with multiple physical, developmental, and physiological difficulties secondary to sequelae associated with a premature birth and resultant postnatal complications. She was referred as an outpatient to the feeding and swallowing team by her gastrointestinal (GI) physician, in order to assist in the weaning process from gastrostomy tube (G-tube) to oral (by mouth) feeds. The members of the feeding and swallowing team included a nutritionist, a feeding therapist (speech and language therapist), an occupational therapist, and a psychology intern working under the supervision of a pediatric psychologist. Initially, D.H.'s swallowing ability was assessed by the feeding and swallowing therapist via a radiological study and found to be within normal limits. She was also found to have appropriate abilities to chew and physically tolerate a variety of solids; however, her years of tube feeding without concurrent oral feeding left her reluctant to try oral eating, and aversive to the smells and sights of certain foods. Her ability to appreciate hunger signals was also suppressed as the result of continuous G-tube feeding directly to her stomach area.

A feeding and swallowing team assessment and case conference yielded the following treatment plan: (a) D.H.'s G-tube caloric intake would slowly be decreased by GI and nutritional services, allowing for the restimulation of a natural hunger response; (b) D.H. would slowly be introduced to a variety of foods, beginning with liquids and soft solids and progressing to hard solids, by the feeding and swallowing therapist; (c) D.H. would learn to tolerate a variety of textures as related to cooking and eating by exploring, cooking, and playing with foods in her occupational therapy sessions; and (d) D.H.'s parents would work with the pediatric psychology team in order to learn how to reframe oral eating as a positive experience for D.H., to decrease their own negative reactions to the feeding process, and to model positive eating behaviors. D.H.'s parents were conceptualized by the team as integral facilitators of the weaning process and had an important role in terms of generating positive feeding behavior from the clinic to the home environment.

In sessions with D.H.'s parents, the psychology intern ascertained how anxious the whole family had become about D.H.'s oral eating, the parental fears regarding failure to thrive, and D.H.'s fondness of and comfort with her own G-tube (which she nicknamed "tubey"). In supervision, the pediatric psychologist suggested positive ways the family could bond around eating and cooking experiences, playful ways to introduce new foods, appropriate ways to reinforce positive eating behaviors and to extinguish negative associations. In addition, the parents were advised by the pediatric psychologist and intern that they needed to keep a comprehensive food diary and were empowered to feel that they could be successful instruments of change.

After many months of teamwork, dedication on the part of D.H.'s parents, positive gains by D.H., and even some significant setbacks, D.H. was able to successfully wean from G-tube to oral feeding, and she was appropriately able to gain and maintain weight through an oral diet. Specifically, D.H.'s diet at the time of discharge consisted of a variety of liquids, soft solids, and mashed solids, in addition to some harder solids such as fruits, chicken, and pretzels. Although she was still reluctant to try new and unfamiliar foods, especially those that required considerable chewing, her family had the clinical tools and confidence to facilitate perseverance on her part. D.H. and her family's discharge plan included periodic re-evaluations with her GI specialist and regular consultation with the nutritionist in order to maintain an appropriate diet. They were also scheduled by the feeding team for periodic check-ins and encouraged to call the team if they had any concerns or setbacks in the future.

In supervision, the school psychology intern learned how to design appropriate behavioral strategies to promote positive feeding and swallowing behavior, ways to empower D.H.'s family to implement these techniques, and how to tolerate and help the family tolerate the inevitable setbacks that naturally occur during feeding therapy. Following termination of treatment, the school psychology intern utilized supervision in order to process feelings of loss and fear of relapse and was able to come to terms with allowing D.H.'s family increased autonomy and self-efficacy.

Case illustration 2: dangerousness and confidentiality issues

The challenge posed by an adolescent who is neurologically impaired and wants to resume driving involves ethical issues regarding the psychologist's duty to protect third parties and client confidentiality (Gordon, 1999). The Tarasoff ruling of a mandated duty to warn has been applied to unspecified victims of impaired drivers and their physicians (Brittain, Frances, & Barth, 1995).

Mr. S., an 18-year-old with a premorbid history of attention deficit/ hyperactivity disorder, suffered a traumatic brain injury as a result of a motor vehicle accident. A magnetic resonance imaging (MRI) scan of the brain revealed a right frontal hematoma. During his inpatient hospitalization, Mr. S. displayed impulsivity, poor judgment, and lack of awareness of his deficits or the impact of his behavior on others. A serious ethical dilemma arose when Mr. S. told his psychology intern that he had driven during his weekend visit home without his parent's knowledge or permission. Mr. S. became agitated when the intern expressed her concern and the need to tell her supervisor and his treating physician. Feedback from neuropsychological testing and discussions with his speech, occupational, and physical therapists regarding his judgment and impulsivity and the potential dangers of his actions had minimal impact, except to increase his determination to drive. The intern and her supervisor decided that a family meeting would be the best forum to discuss these issues. A team meeting was held among Mr. S.; his parents; psychology intern and supervisor; and speech, occupational, and physical therapists. At this meeting, Mr. S. was able to express his anger and frustration over his lack of independence and his parents' overprotective response to his injury. The supervising psychologist posed the question to Mr. S. of how he would feel if his best friend was seriously injured by an impaired driver. This hypothetical question and the subsequent discussion regarding his family's fears and anxieties regarding his future resulted in a mutual decision to enter family therapy and to have Mr. S. complete a comprehensive driver's evaluation with a specialist in the field.

Case illustration 3: conflicts among clients, families, and staff

Among the most complex and challenging situations confronting psychologists in rehabilitation settings are conflicts among clients, families, and the treatment team regarding issues about goal-setting and discharge plans. These conflicts often involve issues of hope, denial, and awareness.

Ms. L., a 16-year-old female, was admitted to an inpatient rehabilitation program because of a brain tumor that impacted on her ability to ambulate and complete activities of daily living and level of endurance. During the first 6 weeks of rehabilitation, Ms. L. made considerable progress in her level of physical strength and endurance when walking. Unfortunately, she suddenly developed uncontrollable seizures, and an MRI scan of the brain revealed that the tumor had returned and was inoperable. After a few weeks where she was not able to fully partake in her psychotherapy and was experiencing a considerable level of fatigue, the intern experienced intense feelings of helplessness and sadness, which were discussed in supervision. There was consensus during a weekly treatment team conference that Ms. L. had plateaued and that there needed to be a shift in her treatment goal toward comfort, the alleviation of pain, and quality of life concerns.

Ms. L. and her parents strongly felt that she needed to continue her intensive inpatient therapies and that to discontinue would mean the loss of all hope. A family meeting was held in which her parents were given the support to express their concerns. Ms. L. attended part of the meeting and stated that she had made close connections with the staff and a number of clients on the unit and would experience a deep sense of loss if she went home. A compromise was reached in which a modified home-based therapy program was initiated. This emotionally challenging case illustrates the importance of maintaining the client's and family's hope, as well as having the family members contribute their unique viewpoints.

SUMMARY AND CONCLUSIONS

The model of psychotherapy, neuropsychological testing, consultation, ethical decision making, and cultural and diversity supervision and training presented emphasizes a focus on the development of the school psychology intern's professional competence. There is an emphasis on both the learning of specific skills and the development of self-awareness, self-reflection, and the maturity of the intern. Schon (1983) emphasized that professional development involves more than the attainment of factual knowledge and the ability to solve problems; it consists of the ability to handle ambiguous situations, tolerate uncertainties, and make moment-to-moment decisions with incomplete information.

Research on the supervision process had tended to focus on the qualities of effective and ineffective supervision, the impact of supervisor and supervisee self-disclosure, and the bidirectional feedback process. Areas of future research include (a) the use of videotaping supervisory dyads to assess the impact of specific interventions and contrasting verbal and nonverbal behaviors, (b) the development of comprehensive models of neuropsychological and psychological testing and ethical decision making on supervisor and supervisee development, and (c) the impact of different supervision training interventions during graduate school and the future effectiveness of supervisors.

RESOURCES

Gray, L. A., Ladany, N., Walker, J. A., & Ancis, J. R. (2001). Psychotherapy trainees' experience of counterproductive events in supervision. *Journal of Counseling Psychology, 48,* 371–383.
This article examines critical issues that may interfere with the supervisory process. Data were collected by interview interns.

Ladany, N., Constantine, M. G., Miller, K., et al. (2000). Supervisor countertransference: A qualitative investigation into its identification and description. *Journal of Counseling Psychology, 47,* 102–115.
Sources of supervisor countertransference are described and defined. The article describes critical issues to be aware of that can impact the supervisory process.

Ladany, N., Hill, C. E., Corbett, M. M., & Nutt, E. A. (1996). Nature, extent, and importance of what psychotherapy trainees do not disclose to their supervisors. *Journal of Counseling Psychology, 43,* 10–24.
This article discusses the factors determining what a supervisee will disclose in supervision, examining the sources of the relationship that might contribute to nondisclosure.

REFERENCES

American Psychological Association. (2003). Guidelines on multicultural, education, training, research, practice and organizational change for psychologists. *American Psychologist, 58,* 377–404.

Anderson, N. B. (1995). Behavioral and sociological perspectives on ethnicity and health: Introduction to the special issue. *Health Psychology, 14,* 589–591.

Arrendondo, P. (2002). Counseling individuals from specialized, marginalized, and underserved groups. In P. Pedersen, J. G. Draguns, W. J. Lonner, & J. E. Trimble (Eds.), *Counseling across cultures* (5th ed., pp. 241–250). Thousand Oaks, CA: Sage.

Aron, L. (1996). *The meeting of minds: Mutuality in psychoanalysis.* Hillsdale, NJ: Analytic Press.

Aron, L. (1999). Clinical choices and the relational matrix. *Psychoanalytic Dialogues, 9,* 1–29.

Barrett, M. S., & Barber, J. P. (2005). A developmental approach to the supervision of therapists in training. *Journal of Contemporary Psychotherapy, 35,* 169–183.

Berman, E. (2000). Psychoanalytic supervision: The intersubjective development. *International Journal of Psychoanalysis, 81,* 273–290.

Brittain, J. L., Frances, J. P., & Barth, J. T. (1995). Ethical issues in the neuropsychological practice reported by ABCN diplomats. *Advances in Medical Psychotherapy, 8,* 1–22.

Brown, M. T., & Landrum-Brown, J. (1995). Counselor supervision: Cross-cultural perspectives. In J. M. Casas & J. G. Ponterotto (Eds.), *Handbook of Multicultural counseling* (pp. 263–286). Thousand Oaks, CA: Sage.

Buechler, S. (1992). Stress in the personal development of a psychoanalyst. *Journal of the American Academy of Psychoanalysis, 20,* 183–191.

Cunningham, M. (2003). The impact of trauma work on social work clinicians. *Social Work, 48,* 451–459.

Caplan, A. L., Callahan, D., & Haas, J. (1987). Ethical and policy issues in rehabilitation medicine. *Hastings Center Report, 17*(Special Suppl.), 1–20.

Deaton, A. V. (1996). Ethical issues in pediatric rehabilitation: Exploring an uneven terrain. *Rehabilitation Psychology, 41,* 33–42.

Elliot, C. (1997). Caring about risks: Are severely depressed patients competent to consent to treatment? *Archives of General Psychiatry, 54,* 113–116.

Falender, C. A., & Shafranske, E. P. (2004). *Clinical supervision: A competency-based approach*. Washington, DC: American Psychological Association.

Falender, C. A., & Shafranske, E. P. (2007). Competence in competence-based supervision practice: Construct and application. *Professional Psychology: Research and Practice, 38*, 232–240.

Falicov, C. J. (1995). Training to think culturally: A multidimensional comparative framework. *Family Process, 34*, 373–388.

Feiner, A. H. (1994). Comments on contradictions in the supervisory process. *Contemporary Psychoanalysis, 35*, 57–74.

Fiscalini, J. (1995a). The clinical analysis of transference. In M. Lionells, J. Fiscalini, C. H. Mann, & D. B. Stern (Eds.), *The handbook of interpersonal psychoanalysis* (pp. 617–642). Hillsdale, NJ: Analytic Press.

Fiscalini, J. (1995b). Transference and countertransference as interpersonal phenomenon. In M. Lionells, J. Fiscalini, C. H. Mann, & D. B. Sterns (Eds.), *The handbook of interpersonal psychoanalysis* (pp. 603–616). Hillsdale, NJ: Analytic Press.

Fiske, A. P., Kitayama, S., Markus, H. R., Nisbett, R. E. (1998). The cultural matrix of social psychology. In D. T. Gilbert & S. T. Fiske (Eds.), *The handbook of social psychology* (4th ed., Vol. 2, pp. 357–411). New York: McGraw-Hill.

Frawley-O'Dea, M. G. (1997). Who's doing what to whom. *Contemporary Psychoanalysis, 33*, 5–18.

Fundidis, T. (2003). Consent issues in medico-legal procedures: How competent are children to make their own decisions? *Child and Adolescent Mental Health, 8*, 18–22.

Gabbard, G. O. (1995). Countertransference: The emerging ground. *International Journal of Psycho-Analysis, 76*, 475–485.

Gans, J. S. (1983). Hate in the rehabilitation setting. *Archives of Physical Medicine and Rehabilitation, 64*, 176–179.

Gill, S. (1999). Narcissistic vulnerability in psychoanalytic supervision. *International Forum of Psycho-Analysis, 8*, 227–232.

Gordon, R. M. (1999). Ethical challenges. In K. G. Langer, L. Laatsch, & L. Lewis (Eds.), *Psychotherapeutic interventions for adults with brain injury or stroke: A clinician's treatment resource* (pp. 45–71). Madison, CT: Psychosocial Press.

Gray, L. A., Ladany, N., Walker, J. A., & Ancis, J. R. (2001). Psychotherapy trainees' experience of counterproductive events in supervision. *Journal of Counseling Psychology, 48*, 371–383.

Gunther, M. S. (1987). Catastrophic illness and the caregivers: Real burdens and solutions with respect to the role of the behavioral sciences. In B. Kaplan (Ed.), *The rehabilitation desk reference* (pp. 219–243). Rockville, MD: Aspen.

Hahn, W. K. (2001). The experience of shame in psychotherapy supervision. *Psychotherapy, 38*, 272–282.

Hansen, N. D., Pepitone-Arreola-Rockwell, F., & Greene, A. (2000). Multicultural competence: Criteria and case examples. *Professional Psychology: Research and Practice, 21*, 652–660.

Holloway, E. L., & Wolleat, P. L. (1994). Supervision: The pragmatics of empowerment. *Journal of Educational and Psychological Consultation, 5*, 23–43.

Hoffman, I. Z. (1983). The patient as interpreter of the analyst's experience. *Contemporary Psychoanalysis, 19*, 389–422.

Janoff-Bulman, R. (1989). Assumptive worlds and the schema construct. *Social Cognition, 7*, 113–136.

Janoff-Bulman, R. (1992). *Shattered assumptions: Toward a new psychology of trauma.* New York: The Free Press.

Kaslow, N. (2004). Competencies in professional psychology. *American Psychologist, 59,* 774–781.

Koltko-Rivera, M. E. (2004). The psychology of worldviews. *Review of General Psychology, 8,* 3–58.

Ladany, N., & Walker, J. A. (2003). Supervisor self-disclosure: Balancing the uncontrollable narcissistic and indomitable altruist. *JCLP/In Session, 59,* 611–621.

Lesser, R. M. (1983). Supervision: Illusions, anxieties, and questions. *Contemporary Psychoanalysis, 19,* 120–129.

McCann, L., & Pearlman, L. A. (1990). Vicarious traumatization: A framework for understanding the psychological effects of working with victims. *Journal of Traumatic Stress, 3,* 131–149.

Moskowitz, S. A., & Rupert, P. A. (1983). Conflict resolution within the relationship. *Professional Psychology: Research and Practice, 14,* 631–641.

Nelson, G. L. (1978). Psychotherapy supervision from the trainee's point of view: A survey of preferences. *Professional Psychology, 9,* 539–550.

Olkin, R. (2002). Could you hold the door for me?: Including disability in diversity. *Cultural Diversity and Ethnic Minority, 8,* 130–137.

Rock, M. H. (1997). Effective supervision. In M. H. Rock (Ed.), *Psychodynamic supervision: Perspectives of the supervisor and supervisee* (pp. 107–132). Northvale, NJ: Jason Aronson.

Roth, L., Meisel, A., & Lidz, C. (1977). Tests of competency to consent to treatment. *American Journal of Psychiatry, 134,* 279–284.

Sarnat, J. E. (1992). Supervision in relationship: Resolving the teach-treat controversy in psychodynamic supervision. *Psychoanalytic Psychology, 9,* 387–403.

Schon, D. A. (1983). *Educating the reflective practitioner.* San Francisco, CA: Jossey-Bass.

Serani, D. (2001). Yours, mine, and ours: Analysis with a deaf patient and hearing analyst. *Contemporary Psychoanalysis, 37,* 655–671.

Sue, D. W., & Sue, D. (2003). *Counseling the culturally diverse.* New York: Wiley.

Worthen, V., & McNeill, B. W. (1996). A phenomenological investigation of "good" supervision events. *Journal of Counseling Psychology, 43,* 25–34.

Wright, B. A. (1983). *Physical disability: A psychosocial approach* (2nd ed.). New York: Harper & Row.

Yerushalmi, H. (1999). Mutual influences in supervision. *Contemporary Psychoanalysis, 35,* 415–436.

6 Promoting university and schools partnership

Transnational considerations and future directions

Chryse Hatzichristou,
Aikaterini Lampropoulou,
Konstantina Lykitsakou, and
Panayiota Dimitropoulou

A clear picture of the status of the profession of school psychology internationally is an essential foundation for building its future (Oakland & Cunningham, 1992). As the field of school psychology continues to develop around the world, it is important to monitor the current trends regarding the interrelated domains of training, role, and responsibilities of school psychologists. Although emphasis is usually placed on provision of services and the role of school psychologists, these domains are equally important, and training is essential in the evolution of school psychology worldwide. On the basis of the concerns described in the relevant literature, a conceptual framework has been presented incorporating science and professional practice competencies influencing school psychological services.

The proposed integrative framework synthesizes and expands the following conceptual domains: (a) the role and specialty definition: professional practice; (b) legal issues (state and federal/national laws and statutes impacting psychology, education, and provision of services, and certification/licensure); (c) education/preparation and accreditation; (d) scientific and professional associations; (e) scientific foundation for practice; and (f) professional identity (Hatzichristou, 2002).

The model emphasizes the fact that these domains are closely interrelated and attempts to provide guidelines for understanding the cultures of individual students, the country, and the school system to determine the service delivery model and the specific school psychology services that are likely to be most useful. When the evolution of school psychology in these domains is examined in different countries, common phases and considerable similarities are identified, showing that a similar dynamic process of change with a different pace is followed in different countries (Hatzichristou, 2002; Ehrhardt-Padgett, Hatzichristou, Kitson, & Meyers, 2004; Jimerson et al., 2004).

As a result of these trends, multiple challenges are raised regarding the profession of school psychology and effective service delivery, including the preparation, training, and practice (practicum and internship) of young professionals in the field. Among these challenges is the creation of a synthetic scheme that incorporates the different theories and approaches of the field in meaningful comprehensive models that could be applied for training and practice of school psychology (SP). Such models could be a response to the similar lack of guiding theories that has been noted in the domain of school-based practices (Baker, Dilly, Aupperlee, & Patil, 2003).

In an effort to produce such a synthesis, a conceptual framework has been developed that incorporates current trends and theories of school psychology internationally and provides basic guidelines for the preparation and training of graduate students of school psychology; the education of undergraduate students of psychology; in-service training of teachers, school administrators, and mental health professionals; and parent education and training. The main theoretical elements of this framework are the following:

1. Current trends of school psychology based on linking theory, research, and intervention in the school community at national and transnational levels (Hatzichristou, 1998, 2002, 2004a, 2004b)
   a. Models of consultation and counseling in the school environment (Brown, Pryzwansky, & Schulte, 2001, 2006)
   b. Current theories on evidence-based intervention and program assessment (Kratochwill & Shernoff, 2004; Kratochwill & Stoiber, 2002)
   c. Evidence-based interventions: prevention programs at primary, secondary, and system levels and crisis intervention (Hatzichristou, 2004a, 2004c, 2004e, 2008a, 2008b; Nastasi, Moore, & Varjas, 2004; Durlak, 2008).
   d. Provision of school psychological services: alternative model of service delivery in the school communities (Ehrhardt-Padgett et al., 2004; Hatzichristou & Lampropoulou, 2004; Hatzichristou, 2004a)
   e. Multicultural awareness and transnational considerations of different levels of diversity in the school environment (Hatzichristou, Lampropoulou, & Lykitsakou, 2006; Hatzichristou, Lykitsakou, Lampropoulou, & Dimitropoulou, in press).
2. Current theoretical approaches in school psychology
   a. Emphasis on reducing risk and enhancing protective factors in the school environment (Henderson & Milstein, 1996)
   b. Theories of multiple and emotional intelligence (Gardner, 1993; Goleman, 1995)
   c. Linking psychosocial competence and learning (Greenberg, Weissberg, O'Brien, Zins, Fredericks, Resnik, & Elias, 2003)

d. Positive psychology and systemic approach with emphasis on concepts such as school community well-being and resilience at the individual and system levels (Doll, Zucker, & Brehm, 2004, 2009; Lampropoulou, 2008; O'Dougherty, Wright, & Masten, 2005).

e. Current theoretical and research approaches on effective schools and schools as caring communities (Battistisch, Solomon, Watson, & Schaps, 1997; Bickel, 1999; Hatzichristou, Lampropoulou, & Lykitsakou, 2004; Gettinger & Stoiber, 2009).

Within this context, this chapter will present ways of bridging the gaps between theory, training, and practice in school psychology through university, school, and community partnership. In particular, in the following sections, an attempt will be made (a) to describe the current situation regarding training and supervision at national and international levels; (b) to describe the development and evolution of an alternative model of school psychological services in a specific cultural and educational setting, the Greek educational system; (c) to present specific projects that were developed for the promotion of university, school, and community partnership; and (d) to elaborate on critical issues and future perspectives regarding the challenge of bridging the gap between theory and practice at national and transnational levels.

MODELS OF TRAINING AND SUPERVISION

Over the last few decades, increased attention has been devoted to school psychological services worldwide. The importance of school psychologists' role and the fact that school psychologists are making a significant contribution to the lives of all members of the school community are increasingly being recognized and have led to a greater focus on the field (Farrell, Jimerson, & Oakland, 2007). The nature of school psychology services provided is largely determined by the preparation school psychologists receive (Hatzichristou, 2002; Oakland & Jimerson, 2007). Therefore, it is quite important to examine certain significant issues that are directly related to the preparation of school psychologists, such as training and supervision.

When examining the preparation of school psychologists internationally, it is evident that considerable variation exists among the different educational and cultural settings regarding important issues such as training, supervision, program courses and content, length of preparation, and nature and duration of practicum and internships (Farrell et al., 2007). These issues are directly related to the differences that exist within and between countries regarding core aspects of school psychology, such as the status and state of school psychology in each setting, the perceived role of school psychologists, and even legal issues.

Several training and supervision models are described in the relevant literature. Special emphasis has recently been given to the multicultural curriculum models because of the increased diverse population that school psychologists are expected to serve. The *separate course model*, which involves offering a single didactic course on multicultural issues within the entire curriculum, the *area of concentration model*, which combines multiple didactic courses on multicultural issues with applied training involving diverse clients, the *interdisciplinary model*, in which students take core multicultural courses in disciplines closely affiliated with psychology, and the *integration* or *infusion model*, which integrates diversity-related information into curricula by infusing multicultural scholarship into all didactic courses and training, are the basic approaches that have been developed aiming at the multicultural training of school psychologists (see Rogers, 2005, for detailed description).

Supervision practices can be also categorized into various models on the basis of the existing theoretical orientations. The first one is referred to as *psychodynamic* supervision, where the focus is on supervisees' learning to use themselves effectively in helping relationships. *Client-centered* supervision, the second approach, aims at establishing conditions between supervisor and supervisee such as congruence, unconditional positive regard, empathy, and warmth. Finally, there are *behavioral* supervision, where the supervisors must teach appropriate behaviors, and *developmental* supervision, where supervisees pass through predictable stages of levels in their course to expertise (Conoley & Bahns, 1995).

PREPARATION AND TRAINING IN SCHOOL PSYCHOLOGY IN THE GREEK EDUCATIONAL SYSTEM

During the last few years, the field of psychology has rapidly expanded in Greece, and a great deal of effort has been put into promoting the discipline of school psychology. The undergraduate studies leading to a bachelor's degree in psychology are 4 years long. The graduate studies leading to a master's degree are 2 years, and 3 additional years are required for the acquisition of the doctoral degree. Attainment of a bachelor's degree typically requires (a) courses and seminars in psychology (compulsory and optional), (b) internship in institutions of applied psychology, and (c) a dissertation (Hatzichristou, Polychroni, & Georgouleas, 2007).

There are two main graduate programs in school psychology leading to a master's degree, one of which is provided by the Department of the Psychology at the University of Athens. The Graduate Program of School Psychology at the University of Athens started in 1993. Throughout the program, the importance of the scientist–practitioner model for professional preparation and practice is emphasized. Attainment of the master's degree typically requires (a) completion of 20 courses, (b) practicum and internship (in regular and special schools, mental health centers, and counseling centers), (c) a master's dissertation, and (d) participation in research and educational activities.

The 20 courses of the program are in accordance with the following domains of school psychology training and practice: (a) core academic knowledge of psychology: developmental psychology, school psychology, developmental neuropsychology, intelligence and learning, social psychology/small group dynamics, and psychology of personality-developmental deviations; (b) assessment: assessment of cognitive skills, assessment of learning disabilities, personality and social assessment, and school career guidance; (c) abnormal psychology and special educational needs; (d) intervention: counseling psychology, psychological consultation, prevention programs, and psychotherapeutic interventions; (e) research methodology and advanced level statistics; and (f) internship and supervision (program outline, 2005–2006; Hatzichristou et al., 2007). These domains are in accordance with the guidelines proposed by Cunningham and Oakland (1998) for the preparation of school psychologists.

A DATA-BASED MODEL FOR THE DELIVERY OF ALTERNATIVE SCHOOL PSYCHOLOGICAL SERVICES

In spite of the progress that can be identified regarding the evolution of school psychology, Greece is still one of the countries with limited provision of school psychological services in mainstream public schools. School psychologists are currently employed only in special schools and private educational settings, as well as in centers for diagnosis, assessment, and support. The lack of school psychological services in the Greek public schools presented a unique opportunity and a great challenge for the development of alternative service delivery models with the goal of filling the system's vacuum (Hatzichristou, 2004a, 2004b).

The development of a data-based model of alternative school psychological services has helped to link theory, research, and training of graduate students and professionals; to implement intervention programs in schools; and to link the university, schools, professional bodies, and institutions mainly through the establishment and activities of the Center for Research and Practice in School Psychology in the Department of Psychology at the University of Athens.

The need for empirically based interventions was a basic presupposition of the proposed model, which was developed in four phases. The three first phases of the model contributed to the recording of the needs of Greek students, teachers and families, as well as their attitudes toward mental health services and professionals. In particular, an empirical database was developed regarding the profiles of school adjustment and performance of "average" Greek students (Phase I), the profiles of at-risk students with unmet needs (Phase II), and the particular needs of specific school districts in a community where various intervention programs were being implemented (Phase III). Throughout the years, each phase was enriched by new research domains and additional goals (for detailed description, see Hatzichristou, 2004a; Hatzichristou, Lampropoulou, & Lykitsakou, 2006).

In Phase IV, the empirical data derived from the first three phases of the model were integrated into a comprehensive prevention–consultation approach that led to the foundation of the Center for Research and Practice in School Psychology (CRPSP) in the Department of Psychology at the University of Athens. The main goals and activities of the center are (a) promotion of university–school–community partnerships and collaboration; (b) education, preservice training, and in-service training for graduate students, school psychologists, teachers, and parents; (c) scientific research and publications; and (d) development, implementation, and evaluation of multilevel interventions in the school community. Within this context, a number of projects have been developed for meeting the needs of the Greek educational system and for promoting the well-being of the school community. On the basis of the findings of the first three phases of the model, as described previously, several primary and secondary prevention programs have been developed, implemented, and evaluated in order to link theory, research, and practice and meet the particular needs of the Greek educational system (Hatzichristou, 1998, 2004a, 2004b).

The members of the scientific team of the center (scientific director, experienced school psychologists, and PhD candidates) are responsible for the coordination and supervision of the intervention teams (school psychologists, PhD candidates, graduate and undergraduate students, teachers, and other volunteers). The intervention teams participated—initially on a volunteer basis and later in the context of European Union projects—in the implementation of the interventions developed. All members of the intervention teams were trained through seminars and courses and were supervised by the members of the scientific team.

The interventions that were developed by the scientific team of the center include (a) programs for the promotion of mental health and learning (Hatzichristou, 2004c, 2004e, 2008a), (b) intercultural programs for the support of immigrant and remigrant students (Giavrimis, Konstantinou, & Hatzichristou, 2003; Hatzichristou et al., 2001), (c) programs for sex and health education, (d) programs for the inclusion of children with special educational needs in mainstream schools (Hatzichristou & Polychroni, 2007), and (e) crisis intervention programs (Hatzichristou et al., 2008a, 2008b).

PROJECTS FOR THE PROMOTION OF UNIVERSITY, SCHOOL, AND COMMUNITY PARTNERSHIPS

Project I: development of prevention programs in the school community

The following sections include description of intervention programs that were developed and implemented at primary, secondary, and tertiary levels in various educational settings in Greece, as well as the involvement of graduate students of school psychology and teachers in these projects (Table 6.1).

Program for the promotion of mental health and learning: social and emotional learning in schools

One of the main prevention programs that was developed and implemented in public mainstream schools of Greece and Cyprus for many years is the Program for the Promotion of Mental Health and Learning: Social and Emotional Learning in Schools. In this section the program will be described in detail.

The Program for the Promotion of Mental Health and Learning integrates empirical data along with the most recent theoretical approaches in

Table 6.1 Promoting University, School, and Community Partnership

Project I: Development of prevention programs in the school community
Program for the promotion of mental health and learning: social and emotional learning in schools
Awareness building on issues of diversity for students and teachers
Crisis intervention in the school community
Cross-cultural program for awareness building on Olympic values and ideals
Psychoeducational intervention for children with learning and emotional difficulties
Project II: Linking the future of school psychology conference and the data-based model of alternative school psychological services
Graduate students of school psychology
Elementary school teachers
Project III: Community outreach: provision of alternative services in the community
Open seminars: psychopaidia
Crisis seminars
Alumni network
Social activities in the context of prevention programs
Publications

school psychology, aiming to promote children's psychosocial competence, mental health, and learning and to create a positive climate in the school environment (Hatzichristou, 2004c, 2004e, 2008a).

The program consists of 10 thematic units: (a) communication skills; (b) identification, expression, and dealing with feelings; (c) self-concept and self-esteem; (d) coping strategies; (e) conflict resolution; (f) diversity in culture; (g) diversity in individual, family, and social characteristics; (h) learning/study skills; (i) social skills; and (j) crisis intervention in the school community. Educational material for three age groups (preschool, primary, and secondary education) has been developed and published. Each issue includes a literature review, practical guidelines for the implementation of the program, and classroom activities with specific goals and methodology for each age group.

Program development: evolution process and levels of intervention

During its evolution process, different modes of program design and implementation have been employed in order to respond to the existing resources, the particular needs of the target populations, and the feedback from the evaluation process of previous phases of implementation. Initially, it was implemented by school psychologists, members of the scientific team of the CRPSP. In the following years, graduate students of school psychology and teachers were trained for the implementation under the supervision of the center's scientific team. Graduate students of school psychology attended university courses regarding primary and secondary prevention, models of consultation, and promotion of children's mental health in the school environment. In addition, they received specialized training for the implementation of the program in the classroom and supervision through the whole process.

In its latest form of implementation in Greek and Cypriot elementary schools, the program is implemented by teachers on two levels. (a) The first level of intervention includes the implementation of the Program for the Promotion of Mental Health and Learning in the classroom. In addition, an initial effort was made to develop a network of the participating schools, which would facilitate the sharing of ideas and experience, as well as dissemination of the program to other members of the school community. At the end of the academic year, parents, students, and teachers participated in a closing ceremony, in which various activities related to the program were presented (Dimitropoulou, Lykitsakou, & Hatzichristou, 2005). (b) At the second level, a wider system level project was designed, titled Program for the Promotion of School Community Well-Being, which included two axes of intervention: (a) the promotion of resilience of the school community and the development of broader network of schools as *caring communities*, and (b) the implementation of the Program for the Promotion of Mental Health and Learning by teachers in their classrooms (this axis remains similar to the first level of implementation).

The theoretical background of this project consisted of elements of systems theory, schools as caring communities, resilience, and well-being. Within the context of the first axis, teachers were trained in using the problem-solving model, which was presented at the Invitational Conference on the Future of School Psychology in order to develop action plans for enhancing the sense of community in the schools (Hatzichristou & Lampropoulou, 2004). Teachers of each school evaluated critical domains of promoting resilience (Henderson & Milstein, 1996, 2008) and set priorities, goals, and specific actions in response to the particular needs of their school. Coordinators (educators and administrators) from each school participated in regular meetings with the scientific team of the CRPSP to share ideas about problems that emerged in the process, as well as possible solutions.

In relation to the second axis, the following strategies were employed: (a) selection of a limited number of school units that would participate in the program, (b) awareness-building workshops and special training of all teachers and administrators of the selected schools on issues related to the promotion of school well-being (instead of selecting a limited number of participants from more schools), (c) implementation of the program in the classrooms, (d) program dissemination to the parents and teachers of other schools, (e) uploading related material to the program Internet site, and (f) preparation of various group projects that were presented by students and teachers in a closing ceremony at the end of the program.

An important component of program design is program evaluation. The CRPSP has developed a multilevel assessment model including process and outcome evaluation; evaluation by teachers and students; assessment before, during, and after the program; and use of a control group. Results of the program evaluation process provide evidence that the program accounts for some significant positive effects and benefits for both teachers and students. In particular, there is evidence that children respond to and benefit from the intervention selectively, according to their particular needs. For example, children with particular sociometric characteristics or from different cultural groups report significant benefits, especially in the acknowledgement and expression of unpleasant feelings (see also Hatzichristou, Dimitropoulou, Lykitsakou & Lampropoulou, in press).

Results also indicate that intervention at a system level has the potential of producing more extended and dynamic effects on school climate and sense of community. These results, though not always clear or robust, definitely provide an encouraging feedback, taking into consideration the limited duration of the particular program (6–7 months). Results from the comparison between the 1st and 2nd year of intervention further support the hypothesis that one would expect to record concrete indications of change after a longer period of program implementation, generally estimated at between 2 and 5 years (Hatzichristou, Lykitsakou, Lampropoulou, & Dimitropoulou, in press). Nevertheless, the evaluation data provide valuable feedback for detecting strengths and weaknesses of the program and for making necessary adjustments to maximize program efficacy (Holtzman, 1992).

Awareness building on issues of diversity for students and teachers

This project includes the development of a publication series for preschoolers and elementary students. These are fairy tales written and illustrated by graduate students of SP and supervised/edited by the scientific team of the CRPSP. The fairy tales aim at building awareness of students on issues of diversity such as physical or mental handicaps and cultural diversity. In order to meet this goal, special educational material has been developed providing guidelines (specific questions, activities, and conversation topics) to parents and teachers for using the material more effectively with children (Hatzichristou & Polychroni, 2007; Hatzichristou, 2009).

Crisis intervention in the school community

As a response to various occasions of natural disasters in Greece (earthquakes, wildfires), the CRPSP has developed and implemented crisis intervention programs in schools in the affected areas. These programs were based on relevant theory and models regarding crisis interventions in the school community, including basic goals, principles, and guidelines of crisis consultation and intervention (Brock, Sandoval & Lewis, 2001, 2005; Hatzichristou, 2008a, 2008b). The intervention in the classroom consists of four phases (providing facts and dispelling rumors, sharing stories, sharing reactions and feelings and empowerment, and developing coping skills). Throughout the whole process of program development and implementation, graduate students of SP were actively involved. In addition, new modules on crisis intervention have been included in the curriculum of relevant graduate and undergraduate courses at the Department of Psychology of the University of Athens.

Cross-cultural program for awareness building on olympic values and ideals

The CRPSP organized a cross-cultural project titled "The Olympic Spirit Through Children's Voice" in cooperation with the International School Psychology Association. The goal of this effort was to enhance children's and adolescents' awareness concerning the Olympic values and ideals in the context of the Athens 2004 Olympic Games. An international communication network among 21 participating countries was developed for the needs of the program. Students from different educational settings (preschools, elementary and secondary schools, special schools, and institutions) joined the program, and pieces of art and literature works were collected. Through the project, children (a) expressed common needs and feelings (the need for security, communication, closeness, and peace); (b) had common perceptions regarding the Olympic spirit and ideals, fairness, and ethical values; (c) realized and expressed their talents and abilities; and (d) felt that they communicate with children from different countries. Moreover, the children's works are offered for a multilevel reading (developmental, cultural, psychological, etc). The whole process aims to promote cross-cultural understanding and highlights the importance of learning, psychological well-being, and competence of children (Hatzichristou, 2004d).

A special publication and a calendar were published including the best art and literature works of the children. Furthermore, exhibitions with children's work was held during the Olympic and Paralympics Games and during the 27th International School Psychology Association Colloquium in July 2005, cohosted by the Department of Psychology of the University of Athens and the International School Psychology Association.

Psychoeducational intervention for children with learning and emotional difficulties

In an effort to meet the specific needs of children with learning and emotional difficulties, members of the scientific team of CRPSP have developed a psychoeducational program that has been implemented on the tertiary level. The program aims at empowering children with learning and emotional difficulties by helping them build communication skills; express and deal with their feelings, especially those associated with the experience of failure in academic or other domains; accept their strengths and weaknesses; learn effective coping strategies; and adjust to their school environment (Dimitropoulou & Hatzichristou, 2005). The activities of the program are implemented on a one-on-one basis, in accordance to the results of a detailed psychoemotional assessment of children. Moreover, the activities are connected with children's personal life events and difficult experiences. An important prerequisite for the implementation of the program is the provision of counseling to parents within the context of psychoeducational assessment and intervention.

Project II: linking the future of school psychology conference and the data-based model of alternative school psychological services

The Invitational Conference on the Future of School Psychology ("Futures Conference") that was held in Indiana in 2004 provided a conceptual framework with an emphasis on issues critical to the future of the profession and a problem-solving model to facilitate the accomplishment of conference goals. Specific key issues were identified at the conference; these issues constituted the focus of future goals and differentiated this meeting from previous ones (e.g., the Spring Hill Symposium and the Olympia Conference; Ehrhardt-Padgett et al., 2004).

The data-based model of alternative school psychological services, as described previously, and the model employed in the Futures Conference have similar aims. Therefore, an attempt was made to combine the problem-solving model and the strategic planning that is followed by the center in order to (a) implement the problem-solving model in a different cultural and professional context, (b) train graduate students of school psychology and teachers in the implementation of the problem-solving model, and (c) promote cross-national collaboration with the aim of meeting the needs of children, schools, and families.

Graduate students of school psychology

The problem-solving model was introduced within the context of an introductory school psychology graduate course in the University of Athens during the academic year 2003–2004. The students applied the model—having in mind the activities of the CRPSP—under consultation and supervision and came up with a number of action plans. Through this effort, students were given a chance to (a) realize the role of school psychologists, (b) examine critical issues, (c) examine the existing threats and opportunities, and (d) come up with ways to achieve the identified outcomes and to turn their ideas into practice. Finally, they were able to examine important issues of school psychology through a multicultural lens and to realize the differences—but mainly the similarities—among different educational and cultural settings.

The process was repeated during the following academic year (2004–2005), including two additional goals: application of the problem solving model (a) within the students' actual working setting and (b) within the context of the International School Psychology Association Colloquium that was held in Athens in July 2005. Finally, during the following years, an additional aim was to link the futures model with students' internship settings. The introduction of the problem-solving model within the context of the graduate course was a challenging process. The effort to combine two different and innovative approaches within the context of the course enabled students to gain a deeper insight into the theory and practice of school psychology and may contribute to the development of a new direction for training school psychologists in Greece.

Elementary teachers

The problem-solving model was also presented to elementary teachers during their training seminars for the implementation of the Social and Emotional Learning (SEL) program, which has been already described, in their classes. The action plans that were developed by teachers were linked with (a) the implementation of the SEL program and (b) the development of a network of schools among the participant teachers. The evolution of this effort regarding elementary school teachers included—apart from the initial goals of the process—an effort to apply the model within the context of the resiliency wheel for the promotion of resiliency in their schools (Henderson & Milstein, 1996, 2008).

This process has been extremely interesting for all the members involved. The cross-national perspective of this approach included (a) the implementation of the problem-solving model in the United States (national level), (b) the introduction of the problem-solving model to Greece (international level), and (c) the adaptation of the model within the Greek context (national level). This cross-national perspective had innovative features and an interactive process that could expand the aim of achieving positive outcomes in educational systems worldwide. It is proposed that school psychologists working in different countries can benefit from each other by sharing information about the effective and ineffective approaches to psychological services that they have used and by being aware of different paradigms, belief systems, and philosophies that operate in different cultural and educational settings.

Project III: community outreach: provision of alternative services in the community

Open seminars (Psychopaidia)

Since 2008, the Graduate Program of School Psychology of the University of Athens, in collaboration with the Division of School Psychology of the Hellenic Psychological Society, has organized open seminars once or twice a month for teachers and parents. These seminars are conducted by faculty members on issues related to children's development, adjustment, and well-being.

Crisis seminars

Apart from the prevention programs that were described earlier, the Center of Research and Practice in School Psychology, in collaboration with the Graduate Program of School Psychology of the University of Athens and the Division of School Psychology of the Hellenic Psychological Society, has organized an international symposium and a specialized 2-day workshop on crisis prevention and intervention in the school community. The symposium was open to all members of the community, whereas the workshop was attended by mental health specialists (trainers, practitioners, faculty members, etc.). The presenters of the symposium and the workshop were a group of well-recognized specialists in the field of crisis intervention from different countries (the United States, Israel, and the United Kingdom). The training has continued this year with a 2-day workshop on Prepare model by NASP on crisis intervention.

Furthermore, training seminars, lectures, and workshops for parents, teachers, students, and mental health specialists have been held in various contexts by the scientific team of the center regarding basic guidelines for the effective support of children after crises in the community, such as wildfires or earthquakes.

Alumni network

The Graduate Program of School Psychology of the University of Athens has initiated an effort to create a network of its graduates, aiming at the evolution of the field of school psychology at both scientific and professional level.

Social activities in the context of prevention programs

Within the context of most prevention programs that were implemented in the school community, a number of social events were also organized. At the end of the academic year, parents, students, and teachers participated in closing ceremonies, where various activities related to the programs were presented (Dimitropoulou, Lykitsakou, & Hatzichristou, 2005). Also, an additional project with community outreach character was the fairy tale "Tender Tiny Wing," which was dramatized by a group of graduate students of school psychology and presented in an interactive way to an open public of parents, teachers, and students on various occasions and in various settings.

Publications

Among the activities of the CRPSP is the preparation and publication of books, educational material, and booklets for students, teachers, parents, and mental health specialists regarding various educational and mental health issues (e.g., prevention programs for social and emotional learning in schools, crisis intervention, awareness building on diversity, etc.; Hatzichristou, 2004c, 2004d, 2004e, 2008a, 2008b; Hatzichristou & Polychroni, 2007; Hatzichristou, 2009). In addition, foreign scientific books that depict the current international trends in the field, such as consultation, prevention programs, resilience in the school community, and crisis intervention, have been translated and published in Greek (Brock, Sandoval, & Lewis, 2005; Brown, Pryzwansky, & Schulte, 2006; Henderson & Milstein, 2008)

DISCUSSION

Linking theory and practice is a challenging issue in the field of SP. The training and preparation of school psychologists is critical for bridging this gap since it provides opportunities for learning, personal and professional development in the secure context of scientific supervision and guidance. Nevertheless, the lack of comprehensive training models that incorporate the major current trends in the field constitutes a substantial barrier in achieving this goal. Such a synthetic theoretical and practical framework is proposed in this chapter, which aims at providing a paradigm for the preparation and training of graduate students of school psychology. The projects described above are presented as examples of applications of the specific framework and depict the multidimensional role of school psychologists. Gaining a wide range of knowledge, skills, and competences during their training and practice (practicum and internship) is essential for young professionals in order to be able to respond to the increasingly diverse demands of various professional contexts by providing alternative school psychological services according to existing resources and needs.

All projects include four basic dimensions. The first is provision of school psychological services through university and school community partnership (school-linked services). The second dimension is preparation of graduate students regarding school psychological services delivery, which consists of (a) academic training enriched by current trends and theories of school psychology, (b) active involvement in different types and levels of intervention, (c) learning through modeling (observing program coordinators during teachers' training and consultation and teachers during implementation of interventions in the schools), and (d) supervision. The third dimension is awareness building and training of teachers on issues regarding the promotion of positive school climate and well-being of the school community. The fourth dimension is community outreach through activities aiming at awareness building and collaboration of all members of the school community.

The development of these projects is based primarily on a holistic approach that takes into consideration both common and diverse needs of members of the school community and employs a broader perspective of diversity. According to this approach, a model has been proposed providing specific guidelines for program development that can be applied in different cultural and educational settings, thus creating a transnational potential of interventions through appropriate modifications that meet the particular needs and goals of each context (Hatzichristou et al., 2006). This transnational orientation could be enhanced further by specific action plans for the evolution of SP internationally. This transnational orientation goes beyond simply multicultural awareness or cross-cultural considerations and provides general guidelines and a conceptual framework regarding the content and mode of training of school psychologists and provision of school psychological services regardless specific cultural or educational contexts.

Universities, being the main agents that bear the responsibility for the preparation of school psychologists, should play a critical role in providing the appropriate modules and opportunities for bridging the gap between academic and practical domains through promotion of partnerships with all school community stakeholders. The collaboration of university trainers, professionals, and students at national and cross-national levels is of critical importance in this effort, as it creates new perspectives and opportunities for change and evolution of the profession.

Training and continuing professional development have a decisive impact on the specialty definition, the role of school psychologists, and the nature of school psychological services provided in the schools. Closer cooperation between national and international professional associations could promote specific action plans to develop (a) opportunities for professional training (i.e., for school psychologists and teachers, and parent training programs); (b) guidelines for cross-cultural educational curricula and competencies with opportunities to share educational materials with suggested readings, and to organize focused themes and training workshops, summer schools, and so forth; and (c) multicultural professional training experiences for school psychologies of developed and developing countries (Hatzichristou & Lampropoulou, 2004). Cross-national collaboration that involves reciprocal knowledge sharing and personal reflection fosters professional development and encourages a visionary and proactive approach for the evolution of school psychology worldwide.

RESOURCES

Cunningham, J. & Oakland, T. (1998). International School Psychology Association guidelines for the preparation of school psychologists. *School Psychology International, 19,*19–30.
This article provides the guidelines for the preparation of school psychologists around the world in order to ensure the highest standards in the provision of services. The guidelines have applicability to any program.

Farrell, P. T., Jimerson, S. R., & Oakland T. D. (2007). School psychology internationally: A synthesis of findings. In S. R. Jimerson, T. D. Oakland, and P. T. Farrell (Eds.), *The handbook of international school psychology* (pp. 501–510). Thousand Oaks, CA: Sage.
This chapter provides an excellent comparative perspective on internationalization of school psychology. The entire volume is an excellent reference source.

REFERENCES

Baker, J., Dilly, L., Aupperlee, J., & Patil, S. (2003). The developmental context of school satisfaction: Schools as psychologically healthy environments. *School Psychology Quarterly, 18*(2), 206–221.
Battistisch, V., Solomon, D., Watson, M., & Schaps, E. (1997). Caring school communities. *Educational Psychologist, 32*(3), 137–151.

Bickel, W. E. (1999). The implications of the effective schools literature for school restructuring. In C. R. Reynolds & T. B. Gutkin (Eds.), *Handbook of school psychology* (3rd ed., pp. 959–983). New York: Wiley.

Brock, S. E., Sandoval, J., & Lewis, S. (2001). *Preparing for crises in the schools: A manual for building school crisis response teams* (2nd ed). New York: Wiley.

Brock, S., Sandoval, J., & Lewis, S. (2005). Διαχείριση κρίσεων στο σχολείο. Εγχειρίδιο για τη δημιουργία ομίδων διαχείρισης κρίσεων στο σχολείο *[Preparing for crises in the schools: A manual for building school crisis response teams]*. C. Hatzichristou (Ed.) (E. Theoharaki, Trans.). Athens, Greece: ΤυπωΘΤτω.

Brown, D., Pryzwansky, W. B., & Schulte, A. C. (2001). *Psychological consultation: Introduction to theory and practice* (5th ed.). Boston: Allyn and Bacon.

Brown, D., Pryzwansky, W. B., & Schulte, A. C. (2006). Ψυχολογική διαλεκτική συμβουλευτική. Εισαγωγή στη θεωρία και την πρακτική εφαρμογή *[Psychological consultation: Introduction to theory and practice]*. C. Hatzichristou (Ed.) (A. Lampropoulou, Trans.). Athens, Greece: Τυπωθήτω.

Conoley, J. C., & Bahns, T. (1995). Best practices in supervision of interns. In A. Thomas & J. Grimes (Eds.), *Best practices in school psychology III* (pp. 111–122). Washington DC: National Association of School Psychologists.

Cunningham, J. & Oakland, T. (1998). International school psychology guidelines for preparation of school psychologists. *School Psychology International, 19,* 19–30.

Dimitropoulou, P., & Hatzichristou C. (2005, December). Psychosocial support of students with specific learning difficulties. The implementation of the program "Social and Emotional Learning" on a tertiary level of intervention. Presentation at the 10th Greek National Congress of Psychological Research, University of Ioannina, Department of Psychology, Ioannina, Greece.

Dimitropoulou, P., Lykitsakou, K., & Hatzichristou, C. (2005, July). Intervention programs: Implementation, training and effectiveness. Symposium at the 27th International School Psychology Colloquium, Athens, Greece.

Doll, B., Zucker, S., & Brehm, K. (2004). *Resilient classrooms: Creating healthy environments for learning.* New York: The Guilford Press.

Doll, B., Zucker, S., & Brehm, K. (2009). Σχολικές τάξεις που προάγουν την ψυχική ανθεκτικότητα. Πώς να δημιουργήσουμε ευνοϊκό περιβάλλον για μάθηση. [Resilient classrooms: Creating healthy environments for learning]. (E. Theoharaki, Trans. of Greek edition, C. Hatzichristou, editor of Greek edition). Athens, Greece: Τυπωθήτω.

Durlak, J. A. (2008). Prevention. In T. Gutkin & C. Reynolds (Eds.), *Handbook of school psychology* (4th ed, pp. 2377–2418). New York: Wiley.

Ehrhardt-Padgett, G., Hatzichristou, C., Kitson, J., & Meyers, J. (2004). Awakening to a new dawn: Perspectives of the future of school psychology. *School Psychology Review, 33*(1), 105–114.

Farrell, P. T., Jimerson, S. R., & Oakland T. D. (2007). School psychology internationally: A synthesis of findings. In S. R. Jimerson, T. D. Oakland, & P. T. Farrell (Eds.), *The handbook of international school psychology* (pp. 501–510). Thousand Oaks, CA: Sage.

Gardner, H. (1993). *Frames of mind: The theory of multiple intelligences,* New York: Basic Books.

Gettinger, M., & Stoiber, K. C. (2009). Effective teaching and effective schools. In T. B. Gutkin & C. R. Reynolds (Eds.), *The handbook of school psychology* (4th ed., pp. 769–790). Hoboken, NJ : John Wiley.

Giavrimis, P. Konstantinou, E. & Hatzichristou, C. (2003). Dimensions of immigrant students' adaptation in the Greek schools: Self-concept and coping strategies. *Intercultural Education, 14*(4), 423–434.

Goleman, D. (1995). *Emotional intelligence.* New York: Bantam Books.

Greenberg, M. T., Weissberg, R. P., O'Brien, M. U., Zins, J. E., Fredericks, L., Resnik, H., Elias, M. J. (2003). Enhancing school-based prevention and youth development through coordinated social, emotional, and academic learning. *American Psychologist, 58,* 466–474.

Hatzichristou, C. (1998). Alternative school psychological services: Development of a databased model. *School Psychology Review, 27*(2), 246–259.

Hatzichristou, C. (2002). A conceptual framework of the evolution of school psychology: Trans-national considerations of common phases and future perspectives. *School Psychology International, 23*(3), 266–282.

Hatzichristou, C. (2004a). Alternative school psychological services: Development of a model linking theory, research, and service delivery. In N. M. Lambert, I. Hylander, and J. Sandoval (Eds.), *Consultee-centered consultation: Improving the quality of professional services in schools and community organizations* (pp. 115–132). Mahwah, NJ: Lawrence Erlbaum.

Hatzichristou, C. (2004b). *Εισαγωγή στη Σχολική Ψυχολογία* [*Handbook of school psychology*]. Athens, Greece: Ελληνικά Γράμματα.

Hatzichristou, C. (Ed.). (2004c). *Πρόγραμμα προαγωγής της ψυχικής υγείας και της μάθησης: Κοινωνική και συναισθηματική αγωγή στο σχολείο (εκπαιδευτικό υλικό για εκπαιδευτικούς και μαθητές πρωτοβάθμιας εκπαίδευσης)* [*Program for the promotion of mental health and learning: Social and emotional learning in school (educational material for teachers and students in primary education)*]. Center for Research and Practice in School Psychology, University of Athens: ΤΥΠΩΘΗΤΩ.

Hatzichristou, C. (Ed.). (2004d). *The Olympic spirit through children's voice.* Athens: Center for Research and Practice in School Psychology, University of Athens.

Hatzichristou, C. (Ed.). (2004e). *Πρόγραμμα προαγωγής της ψυχικής υγείας και της μάθησης: Κοινωνική και συναισθηματική αγωγή στο σχολείο (εκπαιδευτικό υλικό για εκπαιδευτικούς και μαθητές δευτεροβάθμιας εκπαίδευσης)* [*Program for the promotion of mental health and learning: Social and emotional learning in school (educational material for teachers and students in secondary education)*]. Center for Research and Practice in School Psychology, University of Athens: ΤΥΠΩΘΗΤΩ.

Hatzichristou, C. (Ed.). (2008a). *Πρόγραμμα προαγωγής της ψυχικής υγείας και της μάθησης: Κοινωνική και συναισθηματική αγωγή στο σχολείο (εκπαιδευτικό υλικό για εκπαιδευτικούς και μαθητές δευτεροβάθμιας εκπαίδευσης)* [*Program for the promotion of mental health and learning: Social and emotional learning in school (educational material for teachers and students— Grades K-3*]. Κέντρο Έρευνας και Εφαρμογών Σχολικης Ψυχολογίας, University of Athens: ΤΥΠΩΘΗΤΩ.

Hatzichristou, C. (Ed.). (2008b). *Στήριξη των παιδιών σε καταστάσεις κρίσεων* [*Supporting children in crisis*]. Center for Research and Practice in School Psychology, University of Athens: ΤΥΠΩΘΗΤΩ.

Hatzichristou, C. (Ed.) (2009). *Οι Φριτ–Φρατ και οι Μικροφτερούληδες. Ένα παραμύθι για τη διαφορετικότητα και τον πολιτισμό. [Frit-frats and the tender tiny-wings: A fairy tale for multi-cultural diversity*]. Text: Th. Karayianni. Athens, Greece: Φαντασία.

Hatzichristou, C., Dimitropoulou, P., Konstantinou, E., & Lampropoulou, A. (2002, July). *School psychological services in the Greek schools: Teachers', students' and parents' perceptions*. Symposium at the Twenty-Fifth Annual International School Psychology Colloquium, Nyborg, Denmark.

Hatzichristou, C., Dimitropoulou, P., Lykitsakou, K., & Lampropoulou, A. (in press). Προαγωγή της ψυχικής ευεξίας στη σχολική κοινότητα: Εφαρμογή παρεμβατικού προγράμματος σε επίπεδο συστήματος. [Promotion of school community well being: Implementation of prevention program at a system level].

Hatzichristou, C., Gari, A., Mylonas, K., Georgouleas, G., Lykitsakou, K., Mpafiti, T., Vaitsi, A., & Bakopoulou, A., (2001). Προσαρμογή παλιννοστούντων και αλλοδαπών μαθητών: Ι. Σχεδιασμός και εφαρμογή ενός προγράμματος ψυχολογικής συμβουλευτικής παρέμβασης. ΙΙ. Αξιολόγηση του προγράμματος ψυχολογικής συμβουλευτικής παρέμβασης [Immigrant and remigrant students adaptation: I. Application of an intervention program. II. Evaluation of the program]. *Νέα Παιδεία, 99*, 13–36.

Hatzichristou, C. & Lampropoulou, A. (2004). The invitational conference on the future of school psychology: A cross-national approach to service delivery. *Journal of Educational and Psychological Consultation, 15*(3&4), 313–333.

Hatzichristou, C., Lampropoulou, A., & Lykitsakou, K. (2004). Ένα διαφορετικό σχολείο: Το σχολείο ως κοινότητα που νοιάζεται και φροντίζει [A different school: School as a caring community]. *Ψυχολογία, 11*(1), 1–19.

Hatzichristou, C., Lampropoulou, A., & Lykitsakou, K. (2006). Addressing cultural factors in development of system interventions. *Journal of Applied School Psychology, 22*(2) 103–126.

Hatzichristou, C., Lykitsakou, K., Lampropoulou, A., & Dimitropoulou, P. (in press). Promoting the well-being of school communities: A systemic approach. In B. Doll, W. Pfohl, & J. Yoon (Eds.), *Handbook of youth prevention science*. New York: Routledge.

Hatzichristou, C. & Polychroni, F. (Eds.). (2007). *Ο Τρυφερούλης Μικροφτερούλης. Ένα παραμύθι για τη διαφορετικότητα* [*Tender Tiny-wing: A fairy tale for diversity*]. Text: Th. Karayianni. Athens, Greece: Φαντασία.

Hatzichristou, C., Polychroni, F., & Georgouleas, G. (2007). School psychology in Greece. In S. R. Jimerson, T. D. Oakland, & P. T. Farrell (Eds.), *The handbook of international school psychology* (pp. 135–146). Thousand Oaks, CA: Sage.

Hatzichristou, C., Vaitsi, A., Dimitropoulou, P., & Falki, B. (2000). Center for School and Family Consultation and Research: A partnership-based framework for the development of alternative school psychological services in the Greek schools. In M. Malikiosi-Loisos (Ed.), *Education, Communication and Counseling* (pp.149–165). Athens: Ellinika Grammata.

Henderson, N., & Milstein, M. (1996). *Resiliency in schools. Making it happen for students and educators*. Thousand Oaks, CA: Corwin Press.

Henderson, N., & Milstein, M. (2008). *Σχολεία που προάγουν την ψυχική ανθεκτικότητα. Πώς μπορεί να γίνει πραγματικότητα για μαθητές και εκπαιδευτικούς.* [Resiliency in schools. Making it happen for students and educators]. (V. Vassara, Trans. of Greek edition; C. Hatzichristou, editor of Greek edition). Athens, Greece: ΤΥΠΩΘΗΤΩ.

Jimerson, R. S., Graydona, K., Farrell, P., Kikas, E., Hatzichristou, C., Bocee, E., Bashie, G., & The Ispa Research Committee (2004). The International School Psychology Survey Development and Data from Albania, Cyprus, Estonia, Greece and Northern England. *School Psychology International, 25*(3), 259–286.

Kratochwill, R. T., & Shernoff, S. E (2004). Evidence-based practice: Promoting evidence-based interventions in school psychology. *School Psychology Review, 33*(1), 165–174.

Kratochwill, R. T., & Stoiber, K. C. (2002). Evidence-based interventions in school psychology: Conceptual foundations of the Procedural and Coding Manual of Division 16 and the Society for the Study of School Psychology Task Force. *School Psychology Quarterly, 17*, 341–389.

Lampropoulou, A. (2008). Υποκειμενική αίσθηση ευεξίας εφήβων: Μια πολυεπίπεδη θεώρηση ατομικών, οικογενειακών και σχολικών παραμέτρων *[Subjective well being of adolescents: A multilevel approach of individual, family and school parameters]*. Unpublished doctoral thesis. Department of Psychology, Faculty of Philosophy, Pedagogy and Psychology, School of Philosophy, University of Athens.

Nastasi, B., Moore, R. B., & Varjas, K. M. (2004). *School-based mental health services creating comprehensive and culturally specific programs*. Washington, DC: American Psychological Association.

Oakland, T. & Cunningham, J. (1992). A survey of school psychology in developed and developing countries. *School Psychology Review, 13*, 99–129.

Oakland, T. D., & Jimerson, S. R. (2007). School psychology internationally: A retrospective view and influential conditions. In S. R. Jimerson, T. D. Oakland, & P. T. Farrell (Eds.), *The handbook of international school psychology* (pp. 453–462).Thousand Oaks, CA: Sage.

O'Dougherty Wright, M., & Masten, A. S. (2005). Resilience processes in development. In S. Goldstein & R. B. Brooks (Eds.), *Handbook of resilience in children* (pp. 17–37). New York: Kluwer Academic/Plenum Publishers.

Rogers, M. R. (2005). Multicultural training in school psychology. In C. L. Frisby & C. R. Reynolds (Eds.), *Comprehensive handbook of multicultural school psychology* (pp. 993–1022). Hoboken, NJ: John Wiley and Sons.

Part III
Difficult dialogues

7 Multicultural competence and diversity

University and field collaboration

Emilia C. Lopez and
Margaret R. Rogers

INTRODUCTION AND RATIONALE

Field-based training that provides future school psychologists with the opportunity to develop skills working with a diverse clientele is a critical responsibility of all school psychology training programs. Field-based training occurs primarily in the public schools, but it also takes place in private schools, medical centers/hospitals, mental health centers, and other mental health settings. For the purposes of the present chapter, our attention will be on applied training aimed at school psychology students that takes place in the public schools, with a focus on clients diverse in ethnicity, race, language background, sexual orientation, gender, religious background, and nationality.

There are significant reasons underscoring the importance of developing school psychology students' cross-cultural competence during field-based training. First, public school enrollments are continuing to show significant demographic changes in the United States, with current estimates indicating that 43% of school-aged youngsters represent a racial or ethnic minority group nationwide, as reported by the U.S. Department of Education's National Center for Education Statistics (NCES, 2008). The data suggest that the fastest growing minority subgroup is Latinos, whose numbers have tripled in the last 30 years. Students who speak English as a second language are also a growing segment of the school-age population, with 20% of the overall student body identifying as English language learners (ELLs; U.S. Department of Education, 2007a). Of those students who speak a second language, Spanish is the most common, followed by Chinese, French, German, and Tagalog (U.S. Census Bureau, 2003a). Other data show that about 18% of children live in poverty (U.S. Census Bureau, 2007a), and about 12% of public school students receive special education services (U.S. Department of Education, 2005). Collectively, the data show that the nation's schools are increasingly diverse.

However, an examination of the geographic distribution of many diverse students across the United States tells a more complex story. The greatest concentrations of African American and Latino students, ELLs, and students living in poverty can be found in central cities and some rural areas in the United States (U.S. Department of Education, 2006). African American students are most concentrated in Washington, DC, and Mississippi, and Latino students in New Mexico, California, and Texas. More than half the total number of ELL students live in the West, and greatest proportions are found in California, Texas, New Mexico, Arizona, and New York (NCES, 2007a). Asian Americans are most well represented in Hawaii, California, New Jersey, and Washington, and American Indians and Alaska Natives in Alaska, Oklahoma, and New Mexico (U.S. Census Bureau, 2007b). Maine, New Hampshire, and West Virginia have the fewest racial and ethnic minority students in the country (NCES, 2007b). Thus, although school-age students are increasingly representing diverse backgrounds nationwide, there are wide swaths of the United States that are primarily White and where comparatively few ELLs attend school. Although all school psychology programs must train their students to deliver services to a diverse clientele, access to diverse clients varies depending on the specific populations present in the geographic location of the program.

The second rationale for addressing multicultural competencies during field-based training stems from professional guidelines and standards in psychology. The American Psychological Association's (APA's) accreditation standards (APA, 2008) and the National Association of School Psychologists (NASP) *Standards for Training and Field Placement Programs in School Psychology* (NASP, 2000) stipulate that training programs will provide school psychology students with training that enables them to deliver psychological services effective in meeting the needs of diverse clients. Programs accredited by the APA and approved by the NASP must conform to these expectations and demonstrate how they do so when seeking and maintaining national accreditation.

The training standards are augmented by several additional guidelines and resolutions produced by the APA and NASP that have implications for training. For example, to raise awareness about the special needs of various groups, experts have collaborated to produce resolutions for the APA or NASP about working with girls and women (APA, 2007); gay, lesbian, and bisexual students (APA, 1999; NASP, 1999); clients living in poverty (APA, 2000); and immigrants (APA, 1998), as well as resolutions about recruiting students of color (NASP, 2003) and addressing racism, prejudice, and discrimination (NASP, 2004a). In addition, the 2003 APA "Guidelines on Multicultural Education, Training, Research, Practice, and Organizational Change for Psychologists" contains six guidelines suggesting that training programs prepare future psychologists to take a culturally informed approach not just in their clinical services but also in their pedagogy, research, and organizational development work. Essentially, this means that a culturally informed approach is expected for psychologists who practice in every conceivable setting, from higher education to private industry, to clinical practice, and beyond.

In addition, the latest edition of *School Psychology: A Blueprint for Training and Practice III* (Ysseldyke et al., 2006) reinforced the need for cross-cultural competence addressed by earlier guidelines but goes farther by stating:

> Competence in all aspects of diversity is not demonstrated by an individual's degree of sensitivity to or level of knowledge about a given culture, but rather by the ability to recognize when, where, and how issues of diversity are manifest and operating within the wide variety of activities in which school psychologists engage. (p. 16)

Thus, per the combined specifications of the APA and NASP training standards, resolutions, and guidelines, including the *Blueprint III*, school psychology programs need to train students to recognize "when, where, and how issues of diversity are manifest" (Ysseldyke et al., 2006, p. 16). This level of awareness implies a demonstrated consciousness about how issues of diversity play a role in the complexities of the organizational milieu. For example, how do they influence the structure of the schools; school policies and practices; agendas established within the school system; social processes that operate in the schools; school culture and climate; and the relationships and dynamics between school staff, students and their families, and classmates? Such a focus draws attention to the need to train students to understand the systemic, individual, and psychosocial forces that operate in the public schools.

It is within this context that school psychology programs design field-based training experiences for students. The purpose of the present chapter is to describe some of the major considerations in collaborating with field settings to develop students' cross-cultural competencies during field-based training. Major approaches to collaboration are presented, and issues in providing multicultural supervision are delineated. The chapter closes with two case studies illustrating different dimensions of diversity as examples of the kinds of challenges that arise when collaborating with field settings and providing a multiculturally informed approach to supervision.

LITERATURE REVIEW

Literature focusing on training professionals for practice in school systems affirms that training in multicultural competencies is best accomplished when a field component is present (e.g., Benner & Barclay-McLaughlin, 2005; Bolick, & Fry, 2004; Burnett, Long, & Horne, 2005; McCaleb, 1998). Sue and Zane (1987) argued that field experiences are central in helping future professionals to acquire cultural competence by transforming their knowledge of cultural issues learned at the university into culturally competent skills (e.g., in field-based experiences) that ultimately translate into culturally responsive services in the field. Emphasized in this literature base is the important role of collaboration between university and field personnel to create appropriate training experiences for culturally competent professionals. Specifically, three types of collaborative approaches are identified as important: collaborative supervision practices, professional development schools, and community-based or service learning partnerships.

Collaborative supervision practices approach

Collaborative supervision practices refer to fieldwork and internship experiences that are designed to expose future professionals to multicultural populations. In this framework faculty in the university training programs work with the field-based personnel to coordinate placements; evaluate the university students' progress in specific areas of competency; and plan fieldwork activities designed to increase the university students' awareness, knowledge, and skills in multicultural issues (e.g., Benner & Barclay-McLaughlin, 2005; Grant & Koskela, 2001). Collaborative supervision practices with a multicultural fieldwork are well documented in the teacher training literature, yet these issues have not been fully explored in school psychology. The benefits and challenges of crafting collaborative partnerships in school psychology training are discussed in a subsequent section of this chapter.

Professional development schools approach

Professional development schools (PDSs) are school settings in "which university faculty, administrators, teachers, and future teachers collaborate to build a learning community" (Bolick & Fry, 2004, p. 57). Bell, McCallum, and Cox (2000) also described PDS experiences for school psychologists as applied settings that provide practicum students and interns with "an opportunity to collaborate with educational professionals from various disciplines. In addition, the PDS brings university and public school personnel together in an applied setting so that research informs teaching and vice-versa" (p. 1). Collaboration between university training programs in PDSs involves formalized partnerships, where training roles are defined and university training programs share resources with schools that become training laboratories and research partners.

Community-based/service learning partnerships approach

Hasslen and Bacharach (2007) defined service learning as well-planned, experiential pedagogy that meets authentic community needs. Belbas, Gorak, and Shumer (1993) also defined it as "an experiential pedagogy that explicitly connects community service with appropriate learning objectives" (p. 36). Community-based training experiences are viewed as ways to link learning opportunities for university students with communities' social needs (e.g., Brown, 2005; Burnett et al., 2005; McCaleb, 1998; Ngai, 2004).

In community-based service learning programs, graduate students actively interact with the communities that they work with by, for example, living within the community, volunteering to provide services, and/or interning in local settings. Service learning experiences have been described as social justice training tools (Hasslen & Bacharach, 2007). Social justice involves "providing equal access and opportunity, being inclusive, and removing individual and systemic barriers" to deliver fair educational and mental health services for clients (Sue, 2001, p. 801). Community-based programs and service learning opportunities that help students to connect with various communities and individuals of diverse backgrounds (e.g., gender, religion, ethnicity, language, socioeconomic status) while becoming immersed in issues about equity in education and mental health are venues to expose future professionals to social justice issues.

Ford (2004) views service learning partnerships as essential in helping schools to address the needs of diverse learners within the context of communities. Service learning experiences have also been found to positively influence teachers' attitudes about teaching inner-city youngsters, and teachers' awareness of the needs of children and families from diverse backgrounds (Hasslen & Bacharach, 2007; Olmedo, 1997). In a review of the literature, Cooper (2007) found that teachers who participated in such programs were more likely to choose to work in similar settings after graduation.

There is a dearth of research about collaborative supervision, professional development schools, and community-based service learning approaches to train future school psychologists to acquire multicultural competencies. Each of these approaches differs in significant ways and must be evaluated as to their utility and outcomes. For example, professional development schools and community-based partnerships may provide more comprehensive and integrated forums by which to coordinate training experiences (e.g., identify competencies and integrate them into courses and fieldwork experiences) and align the needs of the university (i.e., to train future professionals), schools, and communities (i.e., provide quality instruction and mental health services to students of diverse backgrounds). Community-based service learning approaches may result in partnerships that more directly benefit schools and communities.

Crafting collaborative partnerships in multicultural training

The literature exploring how to foster collaboration between the university and the field to train students to acquire multicultural competency is scarce and is drawn primarily from teacher training models (e.g., Bell et al., 2000; Hasslen & Bacharach, 2007; McCaleb, 1998; Wiggins, Follo, & Eberly, 2007). Areas for collaboration discussed in this literature include (a) codeveloping courses, course content, and field experiences; (b) coidentifying areas of training and multicultural competencies; (c) codelivering workshops and seminars for university students; (d) co-observing university students during fieldwork activities; (e) codelivering services (e.g., university faculty and teachers participating in coteaching); (f) codeveloping programs and interventions; (g) coconducting research; and (h) co-outlining efforts to reach common outcomes (Benner & Barclay-McLaughlin; Bolick & Fry, 2004; Hasslen & Bacharach; McCaleb; Ngai, 2004). In addition, collaborations were also accomplished by providing reciprocal support and consultation, attending mutual meetings (e.g., university faculty attending district faculty meetings to become better acquainted with schools), interacting with parents, and teaching continuing education courses at the fieldwork site (Bolick & Fry; Hasslen & Bacharach; Wiggins et al.). Benner and Barclay-McLaughlin (2005) reported that these are the types of activities helpful for faculty in getting to know the district settings and the communities, and infusing field-based issues into university-based courses and supervision sessions.

Benefits of collaboration

The benefits of university and field collaborations for university students include (a) obtaining knowledge and skills in multicultural issues; (b) acquiring an understanding of how theory and practice are connected; (c) acquiring awareness of their own values, beliefs, and attitudes about working with clients of diverse backgrounds; (d) learning about the schools, communities, and settings affiliated with fieldwork experiences; and (d) providing exposure to social justice issues (Bell et al., 2000; Brown, 2005; Burnett et al., 2005; Ford, 2004; Hasslen & Bacharach, 2007). To date, the bulk of research focuses on the benefits to the university students. Less attention is devoted to benefits for children, teachers, and communities, such as receiving culturally responsive educational and psychological services. The research has also not yet addressed the potential benefits of collaboration for university training programs, faculty, university-based supervisors, and field-based supervisors. The potential benefits of such collaborations for university training programs may include university faculty infusing more authentic multicultural experiences into their courses and university programs increasing their resources (e.g., courses, faculty, materials, capacity to retain graduate students of diverse backgrounds) to address multicultural training issues. University faculty and supervisors can also benefit by increasing their own knowledge, skills, and levels of awareness related to multiculturally responsive practices, which will ultimately affect training.

Barriers to collaboration

There are multiple barriers to establishing collaborative partnerships for training for multicultural competence. Some barriers discussed in the literature include negotiating (a) the cultural divide that can separate the university and field settings; (b) a lack of connection between knowledge gained at the university program and the practices in the field; (c) the time-consuming nature of collaboration; (d) agreements between settings as to how to structure field experiences for students to acquire multicultural skills; (e) clear objectives that meet the needs of both the university students and the fieldwork placements (e.g., needs of schools, supervisors, and clients); (f) key components within the university curriculum and fieldwork experiences that incorporate multicultural issues in substantive ways (e.g., infusing multicultural issues into multiple courses and providing appropriate supervision in multicultural areas); (g) commitment and action from university faculty and supervisors to develop their own knowledge, skills, and awareness about multicultural issues; and (h) a lack of funding to support collaborative efforts (e.g., release time for faculty and supervisors, travel funds) (Benner & Barclay-McLaughlin, 2005; Bolick & Fry, 2004; Brown, 2005; Burnett et al., 2005; Grant & Koskela, 2001; Hasslen & Bacharach, 2007; McCaleb, 1998; Wiggins et al., 2007). Each barrier presents a need for coordinated and sustained efforts from all parties.

University training programs and school settings remain distinct organizational systems, each with their own emphases (e.g., university training programs emphasize evidence-based practices, whereas practitioners emphasize practical interventions), structures (e.g., administrative frameworks with top-down practices as compared with individualized governing), knowledge bases (e.g., university programs emphasize theoretically informed decision making, and practitioners emphasize solution focused outcomes), priorities (e.g., needs of university students vs. the needs of the district), and tasks (e.g., universities train future professionals, whereas schools educate children). According to Bolick and Fry (2004), the "cultural divide" between universities and public schools can provide obstacles for successful school–university collaborations. However, research is needed to understand how those organizational differences impact the training of future school psychologists to work with diverse student populations (Sue, et al., 1998).

Techniques to address the research gaps

The research focusing on collaboration between university training programs and school settings to enhance school psychology students' multicultural skills is clearly lacking. The available studies are drawn from the teacher training literature and are mostly qualitative investigations that use interview techniques to explore preservice teachers' attitudes and beliefs about multicultural issues. Empirical research is needed in school psychology using quantitative and qualitative research methods to investigate the potential outcomes of using a variety of collaborative frameworks (e.g., collaborative supervision practices, PDSs, and community-based/service learning partnerships). University student outcomes should include specific multicultural areas of awareness, knowledge, and skills learned as a result of collaborative training efforts between university programs and school psychology supervisors. Similarly, faculty and supervisor knowledge, skills, and awareness acquired via collaborative frameworks can be measured. Identifying and measuring organizational gains (e.g., faculty, supervisors, and other school professionals sharing multicultural resources that improve children's educational and mental health functioning) will be helpful to university training programs and school districts in order to understand the gains associated with their collaborative experiences. Qualitative and action-based research methodologies should be particularly helpful in enhancing our understanding of how collaboration occurs and how it can be improved to address issues of diversity for graduate students, faculty, school personnel, and children.

SUPERVISION ISSUES

General framework for supervision

Providing high-quality supervision to school psychology trainees is a complex and multilayered process. Considerations include selecting field-based supervisors and training sites, planning for and partnering with field-based supervisors, conducting university-based and field-based education, and carving out a role as a multicultural supervisor. Both the APA and NASP provide faculty with guidance in articulating the role and responsibilities of supervisors in field-based settings. Supervision is addressed in the most recent ethical principles and codes of conduct (APA, 2002; NASP, 2000) and in the latest training standards (APA, 2008; NASP).

The NASP (2000) *Guidelines for the Provision of School Psychological Services* are also helpful in discussing parameters of supervision including eligibility criteria, evaluation procedures, and what are considered to be appropriate conditions for applied training. Specifically, NASP recommends supervisors have at least 3 years' experience, hold appropriate credentials (e.g., state certification as school psychologist), and be regarded as "appropriate role models" (p. 58). More recently, NASP (2004b) published a *Position Statement on Supervision in School Psychology* that defines the nature of the supervisory relationship, distinguishes between administrative and professional (i.e., clinical) supervision, identifies recipients of supervision (novice and advanced students, beginner and experienced practitioners), explores supervisory techniques, and discusses the training and evaluation of supervisors. As a collection, these resources provide a general and valuable orientation to supervision; however, they do not discuss a multiculturally informed approach to supervision, nor do the definitions of administrative or professional supervision sufficiently capture the supervisors' professional obligations relevant to psychological service delivery to diverse clients.

Multicultural approach to supervision

APA's and NASP's ethical codes promote values relevant to work with diverse clients and serve as a framework for understanding multicultural supervision. As Sandoval (2007) notes in his discussion of the ethical codes that have special significance for work with diverse populations, APA's principle of justice and APA's and NASP's principle of respect for people's rights and dignity are most relevant. The first, APA's (2002) Principle D—Justice, states:

> Psychologists recognize that fairness and justice entitle all persons to access to and benefit from the contributions of psychology and to equal quality in the processes, procedures, and services being conducted by psychologists. Psychologists exercise reasonable judgment and take precautions to ensure that their potential biases, the boundaries of their competence, and the limitations of their expertise do not lead to or condone unjust practices. (p. 3)

The principle calls for supervisors to use a framework of justice in critically examining who has access to psychological services, how clients needs are addressed, and what the impact of those services are for clients. It also calls for supervisors to be mindful of their biases and their boundaries of competence and take action should their limitations lead to differential access to services or differential outcomes for clients.

The second relevant principle, addressed by both APA (2002) and NASP (2000) and here drawn from APA, states:

> Psychologists respect the dignity and worth of all people, and the rights of individuals to privacy, confidentiality, and self-determination. Psychologists are aware that special safeguards may be necessary to protect the rights and welfare of persons or communities whose vulnerabilities impair autonomous decision-making. Psychologists are aware of and respect cultural, individual, and role differences, including those based on age, gender, gender identity, race, ethnicity, national origin, religion, sexual orientation, disability, language, and socioeconomic status and consider these factors when working with members of other groups. Psychologists try to eliminate the effect on their work of biases based on those factors, and they do not knowingly participate in or condone activities of others based upon such prejudices. (p. 4)

As Sandoval (2007) suggested, the important features of this principle are that school psychologists have an obligation to consider how human diversity influences quality of life, to counteract the forces of bias in self and others, and to advocate for those whose rights have been compromised. Supervisors who ground their philosophical orientation, their professional practices, and their approach to supervision using these two principles take a multiculturally informed stance in their work.

With these principles in mind, we define multicultural supervision as an approach to supervision that (a) provides a forum for examining how human diversity influences quality of life and (b) uses that knowledge to improve effectiveness of services, with the goal of ensuring a just and fair environment for clients. Within the supervision relationship, supervisors assess supervisee skills, provide feedback to improve skill development, and evaluate supervisee performance to meet the goal of improved performance of the supervisee, the supervisor, and the whole school community. This definition blends elements of previous definitions of supervision from McIntosh and Phelps (2000) and NASP (2004b), and multicultural supervision from D'Andrea and Daniels (1997). It contrasts with other definitions widely used in the multicultural supervision literature that frame multicultural supervision as occurring between a supervisor and a supervisee who are ethnically different and are thus too narrow to capture the complexities of the roles and missions of multicultural supervisors in school psychology contexts (e.g., Constantine, 1997; Dressel, Consoli, Kim, & Atkinson, 2007; Leong & Wagner, 1994).

Although the closely related specialty of counseling psychology has begun to establish a thriving research base about multicultural supervision, the knowledge base in school psychology has been notably silent. The following section applies the research findings about multicultural supervision from the counseling psychology literature to discuss the advantages and challenges of multicultural supervision within a school psychology context.

Advantages of multicultural supervision

There are several advantages of a multiculturally informed approach to supervision. Most notably, researchers have shown that multiculturally informed services lead to improved outcomes for clients, and supervisors who model cross-cultural competence by delivering informed services demonstrate to supervisees how to provide optimal services. In a recent meta-analysis about the effectiveness of culturally sensitive mental health interventions, Griner and Smith (2006) found that services delivered in the client's native language were twice as effective as those delivered in English, and interventions tailored to a specific racial group were 4 times as effective as those not directed at specific racial groups. Delivering culturally sensitive services and showing supervisees how to do the same meets the dual goals of high-quality service provision to clients and high-quality training for supervisees.

Second, multicultural supervision leads to supervisees feeling more effective in delivering services to diverse clients (Constantine, 2001). For example, teaching supervisees to engage in honest reflection about their own biases and beliefs helps university students to confront those beliefs constructively. Supervisors who model cross-cultural competence demonstrate to their supervisees how to critically analyze themselves and their work environments, gather important culturally relevant information and resources, make decisions, and deliver culturally informed services. Indeed, practica students who learn during supervision how to explore their feelings and beliefs about sexual orientation when presented with gay clients can begin to develop a heightened awareness of prejudices they may hold toward gay and straight clients so that they can learn how to address those beliefs. In responding to the needs of a specific high school client (e.g., a gay student who is struggling to fit in at high school), the practica student will also have the chance to look for, access, and use an array of gay, lesbian, bisexual, and transgender resources and supports that offer the opportunity to become better equipped to fill the needs of other gay clients with similar issues.

Third, researchers have shown that a multicultural supervision approach improves supervisees' level of satisfaction and positively influences their perceptions of the quality of supervision (Duan & Roehlke, 2001). A fourth advantage is that it provides supervisees with a forum for exploring individual, organizational, and societal expressions of bias, prejudice, and oppression. Multicultural supervision provides lessons about how to advocate for underrepresented clients, and challenge and address oppressive behaviors, social systems, and institutions. Furthermore, it gives supervisees the advantage of learning how to critically analyze institutions, examine the process of organizational development, and understand how systems change. A fifth advantage is that it has the potential to create more just organizations (i.e., schools) and social systems within the schools, because the supervisor will be working to ensure more equitable environments in support of diverse clients.

Challenges of multicultural supervision

There are also challenges and obstacles in multicultural supervision. One obstacle is that supervisors will vary in their cross-cultural skills and their skills as supervisors. If the cross-cultural skills of the supervisors are not adequately developed, or if the supervisors are culturally encapsulated, are biased, are resistant to change, lack self-awareness, or are uninformed and uninterested in furthering their knowledge in specific domains, this will compromise the success of the supervision experiences. A second challenge is the possibility that few supervisors presently operate from a multiculturally informed position. Research indicates that there is a shortage of bilingual psychologists (Castaño, Biever, Gonzalez, & Anderson, 2007), and in counseling psychology, far fewer supervisors (30%) than students (70%) have taken multicultural course work, suggesting that most supervisors are not as informed about the latest theory and research about diversity issues as their supervisees are (Constantine, 1997). Among school psychology supervisors, no data are presently available about the use of multicultural supervision.

Some obstacles indirectly influence the potential successes of multicultural supervision. An organizational culture and climate that actively resists change in the face of compelling evidence of inequities can impede multicultural supervision by creating training environments that do not support growth in multicultural awareness, knowledge, and skills. For example, a school setting that tolerates racially derogatory remarks made by members of the administration, promotes sexist depictions of young women, engages in language-based discrimination, and fails to take steps to redress these inequities and replace a hostile environment with a healthy one will prove difficult and stressful to the supervisors who are trying to create a just training environment. Ultimately, the aim of multicultural supervision is to help students acquire cross-cultural competencies while simultaneously improving the services delivered to diverse clients. The next section of the chapter presents two cases that illustrate the types of cross-cultural dilemmas faced during field-based training of school psychology students.

CASE ILLUSTRATIONS

Case involving gender-related issues

While participating in a biweekly meeting on campus for supervision purposes, a practicum student disclosed to her classmates and university supervisor an interchange that she had witnessed involving her field supervisor at her field-based placement. In a conversation with the school principal, the field supervisor spoke about the mother of a youngster who had been receiving special education services. As the two men talked, the supervisor commented on the mothers' physical appearance, making pointed comments about her breasts and other physical attributes. The practicum student stood by listening to the interchange and was stunned and offended by these comments but, not knowing how to respond, said nothing.

After learning of this interchange, the university supervisor contacted the psychological supervisor for the district, explained the student's report, and offered to begin to offer a series of workshops within the district starting with one on sexual harassment identification and prevention for the mental health service providers in the district. It was jointly agreed that the workshop would be conducted the next professional development day and attended by all district school psychologists. As part of the workshop, case scenarios were distributed and included an example identical to the practicum student's report. As workshop participants read the case scenarios aloud, the supervisor heard his own words and exclaimed, in a candid moment of self-awareness, "I've done that!"

Case involving bilingual and community issues

A university training program with a multicultural specialization identified school settings with children from various culturally and linguistically diverse backgrounds as possible fieldwork settings and collaborated with bilingual supervisors speaking various languages. One of the students who needed to be placed in a bilingual internship spoke Urdu, a language spoken in Middle Eastern countries such as Pakistan and India. The university training program was not able to locate a bilingual Urdu-speaking school psychologist but was able to identify a school setting with an Urdu-speaking population. The same school setting employed a Spanish-speaking school psychologist who had been trained to provide bilingual services to children and families. The university faculty and field-based supervisor explored the general skills that the intern needed to acquire as a school psychologist. They also discussed the specific skills that the intern needed to become proficient as a bilingual school psychologist and designed training activities to meet that goal (e.g., translating for the school psychologist [i.e. for the student's supervisor] to communicate with Urdu-speaking students and families, providing educational and psychological services to the Urdu-speaking children and families while being supervised). The field supervisor agreed to supervise the Urdu-speaking student for all cases, including bilingual Urdu cases.

During the university-based group supervision meetings, the intern shared with peers and the university supervisor that although the field supervisor was supportive, the intern was having a very difficult time connecting with the Urdu-speaking community. The intern did not feel that the Urdu-speaking children and families viewed her as a resource. The university supervisor and peers provided the intern with suggestions as to how to make connections with the community: writing a letter to the parents in Urdu with information about the school and an invitation to call her, approaching the supervisor about creating a parenting group, and including a column in the school newspaper in Urdu. The student felt more empowered to make a connection with the community and approached the supervisor to discuss possible strategies. In addition, the university supervisor met with the field supervisor to discuss the challenges of providing bilingual services to a community that had a different cultural and language background than the supervisor. They also explored other ways to help the intern reach out to the Urdu-speaking community.

SUMMARY AND CONCLUSIONS

Demographic changes in the United States reflect increasing diversity in our schools in ethnicity, race, sexual orientation, gender, language, and religious backgrounds. Training standards and guidelines in our profession provide an ardent call for university programs to prepare future school psychologists to demonstrate a number of multicultural competencies that are pivotal to providing culturally responsive services to children and families from diverse backgrounds; however, university programs cannot provide multicultural training in isolation. Collaborative partnerships with field-based settings are imperative in order to bridge theoretical and background knowledge with practical skills and applications used in the professional practice of school psychologists.

Given the unique characteristics of school settings and the array of multicultural competencies needed by school psychologists to function within a wide range of roles and functions, future research is needed to explore issues relevant to multicultural supervision and fieldwork settings. Among the initial questions that can be researched are (a) What competencies are needed by supervisors to provide culturally competent supervision to school psychology students? (b) How do systemic and organizational characteristics of fieldwork settings impact the process of multicultural supervision and students' multicultural competencies? (c) How can university training programs and fieldwork settings collaborate to provide optimal learning experiences in multicultural school psychology? Since our ultimate goal is to improve children's academic, social, and mental health functioning, future research must also explore how multicultural training, competencies, and practices impact the quality of services that school psychologists provide to children and families within a multiculturally responsive framework.

RESOURCES

American Psychological Association. (2003). Guidelines on multicultural education, training, research, practice, and organizational change for psychologists. *American Psychologist, 58*, 377–402.

The guidelines are an excellent resource for practitioners, researchers, and trainers in presenting a rationale for multiculturally informed practice, synthesizing current research, and discussing major issues affecting the profession of psychology and the delivery of psychological services.

Benner, S. M., & Barclay-McLaughlin, G. (2005). Simultaneous curricular reform in urban education and teacher preparation: A partnership approach. *Teacher Education and Practice, 18*, 96–112.

The authors discuss a partnership approach in which a teacher preparation program and elementary school ventured into reforming curriculum at both the university and school levels with the ultimate goal of improving student outcomes. This resource provided a context for understanding the process of collaboration to achieve change in multicultural contexts.

Lopez, E. C., & Rogers, M. R. (2007). Multicultural competencies and training in school psychology: Issues, approaches, and future directions. In G. Esquivel, E. C. Lopez, & S. Nahari (Eds.), *Handbook of multicultural school psychology: An interdisciplinary perspective* (pp. 47–67). Mahwah, NJ: Lawrence Erlbaum.

This chapter provides a historical overview of multicultural training issues in school psychology. Research is discussed relevant to multicultural training. The authors provide suggestions to address the challenges of investigating and validating cross-cultural competencies, and meeting training needs.

Norton, R. A., & Coleman, H. L. K. (2003). Multicultural supervision: The influence of race-related issues in supervision process and outcome. In D. B. Pope-Davis, H. L. K. Coleman, W. M. Liu, & R. L. Toporek (Eds.), *Handbook of multicultural competencies in counseling and psychology* (pp. 114–136). Thousand Oaks, CA: Sage.

This chapter is especially helpful in discussing what is presently known and what is not yet established empirically about multicultural supervision. It focuses on theory and research about the role of race and ethnicity in supervision contexts, relationships, processes, and outcomes.

Rogers, M. (2006). Exemplary multicultural training in school psychology programs. *Cultural Diversity and Ethnic Minority Psychology, 12,* 115–133.

The investigator examined the characteristics of 17 school psychology programs that emphasize multicultural training. The programs exposed graduate students to multicultural clients in fieldwork placements, course work in diversity issues, knowledge about specific cultural groups, and faculty of diverse culture and languages.

REFERENCES

American Psychological Association. (1998). *Resolution on immigrant children, youth, and families.* Retrieved July 1, 2009, from http://www.apa.org/pi/cyf/res_imm.html

American Psychological Association. (1999). *Resolution on lesbian, gay, and bisexual youth in the schools.* Retrieved July 1, 2009, from http://www.apa.org/pi/lgbc/policy/youths.html

American Psychological Association. (2000). *Resolution on poverty and socioeconomic status.* Retrieved January 8, 2008, from http://www.apa.org/pi/urban/povres.html

American Psychological Association. (2002). *Ethical principles of psychologists and code of conduct.* Retrieved July 1, 2009, from http://www.apa.org/ethics/code.html

American Psychological Association. (2003). Guidelines on multicultural education, training, research, practice, and organizational change for psychologists. *American Psychologist, 58,* 377–402.

American Psychological Association. (2007). Guidelines for psychological practice with girls and women. *American Psychologist, 62,* 949–979.

American Psychological Association. (2008). *Guidelines and principles for accreditation of programs in professional psychology.* Washington, DC: Author.

Belbas, B., Gorak, K., & Shumer, R. (1993). *Commonly used definitions of service learning. A discussion piece.* Scotts Valley, CA: National Service Learning Clearinghouse.

Bell, S. M., McCallum, S., & Cox, E. (2000, April). *Promoting academic and behavioral growth: Collaboration at a professional development school.* Paper presented at the annual conference of the National Association of School Psychologists, New Orleans, LA.

Benner, S. M., & Barclay-McLaughlin, G. (2005). Simultaneous curricular reform in urban education and teacher preparation: A partnership approach. *Teacher Education and Practice, 18,* 96–112.

Bolick, M. E., & Fry, J. (2004). Inquiry into the influence of a partnership on the beliefs and practice of preservice teacher. *Teacher Education and Practice, 17,* 56–70.

Brown, E. L. (2005). Service-learning in a one-year alternative route to teacher certification: A powerful multicultural teaching tool. *Equity & Excellence in Education, 38,* 61–74.

Burnett, J. A., Long, L. L., & Horne, H. L. (2005). Service learning for counselors: Integrating education, training, and the community. *Journal of Humanistic Counseling, Education and Development, 44,* 158–167.

Castaño, M. T., Biever, J. L., Gonzalez, C. G., & Anderson, K. B. (2007). Challenges of providing mental health services in Spanish. *Professional Psychology: Research and Practice, 38,* 667–673.

Constantine, M. G. (1997). Facilitating multicultural competency in counseling supervision: Operationalizing a practical framework. In D. B. Pope-Davis & H. L. K. Coleman (Eds.), *Multicultural counseling competencies: Assessment, education and training, and supervision* (pp. 310–324). Thousand Oaks, CA: Sage.

Constantine, M. G. (2001). Multiculturally-focused counseling supervision: Its relationship to trainees' multicultural counseling self-efficacy. *The Clinical Supervisor, 20,* 87–98.

Cooper, J. E. (2007). Strengthening the case for community-based learning in teacher education. *Journal of Teacher Education, 58,* 245–255.

D'Andrea, M., & Daniels, J. (1997). Multicultural counseling supervision: Central issues, theoretical considerations, and practical strategies. In D. B. Pope-Davis & H. L. K. Coleman (Eds.), *Multicultural counseling competencies: Assessment, education and training, and supervision* (pp. 387–405). Thousand Oaks, CA: Sage.

Dressel, J. L., Consoli, A. J., Kim, B. S. K., & Atkinson, D. R. (2007). Successful and unsuccessful multicultural supervisory behaviors: A Delphi poll. *Journal of Multicultural Counseling and Development, 35,* 51–64.

Duan, C., & Roehlke, H. (2001). A descriptive "snapshot" of cross-racial supervision in university counseling center relationships. *Journal of Multicultural Counseling and Development, 29,* 131–146.

Ford, B. A. (2004). Preparing special educators for culturally responsive school-community partnerships. *Teacher Education and Special Education, 27,* 224–230.

Griner, D., & Smith, T. B. (2006). Culturally adapted mental health interventions: A meta-analytic review. *Psychotherapy: Theory, Research, Practice, Training, 43,* 531–548.

Grant, C. A., & Koskela, R. A. (2001). Education that is multicultural and the relationship between preservice campus learning and field experiences. *Journal of Educational Research, 79,* 197–204.

Hasslen, R. C., & Bacharach, N. (2007). Nurturing multicultural competence in an early childhood graduate teacher licensure program. *Action in Teacher Education, 29,* 32–41.

Leong, F. T. L., & Wagner, N. M. (1994). Cross-cultural supervision: What do we know? *Counselor Education and Supervision, 34,* 117–132.

McCaleb, S. P. (1998). Connecting preservice teacher education to diverse communities: A focus on family literacy. *Theory Into Practice, 37,* 148–154.

McIntosh, D. E., & Phelps, L. (2000). Supervision in school psychology: Where will the future take us? *Psychology in the Schools, 37,* 33–38.

National Association of School Psychologists. (1999). *Position statement on gay, lesbian, bisexual, transgender, and questioning youth.* Retrieved July 1, 2009, from http://www.nasponline.org/about_nasp/pospaper_glb.aspx

National Association of School Psychologists. (2000). *Standards for training and field placement programs in school psychology.* Bethesda, MD: Author.

National Association of School Psychologists. (2003). *Position statement on minority recruitment.* Retrieved July 1, 2009, from http://www.nasponline.org/about_nasp/position_papers/minrecruit.pdf

National Association of School Psychologists. (2004a). *Position statement on racism, prejudice, and discrimination.* Retrieved July 1, 2009, from http://www.nasponline.org/about_nasp/position/papers/racism.pdf

National Association of School Psychologists. (2004b). Position statement on supervision in school psychology. Retrieved August 27, 2008, from http://www.nasponline.org/about_nasp/pp_supervision.aspx

Ngai, P. B. (2004). A reinforcing curriculum and program reform proposal for 21st century education: Vital first steps for advancing K-12 multicultural education. *Equity & Excellence in Education, 37,* 321–331.

Olmedo, I. M. (1997). Challenging old assumptions: Preparing teachers for inner city schools. *Teaching and Teacher Education, 13,* 245–258.

Sandoval, J. H. (2007). Professional standards, guidelines, and ethical issues within a multicultural context. In G. B. Esquivel, E. C. Lopez, & S. G. Nahari (Eds.), *Multicultural handbook of school psychology: An interdisciplinary perspective* (pp. 29–45). Mahwah, NJ: Lawrence Erlbaum.

Sue, D. W. (2001). Multidimensional facets of cultural competence. *The Counseling Psychologist, 29,* 790–821.

Sue, D. W., Carter, R. T., Casas, J. M., Fouad, N. A., Ivey, A. E., Jensen, M., et al. (1998). *Multicultural counseling competencies: Individual and organizational development.* Thousand Oaks, CA: Sage.

Sue, S., & Zane, N. (1987). The role of culture and cultural techniques in psychotherapy: A reformulation. *American Psychologist, 42,* 37–45.

U.S. Census Bureau. (2003a). *Language use and English-speaking ability: 2000.* Retrieved January 7, 2008, from http://www.census.gov/population/www/cen2000/phc-t20.html

U.S. Census Bureau. (2003b). *Language use, English ability, and linguistic isolation for the population 5 to 17 years by state: 2000.* Retrieved July 1, 2009, from http://www.census.gov/population/www/cen2000/briefs/phc_t20/index.html

U.S. Census Bureau. (2007). *Poverty: 2006 highlights.* Retrieved January 1, 2008, from http://www.census.gov/hhes/www/poverty/poverty06/pov06hi.html

U.S. Department of Education. (2005). *Twenty-fifth annual (2003) report to Congress on the Implementation of the Individuals with Disabilities Education Act* (Vol. 1). Office of Special Education and Rehabilitative Services, Offices of Special Education Programs. Washington, DC: Author.

U.S. Department of Education, National Center for Education Statistics. (2006). *Participation in education: Elementary/secondary education: Concentration of enrollment by race/ethnicity and poverty.* Retrieved July 1, 2009, from http://nces.ed.gov/pubs2006/2006071.pdf

U.S. Department of Education, National Center for Education Statistics. (2007a). *2006 American Community Survey.* Retrieved July 1, 2009, from http://nces.ed.gov/pubs2007/2007064.pdf

U.S. Department of Education, National Center for Education Statistics. (2007b). *Racial/ethnic distribution of public school students.* Retrieved July 1, 2009, from http://nces.ed.gov/pubs2007/2007064_Appl.pdf

U.S. Department of Education, National Center for Education Statistics. (2008). *The condition of education 2008.* Retrieved July 1, 2009, from http://nces.gov//pubs2008/2008031.pdf

Wiggins, R. A., Follo, E. J., & Eberly, M. B. (2007). The impact of a field immersion program on pre-service teachers' attitudes toward teaching in culturally diverse classrooms. *Teaching and Teacher Education, 23,* 653–663.

Ysseldyke, J., Burns, M., Dawson, P., Kelley, B., Morrison, D., Ortiz, S., et al. (2006). *School psychology: A blueprint for training and practice III.* Bethesda, MD: National Association of School Psychologists.

8 Problematic behaviors
Mediating differences and negotiating change

Tracy K. Cruise and Mark E. Swerdlik

Although the majority of graduate students in school psychology training programs either possess or develop the necessary skills, attitudes, values, and beliefs to function effectively as school psychologists, there is a small percentage of trainees who are delayed in meeting these competencies and/or require more direct intervention to meet exit criteria. These few trainees seem to demand more time and energy from supervisors and trainers, thus often distorting the perception of how prevalent professional competence problems are among the field. The impact of these inadequacies cannot be minimized, however, as they can have a detrimental effect on the recipients of services, the public, the training program, and the profession.

School psychology, as one specialty of professional psychology, is part of the movement toward competency-based education and training. Although professional ethics codes have long required practice within the boundaries of and maintenance of one's competence, psychology is taking a direct role in advancing competency-based education, training, and credentialing (Rubin et al., 2007). The 2002 Competencies Conference: Future Directions in Education and Credentialing in Professional Psychology and the ongoing work of the American Psychological Association (APA) Task Force on the Assessment of Competence in Professional Psychology are fostering an emphasis on competency-based assessments in psychology training programs. School psychology training programs are being encouraged to adopt specific measures of competency at all stages of training in order to ensure quality graduates and early identification of trainees with personal or performance difficulties.

The latest edition (January 2008) of the APA *Guidelines and Principles for Accreditation of Programs in Professional Psychology* and the National Association of School Psychologists' (2000a) *Standards for Training and Field Placement Programs in School Psychology* outline necessary procedures for documenting performance-based assessment of candidate professional skills. Domain E of the doctoral graduate programs and internship sections of the APA criteria describes program responsibilities in providing written policies and procedures, time frames for evaluation, and methods of written notification and remediation of competency concerns. Similarly, Standard IV: Performance-Based Program Assessment and Accountability of the National Association of School Psychologists program approval guidelines states that all programs must employ

> a systematic, valid process to ensure that all candidates, prior to the conclusion of the internship experience, are able to integrate domains of knowledge and apply professional skills in delivering a comprehensive range of services evidenced by measurable positive impact on children, youth, families, and other consumers. (p. 20)

Demonstration of trainee competence is required not only of training programs through accreditation processes but also of professional credentialing bodies as they certify individual competence. At the broadest professional level, competence evaluation is ethically and legally mandated. The ethical and professional codes of conduct for the National Association of School Psychologists (NASP) and the APA directly address the issue of competence, and court decisions have confirmed that professionals must acquire and maintain appropriate levels of knowledge and skills (APA, 2002; NASP, 2000a). For example, the *NASP Professional Conduct Manual* states, "School psychologists recognize the strengths and limitations of their training and experience, engaging only in practices for which they are qualified. They must continually obtain additional training and education to provide the best possible services to children, families, schools, communities, trainees, and supervisees" (NASP, 2000a, p. 622). The current APA ethics code offers two relevant statements regarding competence: "(a) Psychologists provide services, teach, and conduct research with populations and in areas only within the boundaries of their competence, based on their education, training, supervised experience, consultation, study, or professional experience"; and (b) "Psychologists undertake ongoing efforts to develop and maintain their competence" (APA, 2002, pp. 1063–1064).

School psychology training programs serve as the initial gatekeepers for the profession, securing public safety and trust. Therefore, educators must carefully assess trainee competence throughout the course of their programs, ensuring early detection of concerns, and provide prompt feedback allowing for effective remediation. Supervision is one avenue most professional training programs utilize to carry out evaluation procedures. The APA ethics code directly mandates this task in section 7.06: Assessing Student and Supervisee Performance:

> (a) In academic and supervisory relationships, psychologists establish a timely and specific process for providing feedback to students and supervisees. Information regarding the process is provided to the student at the beginning of supervision.

(b) Psychologists evaluate students and supervisees on the basis of their actual performance on relevant and established program requirements. (APA, 2002, p. 1069)

This chapter reviews the literature related to professional competency problems among school psychology trainees and explores how the training program, including the supervisory relationship, can play a significant role in assessing and intervening with such behaviors. Also offered is a best practices training model aimed at addressing competence, beginning with the initial trainee contact and continuing through the completion of the school psychology professional training program.

DEFINING COMPETENCE

School psychologists must acquire the appropriate education, training, and supervision to function ethically in their roles. During formal academic training, trainees must demonstrate competence in several broad areas, including academic skills, assessment/clinical skills, clinical judgment, ethics, interpersonal skills, and response to supervision (Forrest, Elman, Gizara, & Vacha-Haase, 1999). Some authors have classified these skills into two categories: foundational (e.g., professionalism, ethical and legal practice, scientific knowledge and methods) and functional (e.g., assessment/diagnosis/conceptualization, intervention, supervision/training) (Kaslow et al., 2007b). Still others have collapsed them into three types of professional functioning: "(1) acquisition and integration of relevant professional standards, (2) development of appropriate professional skills, and (3) monitoring of personal functioning" (Lamb & Swerdlik, 2003, p. 96). Although it may be easier and clearer to think of these as discrete units of competence to be evaluated, it is the integration of these knowledge, skills, and attitudes that yields a more complete picture of professional behavior.

In order for training programs to meet their ethical, legal, and moral obligations of producing competent professionals, faculty need to clearly define tasks and levels of skill that trainees must meet to be deemed competent. Kaslow et al. (2007) refer to these as "benchmarks" and emphasize that behavioral descriptors need to be measurable. Assessing trainee knowledge and specific skills (e.g., report writing, problem identification) seems easily managed for many programs through the use of course examinations, comprehensive written exams, case studies, and performance appraisals; however, evaluating personal dispositions and interpersonal qualities seems to pose a greater challenge for many faculty. Most educators of school psychologists recognize certain personality qualities and interaction patterns among trainees that will negatively impact performance, but they express concern about formally evaluating these characteristics and providing individual feedback. Courts have upheld faculty decisions in this venue by stating that academic and interpersonal skills are essential in the trainee's "capacity to perform the tasks of the profession" (Forrest et al., 1999, p. 659). Specific court rulings have supported dismissal decisions where trainees were performing well academically but demonstrated interpersonal qualities that negatively impacted their practical work (Forrest et al.; Knoff & Prout, 1985).

Training programs must ensure that trainees are provided with the expected competencies of the program; the evaluation procedures that will be used throughout training, including a timeline of when and how individualize feedback will be provided; approaches for remediation; and procedures for due process (Forrest et al., 1999; Kaslow et al., 2007b). When all of these components are explicitly provided to trainees, courts have expressed no desire to second-guess faculty dismissal decisions as long as the decisions were nondiscriminatory and not capricious. Although most trainees advance through training achieving program outcomes, a minority of trainees will exhibit deficiencies, incompetence, or what has in the past been referred to as impairment. There is a current movement to avoid using the term *impairment,* as it is legally related to a disability, and instead to use descriptors such as *professional competence problems* or *problematic professional competence* (Elman & Forrest, 2007). Other terms appearing in the literature include *problem trainees* (Cobb, 1994) and *inadequate* (Bernard, 1975; Olkin & Gaughen, 1991), *unsatisfactory* (Biaggio, Gasparikova-Krasnec, & Bauer, 1993), *deficient* (Gaubatz & Vera, 2002), or *substandard* (Baldo, Softas-Nall, & Shaw, 1997) behavior. Competence problems may be specific (e.g., report writing skills) or global (e.g., unprofessional conduct, failure to respond to feedback). They may be expected developmentally (e.g., skill practice, immaturity) or due to lack of academic/skill acquisition or personality/interpersonal dynamics, and they may stem from one etiological factor or be multidetermined (Kaslow et al., 2007a). Competence problems may present when trainees do not have adequate education or experience, repeatedly fail to respond to feedback, have difficulty managing personal concerns and professional development, have problems with interpersonal relationships, or have mental health difficulties. Most academic and internship programs (66–95%) reported having at least one "impaired" trainee during the past 5 years, with annual impairment rates ranging from 4.2% to 4.8% (Forrest et al., 1999). More than half (52–86%) of these programs reportedly dismiss at least one trainee every 3 to 5 years (Forrest et al.). Although there seems to be great variability in the performance categories evaluated by training programs, the most commonly reported professional competency problems include clinical deficiencies, interpersonal problems, problems in supervision, and personality disorders (Forrest et al.).

A range of remediation options have been used by doctoral and master's level institutions; however, the most commonly reported recommendation was personal therapy (Forrest et al., 1999). Other remediation plans include increased supervision with the same or other supervisors or a change in the focus of supervision, reduction of the trainee's workload, course repetition, additional course or applied work, denial of admission to an advanced sequenced course, and self-structured behavioral modification plans (Biaggio, Gasparikova-Krasnec, & Bauer, 1983; Kutz, 1986; Lamb, et al., 1987; Olkin & Gaughen, 1991; Wilkerson, 2006). Documentation of a trainee's problematic behaviors often include written warnings, formal probation, a leave of absence, disciplinary action (e.g., penalties for cheating, no advancement in program sequence), and program dismissal. Some common training program assessment and intervention procedures put in place to address trainees with competency problems include (a) providing definitions of competence and performance areas to be evaluated, along with clear statements about program expectations or benchmarks; (b) inclusion of definitions and criteria in policies and procedures that also illustrate assessment procedures, evaluation timelines, and methods of communication of assessment results; (c) an outline of procedures used to identify and subsequently notify trainees when performance concerns are beyond those developmentally expected; (d) methods of formally documenting trainee concerns; (d) procedures and timelines for implementing and evaluating interventions/remediation plans; (e) follow-up review procedures to evaluate trainee progress; (f) sequence of steps to follow if program dismissal is warranted; and (g) an explanation of due process rights and communication of limitations to trainees' rights to confidentiality (Bemak, Epp, & Keys, 1999; Forrest et al., 1999; Kaslow et al., 2007b; Wilkerson, 2006). Although this list covers the majority of competency concerns that training faculty face, it is important to note that trainers and supervisors must also consider the impact individual and cultural differences may have on the identification of problematic behaviors and in the development of remediation plans (see Brown & Landrum-Brown, 1995; Haynes, Corey, & Moulton, 2003).

Although developing necessary policies and procedures for competency assessment and intervention seems straightforward, training programs often struggle with implementation and follow-through. Some supervisors express hesitation at evaluating performance beyond academic knowledge, where they can be clear that a trainee either has acquired pertinent knowledge or is deficient. However, personality characteristics and interpersonal approaches may vary considerably among competent professionals, making the distinction between what is an acceptable individual difference and problematic behavior less clear. Some supervisors are also reluctant to provide negative feedback to trainees. Supervisors cite (Gizara & Forest, 2004) difficulty with handling conflict or fear of litigation as reasons for their avoidance. The following best practices guidelines are specific suggestions for incorporating the competency definition and evaluation components listed above and may clarify how to offer support in addressing problems of professional competence among school psychology graduate students.

Specific examples of evaluation forms and policy wording are also provided in the next section of this chapter. Although these examples were developed for a doctoral program in school psychology, they can be easily adapted for use in a specialist level school psychology training program.

BEST PRACTICES IN EVALUATING, ASSESSING, AND INTERVENING WITH TRAINEE COMPETENCY PROBLEMS

A training program's evaluation policy and procedures that include clear expectations, criteria and procedures for evaluation, and due process should be available to all potential and current graduate trainees. These policies and procedures should also be congruent with APA and NASP professional ethics and codes of conduct and accreditation/program approval standards. Policies and procedures (instructions) regarding how they can be accessed should be available in all recruitment and acceptance materials and program-operating handbooks. Policies and procedures should undergo regular review by program faculty to ensure that they are current, congruent, fair, and consistent.

The program handbooks should include copies of the rating scales/evaluation forms used to assess trainee progress focusing on knowledge, skills, and dispositions (see sample trainee progress form in Figure 8.1). Faculty should confirm that trainees have received and reviewed these materials by collecting the trainee's signature documenting the process.

To increase the value of the professional evaluation process for professional development and to promote real-time, in-depth understanding, the program evaluation policies and procedures (e.g., case examples of problematic behaviors) should be discussed throughout the trainee's graduate program. Early course work, such as an introductory professional school psychology seminar, provides the opportunity to establish policies and procedures related to evaluation. Required readings from program handbooks and related literature establish the importance of these documents for a trainee's career in the program. Subsequent discussion can then center on areas such as the effective use of supervision, expectations for supervisees, legal–ethical issues, and evaluation over the course of the trainee's professional training.

All evaluation policies and operating procedures should be guided by a coherent and agreed-upon philosophy of evaluation. These policies and procedures should be discussed in detail and formally agreed upon by program faculty. It is also recommended that the university attorney, graduate school personnel, and/or representatives from the university office involved in reviewing faculty decisions related to dispute resolution and dismissal from a program of study or the university have reviewed evaluation procedures.

School Psychology Program
Student Evaluation Form: Professional Development
(Completed at the end of each first, second, third, and fourth year of study by Instructor)
Based on a form developed by the School Psychology Program at the University of Texas at Austin.

Student: _____ Date: _____
Year in Program: _____ GPA: _____
Faculty/Evaluator: _____

Courses and practica with student _____

Please rate the above named student in those areas below for which you have information. Each evaluator is encouraged to provide additional comments at the end of this form. Ratings will be averaged and communicated to the doctoral student.

	Superior	Above Average	Average	Needs Improvement	No Knowledge
I. Communication Skills					
Oral	____	____	____	____	____
Written	____	____	____	____	____
II. Independence/ Initiative (GA, courses, including practicum)	____	____	____	____	____
III. Knowledge of the Literature	____	____	____	____	____
Knowledge of Prof. Standards and Conduct	____	____	____	____	____
IV. Quality of Professional Interpersonal Relationships With:					
Instructor	____	____	____	____	____
Peers	____	____	____	____	____
Clients	____	____	____	____	____
Staff	____	____	____	____	____
Other professionals	____	____	____	____	____
V. Discharging Professional Responsibilities:					
Preparation for assignments	____	____	____	____	____
Work completed in appropriate time frame (class assignment, thesis proposal, GA responsibilities, ability to schedule and keep appointments in practicum	____	____	____	____	____
Quality of clinical work	____	____	____	____	____
Responsiveness to feedback from instructor	____	____	____	____	____
Responsiveness to feedback from peers	____	____	____	____	____
Effectiveness offering feedback to peers	____	____	____	____	____
Ability to balance/regulate pressure and demands	____	____	____	____	____
Ability to make sound professional judgments	____	____	____	____	____
Appropriate involvement and objectivity	____	____	____	____	____

Figure 8.1 Sample formative evaluation form.

	Superior	Above Average	Average	Needs Improvement	No Knowledge
VI. Professional Qualities:					
Appropriate professional appearance and self-presentation	___	___	___	___	___
General emotional maturity	___	___	___	___	___
Appropriate empathy	___	___	___	___	___
Appropriate assertiveness	___	___	___	___	___
Self-motivation	___	___	___	___	___
Reliability	___	___	___	___	___
Promptness	___	___	___	___	___
Resourcefulness and resiliency (coping skills, handling stress)	___	___	___	___	___
Creativity	___	___	___	___	___
Self-confidence	___	___	___	___	___
Awareness of strengths and weaknesses	___	___	___	___	___
Openness to professional growth	___	___	___	___	___
Sensitivity to multicultural issues	___	___	___	___	___

Comments:

Summary
Potential for Successful Teaching (consider fulfilling GA responsibilities, oral communication skills, knowledge, etc.)

_____

_____

_____

_____

Research Potential (consider quality of thesis proposal, GA responsibilities, conference presentations, workshop/in-service activities, initiative for research collaboration, contributions to Research Interest Group)

_____

_____

_____

_____

Potential For Independent Practice

_____

_____

_____

Figure 8.1 (Continued)

ARTICULATING AN OVERALL PROGRAM PHILOSOPHY OF EVALUATION

An important feature of any written evaluation policy describes the overall philosophy of the program. The philosophy should address the responsibility of faculty members to address professional competence throughout the training program in their role as gatekeepers for the profession. Policies and procedures for addressing trainee deficits should also be presented.

Determining the continuum of competence is important, as many faculty may agree what constitutes a significant difficulty or distinctive performance, but the minimal threshold of competence can remain elusive (Elman & Forrest, 2007). Articulating minimum threshold criteria in graduate training is important for the ongoing professional competence assessment that individuals are ethically required to conduct throughout the course of their professional careers.

GENERAL EVALUATION POLICIES AND PROCEDURES

The program's evaluation policies and procedures should include regular, specific, and direct feedback from faculty to individual trainees on both formative and summative data. Formative evaluations often focus on developmental trainee skills, where trainee performance on expected professional trajectories is noted directly and specific feedback is provided for the purpose of supporting the trainee to attain higher levels of competence (Kaslow et al., 2007a; Wilkerson, 2006). Formative evaluations encourage trainees to note and then adjust their behaviors as they increase their academic and clinical skills. Close monitoring of trainee performance through formative assessment also serves to detect patterns of difficulty and early identification of problematic behaviors. Program faculty can then develop support plans to address these identified skill deficits and/or uneven development of professional behaviors.

Summative evaluation answers the question of whether important benchmarks have been attained. Although both formative and summative evaluation focuses on a school psychology trainee's strengths and relative weaknesses, summative evaluations serve to note whether skills are met at that time. Programs may have more than one summative evaluation (e.g., comprehensive exams, internship, graduation, standardized tests scores such as the Praxis or Examination for Professional Practice in Psychology), where retention decisions are based on benchmarks. More than one summative approach is recommended to meet the goal of enhanced competence; these approaches are most useful when combined with a formative component (Weber, 2000).

SKILLS ASSESSED

Program policy should also describe skills and professional behaviors that will be assessed as part of formative and summative evaluations. Assessment should focus on areas such as knowledge, practice-based skills, personal work characteristics (e.g., professional deportment, openness to supervision, management of personal stress), and the integration of these areas that allow for effective task performance (Kaslow et al., 2007b). Competence assessment should reflect the continuum on which performance development lies, and programs should delineate the level of knowledge, skills, and work characteristics expected at each stage. Figure 8.1 is a sample formative assessment completed annually by school psychology trainees at one of the author's APA-accredited and NASP-approved training programs. Table 8.1 provides a sample policy related to types of skills assessed in a school psychology professional training program.

ASSESSMENT METHODOLOGY

Formative and summative evaluations should be both multitrait and multimethod, gathered from a variety of informants (Kaslow et al., 2007b). Multitrait evaluations focus on knowledge, skills and attitudes, performance, and their integration. For example, skill in behavioral consultation would include demonstrating observable actions defined within the behavioral consultation processes. For example, trainees should begin with defining the problem in operational terms; demonstrate a theoretical understanding of the assumptions that define the model and familiarity with empirical and clinical data collected in a behavioral consultation situation; and then integrate this knowledge to result in an effective consultation interaction with teachers. Determining whether a trainee is able to perform a behavioral consultation is assessed through multiple methods, such as oral and written examinations as part of course work, a comprehensive examination question, supervisor ratings of actual field performance, self-evaluations/reflections, and permanent work products (e.g., videotapes or audiotapes) that are often collected as part of a trainee's portfolio. Using multiple informants, beyond one supervisor, from diverse environments, is also important in yielding a reliable and valid assessment of trainee competence. These informants might include course instructors, field supervisors, peers, and self evaluations. Evaluation methods should be developmentally appropriate. For example, early in the training program, paper and pencil tools may represent the most reliable and valid method to assess knowledge, whereas an evaluation of skills and attitudes later in training is best accomplished through more direct observations of actual or case simulations (Kaslow et al., 2007b). Multiple samples of behavior observed by multiple evaluators using multiple methods leads to the most reliable and

Table 8.1 Sample Program Policy Listing of Relevant Professional Skills

Course work includes both academic and skill-related (e.g. diagnostic assessment, intervention, report writing) training. In addition to traditional academic and skill-related growth in graduate professional training, personal and professional growth is critical for future effective functioning as a school psychologist.

Personal and Professional Skill Areas

Professionally related interpersonal/professional skills include the following:

Ethics

1. Demonstration of knowledge/application of APA/NASP ethical guidelines
2. Moral reasoning
3. Demonstration of knowledge/application of other statutes regulating professional practice
4. Demonstration of appropriate level of concern for client welfare
5. Demonstration of appropriate client–school psychologist relationships
6. Empathy
7. Teamwork

Professional Deportment

1. Appropriate manifestation of professional identity (e.g., attire, behavior)
2. Appropriate involvement in professional development activities (e.g., professional associations)
3. Appropriate interaction with peers, faculty, staff, parents, and other professionals
4. Awareness of impact on colleagues (faculty and students)

Sensitivity to Client/Diversity Issues

Acknowledgment and effective dealing with children, parents, teachers, school administrators, and other school staff (e.g., social workers, guidance counselors, speech therapists) of diverse ethnic and racial groups, life styles, and other diverse choices

Use of Supervision

1. Appropriate preparation
2. Accepts responsibility for learning
3. Openness to feedback/suggestions
4. Application of learning to practice
5. Willingness to self-disclose and/or explore a personal issue that affects professional process functioning
6. Appropriately self-reliant
7. Appropriately self-appreciative and self-critical

Other Trainee Issues

1. Effective management of personal stress
2. Appropriate boundaries between personal adjustment problems and/or emotional responses and professional practice
3. Formulation of realistic professional goals for self
4. Appropriate self-initiated professional development (e.g., self-initiated study, going beyond course work requirements for learning)

valid assessments that reduce bias and have fidelity (Kaslow et al., 2007b). All assessment methodologies need to be culturally sensitive to prevent errors from occurring in interpreting culturally normative behaviors as problematic. In addition, assessments must address the important area of developing cultural competency across the domains of age, gender, disability status, race/ethnicity, social class, and sexual orientation (see Brown & Landrum-Brown, 1995; Haynes et al., 2003).

Self-assessment represents a skill that it is critical for school psychology trainees to develop during their professional training, as it relates to life-long professional development. Although self-assessment may not be consistent with other assessment methods and is generally poorly correlated with performance measures, trainees can be trained in this skill (Davis et al., 2006). In fact, since school psychologists are ethically obligated to self-monitor competencies after graduate training (APA, 2002; NASP, 2000a), this is an essential step in professional development. Evaluation policies and procedures should provide an opportunity for trainee self-assessments to be monitored, with trainees receiving feedback from external sources such as professors, supervisors, and peers, who can assist them in integrating their self-assessments with other feedback from these external sources (Kaslow et al., 2007b; Roberts, Borden, Christiansen, & Lopez, 2005).

IDENTIFYING PROBLEMATIC BEHAVIORS

As discussed, program faculty must agree upon, define, and document terminology to be used with trainees who show competency concerns. Professional competence problems may be divided into three descriptive levels of severity: simple/developmentally inappropriate, chronic/substandard behavior(s), and gross ethical violation(s)/professional negligence. Faculty response should be proportionate to the level of severity demonstrated by the trainee.

A program's policy and procedure manuals should distinguish behaviors or personality traits that are best described as simple situational concerns, expected developmental growth patterns that can be part of the learning process. These behaviors often require support for a positive trajectory but are not considered excessive or inappropriate and do not represent atypical aspects of a trainee's learning experience. Although this professional growth experience may still be characterized as problematic, often course instructors or practicum supervisors handle the trainee's developmental needs within the supervisory relationship without formal concern to the program faculty. Examples useful to provide in the program handbook include performance anxiety that results in greater dependency in supervision; expressed worry about supervisor evaluations; temporary regression in previously acquired skills; discomfort with clients of diverse lifestyles and ethnic backgrounds that results in trainees avoiding discussing these aspects of their clients in supervision, avoidance of discussing personal reactions to diverse clients in supervision, or selectively choosing ethnically similar individuals with whom to work; or lack of appreciation of agency norms that results in incomplete or untimely paperwork, inappropriate professional attire, or tardiness for supervision or agency meetings. Problems of this nature are usually felt to be transitory and can be remediated with appropriate support for the trainee.

Conversely, significant substandard or problematic behavior(s) that interfere with the trainee's ability to perform academically or clinically requiring intensive intervention (Wilkerson, 2006) are dealt with by the entire training program faculty. These types of behaviors are chronic (i.e., have not responded to previous support interventions) or do not lead to behavioral change that is consistent or acceptable to professional demeanor. Often, inflexible personality characteristics or problem behaviors have been unresponsive to supervisory input. For example, a trainee may exhibit continued defensiveness in supervision, an inability to be self-appreciative and self-critical, or continued abrasiveness in professional interpersonal relationships. Finally, serious substandard or problematic types of behaviors should also be specified. These might include (a) the trainee does not acknowledge, understand, or address the problem when it is identified; (b) the problem is not merely a reflection of a skill deficit that could be addressed by additional academic or didactic training; (c) the quality of services delivered by the trainee is sufficiently negatively affected; (d) the problem is not restricted to one area of professional functioning; (e) a disproportionate amount of attention by training personnel is required; (f) the trainee's behavior does not change as a function of feedback and informal remediation efforts; and/or (g) the problematic behavior has the potential for ethical or legal ramifications if not addressed (Lamb, et al., 1987). This level of severity would warrant an immediate formal remediation plan to ensure that trainees are aware of faculty concerns, given the opportunity to modify their behavior, and understand the consequences of inadequate or incomplete behavioral changes.

In rare circumstances, a trainee will engage in serious professional misconduct (e.g., a sexual relationship with a client) or gross professional negligence (e.g., knowingly choosing not to report child maltreatment). The severity of these behaviors may warrant an immediate dismissal from the program provided that trainees are informed of their misbehaviors and appropriate documentation is completed.

ACTION LETTERS AND REMEDIATION PLANS

Once problematic behaviors are noted as part of an evaluation, concerns must be communicated both orally and in writing through an action letter to the trainee. One approach is to schedule an individual conference with the trainee and provide a written summary of the problematic behaviors and/or skill deficits at the onset requesting, the trainee to initially read the concerns expressed in writing and then discuss in more depth the contents of the letter and develop a remediation plan. This sequence of communicating the concerns is important because trainees often do not "hear" or fully comprehend the concerns, and presenting them in writing increases the probability that the trainee will understand the problematic behaviors he or she is exhibiting.

The action letter should describe the problematic behavior in language that is observable and measurable, and provide the explicit criteria/standards used in arriving at the conclusion that the behavior is a significant concern. Remediation plans should be written with a constructive (focusing on the replacement behaviors for the deficits noted) and educative focus. All relevant ethical codes should also be noted. Specific interventions should be presented with sufficient detail, describing the nature of the interventions and their expected outcomes. Interventions may occur concurrently or in a specialized sequence determined by the needs of the trainee. For example, a trainee may need to seek interpersonal counseling about anger management or acquire more practice in the problem-solving steps of consultation before completing a course with a field experience.

The individualized remediation plan should also be unambiguous, listing the time frame for remediation, the roles and responsibilities of all of the parties (e.g., who is providing additional training, supervision, feedback), the context in which behaviors should be exhibited, the type of evaluation (e.g., work samples and performance observations) that will be used to determine whether goals have been met, and the consequences to the trainee should the trainee fail to perform at the level of competence expected for his or her level of professional development (e.g., intern, 1st-year trainee) especially if there has been some, albeit inadequate, progress toward behavioral expectations. Table 8.2 provides an example of an action letter.

If a trainee's competence is so deficient that his or her standing in the program should be adjusted to probationary, the action letter and remediation plan must communicate changes in the trainee's responsibilities, along with a description of due process rights. Although supervisors and/or program faculty typically draft the remediation plan under the premise that they know what behaviors need to be addressed, trainee ideas for the change process should be invited and incorporated into the plan where appropriate. Faculty should make an effort to modify the plan to increase the effectiveness of the interventions. Once trainee needs have been identified and a remediation plan developed, confidentiality is critical. It is important to clearly delineate who will have access to the trainee's remediation plan. For example, should the practicum and internship field supervisors be informed? These decisions should be based on whether or not such disclosures would facilitate or hinder trainee progress.

Table 8.2 Sample Remediation Plan, Including Use of Personal Therapy and Due Process Rights

---

DATE:

Dear Elizabeth:

As you know, you have missed another deadline (i.e., the end of summer 2007) regarding the completion of your master's thesis or doctoral Research Apprenticeship project. Consequently, you are now officially prevented from sitting for the fall semester administration of the doctoral comprehensive examination. The School Psychology Coordinating Committee (SPCC) has met to discuss your failure to meet this deadline. The SPCC, consistent with our Graduate Student Evaluation and Remediation Policies and Procedures, has identified your pattern of behavior as indicative of problematic professional competence in the areas of time management, decision making, and self-evaluation/appraisal.

Our concerns about these problematic behaviors have been shared with you in your annual feedback sessions. Regrettably, the problems have not been ameliorated. Indeed, your performance regarding the research requirement in the PhD program creates the impression you are unresponsive to feedback from faculty in School Psychology. As of this date, the SPCC is no longer willing to accept your unfinished master's thesis as potential credit in lieu of the doctoral Research Apprenticeship.

Even though you have many assets considered important for one entering a helping profession, including strong interpersonal skills and intelligence, the SPCC believes your problematic behaviors have high potential to negatively impact your future professional functioning as a doctoral-level school psychologist. Based upon our identification of competency concerns in the areas specified above, the SPCC has determined that your status in the doctoral program is Probationary, and remediation is necessary. As such, the SPCC has developed a remedial plan for you. The plan has the following requirements:

1. You must immediately begin to meet weekly with Dr. Competent, Chair of your doctoral advisory committee, to set goals related to the completion of your Research Apprenticeship project. These weekly meetings must continue until you have officially selected a research mentor to direct your Apprenticeship. This selection must occur no later than October 1, 2007. Once your research mentor is selected, you are required to meet weekly with him/her until the *completion* of your research project, or until your research mentor has determined these weekly meetings are unnecessary. Failure to make and/or keep these weekly appointments will lead the SPCC to conclude that your remediation plan is unsuccessful.

2. You must immediately seek personal therapy (available at no cost from the University Student Counseling Center or at an agency of your choice). Treatment goals must include improved time management, more realistic self-evaluation/ assessment of your current functioning and future goals, and improved decision making. You must inform the SPCC of the date of your first therapeutic session. Although the details of your work with the therapist will be confidential, you must provide documentation to the SPCC that you are regularly attending these counseling sessions. Failure to *immediately* seek professional therapy, and failure to document your regular attendance at these therapeutic sessions, will lead the SPCC to conclude that your remediation plan is unsuccessful.

Table 8.2 Sample Remediation Plan, Including Use of Personal Therapy and Due Process Rights (*Continued*)

3. You must have an officially approved Institutional Review Board (IRB) proposal for the Research Apprenticeship project no later January 1, 2008. This deadline requires that you submit your proposal to the IRB in time for its December meeting. Once submitted and approved, you will be required to provide the SPCC the official IRB approval number. If you fail to meet this IRB proposal submission deadline, you will be summarily dismissed from the doctoral program. Most importantly, you must complete *all* requirements for the Research Apprenticeship no later December 15, 2008. These requirements include, but are not limited to, a colloquium presentation of your project to the Department of Psychology during the fall semester of 2008. If you fail to complete all requirements of the Research Apprenticeship by the stipulated deadline, you will be summarily dismissed from the doctoral program.

If you satisfy *all* requirements specified in the three paragraphs above, you will be restored of Full status in the PhD program (i.e., no longer on Probation). Once you are restored to Full status, the SPCC will determine when it is appropriate for you to take the doctoral comprehensive examination. If, however, one or more of the above requirements is not satisfied, you will be summarily dismissed from the doctoral program.

If you accept all terms of this remedial plan, please indicate such in writing addressed to the SPCC no later than August 22, 2007. If the Committee does not receive such notice by that date, you will be summarily dismissed from the doctoral program. Consistent with program policies, you may appeal this action by contacting Dr. Merit, Department Chair, within 14 days of receipt of this letter or to the Office of Student Dispute Resolution Services <http://www.linktowebsite.edu/>

Elizabeth, we feel you have numerous strengths. As such, the faculty in School Psychology stands ready to assist you in completing this remedial plan, including your Research Apprenticeship, so you may continue in the doctoral program.

For the School Psychology Coordinating Committee:

Jared Competent, PhD

Coordinator, Graduate Programs in School Psychology
Professor of Psychology

SPECIAL CONSIDERATION: PSYCHOTHERAPY AS REMEDIATION

Because many remediation plans for deficient professional attitudes/behaviors include the completion of personal psychotherapy, a separate consideration of these issues is warranted. Personal psychotherapy can represent a valuable component of a remediation plan. However, many trainees need assistance in understanding why the issues to be addressed in personal psychotherapy reflect competency problems or require assistance in overcoming psychological barriers that prevent them from making necessary changes. Although research on the effectiveness of employee assistance programs suggests that psychotherapy can positively enhance work performance (Preece,

Cayley, Scheuchl, & Lam, 2005), there is no research on the effectiveness of this component of many remediation plans or the most effective balance between therapist–client confidentiality and accountability to the program and the public related to disclosure of information; however, when problematic behaviors are inconsistent with professional standards, the right to confidentiality can be limited because of the significant future risk to the public and the profession. The APA ethical code requires trainees to disclose personal information that may prevent them from competently performing professional duties or would pose a threat to the public. Programs must still give careful consideration to whether a referral for personal psychotherapy represents an appropriate part of the remediation plan, as some students may be able to make necessary changes without formal therapy, and others may not have a clear understanding of how therapy will help them meet their goals. Trainees should be advised of their ethical and due process rights in these circumstances. Furthermore, consideration must be given to the importance of informed consent, the avoidance of dual relationships, attention to cultural background of the parties, use of qualified providers, clarification related to confidentiality, and financial considerations.

If personal therapy is a component of a remediation plan, all parties, including the trainee, program faculty, and therapist, must agree in advance upon what information from the therapist is to be shared with the program. Similar to the procedures used with employee assistance program, disclosures would be made to only those who need to know and would be limited to attendance and the fact that issues related to professional functioning are being addressed; specific content of sessions would not be disclosed. In order to secure such an exchange of information between the program faculty and the trainee's therapist, a release of information according to Family Educational Rights and Privacy Act requirements must be signed. A sample release is provided in Table 8.3.

If an evaluation of the emotional well-being of the trainee is needed, an independent source, other than the therapist, should be secured to avoid a conflict of interest and possible negative effects on the therapeutic relationship. Table 8.2, described previously, also includes a sample of the language used in a letter to a trainee outlining a remediation plan that includes personal therapy and reflects the limitations related to exchanging confidential information about the personal therapy of this trainee.

SUCCESSFUL OUTCOME OR DISMISSAL

If remediation plans are successful, this should be documented in the trainee's record, along with a written recommendation to return to full status in the program. If outlined remediation program goals are not met, program dismissal must be considered. As stated, courts have upheld faculty dismissal decisions that were not capricious. In short, the steps leading to the dismissal decision were documented, and the trainee was informed about

Table 8.3 Sample Release of Information Form

I (name of student and date of birth) hereby give permission for the representative of (name of academic institution) and representative of (name of counseling agency) to mutually release information to each party regarding attendance and domains of my competence for the purpose of coordinating efforts toward helping me develop appropriate professional competence. If I do not agree to this release, information will not be shared between the training program and the counseling agency, which may result in unsuccessful completion of my remediation plan. This authorization will expire on (date). I understand I may revoke this authorization at any time, for any reason, by notifying (name of counseling agency) in writing, except to the extent this agency has already taken action in reliance on the consent.

Trainee Signature: Date:

_____

Witness to Signature: Date:

_____

Source: Modified from Kaslow et al. (2007b). *Psychology: Research and Practice, 38,* 479–492.

the consequences of his or her ongoing actions and given adequate notice of formal appeal processes. Legal implications of terminating trainees from training programs can be found in Bernard (1975), Cobb (1994), Knoff & Prout (1985), and Olkin & Gaughen (1991).

In general, dismissal from a training program should represent the last option after other interventions have failed to result in meaningful changes in the trainee's professional behavior. However, if a trainee engages in egregious behavior, such as sexual violations or child abuse, immediate dismissal would be warranted. Program faculty must serve to protect the public by faithfully addressing legal and ethics violations of their trainees. Furthermore, the faculty are responsible for acting in a manner that supports trainees when appropriate and will be decisive when the trainee requires probationary status, suspension, or dismissal from the program. When dismissal is imminent, it is recommended that programs consider helping trainees to make their own decision to voluntarily withdraw from their program.

DUE PROCESS RIGHTS

Due process rights are often established at the university level. If a training program has a separate due process procedure, every effort should be made to make sure that these do not conflict. University and program process should be cross-referenced in the remediation plan. Student due process rights should be clearly articulated in evaluation policies and procedures. These rights should also address confidentiality and a formal appeals process. Table 8.2 includes language related to due process rights of a trainee who is the subject of a remediation plan.

Once all of the components of a program's evaluation policy and operating procedures are articulated and ready for implementation, they must be integrated together into a coherent evaluation or assessment plan. What follows is a description of an evaluation plan that takes a preventative approach, divided into predictable phases at various points in a student's progress through his or her training program (Bemak et al., 1999; Kaslow et al., 2007b; Wilkerson, 2006).

A PHASE MODEL OF TRAINEE ASSESSMENT: A PREVENTATIVE APPROACH

The process begins at the preadmission stage, at which time program faculty assess for predictors of professional behaviors through a review of letters of recommendation, review of personal statements for concerns such as poor boundary development, and during interviews and observations of group processes. Although this process is routinely used in training programs, there is little evidence that this type of admission process can successfully predict which trainees will experience deficits (Wilkerson, 2006). Although there is a relationship between aptitude scores and future academic rankings by faculty in a mental health training program (Hosford, Johnson, & Atkinson, 1984), the relationship between aptitude scores and clinical competency ratings is minimal. The goal, however, remains to reduce the number of trainees exhibiting significant problematic behaviors by admitting qualified trainees with both the cognitive/academic and interpersonal competencies to be successful in the training program.

The second phase of assessment occurs when a trainee is accepted into a school psychology training program; informed consent for evaluation as part of professional training should be obtained from each trainee. This can occur when evaluation policies and procedures are shared with the potential trainee; inherent risks and potential benefits from completing the professional training program in school psychology should also be shared (Knoff & Prout, 1985). This approach promotes trainee awareness of the importance of informed consent.

The third phase involves ongoing evaluation, which is critical to the development of trainee competency and reaching the goal of successful completion of the training program. Feedback during each semester as part of individual courses should be a part of the assessment and evaluation process. Specific, individualized feedback related to the development of professional knowledge, skills, and professional behaviors described above should be provided as a part of all courses. Practicum or internship evaluations from site supervisors, a method of formative evaluation, could be completed during and at the end of each semester. A comprehensive formative assessment should also be conducted on an annual basis. The program faculty can provide formative feedback using the multimethod and multisource assessment process at the end of each academic year, with oral and written feedback provided to each trainee.

Finally, prior to graduation or for inclusion in a professional portfolio, program faculty should provide their trainees with a summative evaluation of their development of relevant professional knowledge, skills, and professional behaviors. Final internship supervisor evaluations and comprehensive exams might be used as independent sources of summative evaluation or integrated into a more complete summary. A sample set of program policy and procedures, including a description of the regular intervals in the training program at which formative and summative assessments are provided to trainees, is included in Table 8.4.

Table 8.4 Sample Program Policies and Procedures Related to Stages of Assessment Process

Evaluation Timelines

Each doctoral student is formally evaluated at least once each year, and the student's continuation in the doctoral program is contingent upon a satisfactory annual evaluation. In addition, reappointment to a graduate assistantship is dependent, in part, upon the results of these annual performance evaluations. In addition to the grades and in-course evaluations, the student will receive as part of his/her courses:

1. A mid-year evaluation after the first semester in the program. All instructors of first-semester courses in which the graduate student is enrolled will complete this form.* The completion of these faculty evaluation forms will occur following the doctoral student's first semester and will culminate in a feedback conference with the program coordinator.

2. At the end of each year of training, the School Psychology Coordinating Committee (excluding student representatives) conducts a formal performance evaluation of each student in the doctoral program. Assessment of performance is based on the student's self-evaluation, course instructor evaluations (see Figure 8.1), practica supervisor evaluations, and performance evaluation of the graduate assistantship. The student's self-evaluation* must be submitted no later than April 15th of each year (see Academic Professional Development Information Form, and Dissertation Progress Monitoring Form). Results of this formal Coordinating Committee evaluation are shared with each doctoral student in an annual meeting with his/her Program Advisor, usually during summer enrollment in the program. In this meeting, evaluation information is summarized in writing using the Annual Program Advisor Meeting Form,* and the student receives a copy of this summary. If problems are identified, more immediate feedback will be provided.

3. Throughout the second year of full-time training, each doctoral student is enrolled in the full-year psychoeducational and psychosocial practica, and frequent feedback is provided on a case-by-case basis. In addition, summative feedback is provided at the end of the first and second semesters.

4. Feedback is also provided as part of all advanced practica.

* Copies of all forms are available from the second author at Department of Psychology, Campus Box 4620, Illinois State University, Normal, IL 61790-4620 or meswerd@ilstu.edu. However, they cover the areas specified in the section Skills Assessed.

SUMMARY

School psychology training programs are accountable to their accrediting bodies and overarching codes of conduct to ensure adequate professional development among their trainees. This chapter has attempted to review the issue of competence among school psychology graduate programs and provide a best practices model for assessing and intervening with trainees exhibiting professional competence problems. The emphasis has been on clear, consistent communication with trainees from their first inquiry about the program, throughout the training experience, and continuing through their initial job placements. Specific, published policies and procedures manuals or trainee handbooks should describe benchmarks, along with criteria and procedures for evaluation. Although the frequency of significant competency problems among trainees is low, graduate educators should be prepared to draft remediation plans outlining objective, measurable goals for such trainees to address. Established procedures for due process should also be included in all written policies, and trainee responsibilities in the appeal process should be addressed. The application of this model may prevent and/or minimize competency problems and allow training programs to have more confidence in their approach to these matters.

RESOURCES

Forrest, L., Elman, N., Gizara, S., & Vacha-Haase, T. (1999). Trainee impairment: Identifying, remediating, and terminating impaired trainees in psychology. *The Clinical Psychologist, 27*, 627–686.
This article provides a thorough overview of the topic of trainee impairment. The authors review research on the prevalence of trainee impairment, the most common problematic areas among trainees, and methods used to address remediation. A literature review of key issues related to defining impairment, evaluating trainees, and ensuring legally appropriate policies and procedures related to competence is the basis for specific recommendations for psychology training programs.

Harvey, V. S., & Struzziero, J. (2008). *Professional development and supervision of school psychologists II*. Thousand Oaks, CA: Corwin Press.
This text provides a comprehensive overview of supervision specific to the field of school psychology. Although the text addresses supervision broadly, much of the literature and practical suggestions offered to supervisors could be directly applied to preventing and intervening competency concerns. Supervisors will find sections targeting performance assessment that may help one determine whether student performance reflects developmental progress or deficiencies of greater concern.

Kaslow, N. J., Rubin, N. J., Forrest, L., Elman, N. S., Van Horne, B. A., Jacobs, S. C., et al. (2007). Recognizing, assessing, and intervening with problems of professional competence. *Psychology: Research and Practice, 38,* 479–492.
This article is from a special section on assessment of competence in the October 2007 issue of *Professional Psychology: Research and Practice.* The article outlines eight proposals to consider in recognizing, assessing, and intervening with problems of professional competence in trainees. Training programs are advised to consider the terminology used to define competency problems, how to encourage self-assessment, and factors to consider when addressing remediation. The article offers practical suggestions related to the impact of culture in competence evaluations and for clear communication to the trainee and other necessary professionals involved in the trainee's professional development.

Wilkerson, K. (2006). Impaired students: Applying the therapeutic process model to graduate training programs. *Counselor Education & Supervision, 45,* 207–217.
This article offers a five-step therapeutic process model for addressing competency concerns among graduate trainees. The author integrates eight common elements of several widely supported program models within a more therapeutic process model beginning with informed consent and progressing through termination. Readers may garner several best practices suggestions for assessing and addressing competency problems in their training programs.

REFERENCES

American Psychological Association. (2002). Ethical principles of psychologists and code of conduct. *American Psychologist, 57,* 1060–1073.
American Psychological Association. (2008). *Guidelines and principles for accreditation of programs in professional psychology.* Washington, DC: Author.
Baldo, T. D., Softas-Nall, B. C., & Shaw, S. F. (1997). Student review and retention in counselor education: An alternative to Frame and Stevens-Smith. *Counselor Education & Supervision, 35,* 245–253.
Bemak, F., Epp, L. R., & Keys, S. G. (1999). Impaired graduate students: A process model of graduate program monitoring and intervention. *International Journal for the Advancement of Counselling, 21,* 19–30.
Bernard, J. L. (1975). Due process in dropping the unsuitable clinical student. *Professional Psychology: Research and Practice, 6,* 275–278.
Biaggio, M. K., Gasparikova-Krasnec, M., & Bauer, L. (1993). Evaluation of clinical psychology graduate students: The problem of the unsuitable student. *Professional Practice of Psychology, 4,* 9–20.
Brown, M. T., & Landrum-Brown, J. (1995). Counselor supervision: Cross-cultural perspectives. In J. G. Ponterotto, J. M. Cassas, L. A. Suzuki, & C. M. Alexander (Eds.), *Handbook of multicultural counseling* (pp. 263–286). Thousand Oaks, CA: Sage.

Cobb, N. H. (1994). Court recommended guidelines for managing unethical students and working with university lawyers. *Journal of Social Work Education, 30*, 18–31.

Davis, D. A., Mazmanian, P. E., Fordis, M., Harrison, R. V., Thorpe, K. E., & Perrier, L. (2006). Accuracy of physician self-assessment compared with other measures of competence: A systematic review. *Journal of the American Medical Association, 296*, 1094–1102.

Elman, N. S., & Forrest, L. (2007). From trainee impairment to professional competence problems: Seeking new terminology that facilitates effective action. *Professional Psychology: Research and Practice, 38*, 501–509.

Forrest, L., Elman, N., Gizara, S., & Vacha-Haase, T. (1999).Trainee impairment: Identifying, remediating, and terminating impaired trainees in psychology. *The Clinical Psychologist, 27*, 627–686.

Gaubatz, M. D., & Vera, E. M. (2002). Do formalized gatekeeping procedures increase programs' follow-up with deficient trainees? *Counselor Education & Supervision, 41*, 294–305.

Gizara, S. S., & Forrest, L. (2004). Supervisors' experience of trainee impairment and incompetence at APA-accredited internship sites. *Professional Psychology: Research and Practice, 35*, 131–140.

Haynes, R. H., Corey, G., & Moulton, P. (2003). *Clinical supervision in the helping professions: A practical guide.* Pacific Grove, CA: Brooks-Cole-Thomson Learning.

Hosford, R. E., Johnson, M. E., & Atkinson, D. R. (1984). Trends and implications for training: Academic criteria, experiential background, and personal interviews as predictors of success in a counselor education program. *Counselor Education & Supervision, 23*, 269–275.

Kaslow, N. J., Rubin, N. J., Bebeau, M. J., Leigh, I. W., Lichtenberg, J. W., Nelson, P. D., et al. (2007a). Guiding principles and recommendations for the assessment of competence. *Psychology: Research and Practice, 38*, 441–451.

Kaslow, N. J., Rubin, N. J., Forrest, L., Elman, N. S., Van Horne, B. A., Jacobs, S. C., et al. (2007b). Recognizing, assessing, and intervening with problems of professional competence. *Psychology: Research and Practice, 38*, 479–492.

Knoff, A. M., & Prout, H. T. (1985). Terminating students from professional psychology programs: Criteria, procedures, and legal issues. *Professional Psychology: Research and Practice, 16*, 789–797.

Kutz, S. L. (1986). Defining "impaired psychologist." *American Psychologist, 41*, 220.

Lamb, D. H., & Swerdlik, M. E. (2003). Identifying and responding to problematic school psychology supervisees: The evaluation process and issues of impairment. *Clinical Supervisor, 22*, 87–110.

Lamb, D. H., Presser, N. R., Pfost, K. S., Baum, M. C., Jackson, V. R., & Jarvis, P. A. (1987). Confronting professional impairment during the internship: Identification, due process, and remediation. *Professional Psychology: Research and Practice, 18*, 597–603.

National Association of School Psychologists. (2000a). *Professional conduct manual: Principles for professional ethics and standards for the provision of school psychological services.* Bethesda, MD: Author.

National Association of School Psychologists. (2000b). *Standards for training and field placement programs in school psychology.* Bethesda, MD: Author.

Olkin, R., & Gaughen, S. (1991). Evaluation and dismissal of students in master's level clinical programs: Legal parameters and survey results. *Counselor Education & Supervision, 30,* 276–288.

Preece, M., Cayley, P. M., Scheuchl, U., & Lam, R. W. (2005). The relevance of an employee assistance program to the treatment of workplace depression. *Journal of Workplace Behavioral Health, 21,* 67–77.

Roberts, M. C., Borden, K. A., Christiansen, M. D., & Lopez, S. J. (2005). Fostering a culture shift: Assessment of competence in the education and careers of professional psychologists. *Psychology: Research and Practice, 36,* 355–361.

Rubin, N. J., Bebeau, M., Leigh, I. W., Lichtenberg, J. W., Nelson, P. D., Portnoy, S., et al. (2007). The competency movement within psychology: An historical perspective. *Psychology: Research and Practice, 38,* 452–462.

Weber, M. L. (2000). Evaluation of learning: An impossible task? *Royal College of Physicians and Surgeons of Canada, 33,* 339–344.

Wilkerson, K. (2006). Impaired students: Applying the therapeutic process model to graduate training programs. *Counselor Education & Supervision, 45,* 207–217.

9 Ethical and legal challenges

Negotiating change

A. Nichole Dailor and Susan Jacob

INTRODUCTION

The decisions made by school psychologists have an impact on children, families, and schools. To build and maintain public trust in school psychologists and and in the field of psychology, every practitioner must be sensitive to the ethical components of his or her work, knowledgeable of broad ethical principles and rules of professional conduct, and committed to a proactive stance in ethical thinking and conduct. In addition, many aspects of school psychological practice are regulated by law. To safeguard the legal rights of pupils and families, practitioners also must know and respect law.

The field of school psychology has demonstrated a long-standing commitment to supporting and encouraging appropriate professional conduct. Both the American Psychological Association (APA) and the National Association of School Psychologists (NASP) have adopted codes of ethics. These codes serve to protect the public by educating practitioners about the boundaries of appropriate conduct and assisting professionals in monitoring their own behavior (Koocher & Keith Spiegel, 1998). Each organization supports an ethics committee that responds to informal inquiries about ethical issues, investigates complaints about possible ethics violations by its members, and imposes sanctions on violators. Both also support activities designed to educate school psychologists about appropriate professional conduct (Jacob & Hartshorne, 2007).

Three broad types of ethical–legal problems arise in professional practice: ethical dilemmas, ethical transgressions, and legal difficulties. Ethical dilemmas occur when "there are good but contradictory ethical reasons to take conflicting and incompatible courses of action" (Knauss, 2001, p. 231). Dilemmas may be created by situations involving competing ethical principles, conflicts between ethics and law, the conflicting interests of multiple clients, or dilemmas inherent in the dual roles of employee and pupil advocate, or because it is difficult to decide how broad ethics code statements apply to a particular situation (Dailor, 2007; Jacob-Timm, 1999). Some dilemmas are quickly and easily resolved; others are troubling and time consuming (Sinclair, 1998). Dailor surveyed a nationally representative sample of public school psychology practitioners and found that almost three fourths of the 208 respondents indicated they had encountered at least one of eight types of ethical dilemmas within the previous year.

Ethical transgressions or violations are those acts that go against expectations for ethical conduct and violate professional codes of ethics. Ethical transgressions can result in harm to students or other clients and create a problematic situation for colleagues who must decide whether and how to confront the misconduct. Unethical conduct may also result in a complaint to NASP or APA and sanctions for ethics code violations. Dailor (2007) found that more than 90% of the respondents in her sample had witnessed at least one type of ethical transgression by a school psychologist within the past year.

Practitioners must also be knowledgeable of law pertinent to practice. Disregard of federal and state law can result in violations of the legal rights of pupils and families; parent-school disputes, especially with regard to special education law; and legal action against the school. Unlawful conduct by a practitioner can also result in loss of certification or licensure to practice.

PRACTITIONER COMPETENCIES IN ETHICS AND LAW

As shown in Table 9.1, a number of desired outcomes of training in ethics and law have been identified. Two paradigms describe how students and new practitioners develop ethical competence: the acculturation model (Handelsman, Gottlieb, & Knapp, 2005) and a stage model (Dreyfus, 1997; also see Harvey & Struzziero, 2008). Handelsman et al. describe ethics training of psychology graduate students as a dynamic, multiphase acculturation process. They suggest that psychology, as a discipline and profession, has its own culture that encompasses aspirational ethical principles, ethical rules, professional standards, and values. Students develop their own "professional ethical identity" on the basis of a process that optimally results in an adaptive integration of personal moral values and the ethics culture of the profession. Trainees who do not yet have a well-developed personal sense of morality, and those who do not understand and accept critical aspects of the ethics culture of psychology, may have difficulty making good ethical choices as psychologists.

The stage model describes a process whereby practitioners progress through five levels: novice, advanced beginner, competent, proficient, and expert (Dreyfus, 1997). In foundational course work, instruction focuses on teaching the basic principles and rules for decision-making and heightening awareness of the ethical–legal aspects of situations. For this reason, novice practitioners are rule-bound and slow to make decisions. With some experience in applying rules of practice, advanced beginners become more capable of identifying multiple aspects of a complex situation and taking

Table 9.1 Desirable Practitioner Competencies in Ethics and Law

1. Competent practitioners are sensitive to "the ethical components of their work" and are aware that their actions "have real ethical consequences that can potentially harm as well as help others" (Kitchener, 1986, p. 307; also Rest, 1984; Welfel & Kitchener, 1992).
2. Competent psychologists have a sound working knowledge of the content of codes of ethics, professional standards, and law pertinent to the delivery of services (Fine & Ulrich, 1988; Welfel & Lipsitz, 1984).
3. Competent practitioners are committed to a proactive rather than a reactive stance in ethical thinking and conduct (Tymchuk, 1986). They use their broad knowledge of codes of ethics, professional standards, and law along with ethical reasoning skills to anticipate and prevent problems from arising.
4. Skilled practitioners are able to analyze the ethical dimensions of a situation and demonstrate a "well-developed ability to reason about ethical issues" (Kitchener, 1986, p. 307). They have mastered and make use of a problem-solving model (de las Fuentes & Willmuth, 2005; Tymchuk, 1981, 1986).
5. Competent practitioners recognize that ethics develop within the context of a specific culture, and they are sensitive to the ways in which their own values and standards for behavior may be similar to or different from those of individuals from other cultural groups. They are aware of their personal values and feelings and the role of their feelings and values in ethical decision making (Corey, Callanan, & Corey, 2002; Kitchener, 1986).
6. Competent practitioners appreciate the complexity of ethical decisions and are tolerant of ambiguity and uncertainty. They acknowledge and accept that there may be more than one appropriate course of action (de las Fuentes & Willmuth, 2005; Kitchener, 1986).
7. Competent practitioners do their best to engage in "positive ethics," that is, they strive for excellence rather than meeting minimal obligations outlined in codes of ethics and law (Knapp & VandeCreek, 2006).
8. Competent practitioners have the personal strength to act on decisions made and accept responsibility for their actions (de las Fuentes & Willmuth, 2005; Kitchener, 1986).

Source: Adapted from Jacob, S., & Hartshorne, T. S. (2007). *Ethics and Law for School Psychologists* (5th ed., pp. 5–6). Hoboken, NJ: Wiley. With permission.

context into account, but they are still focusing on technical mastery of their skills. Competent practitioners are better able to identify key elements of a situation, see relationships among elements, recognize subtle differences between similar situations, balance skills and empathy, and consider the long-term effects of their decisions. However, because they are more skilled in considering relevant elements, competent practitioners are at times overwhelmed by the complexity of real-world problems. Practitioners who are proficient recognize situational patterns and subtle differences more quickly, and they are able to prioritize elements in decision making more effortlessly. Because proficient practitioners no longer need to study the elements of a situation and deliberate on alternatives, they may not be conscious of the knowledge and thinking processes that provide the foundation for choices. Finally, because of many experiences with diverse situations, experts are able to rely on past decisions to inform future decisions, base decisions on subtle qualitative distinctions, and often have an intuitive grasp of what needs to be done without extensive analyses. On the basis of their review of research on expert performance, Ericsson and Williams (2007) suggest that expertise involves mastery of complex skills acquired by early supervised practice coupled with deliberate practice over an extended period of time, usually 10 years.

TRAINING, PEDAGOGICAL, AND SUPERVISORY ISSUES

Prior to the late 1970s, the training of school psychologists in ethics and law often occurred only in the context of practica and internship supervision (Handelsman, 1986). A shortcoming of this approach, however, is that student learning is limited by supervisor awareness and knowledge of ethical–legal issues and the types of situations encountered in the course of supervision. Consensus now exists that ethics, legal aspects of practice, and a problem-solving model need to be explicitly taught during graduate training (Hass, Malouf, & Mayerson, 1986; Jacob & Hartshorne, 2007; Tryon, 2001; Tymchuk, 1985). Both NASP and APA graduate program training standards require course work in professional ethics. NASP's *School Psychology: A Blueprint for Training and Practice III* identifies competence in professional, legal, ethical, and social responsibility as a foundational domain, one that permeates "all areas of practice for every school psychologist" (Ysseldyke et al., 2006, p. 15).

Growing professional support also exists for a planned, multilevel approach to training in ethics and law (Conoley & Sullivan, 2002; Fine & Ulrich, 1988; Meara, Schmidt, & Day, 1986). In her national survey, Dailor (2007) asked school psychology practitioners to describe their graduate school preparation in ethics. More specifically, respondents were asked to indicate whether they had completed a course in ethics, whether ethical issues were discussed in multiple courses, and whether ethical issues were addressed during practica and internship. Slightly more than half of the respondents (55%) had completed one or more courses in ethics as part of their graduate training.

Tryon (2000) and others (Jacob-Timm, 1999) recommend that formal course work in ethics and law be required at the beginning of graduate training to prepare students to participate in discussions of ethical and legal issues throughout their program. Because many aspects of school-based practice are regulated by law as well as professional codes of ethics, Jacob and Hartshorne (2007) recommend integrated rather than separate instruction in ethics and law. Practitioners are ethically obligated to know and respect federal and state law and school policies; furthermore, key concepts such as privacy, informed consent, and confidentiality have roots in both law and ethics. A foundational course can introduce students to broad ethical principles, codes of ethics, the major provisions of federal law pertinent to practice, significant relevant court rulings, and an ethical–legal decision making model. Knowledge of the major provisions of federal law provides a cognitive framework for students to build on when they are required to read and apply state regulations during practicum and internship. In addition, Handelsman et al. (2005) recommended that early course work include activities to heighten self-awareness of personal values and beliefs. For example, they suggested asking students to write an ethics autobiography in which they reflect on their own values, those of their family, and those of their culture of origin and consider what it means to be an ethical professional.

As noted previously, experts in the field of ethics education generally agree that a problem-solving model should be explicitly taught during graduate training (Haas et al., 1986; Handelsman, 1986; McNamara, 2008; Tryon, 2001; Tymchuk, 1985; Williams, Armistead, & Jacob, 2008). Eberlain (1987) and others (Kitchener, 1986; Knapp & VandeCreek, 2006; Tymchuk, 1985) suggested that mastery of an explicit decision-making model may help the practitioner make informed, well-reasoned choices when dilemmas arise in professional practice. Tymchuk (1985) noted that use of a systematic problem-solving strategy also allows a practitioner to describe how a decision was made, which may afford some protection if difficult decisions are later challenged and scrutinized by others. Furthermore, a systematic decision-making model can be helpful in anticipating problems and preventing them from occurring (Sinclair, 1998). Use of a decision-making model may also help practitioners chose an appropriate course of action in response to societal, technological, or other changes that create ethical–legal concerns (see Case Illustration: Negotiating Change).

A foundational course can also provide opportunities for students to apply what they are learning about the ethical–legal aspects of practice by role-playing difficult situations and analyzing case incidents. Individual or small group problem-solving followed by class discussion is an excellent way to engage trainees in learning. As students challenge each other to take into account relevant ethical principles, legal issues, and salient cultural factors, and to consider the parties potentially affected by a decision, they are likely to become more sensitive to the ethical–legal components of problem situations, aware of their own values and standards and those of others, and more skilled in analyzing complex situations. As a result, such classroom experiences may help promote the transition from novice to advanced beginner. Williams et al. (2008) and Jacob and Hartshorne (2007) provided case vignettes for students to analyze using a problem-solving model.

A number of ethical decision-making models have appeared in the literature (Cottone & Claus, 2000; McNamara, 2008; Koocher &

Keith-Spiegel, 1998). Although many appear useful, only limited research has explored whether use of a decision-making model improves the quality of practitioner choices (Cottone & Claus, 2000). Gawthrop and Uhlemann (1992) found that undergraduate students who received specific instruction in ethical problem solving demonstrated higher quality decision making in response to a case vignette than students who had not received the instruction.

A graduate course in ethical and legal issues provides a critically important foundation for subsequently training, but it is not sufficient to achieve desired practitioner competencies in ethics and law. If students have only one course, they may not be prepared to apply this knowledge across various domains of practice (Dreyfus, 1997; Meara et al., 1996). In order for students to progress beyond the stage of advanced beginner, discussion of ethical–legal issues associated with diverse situations and professional roles must be a component of course work in assessment, academic remediation, behavioral interventions, counseling, and consultation. For this reason, Tryon (2000) recommends that all graduate faculty discuss ethical issues related to their specialty area. Dailor (2007) found that about half of her survey respondents (54%) reported that ethics were taught in multiple graduate classes.

Supervised field experiences provide a vitally important opportunity for students to apply their knowledge to multiple real-world situations (Harvey & Struzziero, 2008). As noted previously, Dreyfus (1997) suggests that experience with multiple situations is necessary to achieve a high level of competence in a problem-solving domain. Similarly, Ericsson and Williams (2007) observed that expertise involves mastery of complex skills acquired by early supervised practice and deliberately practiced over an extended period of time. With appropriate supervisory support, internship is "a prime time to develop ethical frameworks that will be useful throughout a professional career" (Conoley & Sullivan, 2002, p. 135). Consistent with this view, most of the respondents in Dailor's study (70%) indicated that ethics were addressed in practicum/internship. Field- and university-based practicum and internship supervisors consequently have a special obligation to model sound ethical–legal decision making and to monitor, assist, and support supervisees as they first encounter real-world challenges (Conoley & Sullivan; Handelsman et al., 2005; Harvey & Struzziero). Analysis of vignettes is an excellent way to extend discussion of problem-solving beyond situations that arise during field experiences (Williams et al., 2008).

Dailor (2007) defined *multilevel university-based ethics training* to mean that respondents reported receiving all three levels of ethics training during graduate study: course work in ethics, discussion of ethical issues in multiple courses, and supervised discussion of ethical issues in practica and internship. Although growing professional support exists for a planned, multilevel approach to graduate preparation in ethics, only 24% of the respondents in Dailor's study reported receiving such training. Dailor also asked survey participants to identify the types of problem-solving strategies they used when handling difficult situations in the previous year. Less than one quarter of respondents reported using a systematic decision-making model. However, respondents who had received multilevel university training were more likely to report use of a systematic decision model than those who had not received multilevel ethics preparation. Use of a systematic decision-making procedure was not associated with degree level (doctoral vs. nondoctoral).

Only a few empirical investigations of the effectiveness of formal ethics training have appeared in the literature (Tryon, 2001; Welfel, 1992). Baldick (1980) found that clinical and counseling interns who received formal ethics training were better able to identify ethical issues than interns without prior course work in ethics. Tryon (2001) surveyed school psychology doctoral students from APA-accredited programs and found that students who had taken an ethics course and those who had completed more years of graduate study felt better prepared to deal with the ethical issues presented than those who had not taken an ethics course and who had completed fewer years of graduate education. Student ratings of their preparedness to deal with the issues presented in the survey were positively associated with the number of hours of supervised practicum experience completed. More recently, Dailor (2007) found an association between the types of university training that school psychology practitioners had received and their preparedness to handle ethical issues on the job, with those who had received multilevel university preparation in ethics reporting higher levels of preparedness to handle ethical issues. Preparedness was not associated with degree level (doctoral or nondoctoral) or years of experience on the job (5 or fewer years, more than 5 years).

School psychologists are ethically obligated to "remain current regarding developments in research, training, and professional practices that benefit children, families, and schools" (NASP, 2000, Principle II.A.4; also APA, 2002, Ethical Standard 2.03). Continued professional training in the area of ethics is required for renewal of a Nationally Certified School Psychologist credential (Armistead, 2006), and many states require continuing education credits in ethics for renewal of licensure. In 2006, NASP's ethics committee began an initiative to support state level efforts to promote ethics education (McNamara, 2006).

Dailor (2007) found that 49% of the practitioners in her study had attended professional development workshops on ethics, 21% had participated in district in-service training on ethics, 36% indicated that ethical issues were discussed at school psychologists' staff meetings, and 44% had engaged in self-study (e.g., read journal articles or books). However, it is important to note that although an association was found between multilevel university preparation in ethics and higher levels of preparedness to handle ethical problems, preparedness to handle problems was not associated with years of experience on the job. Because Ericsson and Williams (2007) suggested that greater expertise can develop over time as a consequence of supervised and intentional practice, the lack of association between preparedness to handle ethical problems and years of experience on the job is somewhat disappointing. It may be that new school psychology practitioners need greater supervisory support in the area of professional ethics than they are currently receiving, including mentoring with the explicit goal of promoting skill development in ethical–legal problem solving (see Harvey & Struzziero, 2008). The lack of association between years of experience and preparedness to handle ethical problems also suggests that a stronger commitment to deliberate continuous professional development in ethics is needed among new practitioners to translate experience into expertise.

Although Dailor's (2007) study found that less than one fourth of practitioners reporting using a systematic problem-solving procedure when faced with a challenging situations, most (66%) reported consulting with colleagues. Creation of an Internet-based discussion group that specifically addresses ethical–legal issues may be a way to provide school psychologists with access to colleagues who have greater expertise in ethics and law, and could be particularly useful for beginning practitioners and those who work in isolated areas.

CASE ILLUSTRATION: NEGOTIATING CHANGE

School psychologists must negotiate frequent changes in codes of ethics, law, and recommended professional practices. The ethics codes of the APA and NASP are revised every 10 years; changes in law are unpredictable. When codes of ethics are revised or laws change, psychologists scrutinize the implications of such changes for school-based practice (e.g., Burns, Jacob, & Wagner, 2008; Fisher, 2003; Flanagan, Miller, & Jacob, 2005; Knapp & VandeCreek, 2003).

School psychologists must also respond to societal changes and technological advances. In addition, a continuous stream of research provides the impetus for introducing new practices that promise to benefit school children. For these reasons, psychologists examine the ways that existing professional standards provide guidance for negotiating societal change (e.g., Bahr, Brish, & Crouteau, 2000), technological advances (e.g., Harvey & Carlson, 2003; Naglieri et al., 2004), and new practices.

School-based practitioners must negotiate change as it affects their role and delivery of services. Use of a systematic decision-making model may assist them in considering the ethical and legal aspects of change. In the paragraphs that follow, Koocher and Keith-Spiegel's (1998) problem-solving model provides the basis for considering the ethical–legal issues associated with accessing information posted on a student's MySpace or Facebook

Web page. (This situation and analysis were suggested by Matthew Lau, Minneapolis Public Schools, and Isadora Szadokierski, doctoral student in the School Psychology Program at the University of Minnesota, and are used with their permission.)

Describe the parameters of the situation: An English teacher at the middle school stopped in to see Hannah Cook, a school psychologist, to discuss concerns about one of her eighth-grade students, Melinda. The teacher reported that Melinda's grades have declined over the past 6 weeks and that she appears sad and tired in class. Because the district's policy allows a student to be seen by any school mental health professional without parent notice to ensure the student is safe and not in danger, the teacher hopes that Hannah has time to meet with Melinda, to make sure she is all right. The teacher believes that Melinda spends quite a bit of time online and mentioned that there is growing concern about cyberbullying among the girls at the middle school. The teacher goes on to suggest that Hannah also gather information about Melinda's well-being by visiting her MySpace page. Hannah was unsure whether this would be appropriate, so she decided to use a problem-solving procedure to consider the ethical–legal issues raised by this suggestion.

Define the potential ethical–legal issues involved: Hannah made a list of questions for consideration: Is it legally permissible and ethically appropriate for me to visit Melinda's Web page and gather information as suggested by the teacher? Should I seek parent permission prior to visiting Melinda's MySpace page, and/or should I seek Melinda's permission to visit her page? Is it permissible to use information from a student's Web page as part of a psychological evaluation?

Consult ethical and legal guidelines that might apply to the resolution of each issue; consider the broad ethical principles as well as specific mandates involved; and consult colleagues as needed: Hannah consulted with her district colleagues and contacted the NASP's Ethical and Professional Practices Committee. On the basis of her own ideas and input from others, she identified multiple sources of ethical and legal guidance that might apply to the resolution of the issues she had identified: NASP's (2000) *Principles for Professional Ethics*; APA's (2002) *Ethical Principles of Psychologists and Code of Conduct*; Children's Online Privacy Protection Act of 1998 (COPPA), a federal law; and several professional publications on legal issues relating to technology use in schools (e.g., Willard, 2007).

Evaluate the rights, responsibilities, and welfare of all affected parties: Hannah identified the following rights and responsibilities of affected parties:

1. Privacy: Psychologists are ethically obligated to avoid undue invasion of privacy (APA, 2002, Principle E; NASP, 2000, Principle III.B.1). Even if material posted in an online community is public and accessible to anyone, "many youth simply do not seem to understand the public nature of these environments" (Willard, 2007, p. 58), and they

are likely to feel that their privacy has been violated when parents or school personnel question them about their postings.

2. Self-determination, autonomy, and consent: School psychologists respect a client's right to self-determine the circumstances under which he or she discloses private information to the psychologist. For this reason, with the exception of emergency situations (i.e., there is reason to suspect a student poses a threat to self or others), ethical principles suggest that a school psychologist should seek a student's permission prior to visiting his or her MySpace page when such actions are part of the practitioner's professional role. Although decisions must be made on a case-by-case basis, COPPA provides some *indirect* guidance regarding whether a school psychologist is also obligated to seek parent permission prior to visiting a child's Web page. COPPA requires a person who operates a commercial Web site, and who collects personal information (e.g., name, e-mail address, or any other identifier) from the users of the Web site, to obtain parent consent for the collection of personally identifying information from children. This means that operators of sites such as MySpace must have parent consent for the collection of personal information from children, and they are also required to take reasonable steps to protect the confidentiality of personal information about children. Parents must be given access to information about their own child, and an operator is required to terminate services to a child whose parent has refused to allow the child to post a Web page. COPPA provisions do not apply to personal information used to respond on a one-time basis to a specific request from the child. Hannah notes that this law defines "child" to mean an individual under the age of 13. Because a person who operates a commercial Web site does not face sanctions for allowing minor ages 13–17 to register and post a Web page without parent notice or consent, COPPA indirectly permits youth age 13 and older to make an independent decision to do so.

After reviewing these ethical and legal guidelines, Hannah has a new appreciation of the ways in which student-created Web spaces raise complex questions regarding how to balance the rights and responsibilities of parents and the school with the interests and needs of teenage youth. Parents have an obligation to supervise their children to ensure that the Internet and other digital technologies are used in safe and responsible ways; similarly, schools often monitor school-based student Internet activities to help ensure safety. Both parents and the schools have a responsibility to teach children to avoid inappropriate disclosure of personal information and how to engage in responsible on-line behavior. At the same time, Internet communication is increasingly important as an educational tool and for participation in the social life of the school. Although children should be encouraged to share and discuss their Web page with parents, teenagers also need some freedom and privacy, within limits, so they can learn to make good decisions when using the Internet on their own (see Willard, 2007).

3. Validity of information gathered for professional purposes: The APA's (2002) Ethical Standard 9.01(a) states that psychologists base their opinions "on information and techniques sufficient to substantiate their findings." Willard (2007) cautions school professionals and parents to recognize that material posted on a Web page may be real and true—or not (2007, pp. 14–15, 53). Consistent with ethical guidelines and sound professional practices, Hannah recognizes the importance of verifying the truthfulness of information posted on a student's Web page prior to using the information in decision making.

4. Welfare of students: School psychologists have a responsibility to promote school policies and practices that enhance student welfare (APA, 2002, Principle B; NASP, 2000, Principle III.A.3). Cyberbullying is a threat to student well-being (Willard, 2007). The English teacher's observations indicate a need to better educate students about responsible online behavior and to consider introducing school district policies that address cyberbullying.

Generate a list of alternative decisions possible for each issue, consider the consequences of making each decision (a risk-benefit analysis), and make the decision: Hannah first considers the questions, "Should I visit Melinda's MySpace page and gather information as suggested by the teacher?" and "Should I seek Melinda's permission to visit her MySpace page?" Because she wishes to respect Melinda's privacy and right to self-determination and to foster trust, Hanah decides to seek Melinda's permission to visit her MySpace page. Furthermore, to get to know Melinda and encourage a positive psychologist–student relationship, Hannah will ask Melinda if they can sit down and view her page together. In this way, if she agrees, Melinda can share her story about the material she posted and clarify what information is really about Melinda rather than an online persona (Willard, 2007). In addition, as a result of their meeting, Melinda may benefit by becoming more aware that what is posted online is seen by others. Hannah also decides that Melinda's permission (assent) to share her Web page with a school psychologist is sufficient if three conditions are met: the Web page is in the public domain, the posted information will not be part of a formal psychological evaluation, and Melinda is age 13 or older.

Hannah also considers whether she should seek parent permission prior to visiting Melinda's MySpace Web page, and whether it is permissible to use information from a student's Web page as part of a psychological evaluation. Although youth often ignore and circumvent online community rules, COPPA suggests that a minor under the age of 13 has no "legal standing" to independently register for a commercial Web page without parent consent. Because the Web page of a child under age 13 is allowed only as an extension of parental authority, Hannah decides that parent consent should be obtained prior to viewing the Melinda's MySpace Web page if she is under age 13, that is, assent of a child under age 13 is desirable but not sufficient. Similarly, if the Web page is not in the public domain (i.e., access is restricted), parent consent to view a student's Web page is advisable. Furthermore, Hannah decides it is not appropriate to gather information from a student's Web page as part of a formal psychological evaluation without parent consent because the individual giving consent should be as fully informed as possible about the anticipated sources of evaluation data.

Make the decision, accept responsibility for the decision made, and monitor the consequences of the course of action chosen: In addition to monitoring the consequences of her decisions, Hannah will seek feedback from colleagues about her resolution of the issues. She will also discuss with others whether there is a need to better educate students in her district about responsible online behavior and explore whether additional district policies are needed to address cyberbullying (see Willard, 2007, for sample policies). Furthermore, Hannah will seek opportunities to update her readiness and competence to address issues associated with student use of the Internet and other digital technologies.

SUMMARY

Ethical–legal decision making applies "to almost everything psychologists do" (Tryon, 2000, p. 278). For this reason, it is critically important for school psychologists to achieve proficiency in the ethical and legal aspects of the delivery of services, particularly those who assume supervisory roles. Growing professional support exists for a planned, multilevel approach to training in the ethical–legal aspects of school psychology practice, and it is generally recognized that practitioners must engage in lifelong continuing education to achieve and maintain expertise in this domain. Explicit instruction in a systematic problem-solving model provides trainees and practitioners with a means to anticipate problems, prevent them from arising, and manage difficult situations when they do occur, and it provides a paradigm for negotiating societal, technological, or other changes that create ethical and legal concerns.

AUTHORS' NOTE

This chapter is based in part on a master's thesis completed by A. Nichole Dailor in fulfillment of requirements for a doctoral degree in school psychology at Central Michigan University (CMU). Funds for the study were provided by a CMU Graduate Student Research and Creative Endeavors Grant to the first author. Nothing in this chapter should be construed as legal advice, and the interpretation of codes of ethics presented here does not reflect the official opinion of any specific professional organization.

RESOURCES

Fisher, C. B. (2003). *Decoding the ethics code.* Thousand Oaks, CA: Sage.
This is a resource for students and school psychologists who wish to gain a better understanding of the APA's 2002 code of ethics.

Jacob, S., & Hartshorne, T. S. (2007). *Ethics and law for school psychologists* (5th ed.). Hoboken, NJ: John Wiley.
This text was specifically written to meet the needs of the psychologist in the school setting. An instructor's guide with a sample syllabus and test bank is available from the publisher.

National Association of School Psychologists. (2000). *Professional conduct manual.* Bethesda, MD: Author. Retrieved October 11, 2006, from http://www. nasponline.org/standards/ProfessionalCond.pdf
This manual includes the *Principles for Professional Ethics* and the *Guidelines for the Provision of School Psychological Services.* It is required reading for school psychologists and supervisors of school psychological services.

Williams, B., Armistead, L., & Jacob, S. (2008). *Professional ethics for school psychologists: A problem-solving model casebook.* Bethesda, MD: National Association of School Psychologists.
This is a collection of case vignettes for use in teaching ethical–legal problem solving in school psychology.

REFERENCES

American Psychological Association. (2002). Ethical principles of psychologists and code of conduct. *American Psychologist, 57,* 1060–1073.
Armistead, L. (2006). *NASP leaders guide to continuing professional development.* Retrieved December 18, 2007, from http://www.nasponline.org/leadership/ CPD_Guide.pdf
Bahr, M. W., Brish, B., & Croteau, J. M. (2000). Addressing sexual orientation and professional ethics in the training of school psychologists in school and university settings. *The School Psychology Review, 29,* 217–230.
Baldick, T. L. (1980). Ethical discrimination ability of intern psychologists: A function of training in ethics. *Professional Psychology, 11,* 276–282.
Burns, M. K., Jacob, S., & Wagner, A. (2008). Ethical and legal issues associated with using responsiveness-to-intervention to assess learning disabilities. *Journal of School Psychology, 46,* 263–279.
Children's Online Privacy Protection Act of 1998, 15 USCS § 6501 (1998).

Corey, G., Callanan, P., & Corey, S. S. (2002). *Issues and ethics in the helping professions* (6th ed.). Belmont, CA: Wadsworth Publishing.

Conoley, J. C., & Sullivan, J. R. (2002). Best practices in the supervision of interns. In A. Thomas & J. Grimes (Eds.), *Best practices in school psychology IV* (pp. 131–144). Bethesda, MD: National Association of School Psychologists.

Cottone, R. R., & Claus, R. E. (2000). Ethical decision-making models: A review of the literature. *Journal of Counseling and Development, 78,* 275–283.

Dailor, A. N. (2007). *A national study of ethical transgressions and dilemmas reported by school psychology practitioners.* Unpublished master's thesis, Central Michigan University, Mt. Pleasant.

de las Fuentes, C., & Willmuth, M. E. (2005). Competency training in ethics education and practice. *Professional Psychology: Research and Practice, 36,* 362–366.

Dreyfus, H. L. (1997). Intuitive, deliberative, and calculative models of expert performance. In C. E. Zsambok & G. Klein (Eds.), *Naturalistic decision making* (pp. 17–28). Mahwah, NJ: Lawrence Erlbaum Associates.

Eberlain, L. (1987). Introducing ethics to beginning psychologists: A problem-solving approach. *Professional Psychology: Research and Practice, 18,* 353–359.

Ericsson, K. A., & Williams, A. M. (2007). Capturing naturally occurring superior performance in the laboratory: Translational research on expert performance. *Journal of Experimental Psychology: Applied, 13,* 115–123.

Fine, M. A., & Ulrich, L. P. (1988). Integrating psychology and philosophy in teaching a graduate course in ethics. *Professional Psychology: Research and Practice, 19,* 542–546.

Fisher, C. B. (2003). *Decoding the ethics code.* Thousand Oaks, CA: Sage.

Flanagan, R., Miller, J. A., & Jacob, S. (2005). The 2002 revision of APA's ethics code: Implications for school psychologists. *Psychology in the Schools, 42,* 433–44.

Gawthrop, J. C., & Uhlemann, M. R. (1992). Effects of the problem-solving approach in ethics training. *Professional Psychology: Research and Practice, 23,* 38–42.

Hass, L. J., Malouf, J. L., & Mayerson, N. H. (1986). Ethical dilemmas in psychological practice: Results of a national survey. *Professional Psychology: Research an Practice, 17,* 316–321.

Handelsman, M. M. (1986). Problems with ethics training by "osmosis." *Professional Psychology: Research and Practice, 17,* 371–372.

Handelsman, M. M., Gottlieb, M. C., & Knapp, S. (2005). Training ethical psychologists: An acculturation model. *Professional Psychology: Research and Practice, 36,* 59–65.

Harvey, V. S., & Carlson, J. F. (2003). Ethical and professional issues with computer-related technology. *School Psychology Review, 32,* 92–107.

Harvey, V. S., & Struzziero, J. A. (2008). *Professional development and supervision of school psychologists.* Thousand Oaks, CA: Corwin Press.

Jacob, S., & Hartshorne, T. S. (2007). *Ethics and law for school psychologists* (5th ed.). Hoboken, NJ: John Wiley & Sons.

Jacob-Timm, S. (1999). Ethical dilemmas encountered by members of the National Association of School Psychologists. *Psychology in the Schools, 36,* 205–217.

Kitchener, K. S. (1986). Teaching applied ethics in counselor education: An integration of psychological processes and philosophical analysis. *Journal of Counseling and Development, 64,* 306–310.

Koocher, G. P., & Keith-Spiegel, P. (1998). *Ethics in psychology* (2nd ed.). New York: Oxford.

Knapp, S., & VandeCreek, L. (2003). An overview of the major changes in the 2002 APA ethics code. *Professional Psychology: Research and Practice, 34,* 301–308.

Knapp, S., & VandeCreek, L. (2006). *Practical ethics for psychologists: A positive approach.* Washington, DC: American Psychological Association.

Knauss, L. K. (2001). Ethical issues in psychological assessment in school settings. *Journal of Personality Assessment, 77,* 231–241.

McNamara, K. (2006). Ethical and Professional Practices Committee activity report as of May 30, 2006. Available from Susan Jacob at jacob1s@cmich.edu

McNamara, K. (2008). Best practices in the application of professional ethics. In A. Thomas & J. Grimes (Eds.), *Best practices in school psychology V* (Vol. 6, pp. 1933–1941). Bethesda, MD: National Association of School Psychologists.

Meara, N. M., Schmidt, L. D., & Day, J. D. (1996). Principles and virtues: A foundation for ethical decisions, policies, and character. *Counseling Psychology, 24,* 4–77.

Naglieri, J. A., Drasgow, F., Schmit, M., Handler, L. Prifitera, A., Margolis, A., et al. (2004). Psychological testing on the Internet. *American Psychologist, 59,* 150–162.

National Association of School Psychologists. (2000). *Principles for professional ethics: Guidelines for the provision of school psychological services. Professional conduct manual* (pp. 13–62). Bethesda, MD: Author. Available from: http://www.nasponline.org

Rest, J. R. (1984). Research on moral development: Implications for training counseling psychologists. *Counseling Psychologist, 12,* 19–29.

Sinclair, C. (1998). Nine unique features of the *Canadian Code of Ethics for Psychologists. Canadian Psychology, 39,* 167–176.

Tryon, G. S. (2000). Ethical transgressions of school psychology graduate students: A critical incidents survey. *Ethics & Behavior, 10,* 271–279.

Tryon, G. S. (2001). School psychology students' beliefs about their preparation and concern with ethical issues. *Ethics & Behavior, 11,* 375–394.

Tymchuk, A. J. (1981). Ethical decision-making and psychological treatment. *Journal of Psychiatric Treatment and Evaluation, 3,* 507–513.

Tymchuk, A. J. (1985). Ethical decision-making and psychology students' attitudes toward training in ethics. *Professional Practice of Psychology, 6,* 219–232.

Tymchuk, A. J. (1986). Guidelines for ethical decision making. *Canadian Psychology, 27,* 36–43.

Welfel, E. R. (1992). Psychologist as ethics educator: Successes, failures, and unanswered questions. *Professional Psychology: Research and Practice, 23,* 182–189.

Welfel, E. R., & Kitchener, K. S. (1992). Introduction to the special section: Ethics education—An agenda for the '90s. *Professional Psychology: Research and Practice, 23,* 179–181.

Welfel, E. R., & Lipsitz, N. E. (1984). Ethical behavior of professional psychologists: A critical analysis of the research. *The Counseling Psychologist, 12,* 31–41.

Willard, N. E. (2007). *Cyberbullying and cyberthreats.* Champaign, IL: Research Press.

Williams, B., Armistead, L., & Jacob, S. (2007). *Professional ethics for school psychologists: A problem-solving model casebook*. Bethesda, MD: National Association of School Psychologists.

Ysseldyke, J., Burns, M., Dawson, P., Kelley, B., Morrison, D., Ortiz, S., et al. (2006). *School psychology: A blueprint for training and practice III*. Bethesda, MD: National Association of School Psychologists.

10 Discrimination, harassment, and other challenging topics

Judith Kaufman and
Tammy L. Hughes

Issues of gender, gender orientation, race/ethnicity, and disability discrimination are prevalent throughout society. Few, if any, institutions are protected from these difficult interpersonal challenges. Incidences of harassment, whether covert or overt, reported or ignored, unfortunately take place with great frequency. It becomes particularly difficult to deal with these issues in settings that are presumed to be enlightened, liberal, and progressive. It was not that long ago that women were called "Baby," "Sweetie," and "Honey," and were expected to flirt and laugh irrespective of how uncomfortable they felt in those situations. It is sometimes presumed that this no longer happens. Sexual harassment is not the only form of abuse that takes place in public settings, particularly our educational institutions. Gender, disability, race, and ethnicity discrimination and harassment, along with peer harassment, are also critical areas to consider. Although the main focus of this chapter is sexual harassment, other relevant areas are discussed; prevention and intervention in all of these areas share common approaches and methodology. We also detail how to teach school psychology students to prepare for the difficult dialogues that may need to occur as part of the business of working in public settings. Finally, a case example and resources are included.

INTRODUCTION

The field of education has typically been seen as providing good jobs for women. Florida, for example, which mirrors national trends, reports that the instructional staff comprises 22% males and 78% females, and 43% males and 57% females are employed as administrators (Florida Department of Education, 2007). Although the majority of the rank and file in education tends to be women, until recently leadership and administrative roles were held predominately by males. In Texas, from 1995 to 2002, there was a 36% increase in women principals (an increase of 947), whereas the number of males in that role decreased by less than 6% (17 principals). Similarly, the National Center for Educational Statistics (Indicator 34,

2007) reported that between 1993–1994 and 2003–2004, the percentage of public school principals who were female increased from 41% to 56% in elementary schools and from 14% to 26% in secondary schools. Although the gap is narrowing between male and female principals, the percentage of female principals remains smaller than the percentage of teachers who are female. That is, researchers have found that the average male teacher is more likely than the average female teacher to become a principal. Similarly, although the percentage of female administrators is on the rise, the gender gap still persists, with the proportion of female administrators remaining well below that of teachers. This gender gap is more pronounced at the elementary level than at the secondary level.

At present, there is no comprehensive national survey of school superintendents that is comparable to the Schools and Staffing Survey providing data on teachers and administrators; however, it is well known that the school administrative staff nationwide is aging, and the average age of school superintendents in 2000 was 52.5 years. The American Association of School Administrators survey (Cooper, Fusarelli, & Caarella, 2000), which is conducted every 10 years, found that this is the oldest average age ever recorded for school personnel. Now, 9 years later, it is suspected that the average is even higher. In 2000, women accounted for 13% of school superintendents, in contrast to 76% of teachers who are women. Although this is still a very small number, it is a marked increase from 1992, when only 5% of superintendents were women. These data show that there appears to be an increase in gender parity; however, the same cannot be said of the racial and ethnic mix, which is particularly evident when contrasted to the demographics of school-aged children. The vast number of administrators are Caucasian; in the past few years, there has been a slight increase in minority representation but not sufficient to reach parity. The field of school psychology also follows these trends. According to a National Association of School Psychologists survey (2004–2005), 93% of their membership identify themselves as Caucasian; 74% are female, and the mean age was 46 years. Data from the same survey showed similar findings for school psychology faculty, where 93% identified themselves as Caucasian and 60% are female. Consistent with all areas of education, there is a dramatic absence of minorities in the profession.

Some may assume that as the number of women who hold leadership roles in educational settings increases, so too would there be an increase in opportunities for women, as well as a decrease in the number of harassment complaints. The sexual harassment data alone, however, show that harassment continues to be a serious problem in the workplace, such that at university and in military settings, 2 in 5 women and 1 in 6 men report at least one episode of sexual harassment in the past 2 years (Street et al., 2007). Both women and men are more likely to experience harassment from men than from women, although the nature of the harassment is different. Women report verbal put downs, unfair or unequal treatment, and physical violation of personal space, whereas men report vulgar comments or negative remarks (Wolfe & Chiodo, 2008). Certainly, since the 1960s, gender discrimination has been recognized as in need of formal remediation. In 1970s, this protection was extended beyond the workplace to the school environment. Since school settings are composed of both employees and students, all individuals must adhere to both employment and academic laws regarding sexual harassment (Ramson, 2006).

DEFINING HARASSMENT WITHIN A SCHOOL CONTEXT

As summarized by Ramson (2006), sexual harassment law is governed by federal civil rights legislation, the Civil Rights Act of 1964. Title VII of the Civil Rights Act prohibits sex discrimination by employers. *The Meritor Savings Bank FSB v. Vinson Supreme Court* case in 1986 defined sexual harassment as a form of sex discrimination. The United States Equal Employment Opportunity Commission (EEOC) implements Title VII by issuing interpretative regulations, handling workplace sexual harassment cases, and providing legal guidance. In 1980, with an amendment in 1990, the EEOC issued regulations for implementing Title VII titled Guidelines on Discrimination Because of Sex. This document (29 C.F.R. section 1604.11) defined two types of behavior that constitute sexual harassment in the workplace. Both types of behavior describe an abuse of power where physical, verbal, or nonverbal conduct relating to sex is unwelcome by the victim. The first type of sexual harassment is quid pro quo, which is defined as occurring when a person with more authority exerts power over a person of less authority by (a) making sexual advances, (b) requesting sexual favors, or (c) engaging in other conduct of a sexual nature. Quid pro quo sexual harassment is an exchange whereby submission to the conduct is made a term or condition of employment or academic evaluation, or whereby submission or rejection of the conduct is used as a basis for an employment or academic evaluation. The second and more common type of sexual harassment is hostile environment sexual harassment. This type occurs between or among individuals of equal power. This type of harassment occurs when conduct unreasonably interferes with the victim's work or academic performance or has the effect of creating an intimidating, hostile, or offensive work or academic environment. Title IX of the Education Amendments of 1972 extends this same protection (prohibiting sex discrimination) to students and other academic community members in public and private educational settings that receive federal funding. Until the late 1990s, academic institutions were not held accountable for sexual harassment claims. In 1998 and 1999, two landmark decisions were handed down by the Supreme Court that opened the door for schools to be monetarily liable in private actions where a student is sexually harassed by a teacher or another student. In *Gebser v. Lago Vista Independent School*

District (1988) and *Davis v. Monroe County Board of Education (1999)*, schools were found to be liable for being indifferent to sexual harassment conduct. Although these cases require a number of conditions to be met in order for schools to be found liable (i.e., school possesses actual notice of the conduct and shows deliberate indifference to that conduct), the door is now open for future sexual harassment suits against schools.

PEER HARASSMENT IN THE SCHOOL CONTEXT

Although the aforementioned cases were instances of adult-to-student harassment in school systems, it is important to note the extent to which older children and adolescents engage in harassing behavior throughout elementary, middle, and high school. The American Association of University Women (AAUW) conducted two extensive studies of harassment in schools between 1993 and 2001. Over 81% of students reported that they had experienced some form of harassment during their school years. In addition, over 50% reported that they had harassed someone during their school years. Not unexpectedly, girls reported a greater frequency of harassment than did boys. In a survey of more than 1,800 9th and 11th graders, Wolfe and Chiodo (2007) concluded that there is ample evidence that harassment and abuse occur frequently among high school students. Many of the behaviors were described as not visible (e.g., passing notes, ignoring in public places, gossiping) but nonetheless as having significant personal and psychological impact on the lives of adolescents. Interestingly, some behaviors (e.g., public name calling, sexual pranks) did decline between 9th and 11th grades; however, students continued to report fears about their own safety as they enter secondary school. Consistent with the literature around bullying, there are many school environments that consider harassment behavior as normative, often dismissing it as a regular feature of adolescent social–sexual development (Terrance, Logan, & Peters, 2004). High schools in particular are being held liable for their negligence due to a lack of responding to sexual harassment (Terrance et al.). School personnel often claim that it is difficult to identify all the behaviors that fall within the rubric of sexual harassment and what defines a hostile environment. Stone and Couch (2004) suggested that adults in school settings are aware of harassment but are doing less than they should to stop the behavior. In Stone and Couch's survey, teachers reported an intolerance of harassment but acknowledged that they typically would not report the harassment to a designated authority or tell the initiator to stop.

For classrooms to be conducive for learning, they must be safe and supportive of students' social emotional well-being and adjustment (Adelman & Taylor, 1998). Conflict and disagreement among children is common, and negotiation skills are among the developmental skills that are learned;

however, when conflicts are accompanied by taunts, physical aggression, and exclusion, children can develop anger, anxiety, sadness, and a sense of isolation (Coie, 2004). Persistent, unwanted harassment can turn a positive educational environment into a nightmare for its victims. Children in our schools are being bullied and victimized at a frightening rate; this victimization can result in serious negative academic and psychological consequences and radically diminished sense of competence and self-esteem (American Psychological Association, 1999; Rigby, 2001). A national study reported that 29% of children said they felt less confident after having been harassed, 23% reported not wanting to attend school, and another 12% stopped attending extracurricular activities (American Civil Liberties Union of Ohio, 2000).

Some children turn to school personnel, including teachers, administrators, school counselors, and school psychologists, for assistance in dealing with the difficulties they are facing. Help-seeking itself may create an additional dilemma for children and may create further victimization (Newman, 2008). That is, what may be considered adaptive help-seeking behavior at the onset of harassment may be reconstituted as learned helplessness when school systems fail to respond to victim reports (Newman). Graham and Juvonen (2001) have shown that children have a greater likelihood of engaging in adaptive help-seeking behavior when children perceive the situation as dangerous, hostile, unprovoked, and uncontrollable. Events can be misperceived, and some children may become accustomed to stressful and painful experience, fail to seek help, and potentially experience greater psychological damage (Ladd & Ladd, 2001). The location of the incident may contribute to help-seeking behavior. Those situations where children perceive themselves to be alone (e.g., playground, bathrooms, hallways) are acceptable venues to seek help from the viewpoint of peers. Regardless, as stated, it is the belief that support is unavailable that increases students' stress (Newman & Murray, 2005).

The definition of what constitutes bullying and harassment may vary across school cultures and thus may systematically impact school policy. For example, some school personnel have negative perceptions of those students seeking help, particularly if reporters are male. Ignoring a child's request may exacerbate anxiety or lead to feelings of shame and embarrassment (Newman, 2008). Having said that, there are adults within the school environment who may be overprotective of particular students and undermine those situations where children should be negotiating on their own (Birch & Ladd, 1998), which can potentially have negative consequences as well. In both designing appropriate interventions and determining prevention procedures, teachers, school administrators, and school psychologists can use these incidents to plan for conflict resolution situations, communicate standards for respectful behavior, and assist the child/victim in developing effective coping strategies.

LESBIAN, GAY, BISEXUAL, OR TRANSGENDER HARASSMENT IN THE SCHOOL CONTEXT

Along with peer harassment or bullying are those situations of verbal harassment and abuse targeted toward students who are or presumed to be gay, lesbian, bisexual, or transgender (GLBT; Kosciw, 2004). In fact, "actual or perceived sexual orientation is one of the most common reasons that students are harassed by their peers, second only to physical appearance" (Novotney, 2008, p. 18). A recent national study indicated that 92% of GLBT youth reported frequently hearing homophobic remarks in school (Kosciw), and students reported that often, teachers and staff were present. Students reported that teachers intervened less than 20% of the time (Kosciw). Almost two thirds of GLBT youth reported feeling unsafe in their schools because of their sexual orientation (Kosciw). Researchers have demonstrated that fear of harassment and experiencing harassment can lead to higher rates of truancy, poor school performance, and school dropout (Fontaine, 1998). Unchecked verbal harassment often leads to physical harassment, such as pushing, hitting, and shoving (Human Rights Watch, 2001). Furthermore, GLBT students are four times more likely to be threatened by a weapon at school than are heterosexual students (Garofalo, Wolf, Kessel, Palfrey, & DuRant, 1998). Thus, the school climate can be seen as hostile and unsafe for GLBT students and can cause serious negative effects on both academic and personal development.

DISABILITY HARASSMENT IN THE SCHOOL CONTEXT

As challenging as it is for all children to deal with peer harassment, these issues become magnified for those with disabilities. It is assumed that individuals working within the public education system are well aware of the legislation providing protections for individuals with disabilities. Many view disability discrimination as thoughtlessness or failure to accommodate individual needs (Weber, 2002). Harassment may be much more endemic, and indeed there may be intentional discrimination, with expressions of overt hostility. When describing the hostility aimed at individuals with disabilities, Weber noted, "nowhere is the injury more common or more severe than in elementary and high schools (2002, p. 2)." Weber argued that well-meaning teachers make a host of mistakes in the name of concern. For example, teachers uncritically committed to inclusion standards, may overly focus on a student's disability to such a degree that they inadvertently shame the student with a disability. Second, students with disabilities may be excluded from routine activities in order to protect them without regard to individualized education program recommendations or involving the students or families in that decision making. Third, some hold the assumption that having a disability is volitional and can be fixed if the individual is sufficiently motivated. Thus, what makes confronting disability discrimination so challenging is that in many cases, it appears to be relatively unconscious yet results in observable discriminatory behavior and/or attitudes. It is difficult for children to avoid reacting to harassment (Weber, 2002). Often students refuse to attend school or develop somatic complaints (e.g., headaches, stomachaches) to facilitate staying home. Associated with harassment, children with disabilities have school dropout rates three times higher than those of nondisabled children (Weber, 2002).

RACIAL AND ETHNIC DISCRIMINATION IN THE SCHOOL CONTEXT

An in-depth analysis of the history of racial and ethnic discrimination and the sociopolitical consequences is beyond the scope of this chapter; however, race and ethnicity discrimination abounds. There are many challenges that school psychologists are likely to face during their careers. As schools play a major role in making positive changes for a community and, ultimately, for society, it is important that attitudes of racial and ethnic intolerance be corrected at an early age. Messages of tolerance and sensitivity to minority concerns, transmitted to students and staff, can play a significant role in changing a culture of intolerance. Focusing on reducing intolerance cannot be accomplished by a single individual or entity but requires a collaborative community effort and potentially town-, city-, or state-wide efforts. A deeper understanding of the debilitating effects of racism on *all* students and staff should be promoted. Often, school administrators are reluctant to confront racism and racial harassment within the school setting; they may deny its presence in their building. Failure to take appropriate steps, to take action against the perpetrators, and to not provide remedies can only support and reinforce the negative and harmful behaviors.

PREVENTION: SEXUAL AND GENDER HARASSMENT IN THE SCHOOL CONTEXT

Sexual harassment attitudes are thought to stem from stereotyped perceptions of aggressive and tough males contrasted by submissive and caring females; these perceptions can result in potentially false and stereotypic gender expectations (Newman, 2008). Although there have been some generational or cultural shifts regarding the perceptions of typical gender characteristics, traditional expectations and values persist within specific groups. Some researchers claim that the only way to end sexual harassment and gender-based violence is through the promotion of gender equity, assuming that if men and women have gender roles that are equally valued, the power relationship would be mitigated and individuals would function in a gender-friendly environment (Chu).

Prevention starts with strong messages, sent through both written policy and the observable actions of individuals within the system, delineating which behaviors will not be tolerated. Many organizations require periodic review of sexual harassment policies and procedures (American Association of University Professors, 2000). First, individuals should be clear as to what conduct constitutes sexual harassment. Second, individuals need to be aware of the institution's harassment policies and procedures when a violation occurs. Third, institutions need to ensure that this information is adequately disseminated throughout the entire community. For example, informational seminars are often used to share knowledge, clarify particular issues, and describe the consequences of any violations. Finally, written policies need to spell out how anonymity will be protected, the process, and individuals responsible for investigating claims. Recommended actions to prevent sexual harassment in the school environment include the following:

- Develop and publicize a sexual harassment policy that clearly states that it will not be tolerated and includes explicit examples of what is considered to be harassment
- Develop and publicize specific grievance procedure for resolving complaints
- Develop methods to inform staff of policies and procedures
- Conduct periodic training for all school staff
- Conduct periodic age-appropriate awareness training for students
- Establish discussion groups for male and female students where they can talk about what harassment is and how to respond to it in the school settings
- Survey students to find out whether any harassment is occurring in the school
- Involve and educate parents to develop effective methods to help their children deal with these issues (Office for Civil Rights [OCR], 2002, pp. 4–5).

As the primary mental health agents in the schools, school psychologist trainees and professionals can play a vital role in supporting these endeavors and in helping schools to implement harassment programs, as well as to evaluate the effectiveness of such interventions. Although these steps begin the process for preventing sexual harassment, there are several real-world complications that graduate students are likely to face. For example, university training programs may have accessible policies and procedures in place, but field-based placement sites may not have congruent policies. Students need to be clear that although harassment may occur in a practicum or internship setting, oversight remains the responsibility of the university in contract with the field-based placement. At the same time, university supervisors need to be aware of district harassment policies in order to protect all parties involved.

Well-articulated policies are a necessary but not sufficient condition to prevent harassment or to stop it if it does occur. Similar to the data presented for children in their school setting, if harassing behavior is ignored or not reported, it is likely to continue, often becoming worse, and have a major lasting negative impact on academic performance, as well as self-esteem, for our adult students (OCR, 2002). Zero-tolerance policies are recommended; inappropriate behavior should be dealt with in a swift and consistent manner, and "boys will be boys" attitudes should be dismissed. Support networks need to be established to assist individuals who do report misconduct, as individuals report that fear of isolation and retribution keeps individuals from reporting sexual harassment. Under these conditions, university students will see the school as a safe place where everyone can learn (OCR, 2002).

PREVENTION: HARASSMENT AND GENDER ORIENTATION IN THE SCHOOL CONTEXT

Dr. Peter Goldblum, a pioneer in the development of mental health programs for the GLBT community, has partnered with the San Francisco Unified School District to help elementary schools promote respect and the acceptance of diversity. In order to help schools address issues of family diversity, gender stereotyping, and harassing behaviors, teachers and administrators receive training on how to respond to challenging student questions and how to set a positive inclusive tone for all students. By beginning this difficult dialogue at the elementary school level and training staff, the negative effects of bias and discrimination can be prevented, not only in elementary schools but throughout a child's schooling experience.

Staff training about sensitivity is an important component of prevention; however, staff and student attitudes require maintenance, so systems should plan routine environmental checks. Similar to the processes outlined for sexual harassment, clear messages need to be sent by the administration about what are appropriate and inappropriate communications, how infractions will be dealt with, and how students can access support in the school. The training programs may partner with school districts to deliver staff development training. Chapter 12 of this volume deals extensively with preparing school psychologists to address the needs of GLBT youth.

TEACHING STUDENTS TO NEGOTIATE DIFFICULT DIALOGUES IN THE SCHOOL CONTEXT

In general, school psychologists do not receive specific training in helping students deal with harassment issues. Not only is it essential for graduate students to understand the importance of clearly articulated policies along with how to implement prevention strategies, but graduate students need to be prepared to face the real possibility that they may be called upon to deal with children and staff who may have been targets of harassment, or that they may be targets themselves.

Certainly, advocacy is a role that is promoted throughout graduate curriculums and central to the function of the school psychologist; however, it can be less clear how to proceed when a school psychologist observes a teacher or administrator engaging in harassing or insensitive behavior. Ethically, school psychologists must utilize standard processes for resolving dilemmas. If there is a school culture that promotes (or accepts) harassment, then the school psychologist will also need to set about a course of promoting an accepting environment. Of course, attitudes about sexual orientation cannot be legislated in the same manner as sexual harassment, so a nuanced balance between developing an inclusive culture, as well as attending to the legal requirements to provide a safe environment, needs to be considered. It is helpful to find sympathetic administrators within the system to help address systemic problems and utilize skills similar to those required for school-wide consultative services. It is also important to prepare students for negative feelings that may be experienced in the position of being the whistle-blower if the system is particularly intractable. Graduate students need to plan to seek their own outside support from mentors, colleagues, and local, state, and national professional organizations. Also, graduate students (and school psychologists) should plan to seek the support of agencies known to improve sensitivity to these topics (e.g., racial discrimination).

Graduate students need to be aware of contra-power harassment, where the person with less power is the harasser. This is noted in a variety of settings. For example, Matcher and DeSouza (2000) found that both males and females faculty were equally harassed in the university setting, although females were reported to receive more sexual attention. These results are contrary to the assumption that females are seen with less power and thus would have been harassed, thus demonstrating contra-harassment. Although the authors concluded that contra-harassment may be more widespread than previously recognized, they noted that if local norms condone or are tolerant of a sexualized environment, then sexual harassment becomes more prevalent (Matcher & DeSouza, 2000). In school systems, contra-harassment is often overlooked when female students harass male teachers or in the case of same sex harassment (Leland, 2000).

Contra-power harassment is not currently protected in Title VII or Title IX. Within the parameters of the law, there is little protection of individuals in power (e.g., a teacher) from a student or a stakeholder with less perceived power (Juliano, 2007). In the case of those with less power harassing those with more power, the traditional thinking on how to handle sexual harassment for the development of legal doctrine becomes unclear; harassment implies a power relationship. Traditionally, sexual harassment is considered to be an abuse of power; therefore, it would seem inconceivable that someone with a lesser status could challenge that power. Some scholars assert that power is better understood as a social construction, that is, accepted behaviors are socialized in the educational institution rather than a simple individual hierarchy (Eyre, 2000). Although this dialogue may prove useful in explaining how contra-harassment occurs, we are not yet at a point where legal guidelines or actions clearly address this issue. In these cases, school psychology students and practitioners not only need to be aware of the complexities but also need to prepare to address victims who are in the power position. Individuals may experience embarrassment and/ or be reluctant to come forward, as they themselves or others in the school setting conclude that adults should know how to handle their students. Professionals may tolerate and/or reinforce unacceptable behavior by their failure to act. Certainly, this type of harassment can negatively impact the professional identity one holds.

Finally, university training programs need to prepare graduate students for the possibility that they will be the targets of harassment. Although there may be a variety of psychological dimensions associated with harassment, students should be familiar with the power relationships inherent with gender bias. In this situation, males typically expect that they would primarily be the initiators of contact and that females should respond in a stereotypical manner. Although graduate students typically have training in setting boundaries around therapeutic relationships, they may be caught off guard by the need to set boundaries where they assumed professional standards applied.

CASE EXAMPLES

Observing harassment

Sarah, a new intern in the middle school, observed a group of fifth-grade boys yelling at, cursing at, and pushing a male classmate in the school cafeteria. Taunts such as "faggot" and "homo" were being yelled at him. They surrounded the boy and attempted to pull down his trousers. At that point, the teacher in charge came over and separated the youngsters. The boys who initiated the conflict received the appropriate punishment for aggressive behavior. Sarah was deeply concerned, first that no one reached out to the child who was being harassed, and second that the issues of potential homophobia were not being addressed, only the aggressive behavior. With her supervisor's permission, Sarah was able to speak with Tom, the boy who was being bullied. In their conversation he indicated that he enjoys spending time with the girls who are his friends and kind to him. Name calling and harassment, he said, "makes me feel like I am a freak and out of the human race." Sarah was able to make arrangements for Tom to have time to speak with the school guidance counselor, and he seemed to welcome the intervention. Sarah was still deeply concerned and, with her supervisor, approached the principal of the school with a proposal to introduce a prevention program for the fifth grade focusing on gender discrimination and harassment issues. She felt that if children were aware and better educated, incidents like the one involving Tom could potentially be prevented. Sarah was fortunate in that the school administration agreed to a trial intervention. Although there may be a clearly articulated policy to deal with overt aggressive behavior, the issues, misunderstandings, and prejudices that are the triggers for such behaviors often are not dealt with.

Being a victim of harassment

Brian is a 27-year-old doctoral intern in Greenbriar Elementary School. He is considered to be attractive by his peers, and although actively dating, is not particularly involved in a relationship at this time. The teaching staff is 99% female and the administrative staff is 75% female, with the principal also female. Brian's supervisor, Nancy, is a 55-year-old woman who received her doctorate 10 years ago; however, she has been *the* school psychologist for the past 25 years. Brian has begun dreading going to work, although he really likes the kids and loves being a school psychologist. Each morning, Nancy pinches his cheek, squeezes his arm, and tells him how "cute" he looks. The principal keeps giving him telephone numbers of her friends' daughters and checks in with him to see if he has called. Although he enjoys the attention of the females, he finds that two particular teachers keep wanting to "consult" with him after school, "over coffee." Brian finds himself sometimes unable to focus on his job, and although he needs supervision, would like to avoid it. He has tried using humor and has thought about inventing a serious relationship or going out for lunch alone; when he has tried to share his concern with the older male assistant principal, he is told, "I should be so lucky." Having made it through the school year, he is offered a position in the school as they are expanding services. When Brian turns the job down and is questioned by his program director, he finally shares what he has been through. Brian was embarrassed and ashamed to admit what was going on and felt that he should have been able to handle the situation.

Brian suffered through a critical year of training as he was unaware or denied seeing that he was being sexually harassed. The school system did not have a clearly stated policy about harassment. Typically, males have difficulty reporting harassment from the opposite sex and are more likely to report bullying and humiliation by other males. Had Brian reported his concerns to the program director or internship coordinator, he would have received support and guidance in negotiating the situation. It is possible that if an uncomfortable work environment persisted after intervention, Brian could have been placed in an alternate setting.

SUMMARY AND CONCLUSIONS

Understanding sexual, gender, and peer harassment is critical for all individuals working in educational settings. Certainly the demographic realities in the school setting indicate that there are more females in positions of lesser power, suggesting the potential for sexual harassment. The issues remain a real concern for the workplace. Additionally, as the responsibility of school systems to prevent and protect their students' increases, sexual, peer, and high-risk group (such as GLBT) harassment needs to be considered simultaneously so that adequate prevention strategies can be put into place.

School psychologists not only need to be equipped to help the educational system prepare for and prevent harassment, they need to be aware how their services may be required for those who are harassed. Additionally, issues of nontraditional harassment, such as peer to peer and contra-harassment, need to be addressed in training programs to prepare future professionals to feel competent in confronting these issues. Training programs also need to have clearly articulated policies to protect their trainees. As more and more research demonstrates the negative cognitive and social emotional consequences of harassment, school psychologists need to reaffirm their commitment to prevention in order to protect the mental of health of the children we serve, our colleagues, and ourselves.

RESOURCES

Newman, R. S. (2008). Adaptive and nonadaptive help seeking with peer harassment: An integrative perspective of coping and self-regulation. *Educational Psychologist, 43*(1), 1–15.
Newman presents an excellent framework for understanding the dynamics of help-seeking behavior of children, which is an important foundation in considering prevention and intervention programs for peer harassment.

Although the following materials were not developed in the United States, they are easily translatable:

Anti-Discrimination and Anti-Harassment Policy Support Materials: Understanding Gender Diversity. (n.d.). Retrieved from http://www.education.tas.gov.au/school/educators/health/inclusive/antidiscrimination/gender
The information included is to help professionals to understand students with gender diversity issues.

Years K-12 Gender Education. (n.d.). Retrieved from http://www.schools.nsw.edu.au/learning/yrk12focusareas/gendered/index.php
This site contains curriculum and support materials for schools.

Department of Education, Queensland, Australia. (1994). *Enough's Enough! Sexual Harassment and Violence: A resource kit for primary schools.*
These materials are well worth reviewing and can be obtained by writing to the Department of Education in Queensland, Australia. The curriculum materials have won several awards and focus on teaching strategies and resources.

REFERENCES

Adelman, H. S., & Taylor, L. (1998). Reframing mental health in the schools and expanding school reform. *Educational Psychologist, 33,* 135–152.

American Association of University Professors. (2002). *Sexual harassment policies.* Retrieved August 26, 2008, from http://www.aaup.org/AAUP/protect/legal/topics/sex-harass-policies.htm

American Association of University Women. (1993). *Hostile hallways: The AAUW survey on sexual harassment in America's schools.* Washington, DC: Harris/Scholastic Research.

American Civil Liberties Union of Ohio. (2000). *Peer harassment and the law.* Columbus: OH: Author.

American Psychological Association. (1999). *Warning signs: A youth antiviolence initiative.* Washington, DC: Author

Birch, S. H., & Ladd, G. W. (1998). Children's interpersonal behaviors and the teacher-child relationship. *Child Development, 34,* 934–946.

Civil Rights Act, 29 C.F.R. § 1604.11 (1990).

Coie, J. D. (2004). The impact of negative social experiences on the development of antisocial behavior. In J. B. Kupersmidt & K. A. Dodge (Eds.), *Children's peer relations: From development to intervention* (pp. 243–267). Washington, DC: American Psychological Association.

Cooper, B. S., Fusarelli, L. D. and Carella, V. A. (2000) Career crisis in the school superintendency? Washington, DC: American Association of School Administrators and the National Center for Educational Statistics.

Davis v. Monroe County Board of Education, No. 526US629 (U.S. Supreme Court, 1999).

Eyre, L. (2000). The discursive framing of sexual harassment in a university community. *Gender and Education, 12,* 293–307.

Florida Department of Education. (2007). Florida Information Note. Tallahassee, FL.

Fontaine, J. H. (1998). Evidencing a need: School counselors' experiences with gay and lesbian students. *Professional School Counseling, 1,* 109–124.

Garofalo, R., Wolf, R. C., Kessel, S., Palfrey, J., & DuRant, R. H. (1998). The association between health risk behaviors and sexual orientation among a school-based sample of adolescents. *Pediatrics, 101,* 895–902.

Gebser v. Lago Vista Independent School District (U.S. Supreme Court, 1988).

Graham, S., & Juvonen, J. (2001). An attributional approach to peer victimization. In J. Juvonen & S. Graham (Eds.), *Peer harassment in school: The plight of the vulnerable and victimized* (pp. 49–72). New York: Guilford.

Ladd, B. K., & Ladd, G. W. (2001). Variations in peer victimization: Relations to children's maladjustment. In J. Juvoenen & S. Graham (Eds.), *Peer harassment in school: The plight of the vulnerable and victimized* (pp. 25–48). New York: Guilford.

Human Rights Watch. (2001). *Lesbian, gay, bisexual, and transgender students in U.S. schools.* New York: Author.

Juliano, A. C. (2007). *Harassing women with power: The case for including contra-power harassment.* Villanova, PA: Villanova Law/Public Policy Research Paper No.2006-15.

Kosciw, J. G. (2004). *The National School Climate Survey: The school related experiences of our nation's gay, lesbian, bisexual and transgender youth.* New York: GLSEN.

Matcher, J., & DeSouza, E. (2000). The sexual harassment of faculty members by students-statistical data included. *Sex Roles: A Journal of Research, 42*(3–4), 1–6.

Meritor Savings Bank FSB v. Vinson (U.S. Supreme Court, 1986).

National Association of School Psychologists. Retrieved from http://sss.usf.edu/Resources/Presentations/2007/NASP/School_Psychology_2004_2005. ppt#326,1,School Psychology, 2004–2005: National and Regional Demographic Characteristics, Professional Practices, Employment Conditions, & Continuing Professional Development

Newman, R. S. (2008). Adaptive and nonadaptive help seeking with peer harassment: An integrative perspective of coping and self-regulation. *Educational Psychologist, 43*(1), 1–15.

Newman, R. S., & Murray, B. (2005). How students and teachers view the seriousness of peer harassment: When is it appropriate to seek help? *Journal of Educational Psychology, 93,* 347–365.

Novotney, A. (2008). Preventing harassment at schools. *Monitor on Psychology, 39,* 18–20.

Office for Civil Rights. (2002). *Sexual harassment: It's not academic* [Pamphlet]. Washington, DC: U.S. Department of Education.

Ramson, A. (2006). Sexual harassment education on campus: Communication using media. *Community College Review, 33,* 38–54.

Rigby, K. (2001). Health consequences of bullying and its prevention in schools. In J. Juvonen & S. Graham (Eds.), *Peer harassment in school: The plight of the vulnerable and victimized* (pp. 310–331). New York: Guilford.

Stone, M., & Couch, S. (2004). Peer sexual harassment among high school students: Teachers' attitudes, perceptions, and responses. *The High School Journal, 88*(1), 1–13.

Street, A. E., Gradus, J. L., Stafford, J. and Kelly, K. (2007). Gender differences in the experience of sexual harassment. *Journal of Consulting and Clinical Psychology, 75*(3), 464–474.

Terrance, C., Logan, A., & Peters, D. (2004). Perceptions of peer sexual harassment among high school students. *Sex Roles: A Journal of Research, 51*(5–6), 479–490.

U.S. Department of Education. (2007). National Center for Educational Statistics Indicator 34. Washington, DC: Author.

Weber, M. C. (2002). Disability harassment in the public schools. *William and Mary Law Review, 43*(3), 1–6.

Wolfe, D., & Chiodo, D. (2007). *Sexual harassment and related behaviours reported among youth from grade 9 to grade 11.* London, Ontario: Report of the CAMH Center for Preventive Science.

11 Developing professional identity

Values, behaviors, and reputation

Lea A. Theodore, Tammy L. Hughes, and Judith Kaufman

INTRODUCTION

The final stages of identity formation within a profession can be conceptualized as embracing a professional identity, promoting professionalism, and building a professional reputation. Although graduate school is an important stage of the educational process and holds exciting future promises, the practicum and internship, along with initial employment, serve to solidify the integration of education and practice.

Students begin their formal path to professional identity in school psychology as they enter graduate training programs. University trainers are in a key position to serve as role models of the profession, to provide the basic knowledge and skills, and to nurture and support the positive social emotional qualities that are the hallmark of any helping profession. In addition to direct instruction regarding the best evidence-based practices in the field and the potential ethical and legal challenges, graduate programs need to model learning environments that support respect and collaboration within the program and with field-based training facilities. Elements of what is considered to be professionalism need to be integrated in all aspect of graduate training and become an essential component of the professional training and practice. The way that professionals present themselves is important in developing a professional reputation but even more important for maintaining public trust in the professional practice of school psychology (Elman, Illfelder-Kaye, & Robiner, 2005; Johnson & Campbell, 2002). The goal of this chapter is to operationalize the concept of professionalism—that is, to examine its components and discuss methods whereby the university and the field can collaborate in developing and supporting the professional school psychologists. Among the critical issues to consider are the operational definitions of the terms *unprofessional* and *incompetent* as the university program sends the student into the field for the culmination of professional training. What are the strategies appropriate to remediate the absence of or difficulty with professionalism? Finally, the outcome of the education of school psychologists is to be involved in ethical and professional practice, whether in schools, hospitals, or clinics or as university trainers; to achieve this outcome, the new psychologist will need to build an integrated professional identity.

LITERATURE REVIEW

Although professionalism is a critical and important component in evolving a professional identity, there is no single agreed upon definition. *The Random House Dictionary of English Language* describes professionalism as "exhibited by one of the professional character, spirit or methods" or the "standing" practice or methods of a professional as "distinguished from an amateur." Among the assumptions in such a definition is that there is a standing practice or methods that exemplify the profession of school psychology. However, being professional involves many layers and levels of functioning and is subject to many interpretations. The media image of the professional is of someone invariably dressed in a suit, carrying a briefcase (or computer), talking on a cell phone, and rushing from one place to another. Alternatively, we walk into an office and observe walls of diplomas and certifications, along with photos with the influential, and conclude, "This is a real professional!" We often hear statements regarding someone's standing in the profession or influence in a school setting as exemplars of his or her professionalism. Students require guidance on how to interpret these types of observations and perceptions and to determine whether they are sufficient to qualify as professionalism. Clearly, although it is important to look as if one is a professional, that does not necessarily make it so (note, for example, the *Dilbert* comic strips, in which office workers with the trappings of professionalism behave in an unprofessional way).

Although the definitions of professionalism may be varied, there is general agreement as to the characteristics, competencies, and expectations associated with professional behaviors. At the core of professionalism is the commitment to ethical conduct, competent and appropriate practice, and character reflective of caring and respect (Johnson & Campbell, 2002). Although academic knowledge and skills are essential in the preparation of school psychologists, the personal, interpersonal, and professional characteristics are equally important, if not more so. University-based trainers independently and in collaboration with field-based trainers have the responsibility of communicating to trainees the need to be professional and to be recognized as such. In order to do so, they need to distinguish themselves through relevant knowledge and skills, and dispositional characteristics. For example characteristics such as openness to professional growth, initiative, dependability, adaptability, respect for human diversity, effective communication skills, and effective interpersonal relations are useful heuristics that university and field-based trainers can use to monitor professional development. Rogers's descriptions of genuineness, empathy, positive regard, mindfulness, and social and emotional intelligence may be useful for discussions about dispositional characteristics (cited in Elman et al., 2005). Additional competencies associated with professionalism include problem-solving capacity, ability to create knowledge as well as having learned it, and commitment to continuous learning and lifelong education.

Although some of these essential personal attributes may be taught, screening out those individuals who clearly do not have these qualities (or the potential to develop them) is the responsibility of university trainers. The first opportunity we have to address personal attributes is with a selective admissions process (Elman, et al., 2005; Fagan & Wise, 2007) by searching for both characteristics reflective of the profession and those that match the culture of the graduate training program. There is, however, a propensity to focus solely on college grade point average and GRE scores, as these are considered to be some of the best predictors of academic success (Sternberg & Williams, 1997). It is important to note that although GRE scores were an adequate predictor of grade point average during the first year of graduate school, these traditional academic abilities did not predict professional performance characteristics (Sternberg & Williams). University and field-based trainers alike who have had experience with highly qualified students can attest to the fact that additional characteristics are essential. The collaborative responsibility is to nurture the positive characteristics that we find important and to be productively critical and remediate throughout the training process to support the development of the professional school psychologist (Fagan & Wise). An extended discussion of screening for competence from preadmission to internship can be found in Chapter 3 of this volume.

Even as admission seems to have been a success and students have earned A's in their course work and excelled in exams and in simulated practice exercises, the introduction to the field experience can result in a crisis. With relative confidence, the student is assigned a practicum placement, and yet chaos ensues. For illustrative purposes it may be useful to consider the case of Robert, who was among the intellectually brightest students in his school psychology program. His work ethic was exceptional and his products outstanding. Instructors described his performance as excellent and stated that he seemed to absorb knowledge "like a sponge." After Robert's ability and performance were observed, he was placed in a practicum site with an extremely competent supervisor. Beginning with the initial contact with the school personnel and his supervisor, Robert launched into a litany of criticism about the professional practices of the staff. His comments included "That's not the way we learned it in my classes," "You're violating the standardization of the instrument," and, quite simply, "You're doing it wrong." When asked a straightforward question, Robert would respond in a pedantic and condescending manner. Although, ironically, Robert was often correct in both his knowledge and assessment of the situation, his information delivery and attitude caused enormous difficulty at his practicum site and required extensive intervention by the training program.

There are many important lessons to be learned from Robert's experience. Most crucial, we believe, is the importance of asking students to be involved in field-based training as early as possible. Simulation under the protective and supportive context of the university is very different from being involved in the culture and personality of an applied setting. All too often, we discover significant problems when a student is well into training and where it becomes even more difficult to help to modify behavior. A second compelling issue that was highlighted was the importance of open communication and collaboration in acknowledging deficits in professionalism and cooperative attempting to eradicate and remediate those deficits.

There is a paucity of extant literature specifically addressing how the components of professionalism should be integrated into the comprehensive school psychology curriculum and field-based experiences, in both practicum and internship. Although most academic competencies and application of skills are relatively easy to quantify, measuring professionalism is somewhat elusive. As it is difficult to arrive at a universal definition, it is more complex to find psychometrically sound measures specifically designed to assess professionalism and the degree to which those values are internalized by the student and expressed appropriate to context (Elman et al., 2005). Reliable and valid instruments designed to measure attitudes, problem solving, and ethical decision making, as components of professionalism, would be beneficial for evidence-based decision making about a student's initial qualities and tracking their subsequent growth and development. Competency-based and criterion-referenced observations and evaluation measures used throughout the training program could contribute enormously to the evaluation and intervention process (see examples in Chapter 3, this volume).

The values of professionalism must be infused throughout the educational process and strategically incorporated throughout the curriculum (Perry & Imig, 2008) and practice settings so that they become standard practice (Golde, 2007; Shulman, 2005). When there are conflicts or mismatched professional practices, these incidents need to be examined and problem solving toward negotiation initiated. For example, when a graduate student reports that a district is using out-of-date testing materials because the district "does not have money to waste on new tests" or a supervisor is "comfortable with what she already knows," this is an opportunity for enacting one's professionalism and ethical responsibility skills through (immediate) negotiation.

Trainers are ideally suited to influence and enhance the personal and professional development of their students. Developing a professional demeanor and reputation takes time, as emotional, social, moral, and cognitive processes evolve into an essential asset to one's career (Elman et al., 2005). These formative years in graduate school allow future school psychologists to hone and sharpen these professional attitudes. Essentially, one's professional reputation begins at the commencement of graduate training and is influenced by professors and classmates. Impressions of one's ability, attitude, and enthusiasm; respect for others and the profession; ethics; and reliability form throughout graduate school (Golde, 2007).

Professionalism is a quality central to maintaining public trust. Trust can only be established over time, by acting with integrity, demonstrating professional and ethical responsibility, and being accountable for your actions (Johnson & Campbell, 2002). Hence, any ethically questionable action or professional integrity problem that impacts a single student has the potential to also negatively impact the profession broadly. How many times have we reviewed case files or read reports of colleagues and been embarrassed to be associated with the profession? Thus, trainers have the responsibility to prepare students to effectively identify and manage ethical situations and dilemmas to ensure that students are trained in field-based settings that reflect congruent values.

ETHICS AND PROFESSIONALISM

Specific courses devoted to teaching professionalism do not exist, although in reviewing curricula of training programs there are often courses entitled Ethics and Professional Practice, Role and Function of the School Psychologist, and Legal and Professional Issues, for example. In general, however, professionalism is typically taught in conjunction with ethics education and serves as the major forum for teaching professional values (Jacob & Taton, 2005). The major driving forces for the academic ethical training are the National Association of School Psychologists (NASP) and American Psychological Association (APA) codes of ethical conduct (Flanagan, Miller, & Jacob, 2005; Jacob & Taton, 2005). Ethics education is considered to be integral to the professional development and to contribute substantially to the development of a professionally responsible attitude and critical thinking skills essential for professional practice (Tryon, 2001; see Chapter 9, this volume).

In ethics training, it is essential to convey that the primary goal of the school psychologist is to protect the overall well-being and the rights of children. The issues of competence and assuming personal responsibility for actions presented above are formally accompanied by expectations for students to develop a respect for multiculturalism and individual differences within an environment of consent and confidentiality (Elman et al., 2005; Jacob & Taton, 2005). Presenting case studies, moral dilemmas, and field-based questions is a way of challenging students to apply academic knowledge in preparation for demonstrating professional conduct. It is particularly useful to provide cases where conflicts might exist between ethical, legal, and moral issues so that problem-solving skills are stimulated along with discussions of values (Tryon, 2001).

There have been few studies evaluating the contribution of ethics education in graduate training. Conclusions regarding the effectiveness of formal ethical training are generally mixed (Tryon, 2001). Specifically, the knowledge base of ethical principles and the individual's ability to effectively address such issues was rated favorably for interns by their APA-accredited program directors (Welfel, 1992). With respect to clinical psychology, graduate students surveyed felt ill prepared to deal with professional ethics (Tymchuk, 1985), whereas counseling psychology doctoral students overwhelmingly (96%) reported that they were well trained and prepared to deal with ethical issues (Wilson & Ranft, 1993).

A recent survey of doctoral level school psychology students in APA-accredited programs examining their perceived ability to deal with ethical issues found that students who were enrolled in courses specifically focusing on ethics felt more prepared to make appropriate decisions when presented with ethical dilemmas (Tryon, 2001). Not surprisingly, advanced level graduate students felt more prepared to address ethical dilemmas. Tryon (2001) suggested that students continued to integrate ethical knowledge throughout the program in combination with field experiences that improved their ability to apply knowledge in a real-world context; however, students reported that they were less prepared to address ethical issues involving child custody cases, aggressive students, and ethical violations and inappropriate behaviors demonstrated by coworkers. Given these data, it would appear that training programs should require a course dedicated to addressing ethics education, as well as placing more emphasis on decision making, attitudes, and dispositions rather than prototypical cases where decision trees are easily applied (Tryon, 2001). Furthermore, involving field-based trainers in ethics seminars might prove effective in providing students with early exposure to the context of ethical decision making in settings where the actors are often known to them.

CURRENT LEGISLATION

Implicit within the scope and sequence of ethical education is the awareness of and responsiveness to current federal and state laws. This is especially warranted for school psychology, which has historically been linked to special education law and where there is a greater propensity of school psychologists to be employed in the public sector (Prasse, 2002). The Individuals With Disabilities Education Act and its subsequent revisions, the Americans With Disabilities Act, and No Child Left Behind have wide-ranging implications for educational interventions, as well as best practices in addressing and treating children with special needs (Prasse, 2002). As the field continues to evolve, the legal sphere of influence serves as a driving force in the roles, functions, and service delivery of school psychological practice. It is essential that training combine exposure to ethical issues, while also taking into consideration the practical reality of current legislation and legal mandates.

The interaction between law and ethics, therefore, is a critical component to professional training. Membership in national, regional, and local organizations provides opportunities for psychologists in training to become aware of any changes in legislation and their implications for practice. There are many training programs that require students to be an affiliate of a professional organization as part of a professional seminar.

PERSONAL CHARACTERISTICS OF PROFESSIONALISM

There are many pragmatic issues and practical questions that emerge when considering issues of professionalism. These issues include the ability to read the culture, knowing how to dress in a variety of contexts, determining how others should address you (e.g., by title, degree or first name) and how to address others, and where and how to socialize with colleagues. With the overwhelming amount of didactic information addressed in graduate programs, many of the pragmatic issues are not articulated; rather, we often assume that our students have the common sense to know what to do. Facilitating the development of the attributes of professionalism is a practical challenge confronting the development of a professional (Elman et al., 2005). Trainers need to clearly indicate that presentation is often as important as academic potential and that a poor personal presentation can easily detract from others' perceptions of a student's professional capability. Efforts devoted to helping graduate students enhance appropriate personal characteristics could potentially have wide-ranging implications for professional conduct. Trainers who have an open dialogue and discussion in a safe environment can deal directly with professional issues, including what it means to demonstrate accountability, duty, integrity, and respect for others. In the application of these principles, students would demonstrate a commitment to the students, staff, and families with whom they work and demonstrate a willingness to learn, take on, and even initiate responsibilities, as well as participate as a member of the support services team. Moreover, students should convey a sense of personal responsibility, while also possessing the positive attributes of being organized and communicating information respectfully and effectively (Fagan & Wise, 2007).

READING THE CULTURE

There are many factors that contribute to an individual being called unprofessional. Although personal and ethical issues are often the major contributory factors, often the culture and expectations of the environment are misread. Thus, an individual may be considered unprofessional when he lacks the ability to understand the context in which he is working. We have seen, for example, individuals jumping into situations and creating change without understanding the climate, while others reflectively study the context, the power structure, and the individuals prior to initiating action.

The typical graduate student coming from a more casual academic environment may not be familiar with the hierarchy and power structure within the school system and may, inadvertently, immediately create a negative impression by not observing the system's customs. Consider the example of Marty, who was considered to be an excellent student, went for an internship interview on a very warm day at the beginning of May. He chose to dress casually and was wearing sandals without socks. Although he ultimately was selected for the internship, the school staff continued to discuss his foot attire!

Students may require (detailed) instruction on how to appropriately dress. Dress and presentation reflect a set of beliefs about the self and regard for the profession. Students should be dressing to emphasize their professionalism, competence, and identity. When in the process of applying and interviewing for practicum placements, internships, and ultimately a job in the field, students need to be cognizant that they are marketing themselves. Generally, a good rule of thumb is to dress conservatively. Neatness counts, and attention to detail is important. Therefore, students should dress the way they want to be seen (see Cialdini et al., 1976), as serious competent professionals. Men and women should have a well-groomed hairstyle, clean and trimmed fingernails, and minimal (if any) cologne or perfume. Additionally, there should not be any gum-chewing or visible body piercings (including tongue-rings) or tattoos. All electronics (cell phones) should be turned off.

Men should wear traditional attire, often a suit with a button-down shirt and a conservative tie (if appropriate to setting) accompanied by dark socks and polished professional shoes. Male students should be aware of how professional clothes are supposed to fit and wear them prior to the interview until they feel comfortable (see Gross & Stone, 2002a). It may be helpful to recall the classic reports by Molloy (1975) showing that men who wear white shirts were considered as smarter.

Women should also wear conservative attire. If dressed in a skirted suit, then the skirt should hit just above the knee. Make-up and jewelry should be kept to a minimum, with body piercings accentuating only the ears. Shirts should not be too sheer, short, or tight (see Gross & Stone, 2002b).

Students should remember that it is important to dress like a serious professional, which means appearance is important. Appearance may impact a school's hiring decision. It is much easier to start with the impression of being too formal and then move to a more casual appearance than to create a negative first impression through a casual appearance. Obviously, dress code varies from setting to setting and as the acculturation process takes place, one's dress can be changed accordingly.

The balance between cultural differences and requirements in the school system need to be dealt with directly by faculty and school-based trainers. For instance, some schools may need to increase their sensitivity and tolerance of cultural expression, whereas students also need to increase their knowledge of the local customs (Butler, 2003). Individuals from multicultural backgrounds should consider how their cultural and/or religious beliefs match with the beliefs and cultural norms of the organization rather than compromise their cultural beliefs for a job. It is important to be aware of the culture of an organization and the extent to which it supports culturally diverse practices. Whether and to what degree one is willing to deviate from one's own cultural practices is a personal choice. For example, many individuals of the Orthodox Jewish faith seek positions as school psychologists in schools where only children and faculty of that particular faith and, consequently, cultural identity are employed.

Just as with dress, what a professional is called and how he or she addresses others is very much determined by the context of the environment. Although it might be appropriate to call a supervisor by first name in supervision, that same individual may want to be more formally addressed in public venues. The context, the age and developmental level of the children, and the custom of the system may also determine what the students call the psychologist. Often, titles and names may be construed as causing problems with boundary issues and may reflect far more than the actual presentation.

Professional image is also reflected in day-to-day conduct and demeanor. Not only the content of what is said but also the manner of delivery is translated into others' judgment about character. Therefore, in order to project a professional demeanor, it is important to refrain from participating in gossip, shouting or speaking loudly (e.g., in cases of disagreement), or sharing inappropriate jokes. Most importantly, consideration of students' confidentiality is critical. Often, information that teachers share in the teachers' lounge would fall under confidential information if the school psychologist shared it; thus, students need to understand the impact of communications shared (e.g., outside a formal problem solving context) that could potentially harm a relationship or have a major impact on the child and family.

Written reports make a lasting impression. It is important to make sure to check for grammar, syntax, and spelling errors. Writing should be clear and jargon should be avoided. This includes the need to proofread any product in order to ensure logical flow, as well as to correct anything that may have been missed. Finally, students need to be aware of the importance of being conscientious. This includes meeting deadlines, taking detailed notes and maintaining appropriate record keeping practices, documenting phone calls and conversations, making written requests, and writing narrative summaries of meetings with parents, teachers, and other professionals involved.

Trainers and student need to discuss appropriate behaviors not specific to the workplace but germane to the community at large. This includes conduct at professional meetings, at social events, and in seemingly private areas such as Internet sites (e.g., Facebook, MySpace). As technology continues to evolve, students need to be conscientious regarding the public nature of information accessible via the Internet. These social networks should be marked *private* for both safety and professional reputation. Furthermore, any editorials or written language, as well as pictures that are posted for public view, should be conservative; that is, no inappropriate clothing/dress, use of alcohol, or inappropriate recreational activities should be posted. Moreover, it is important to have a professional e-mail address that does not include nicknames or terms of endearment.

BUILDING A PROFESSIONAL REPUTATION

Having a good reputation is not achieved overnight; a reputation is a product of consistent behavior over time. Most individuals want to be well thought of, not only on a personal level but on a professional one as well. To be professionally well thought of is the hallmark of the interaction of the educational process and personal and professional characteristics. How a person begins his or her involvement in a situation and how that situation is left often provide the foundation of how others see a person. Having a stormy exit may not serve well in networking and reconnecting in the future.

Williams-Nickelson (2007) provided excellent suggestions in providing the foundation for building a positive professional reputation. Among the suggestions she offers is honoring obligations. Too often, while trying to create a positive impression in a work environment, there is a tendency to say yes to everything, thus overpromising, overextending, or overdoing. Although there may be many exciting and intriguing opportunities, it is important to know our limitations. Not fulfilling a responsibility can have a negative impact on how we are seen.

It is always important to communicate professionally (Williams-Nickelson, 2007), whether orally, in writing, or electronically. It is possible to be passionate about a topic while taking into account the opinions of others and not being condescending or insulting. There are individuals who have literally destroyed their reputation through responses on an e-mail list.

Sharing credit and giving credit where it is due can contribute to how others see a person. It is important to acknowledge those who have contributed to one's development. Sharing accomplishments with those who have contributed on the team and giving appropriate credit for an ideas or achievement are essential in creating a reputation. The credit that a professional reflects back on those who have helped him or her along the way can influence the perception of that person as a collaborator or a loner. We all need each other's special skills, and we all need to part of a contributing team.

Participating in professional development and continuing education (which in some states and for credential renewal is mandated) is essential in building a professional reputation. Striving to maintain professional competence and expand knowledge beyond formal education and training is critical (Elman et al., 2005). This may be accomplished through continuing education activities designed explicitly to promote and enhance professional development or may be accomplished through self-development activities, such as reading current literature. In essence, a professional recognizes that lifelong learning is fundamental to the practice of any profession, including school psychology (Elman et al., 2005; see Chapter 14, this volume). As professionals, it is important to convey that students need to consistently keep up with advances in the field, as well as to monitor changes in the laws. In addition, trainers should encourage active participation in professional societies by promoting membership in both national and state psychological associations. Membership in professional associations demonstrates that one is serious about the profession and also provides educational and networking opportunities. Moreover, it allows one to network in other ways, such as attending seminars, professional events, charity functions, and social hours. Professional development may also be fostered by attending workshops and participating in continuing education programs. Finally, professionalism may be promoted through personal experiences such as serving on professional boards (e.g., journal reviewer; community agency), serving as a supervisor for practicum and/or internship students, and mentoring early career psychologists (Elman et al., 2005).

PEDAGOGICAL AND SUPERVISORY ISSUES

Many programs rely on field-based experiences to provide formative feedback regarding professional behaviors. Field-based experiences are integral in that they provide a real-world context and serve as a culminating experience of graduate training. Therefore, the selection of adequate supervisors is essential (Fischetti & Lines, 2003). When choosing supervisors, it is suggested that the following criteria should be considered: years of experience, ability to provide experiences consistent with the program model, ability to give authentic feedback and supervision regarding strengths and weaknesses based on student performance for the purpose of professional growth, and ability to serve as models of ethical and professional conduct. Upon completion of the field-based experience, practicum, and/or internship, students should provide feedback as to the quality of the experience. This is done to ensure the maintenance of high-quality supervisors and the elimination of sites where supervision and/or experiences are no longer in concert with university and accreditation standards. Areas of evaluation include amount, quality, and usefulness of supervision; the types and various experiences provided (e.g., assessment, consultation, intervention, counseling); and exposure to and communication within the school setting, as well as with outside agencies (Welsh, Stanley, & Wilmoth, 2003).

Although this is certainly an appropriate time to address professionalism, there are many problems with waiting until a field experience to start these types of discussions with students. In the best of circumstances, field experiences provide a source of stress that can compete with a focus on professional behaviors. Furthermore, if there is a problem at this point, students may feel they are being unfairly targeted or that the supervisor does not like them, or they may dismiss concerns about their professional behaviors as simply a clash between professional preferences (Ladany, Friedlander, & Nelson, 2005). The signature training experiences that result in professionalism for school psychology students are accomplished through programs that intentionally design a sequence of courses (e.g., ethics and legal training) in which knowledge is presented and then supplemented by applied experiences (e.g., fieldwork, practicum, and internship) in which skills can be practiced. There is also a need for explicit promotion of students' behavioral and social–emotional presentation. Promoting professional characteristics can be accomplished through a structured learning environment (Perry & Imig, 2008) in which professional practices are modeled by faculty, students are actively mentored, and supervision activities are comprehensive. Students may require support to improve specific dispositions such as openness to professional growth, initiative and dependability, adaptability, respect for human diversity, effective communication skills, and effective interpersonal relations, among others. Although some experiences may need to be tailored for an individual student, they should be aimed at promoting the shared habits of professionalism (Golde, 2007; Shulman, 2005) that are the foundation for building a reputation and public trust.

Faculty should not only lead by example but also explicitly state their decision-making processes regarding professional behaviors. For example, when appropriate, faculty may discuss how they handle their own professional conduct (e.g., giving students space for their own learning rather than providing answers, addressing disagreements with other professionals), as well as the costs and benefits of monitoring their own professional conduct. It is also helpful to describe the public impact when professionalism is compromised. Although many students will internalize behaviors that constitute professional conduct, others require direct instruction on how attitudes and dispositional qualities impact their ability to manifest professional behaviors. Programs should plan for this eventuality, as stress and life events can negatively impact even the most stable student dispositions, not to mention the few students who may turn out to be less well developed than they seemed at the admissions interview (Ladany et al., 2005). Establishing this type of routine feedback provides the essential background for students to be able to benefit from the formative feedback in course work, as well as their ability to seek and benefit from this type of feedback during practicum and internship supervision. Formative feedback should be provided through practicum and internship supervision reviewed by students, faculty, and field-based trainers; summative feedback should be provided in writing at least annually.

Faculty should also be prepared to address known and unknown potential obstacles influencing a student's professionalism. First, faculty should address discrimination issues that students may face in both school and academic-based settings (Adams & Bourgeault, 2003; Cuddy, Fiske, & Glick, 2004). Second, faculty should prepare for the less common, yet time-intensive, impact of the difficult-to-remediate student. Anticipating the need to develop solutions for these challenges is an important component of promoting student professionalism, as well as providing comprehensive training (see also Chapter 8, this volume).

FEMALE STUDENT CHALLENGES

Women in professional practice can face issues of inequality (different treatment) and also inequity (different treatment that are unnecessary and avoidable and also considered unfair and unjust) that may negatively impact their professional development and reputation. With women representing a majority in school psychology (Curtis, Grier, & Hunley, 2004), it is important for faculty to prepare students to determine whether sexism is present and, if so, how to assert themselves effectively.

The data have consistently shown salary differences favoring male psychologists. For example, APA's 2007 data shows that men reported higher salaries regardless of their years of experience, and the difference became more pronounced over 15–19 years and 25–29 years of work experience (Xiaofan, Wicherski, & Kohout, 2008). Similarly, female school psychology trainers reported earning less than their male peers, regardless of years of experience (Crothers et al., 2009). These findings are consistent with the American Association of University Women (2007) report that women have poorer access to organizational resources (e.g., salary, opportunities for promotion, benefits) in comparison with men. Similarly, most women entering the profession of school psychology assume lower salary practitioner roles or choose an academic career in nondoctoral institutions (Akin-Little, Bray, Eckert, & Kehle, 2004). Given these trends, training female students to engage in comprehensive negotiation skills is a requisite component of their professional development.

Female students should also understand that there is some evidence that gender can compete with others' perception of their professionalism. In one study comparing the success of a fictional junior faculty member, authors found that when women were reported to have articles accepted for publication, they were viewed as more professional than those who did not receive a publication, but also less feminine (Cuddy et al., 2004). Similarly, when examining the transition to and from being a professional and being a working mother, Adams and Bourgeault (2003) found that mothers who work risk being reduced to one of two subtypes: homemakers, viewed as warm but incompetent, or female professionals, viewed as competent but cold. Men were not characterized in this way. Instead, when men become fathers, they gained perceived warmth while maintaining perceived competence. Importantly, the characteristic of perceived competence predicted hiring, promotion, and selection for additional education. Unfortunately, results also showed that there is less interest in hiring, promoting, and educating working mothers relative to working fathers and childless employees. Authors from these studies concluded that gender did influence perceptions of professional competence. These results, taken together with recent popular books (e.g., *See Jane Lead* and *Play Like a Man, Win Like a Woman*) promoting the unique success that women can have in leadership positions by highlighting feminine characteristics, such as relationship building, show that female graduate students require preparation for negotiating these complex experiences.

CHALLENGES OF THE DIFFICULT STUDENT

Faculty are typically familiar with and comfortable in remediating student skill difficulties by requiring additional course work, detailed progress monitoring, and reparative work to show mastery. What becomes more difficult is when faculty members suspect a student is not progressing because of a characterological or intractable difficulty (see also Chapter 9, this volume). At some point, the members of the training program realize that they need to determine whether a student's difficulty is due to an impairment, incompetence, or disability. Although these categories do not have an empirical basis that clearly separates these descriptive groups, they are a useful heuristic for training programs to use for planning remediation and in considering dismissal.

The case of impaired performance is characterized by a student who had adequate functioning prior to experiencing psychological instability (Forrest, Elman, Gizara, & Vacha-Haase, 1999). Often trainers may require support services (e.g., psychotherapy or medication compliance) aimed at restoring adequate functioning. Although there is limited empirical support to show that psychotherapy support is an effective intervention for managing the stresses of graduate training (Ladany et al., 2005), program faculty are often satisfied with helping these students remain in their programs. Incompetence describes the student who has never achieved a baseline of competence; this status may be due to characterological or chronic emotional difficulties (Forrest et al., 1999), but it may or may not reach disability status as defined and protected by the Americans With Disabilities Act. In this case, programs are faced with determining whether the student's difficulty interferes with his or her ability to perform essential functions of the professional practice (Ladany et al., 2005). If so, trainers need to be prepared to document the totality of the difficulty. It is also recommended that faculty consult with colleagues, professional organizations (e.g., APA and NASP), and university legal counsel (Ladany et al., 2005). At this point, faculty often consider helping the student to see that the difficulty does not allow for him or her to complete a professional practice program. Counseling a student out of the program may be effective for those students with insight into their functioning. For those students who do not share the concerns of the faculty, dismissal options need to be explored. Faculty who have documented all of the criteria on which all students will be evaluated, as well as detailing the types of disabilities that they can support in their student rights and responsibilities, due process, and grievance policies, have the best ethical and legal standing for dismissing the difficult-to-remediate student (Ladany et al., 2005).

CASE EXAMPLE

Consider the following (real) case example meant to highlight discussions around negotiating discrimination of female students. This was selected because of the high percentages of women entering in to the profession. Issues of cultural and race discrimination may follow a similar model but likely will have to be adapted around the cultural realities of their life circumstances and the setting (e.g., district, university).

Excellent students Jane and John apply for a prime school psychology position at a local district as they are completing internship requirements. There are two positions, and both are thrilled to receive an offer. The administrative salary is not regulated by the union and is determined on the basis of their individual responsibilities. In addition to psychological services, John has agreed to monitor the district's ability to meet state standards by tracking state and national student test scores; Jane has agreed to implement a response to intervention tracking system to determine the adequacy of the reading program. John is offered a salary that is 12% higher than Jane's.

Fortunately, Jane is aware of and has prepared for the possibility of salary inequities. Although she is disappointed (and angry), she is able to put together a strategy for negotiating her current offer, as well as a plan to mark milestones that result in salary increases and leave the door open for additional communications to revisit the plan's success. In her training, she has practiced assertive communication; she is aware that perceived competence can be related to job advancement and as such highlights what she brings to the district with the superintendent. She has practiced conveying the expectation that she deserves a better package, and she is able to manage her feelings that are a result of her feminine role socialization (i.e., demands for her to be thankful; take the one-down position). Although Jane does have some success in the negotiation, she does not get all that she has asked for in the package. Practiced, she is able to hear the superintendent's "no" as "no, not now," rather the often socialized response "no, and that is the final word" that women may ascribe to business interactions. Jane is aware that she will need to highlight her achievements and competence regardless of her feeling that she is bragging or instincts to let others notice her skills. Jane promptly sets out to establish good working relationships with the teachers and administrators in her building, knowing that relationship building can help her to reach the milestones she set. Jane is prepared to balance the business of getting her needs met with her personal preferences for recognition (e.g., salary, status) that are based on her work performance alone. It is important to note that this learning experience is not about targeting John or other men. In this case, John's skills have taken him far and likely will continue to work for him. His habits have resulted in a well-developed professional demeanor. Rather, the purpose is to train for developing professionalism in all students, while facing potential realities.

SUMMARY

Fundamental to the training of future professionals is a combination of education, experience, and appropriate character development designed for building a professional identity and ultimately a professional reputation. Educators have an obligation to instill, develop, and cultivate professional values among graduate students. University and field-based trainers need to share explicit expectations regarding attributes associated with professionalism, such as honesty, integrity, and a commitment to a code of ethics. We have an immense opportunity to influence the formation of behaviors that will serve to drive professional actions. In a broad sense, professionalism may be viewed as a developmental process whereby values and characteristics are fostered and a social-developmental hurdle is passed to cumulatively influence behavior. The importance of nurturing and fostering professionalism throughout graduate school is integral to upholding public trust in the profession of school psychology, as well as within the broader context of psychology.

In sum, this chapter is intended to extend the scope and application of graduate training to explicitly include an important and challenging role of teaching professionalism. The field of school psychology is continually evolving, and as trainers, we need to be able to meet the needs of these changing roles and functions. Graduate training programs should not only keep up with the changing times by modifying their academic training to meet the day-to-day demands and practical needs of practitioners but also cultivate character traits of professionalism. The success of consummate professionals rests on the manner in which they demonstrate their professional values, attitudes, and competencies. This is particularly warranted so that graduates can be marketable and competitive in the pursuit of employment.

RESOURCES

Elman, N. S., Illfelder-Kaye, J., & Robiner, W. N. (2005). Professional development: Training for professionalism as a foundation for competent practice in psychology. *Professional Psychology: Research and Practice, 36*, 367–375.
This article discusses elements of professionalism and professional development and the manner in which they may potentially be assessed within training programs. Moreover, it includes recommendations and practical implications for educators in the promotion of competent psychological practice.

Fagan, T. K., & Wise, P. S. (2007). *School psychology: Past, present, and future* (3rd ed.). Bethesda, MD: National Association of School Psychologists.
This text provides a detailed overview of the roles and functions of school psychologists. It discusses pertinent topics and concepts, including the history, demographics, and current and future trends of the field and practice of school psychology.

REFERENCES

Adams, T. L., & Bourgeault, I. L. (2003). Tension between ideals of feminism and ideals of professionalism, that has the potential to undermine female professional projects. *Women and Health, 38*, 73–90.

Akin-Little, A., Bray, M. A., Eckert, T. L., & Kehle, T. J. (2004). The perceptions of academic women in school psychology: A national survey. *School Psychology Quarterly, 19*, 327–341.

American Association of University Women. (2007). *Behind the pay gap*. Retrieved May 2008 from http://www.aauw.org/research/behindPayGap.cfm

Butler, S. K. (2003). Multicultural sensitivity and competence in the clinical supervision of school counselors and school psychologists: A context for providing competent services in a multicultural society. *The Clinical Supervisor, 22*, 125–144.

Cialdini, R. B., Borden, R. J., Thorne, A., Walker, M. R., Freeman, S., & Sloan, L. R. (1976). Basking in reflected glory: Three (football) field studies. *Journal of Personality and Social Psychology, 34*, 366–375.

Crothers, L. M., Hughes, T. L., Schmitt, A. J., Theodore, L. A., Bloomquist, A. J., Lipinski, J., et al. (2009). Has equity been achieved? Salary and promotion negotiation practices of a national sample of school psychology university trainers. Manuscript in preparation.

Cuddy, A. J. C., Fiske, S. T., & Glick, P. (2004). When professionals become mothers, warmth doesn't cut the ice. *Journal of Social Issues, 60*, 701–718.

Curtis, M. J., Grier, G. E. C., & Hunley, S. A. (2004). The changing face of school psychology: Trends in data and projections for the future. *School Psychology Review, 33,* 49–66.

Elman, N. S., Illfelder-Kaye, J., & Robiner, W. N. (2005). Professional development: Training for professionalism as a foundation for competent practice in psychology. *Professional Psychology: Research and Practice, 36,* 367–375.

Evans, G. (2001). *Play like a man, win like a woman: What men know about success that women need to learn.* New York: Bantam Books.

Fagan, T. K., & Wise, P. S. (2007). *School psychology: Past, present, and future* (3rd ed.). Bethesda, MD: National Association of School Psychologists.

Fischetti, B. A., & Lines, C. L. (2003). Views from the field: Models for school-based clinical supervision. *The Clinical Supervisor, 22,* 75–86.

Flanagan, R., Miller, J. A., & Jacob, S. (2005). The 2002 revision of the American Psychological Association's Ethics Code: Implications for school psychologists. *Psychology in the Schools, 42,* 433–445.

Forrest, L., Elman, N., Gizara, S., & Vacha-Haase, T. (1999). Trainee impairment: A review of identification, remediation, dismissal, and legal issues. *Counseling Psychologist, 27,* 627–686.

Frankel, L. P. (2007). *See Jane lead: 99 ways for women to take charge at work.* Boston: Hachette Book Group.

Golde, C. M. (2007). Signature pedagogies in doctoral education: Are they adaptable for the preparation of education researchers? *Educational Researcher, 36,* 344–351.

Gross, K. J., & Stone, J. (2002a). *Chic Simple Dress Smart Men: Wardrobes that Win in the New Workplace.* New York: Warner Books, Inc.

Gross, K. J., & Stone, J. (2002b). *Chic Simple Dress Smart Women: Wardrobes that Win in the Workplace.* New York: Warner Books, Inc.

Jacob, S., & Taton, J. (2005). Ethical issues in school psychology. In S. W. Lee (Ed.), *Encyclopedia of School Psychology* (pp. 191–195). New York: Macmillan.

Johnson, W. B., & Campbell, C. D. (2002). Character and fitness requirements for professional psychologists: Are there any? *Professional Psychology: Research and Practice, 33,* 46–53.

Ladany, N. L., Friedlander, M. L., & Nelson, M. L. (2005). *Critical events in psychotherapy supervision: An interpersonal approach.* Washington, DC: American Psychological Association.

Molloy, J. T. (1975). *Dress for Success.* New York: Warner Books.

Perry, J., & Imig, D. (2008). A stewardship of practice in education. *Change, 40,* 42–48.

Prasse, D. P. (2002). Best practices in school psychology and the law. In A. Thomas & J. Grimes (Eds.), *Best practices in school psychology IV* (Vol. 1, pp. 57–75). Silver Spring, MD: National Association of School Psychologists.

Shulman, L. S. (2005). Pedagogies of uncertainty. *Liberal Education, 91,* 18–25.

Sternberg, R. J., & Williams, W. M. (1997). Does the Graduate Record Examination predict meaningful success in the graduate training of psychology? A case study. *American Psychologist, 52,* 630–641.

The Random House Dictionary of English Language (2nd ed.). (1987). (p. 1554). New York: Random House.

Tryon, G. S. (2001). School psychology students' beliefs about their preparation and concern with ethical issues. *Ethics and Behavior, 11,* 375–394.

Tymchuk, A. J. (1985). Ethical decision-making and psychology students' attitudes towards training in ethics. *Professional Practice of Psychology,* 6, 219–232.

Welfel, E. R. (1992). Psychologist as ethics educator: Successes, failures, and unanswered questions. *Professional Psychology: Research and Practice, 23,* 182–189.

Welsh, J. S., Stanley, J. D., & Wilmoth, C. (2003). Competency-based pre-internship supervision of school psychologists: A collaborative training model. *The Clinical Supervisor, 22,* 177–190

Williams-Nickelson, C. (2007). Building a professional reputation. *gradPSYCH,* 5(2), 1–2.

Wilson, L. S., & Ranft, V. A. (1993). The state of ethical training for counseling psychology doctoral students. *The Counseling Psychologist, 21,* 445–456.

Xiaofan, L., Wicherski, M., & Kohout, J. (2008, March). *Report of the 2007 APA Salary Survey.* Retrieved December 13, 2008, from http://research.apa.org/salaries07.html#faculty

12 Preparing school psychologists to address the needs of gay, lesbian, bisexual, transgender, and questioning youth

Susan Jacob, Daniel D. Drevon, Christine M. Abbuhl, and Jonnie L. Taton

INTRODUCTION

Jamie Nabozny was continually harassed and physically abused by his fellow students throughout his middle school and high school years because he is homosexual. Classmates called him "faggot" and "queer." In seventh grade, two students performed a mock rape on him in science class in front of 20 other students, who looked on and laughed. When Jaime reported the incident, the principal told him that "boys will be boys" and that he should expect such treatment from his fellow students if he is going to be openly gay. No action was taken against the students involved. In eighth and in ninth grades, Jamie suffered assaults in the school bathroom, including an incident in which he was pushed into a urinal and urinated on by his attackers. In 10th grade, he was pelted with steel nuts and bolts. The same year, he was beaten in school by eight boys while other students looked on and laughed. When Jamie reported the incident, the school official in charge of discipline laughed and told him that he deserved such treatment because he is gay. He later collapsed from internal bleeding that resulted from the beating (Nabozny v. Podlesny, 1996). Jamie subsequently filed a Section 1983 lawsuit in federal court against school officials at his school.

*

School can be a cruel and dangerous place for students who are gay, lesbian, bisexual, or transgender (GLBT) or who differ from their classmates in gender expression. Not only do they face rejection, harassment, and victimization by peers (Massachusetts Department of Education [Mass. DOE], 2006; Swearer & Espelage, 2008), but many teachers are not supportive of sexual minority youth (Russell, Seif, & Truong, 2001). Adolescence also poses special challenges for "questioning" (Q) youth, who are unsure of their own sexual orientation. Partly in recognition of the difficulties

GLBTQ students experience at school, the National Association of School Psychologists (NASP) and the American Psychological Association (APA) developed a joint position statement encouraging school psychologists to take a leadership role in promoting the acceptance of gay, lesbian, and bisexual youth (APA, 1993). Similarly, a NASP (2008) position statement called on practitioners to take steps to ensure that all youth can attend school, learn, and develop their personal identity in an environment free from discrimination, harassment, violence, and abuse.

Based on a survey of members of the NASP, Savage, Prout, and Chard (2004) found that school psychologists generally have positive attitudes toward sexual minority students but low-to-moderate knowledge about gay and lesbian issues. Although willing to address the needs of GLBTQ students, respondents felt inadequately prepared to do so. Consistent with this finding, researchers suggest that graduate psychology programs often provide little training or supervised experience in the area of GLBTQ youth issues (Bahr, Brish, & Croteau, 2000).

LITERATURE REVIEW

For the purpose of this review, the simple abbreviation GLB will be used unless questioning (Q) or transgender (T) youth were specifically included as participant groups in the research cited. The term *sexual orientation* here means a person's physical or sexual attraction to someone of the same or opposite gender. Strong evidence now exists that sexual orientation is determined during the prenatal period by the influence of hormones on the developing hypothalamus, an old part of the brain (in an evolutionary sense) that mediates biological functions (Morris, Gobrogge, Jordan, & Breedlove, 2004). *Sexual behavior* refers to what a person does sexually and with whom. Sexual behaviors that involve perception, memory, and judgment, such as choosing a specific partner and signaling interest, are under the control of the brain's more recently developed center of thought and decision making, the cerebral cortex (Westheimer & Lopater, 2005). Sexual behavior is not always an accurate indicator of sexual orientation. The terms *masculinity* and *femininity* refer to expectations for appearance and behavior based on biological sex. Both biological and environmental influences contribute to the expression of masculine or feminine behaviors (Diamond & Sigmundson, 1997; Hendricks, 2000). Research suggests that the timing, duration, and levels of prenatal hormones impact differentiation of external genitalia, sexual orientation, and masculine or feminine behavior.

Gender identity is a person's deepest inner sense of being male or female. Most individuals, including gays and lesbians, have a gender identity consistent with their biological birth gender, that is, most gay men have an inner sense of being male (a male gender identity); most lesbians have a female gender identity. *Transgender* is an umbrella term used for persons who exhibit gender-nonconforming behaviors and identities (Grossman & D'Augelli, 2006). Transgender persons may be heterosexual, bisexual, or homosexual.

More than 60 years ago, Kinsey, Pomeroy, and Martin (1948) observed that sexual orientation exists as a continuum, not a dichotomy, ranging from exclusively heterosexual, to predominately heterosexual with some same-sex sexual attraction, to bisexual, to predominately homosexual, to exclusively homosexual. Subsequent research supports their findings (Laumann, Gagnon, Michael, & Michaels, 1994; also see LeVay, 1996). Because individuals in the middle range of the continuum experience attraction to both males and females, they may select same-sex or opposite-sex partners at different points in their lives.

It is difficult to estimate how many sexual minority youth attend the nation's schools. The Massachusetts Department of Education (2006) surveyed high school students about their same-sex sexual contacts and whether they identify themselves as gay, lesbian, or bisexual. Results combined over multiple years indicated that 5.3% of students reported same-sex sexual contact; a lesbian, gay, or bisexual identity; or both. Williams, Connolly, Pepler, and Craig (2005) estimated that about 2% of adolescents are uncertain of their sexual attractions, the subgroup of sexual minority youth referred to as questioning. Lock estimates that transgendered youth are "considerably less" than 1% of the population (2002, p. 78).

Youth often are aware of their sexual orientation and gender identity during the elementary school years, much earlier than teachers or parents might expect. Many report feeling "different" from their age-mates in early childhood, often as early as the preschool years. For boys, awareness of sexual orientation occurs around age 9 years; for girls, about age 10 (Troiden, 1998). Self-identification as gay or lesbian occurs at a median age of about 16, with a wide range of individual variability (Floyd & Stein, 2002). Several different models of sexual orientation identity formation have been proposed (e.g., Cass, 1979; Troiden). According to these models, gay or lesbian identity formation involves developmental phases that include questioning one's sexual orientation, accepting the possibility and then the probability of being homosexual, and identity acceptance. For many, identity acceptance is followed by identity pride, a time of immersion in the gay and lesbian culture. During this phase of the coming out process, anger about societal discrimination may be experienced and expressed, and some young adults appear to flaunt their sexual minority status. The milestone experience of immersion in gay and lesbian social networks is typically followed by the final stage of identity synthesis, a time when sexual orientation and gender identity become integrated as one part (but not the only defining part) of self-concept. Floyd and Stein identified varied developmental paths in the coming out process, with some trajectories associated with more positive long-range adjustment.

As noted previously, school can be a cruel place for students who are GLB, or perceived to be by their classmates (Lock, 2002; Swearer & Espelage, 2008). Compared with their heterosexual peers, GLB youth are more likely to be threatened or injured with a weapon at school and to stay home from school or drop out because of feeling unsafe (Mass. DOE, 2006). School environments are most dangerous for males perceived to be effeminate, with the extent of their victimization, peer rejection, and ridicule being proportionate to the degree of their perceived femininity (Martin & Hetrick, 1988; Remafedi, Farrow, & Deisher, 1991). GLB youth also are at increased risk for physical assault at home and in the community compared with their non-GLB age-mates (Lindley & Reininger, 2001; Lock, 2002; Remafedi, 1999).

GLBQ youth are at higher risk for a number of health and developmental problems compared with their non-GLBQ peers, including anxiety, depression, suicide ideation and attempts, alcohol and drug abuse, self-hatred and low self-esteem, sleep and eating disorders, loneliness, life dissatisfaction, teen pregnancy, and sexually transmitted infections (D'Augelli & Hershberger, 1993; Espelage, Aragon, Birkett, & Koenig, 2008; Lock & Steiner, 1999; Mass. DOE, 2006; Williams et al., 2005). Researchers suggest that GLB youth may develop mental health problems in response to the prejudice, discrimination, victimization, and violence they regularly encounter (Meyer, 2003; Ryan & Rivers, 2003).

Studies with population-based samples have consistently found that GLB youth think about and attempt suicide significantly more than non-GLB comparison groups (Garofalo, Wolf, Kessel, Palfrey, & DuRant, 1998; Mass. DOE, 2006; Remafedi, French, Story, Resnick, & Blum, 1998). For example, Garofalo et al. found that 35% of GLB youth reported a suicide attempt within the last year, whereas only 10% of non-GLB youth made such reports. Although young lesbians and bisexual females often express a desire to hurt themselves, gay males are more likely to attempt suicide (D'Augelli, Hershberger & Pilkington, 2001; Remafedi et al., 1998). Youth who recognize or disclose their orientation at younger ages, and those who report sexual experiences at younger ages, were found to be at greatest risk for suicide attempts. In addition, among boys, having a more effeminate appearance increases suicide risk (Pilkington & D'Augelli, 1995; Remafedi, 1999).

Substance use and abuse also is more common among GLB students than their non-GLB age-mates, including use of cigarettes, marijuana, cocaine, inhalants, anabolic steroids, and injectable drugs (Garofalo et al., 1998). Furthermore, GLB youth are more likely to begin using alcohol and illicit drugs before the age of 13 (Garofalo et al., 1998). Risky sexual behavior among GLB youth, such as sexual intercourse before age 13 and sexual contacts with more partners, is also well documented (Garofalo, et al., 1998; Lock & Steiner, 1999; Mass. DOE, 2006; Rotheram-Borus, Rosario, Van Rossem, Reid, & Gillis, 1995; Savin-Williams, 1994).

Many GLB youth experience family discord following the disclosure of their sexual minority status, including negative family reactions, abandonment, and victimization and violence against disclosed youth (D'Augelli, Hershberger, & Pilkington, 1998; Lock, 2002; Savin-Williams, 1994). GLB youth who decide to reveal their orientation to their families risk being forced to leave home. It is estimated that as many as 40% of all homeless youth are GLB (Lindley & Reininger, 2001). D'Augelli et al. (1998) explored family reactions to GLB youth who had disclosed their sexual orientation in a convenience sample of 194 GLB youth ages 14–21. Among youth who had disclosed, 10% of mothers, 26% of fathers, and 15% of their siblings were reported to be actively rejecting. On the other hand, 51% of mothers, 27% of fathers, and 57% of siblings were reported to be fully accepting. These results suggest that family members display a range of reactions to the disclosure of a family member's sexual minority status. Although most family members are fully accepting, a significant percentage are actively rejecting. Moreover, various family members react differently to disclosure.

These studies describing the mental health, physical health, and school and family problems experienced by GLB youth paint a fairly bleak picture. However, it is important to remember that the majority of GLB youth develop into successful and competent individuals despite exposure to varying levels of victimization and violence (Savin-Williams, 1994), that is, they are resilient. Resilience research conducted exclusively with sexual minority youth is limited; however, the available studies suggest that a positive school climate, support from others, positive role models, and high self-esteem are protective (Eisenberg & Resnick, 2006; Espelage et al., 2008; Fenaughty & Harré, 2003; Hershberger & D'Augelli, 1995; Murdock & Bolch, 2005; Oswald, 2002; Williams et al., 2005). Knowledge of modifiable protective factors allows school psychologists to design and implement interventions to enhance resilience among GLB students.

Murdock and Bolch (2005) examined the relationship between measures of school climate (GLB inclusion, victimization, teacher support) and school adjustment, and found that school climate measures were predictive of school adjustment among GLB students. Williams et al. (2005) examined the effects of peer victimization and social support (trust and companionship) from peers and family on psychosocial adjustment in a school-based sample of 97 GLBQ youth and found that social support and level of victimization mediated the relationship between sexual minority status and psychosocial adjustment among male and female participants. Espelage et al. (2008) found that positive school climate and parent support were protective against depression and use of alcohol and drugs. Eisenberg and Resnick (2006), too, found that family connectedness, teacher caring, and school safety were protective against suicide ideation and attempts among GLB youth. Similarly, Hershberger and D'Augelli (1995) found mediating effects of family support on the relationship between victimization and mental health problems and suicide. On the basis of semistructured interviews with gay men, Fenaughty and Harré (2003) suggested that the availability of positive role models may reduce the alienation and isolation that GLB students often experience, particularly among youth who do not know anyone who has openly identified him or herself as being GLB.

Available research suggests that school support groups for GLB students and their allies can be beneficial in a number of ways (Camille, 2002; Goodenow, Szalacha, & Westheimer, 2006). Camille used structured interviews to examine the effects of belonging to a high school gay–straight alliance (GSA) in seven youths, ages 15–18, who self-identified as GLB. Participants reported better attendance and better grades, and they were found to set more ambitious long-range schooling plans after joining the GSA. In addition, participants reported more positive relationships with family, friends, school personnel, and teachers and that they felt safer at school because of their involvement in the GSA.

Goodenow et al.'s (2006) study confirmed these findings using a representative school-based sample of 202 GLB youth. GLB youth attending schools with a support group were less than half as likely to report being threatened or injured with a weapon at school, skipping school because they felt unsafe, and dating violence (defined as being hurt physically or sexually by a date or someone you were going out with) compared with GLB students attending schools without such support groups. Additionally, GLB students attending schools with support groups were less than a third as likely to report two or more suicide attempts during the past year. It appears then that the presence of school support groups is beneficial in that they are associated with less victimization and violence and positive outcomes such as improved academic performance; however, it is not possible to determine whether GSAs played a causal role in the positive outcomes reported, because schools with GSAs may have had a more accepting overall climate than schools without GSAs.

Finally, it is important to note that the simple availability of one caring adult at school has been found to have a positive impact on academic, social, and behavioral indicators among GLB students. GLB students who reported there was a supportive teacher or other staff members at school to talk to about their problems were less likely to use injected drugs or alcohol, and less likely to skip school, than those without such support (Mass. DOE, 2002).

TRAINING FOR PROFESSIONAL ROLES AND FUNCTION

Recent years have witnessed rapid growth in the literature on GLBTQ youth across multiple disciplines. One strategy for providing training to school psychologists on sexual orientation and gender identity is to offer a specialized short course (i.e., 1 credit hour) taught by faculty with expertise in GLBTQ issues. An advantage of this approach is that it allows students to develop in-depth foundational knowledge regarding GLBTQ youth and issues (Bahr et al., 2000). Another approach is to integrate training on GLBTQ youth into existing course work such as graduate classes on child development, diversity, counseling, consultation, practica, and internship. This approach offers the advantage of teaching knowledge and skills specifically relevant to professional roles and practice situations.

There is consensus that training on GLBTQ youth issues should include an affective learning component, a foundational knowledge component, and instruction and supervision in role-specific knowledge and skills (Eliason, 1996; Besner & Spungin, 1998). The affective learning component includes activities and instruction designed to enhance awareness of and emotional sensitively to the experiences of GLBTQ youth, promote increased comfort and confidence when working with GLBTQ youth, heighten learner awareness of their own beliefs and biases regarding GLBTQ persons, and foster a commitment to advocating for the needs and rights of GLBTQ students. Use of the following methods and materials have demonstrated effectiveness in promoting positive attitudes toward GLBTQ persons, as well as challenging stereotypes: panel presentations by GLBT youth (Schreier, 1995); GLBT guest speakers (Bailey, Jacob, & Dobbs, 2008); role plays and guided discussions (Christensen & Sorensen, 1994); assigned readings, including essays by sexual minorities (Athanases & Larrabee, 2003); and providing up-to-date information about human sexuality, particularly regarding the biological foundations of sexual orientation (Bateman, 1996; Ernulf, Innala, & Whitam, 1989; Furnham & Taylor, 1990; Hewitt & Moore, 2002). In addition, opportunities to interact with GLBT faculty, supervisors, and youth are likely to promote understanding among school psychology trainees and heighten their confidence to address sexual minority youth issues in the schools (Bahr et al., 2000).

To provide competent consultation to teachers, parents, and schools, about services that benefit GLBTQ students, school psychologists also need knowledge in the areas of GLBTQ terminology; homophobia and heterosexism; sexual orientation identity formation among GLBTQ youth; the etiology of sexual orientation; educational, physical, and mental health risks confronting GLBTQ youth; and the family as a source of stress or resilience. Practitioners must be prepared to counter outdated ideas and myths about homosexuality that continue to be common even among mental health professionals (Eliason, 1996; see Table 12.1).

Developing role-specific knowledge and skills is the third necessary component of training. Practitioners need to be well informed about evidence-based school interventions and support services that promote resilience among GLBTQ students; familiar with community, state, and national resources to support GLBTQ students; knowledgeable of the legal rights of GLBTQ students and how to foster school policies that safeguard those

Table 12.1 Common Misperceptions Regarding Homosexuality and Transgenderism

---

Homosexuality Is Unnatural

Same-sex sexual behaviors have been found in every human society studied, across cultures and historically (Ford & Beach, 1951). Homosexuality, including same-sex pair bonding, is found among many mammals and birds (Bagemihl, 1999). For example, about 6–8% of rams display a lifelong preference for mating with males rather than females (Roselli, Larkin, Resko, Stellflug, & Stormshak, 2004).

Homosexuality Is Caused by Parent Characteristics and Behavior

On the basis of retrospective clinical case studies, psychoanalysts once theorized that male homosexuality was the result of a boy being raised by overly attentive mother and emotionally withdrawn father; female homosexuality was the result of an over-controlling mother and a detached, passive father (e.g., Bieber & Wilbur, 1962). Subsequent population-based studies have not found any specific family factors that appear to influence sexual orientation (Bell, Weinberg, & Hammersmith, 1981). Psychoanalytic theorists may have failed to consider the bidirectionality of effects, namely, that a father might withdraw from a feminine son, and mothers may attempt to rein in girls who do not conform to gender-role expectations.

Homosexuality Is a Choice

In mammals, compelling research evidence exists that the structure of the anterior hypothalamus influences sexual orientation and that structural differences in this brain region are determined during the prenatal period by the influences of hormones on the developing brain (Morris et al., 2004). In humans, the third interstitial nucleus of the anterior hypothalamus is larger in heterosexual men and smaller in women and homosexual men (Allen & Gorski, 1991, 1992; LeVay, 1991, 1996, Swaab & Hofman, 1990). Parallel findings with sheep show a large interstitial nucleus of the anterior hypothalamus in rams that mate with ewes, but a smaller structure in ewes and rams that attempt to mate only with other rams (Roselli et al., 2004). Hormones can influence prenatal sexual differentiation of the developing brain by means of four pathways. The first is maternal hormone production. A possible link between atypical maternal hormone production and sexual orientation in boys has been identified (e.g., Blanchard, Cantor, Bogaert, Breedlove, & Ellis, 2005). Hormones produced by the developing fetus provide a second possible pathway to atypical influences on sexual differentiation of the brain; a third possibility is individual variability among fetuses in receptivity to hormones. A fourth possibility is that prenatal environmental influences such as medications result in atypical hormonal influences (e.g., Meyer-Bahlburg et al., 1995).

Evolution Would Not Favor Homosexuality, So It Can't Be Genetic

A familial genetic basis for male homosexuality has been found among some, but not all, gay men (Hamer et al., 1993). Hu et al. (1995) identified a link between a small segment of DNA called Xq28 and male homosexuality. This genetic marker is X-linked, meaning that it is carried by females but expressed in males, and could influence sexual differentiation of the brain by influencing hormone production or receptivity in the developing baby.

Homosexuality Can Be "Cured"

Research suggests that reparative or conversion therapies may alter sexual behavior, but the change often is temporary because such therapies do not alter underlying sexual attraction. The American Psychiatric Association cautions that reparative therapists "have not produced any rigorous scientific research to substantiate their claims" of curing homosexuality (1998, p. 2). While counseling may be helpful for reasons other than changing sexual orientation, some clients report that reparative therapies caused them psychological harm (Shidlo & Schroeder, 2002).

Transgender Youth Simply Mislabeled Their Gender in Childhood and Identified With the Wrong Parent

Studies of psychological outcomes of babies born with intersex conditions have prompted researchers to rethink the roles of nature and nurture in shaping gender identity and expression. Prior to the 1990s, and consistent with then-prevailing theories, psychologists believed that gender identity and expression were learned through self-labeling as male or female and identification with the same-sex parent. However, in 1997, Diamond and Sigmundson challenged the long-accepted view that gender identity is learned and malleable, and today there is greater recognition that prenatal differentiation of the brain likely plays a critical role in gender identity and expression. "The sense of who one is—[boy or girl]—is powerful and inborn" (W. Reiner, quoted in Hendricks, 2000, p. 3).

---

rights; skilled in strategies to stop harassment and bullying and promote a positive school environment for all students; and knowledgeable of resources to develop a curriculum inclusive of diversity in sexual orientation and gender expression. The paragraphs that follow explore specific supportive roles that practitioners are likely to hold when working with GLBTQ students and their families and the promotion of school policies to protect GLBTQ students.

PROVIDING SUPPORT AND COUNSELING TO GLBTQ STUDENTS

> Youths with same-sex attractions are similar to all youths, independent of sexual desires. That is, an adolescent is an adolescent, is an adolescent. This should be our basic assumption. (Savin-Williams, 2001, p. 6)

One essential component in supporting GLBTQ students is creating a safe and supportive space for them to be heard and accepted. Nesmith, Burton, and Cosgrove (1999) found that the majority of supportive adults in the lives of GLBTQ youth are non-family members. Practitioners who feel competent and comfortable working with GLBTQ students are encouraged to post a symbol (e.g., an inverted pink triangle sticker) or a GLBT diversity poster (available from http://www.naspweb.org/advocacy/glbt-posters.aspx) to signify that their office is a safe place for students to talk to a caring and nonjudgmental adult. Also, practitioners are encouraged to have information and books on GLBTQ-related topics available so that youth can learn about themselves and as a resource for others. (See Gay, Lesbian, and Straight Education Network in the Resources section.)

GLBTQ adolescents who seek counseling from a school psychologist are confronting sexual attraction and gender identity issues that are part of a normal process of adolescent development; however, these student–clients must cope with the special challenges of self-acceptance and disclosure of a GLBT identity in a heterosexist and homophobic society. The goal of counseling GLBTQ students is to encourage self-understanding and acceptance, reduce the likelihood of risky behaviors, and support the student in making safe and thoughtful choices about disclosure of GLBT status. When working with sexual minority youth, practitioners must take care to safeguard student privacy; school psychologists have an ethical and legal obligation to ensure that a student's sexual orientation or transgender identity status is not disclosed to others without his or her permission (Jacob & Hartshorne, 2007; *Sterling v. Borough of Minersville*, 2000).

Lemoire and Chen (2005) make a compelling case for using Carl Roger's (1987) person-centered counseling as a framework for working with GLBTQ adolescents, with adaptations to meet the unique needs of this group of youth. Consistent with this approach, the psychologist provides unconditional positive regard and empathy; is genuine and open; is sensitive to the student's perception of his or herself and situation; encourages the student to adapt an internal locus of self-evaluation; and provides the student with opportunities for self-exploration and growth at his or her own pace, recognizing that premature disclosure of sexual minority status may be detrimental (Lemoire & Chen). In addition, Lemoire and Chen recommend that person-centered therapy be adapted to GLBTQ youth by incorporating three additional essential elements. The first is providing immediate and explicit validation that being gay, lesbian, or bisexual is a common and healthy variation in sexual orientation. Although less common and not well understood, a transgender identity is most likely a biologically based variation in gender identity and expression (Table 12.1).

The second essential element in counseling GLBTQ youth is providing guided risk assessment regarding disclosure (Lemoire & Chen, 2005). Lipkin (2004) suggested that coming out can contribute to resilience if the response from others, particularly family, is supportive. Although disclosure can result in increased stress, especially at school, over time being out can lead to improved relationships with others, pride, and better mental health. The school psychologist needs to help the student explore how family and friends will react to disclosure and prepare for their reactions, including possible rejection. As noted previously, GLBT students must plan for the possibility that family rejection might mean a loss of emotional and financial support. Family rejection has contributed to the current crisis in homelessness among GLBT youth (Ray, 2006). In addition, GLBT students need to know that it will likely take time for family members to understand and accept their sexual minority status.

The third critically important component in counseling GLBTQ students is identifying support groups for youth where they can make friends, be accepted, socialize, learn about themselves in a safe environment, and have opportunities to interact with GLBT adult role models (Lemoire & Chen, 2005). GLBTQ students who do not have access to youth-oriented support groups may attempt to meet others through risky venues such as the Internet (Lipkin, 2004; Snively, 2004).

WORKING WITH FAMILIES OF GLBTQ STUDENTS

Even when parents are initially accepting of their child's sexual orientation or variant gender expression, full acceptance is a process that takes time. As Lipkin (2004) observed, parents may go through a grieving period during which they mourn the death of the child they thought they had and of their own dreams for their son or daughter. Common emotions include denial, bargaining, guilt, anger, and regret. By explaining that sexual orientation and aspects of gender expression are most likely determined at birth, practitioners can help parents understand that they are not "at fault" for their child's sexual minority status, and hopefully ease the feelings of shame and guilt that some experience.

The goal of counseling the family of a GLBT student is "complete and equal inclusion of the gay student in the family" (Lipkin, 2004, p. 80). However, each family member may progress through the acceptance process in different ways, resulting in within-family alliances, secrets, and tensions that complicate the coming out process and delay full inclusion of a GLBT youth within the family. Families may wish to contact Parents, Friends, and Families of Lesbians and Gays (PFLAG). PFLAG has more than 500 local chapters that provide encouragement and resources to parents, families, friends, as well as GLBT people themselves (http://www.pflag.org).

For parents, allowing a gay child the freedom to meet and date same-sex friends while setting age-appropriate limits on freedom can be challenging. Parents should be encouraged to adopt the same dating rules for a gay teen that they would have for a heterosexual one (Lipkin, 2004); however, it also is important to remember that GLBT adolescents may have more difficulty than their heterosexual peers finding a safe place to socialize. For this reason, the families of GLBT teens should be encouraged to allow their child to attend a youth support group and, if comfortable with GLBT diversity, ensure that their home is welcoming to the GLBT friends of their son or daughter.

SCHOOL- AND COMMUNITY-BASED
GLBTQ YOUTH SUPPORT GROUPS

Because participation in a GLBTQ support group is associated with improved mental health and better school attendance, school psychologists are encouraged to help interested students organize a school-based GSA and to provide guidance to the group. The Equal Access Act of 1984 requires public secondary schools that receive federal funds and that allow other noncurricular student clubs to also permit students to form a club or group to address GLBTQ issues if the request for such a club is initiated by a student. GLBTQ student groups must be treated equally compared with other noncurricular groups; that is, they must be allowed the same access to bulletin boards and meeting space.

Many school districts do not allow noncurricular clubs, however, and even where they are allowed, GLBTQ students may not attend because it increases their visibility at school. Community-based GSAs offer several advantages in comparison with school-based clubs, including anonymity and control over disclosure of GLBTQ status, opportunities to meet students from other schools and to assume leadership and activism roles not feasible in the school setting, and the availability of openly gay or transgender adult role models who typically are not present in rural schools (Snively, 2004).

Students who participate in GSAs may feel empowered to speak up for their own rights. However, it is important for adults to remember that GLBTQ students have limited power, and they may not be developmentally ready for political activism within their school and community. The responsibility to create healthy environments for children and adolescents rests with adults, not youth. Support groups that simply provide an opportunity for fun and acceptance in a safe environment play an important role in fostering healthy development among GLBTQ youth.

ADVOCATING FOR SCHOOL POLICIES
TO PROTECT GLBTQ STUDENTS

Federal statutory law protects public schools students from harassment or hate crimes based on race, color, national origin, sex, and disability. These laws make schools responsible for taking reasonable steps to remedy harassment based on the enumerated characteristics (see Jacob & Hartshorne, 2007). Federal statutory law does not specifically protect students from harassment based on sexual orientation or gender expression. However, some state laws protect GLBTQ students, and in *Nabozny v. Podlesny* (1996; see introductory case scenario), a federal court ruled that under the 14th amendment of the U.S. Constitution, schools must take steps to prevent student-on-student harassment based on sexual orientation. In the years since *Nabozny*, similar lawsuits have been decided or settled in many jurisdictions. These lawsuits were based on claims that school staff violated Title IX of the Education Amendments of 1972 and/or the U.S. Constitution by being deliberately indifferent to student harassment based on sexual orientation or gender expression (e.g., *Flores v. Morgan Hill Unified School District*, 2003; *Theno v. Tonganoxie Unified School District*, 2005; a summary can be found at http://www.aclu.org). In short, school personnel can be held liable for failure to take reasonable steps to protect sexual minority youth. Jamie Nabozny was ultimately awarded $1 million in damages.

As systems level consultants, practitioners can advocate for district antibullying policies that explicitly protect students from harassment and bullying based on sexual orientation and gender expression (see Michigan State Board of Education, 2006, for recommended language). This policy should be disseminated to all district staff, parents, and students. To translate policy into practice, staff must be trained in strategies to stop and prevent bullying, a staff member responsible for receiving and investigating complaints should be identified, and all students must be informed of the likely consequences for violating the district's antibullying policy.

CASE ILLUSTRATION

> When I'm at STRUTS, I have such a good time that I start to wonder "do we really need all of this, just because we're gay?' Then I remember what it's like at school and I know we do need it. It makes us feel like we belong.
>
> Strengthening Teen Resilience Under Tough Situations (STRUTS) youth program participant

Central Michigan University (CMU) is located in Mt. Pleasant, a rural community with a population of about 25,000. Area K–12 schools, especially those in the surrounding communities, have not been accepting of diversity in sexual orientation and gender expression. Beginning fall 2006, a multidisciplinary team of six CMU faculty received a 2-year internal grant to explore ways to promote resilience among GLBTQ teenagers and improve teacher training in the area of GLBTQ youth issues. Biweekly meetings of team faculty and school psychology graduate assistants the 1st year focused on developing an on-campus GLBTQ support program for area youth. In early 2007, a part-time coordinator was hired to develop and oversee the GLBTQ youth program.

The resulting youth program is called STRUTS. STRUTS is a free activity/ social group open to area teenagers ages 13–18, with a special invitation to students who are experiencing stress at school or home because of sexual orientation or gender expression. Activities have included bowling, crafts, cookouts, board games, videos, and attending the Michigan Pride Festival. In addition to providing support for GLBTQ youth and their families,

STRUTS offers consultation to area schools on how to better address the needs of GLBTQ youth.

School psychology students helped plan the STRUTS program, located potential sources of funding, created a GLBTQ reference collection for research purposes, and reviewed and selected age-appropriate books on GLBTQ issues to lend to STRUTS participants. In addition, they participated in evaluation of an instructional intervention designed to foster acceptance of diversity among high school students and evaluation of a state-wide initiative designed to help parents talk to their children about sexuality. School psychology trainees also are pursuing research related to GLBTQ issues, including the effects of the STRUTS program on resilience, school outcomes, and victimization and how to better prepare teachers to meet the needs of GLBTQ students. A doctoral student cofacilitates STRUTS meetings, and additional direct involvement of school psychology trainees is anticipated.

LESSONS LEARNED: RESISTANCE, SUCCESSES, AND SURPRISES

During its first year, school psychology students were privy to team efforts to garner support from area schools for a university-based GLBTQ youth program. In one school, counselors, social workers, and psychologists who initially were enthusiastic about the program were reluctant to write support letters after being told by their principal that "heads would roll" if they did so; however, several did write letters supporting the program in spite of administrative pressure. School psychology students thus had firsthand experience of the negative attitudes toward GLBTQ youth issues that exist in some schools and resistance to change.

School psychology students also were privy to the biweekly meetings of faculty committed to a shared vision, goal-setting sessions led by a consultant with expertise in team leadership, meetings with community agencies and K–12 school representatives, discussions of risk-management of the youth program, and presentations by grant officers. These experiences may help future school psychology practitioners better understand and participate in positive change that involves collaboration among schools, families, and community, and securing funding.

Faculty and school psychology trainees learned from their experiences with STRUTS youth and college-age mentors. We initially worried that only GLBTQ children of CMU-affiliated families would attend STRUTS. However, to our surprise, many STRUTS youth are from low-income rural families. Among youth participants, parental acceptance of their child's GLBT status ranges from very supportive to barely tolerant. Many of the teens withdrew from their neighborhood school because they did not fit in, and they subsequently enrolled in alternative schools or are home-schooled.

In addition, prior to their involvement in STRUTS, some had never traveled outside of their rural community or visited a college campus. The STRUTS program thus allowed participants to experience settings that are affirming of their GLBTQ status, and some are now motivated to attend college.

Five undergraduate student volunteer mentors were recruited and trained for the STRUTS program. These mentors are diverse in sexual orientation, gender expression, and race, and they have formed positive and supportive bonds with STRUTS youth. By involving undergraduate student mentors, STRUTS is able to provide excellent role models for its youth participants, even though many of the faculty and staff involved are not GLBT persons. Overall, we believe that STRUTS has fostered competencies among school psychology trainees and undergraduates that will follow them into their professional lives.

SUMMARY

A *Blueprint for Training and Practice III* identifies diversity awareness and sensitive service delivery as a foundational competence for school psychologists (Ysseldyke et al., 2006, p. 15). In addition, practitioners are expected to be competent in enhancing the capacity of school systems to promote mental health. This chapter explored ways of training school psychologists to better understand and address the needs of GLBTQ students. Strategies to promote a school climate that is affirming of GLBTQ youth were identified.

AUTHORS' NOTES

This research was supported by a Central Michigan University Faculty Insight Team grant and a Michigan Campus Compact Investing in College Futures Brighter Futures grant.

RESOURCES

Lipkin, A. (2004). *Beyond diversity day: A Q & A on gay and lesbian issues in the schools*. Lanham, MD: Rowman & Littlefield Publishers.
This is a readable book for teachers, principals, and school mental health professionals with answers grounded in research and the author's considerable expertise in the area of GLBTQ student issues.

National School Boards Association. (2004). Dealing with legal matters surrounding students' sexual orientation and gender identity. Available from http://www.nsba.org

This is a comprehensive and clearly written guide to legal aspects of schooling for GLBTQ students.

Swearer, S. M., & Espelage, D. L. (Eds.). (2008). *Homophobia and bullying: Addressing research gaps* [Special series]. *School Psychology Review, 37,* 155–227.
This series of articles is devoted to integrating research on bullying and homophobia.

Web Sites

American Psychological Association. (2009). *Healthy Lesbian, Gay, and Bisexual Students project.* Retrieved May 20, 2009, from http://www.apa.org/pi/lgbc/ hlgbsp
Encourages research and disseminates information to address the needs of lesbian, gay, and bisexual students.

Parents, Families and Friends of Lesbians and Gays. (2006). *Home page.* Retrieved May 20, 2009, from http://www.pflag.org
PFLAG is a support, education, and advocacy group.

Gay, Lesbian, and Straight Education Network. (2009). *Home page.* Retrieved May 20, 2009, from http://www.glsen.org/cgi-bin/iowa/all/home/index.html
The Gay, Lesbian, and Straight Education Network is a national organization working toward ending antigay bias in America's schools. This group's Booklink identifies GLBTQ books and resources for grades K–6, grades 7–12, and adults.

REFERENCES

Allen, L. S., & Gorksi, R. A. (1991). Sexual dimorphism of the anterior commissure and massa intermedia of the human brain. *Journal of Comparative Neurology, 312,* 97–104.
Allen, L. S., & Gorski, R. A. (1992). Sexual orientation and the size of the anterior commissure in the human brain. *Proceedings of the National Academy of Sciences of the United States of America, 89*(15), 7199–7202.
American Psychological Association. (1993). *Policy statement on lesbian, gay, & bisexual youths in the schools. Also adopted by the National Association of School Psychologists.* Retrieved June 25, 2009, from http://www.apa.org/pi/ lgbc/policy/youths/html
American Psychiatric Association. (1998). *Position statement on therapies focused on attempts to change sexual orientation (reparative or conversion therapies).* Retrieved June 24, 2009, from http://www.psych.org/Departments/EDU/ Library/APAOfficialDocumentsandRelated/PositionStatements/200001.aspx
Athanases, S. Z., & Larrabee, T. G. (2003). Toward a consistent stance in teaching for equity: Learning to advocate for lesbian- and gay-identified youth. *Teaching & Teacher Education, 19,* 237–261.
Bagemihl, B. (1999). *Biological exuberance.* New York: St. Martin's Press.

Bahr, M., Brish, B., & Croteau, J. (2000). Addressing sexual orientation and professional ethics in the training of school psychologists in school and university settings. *The School Psychology Review, 29*(2), 217–230.

Bailey, N. Jacob, S., & Dobbs, T. (2008). *What do preservice teachers learn from a lesbian guest speaker?* Unpublished manuscript.

Bateman, J. I. (1996). A treatment strategy for changing preservice teachers' attitudes toward homosexuality. *Dissertation Abstracts International: Section B: The Sciences & Engineering, 56*(8-B), 4637.

Bell, A. P., Weinberg, M. S., & Hammersmith, S. K. (1981). *Sexual preference.* Bloomington, IN: Indiana University Press.

Besner, H. F., & Spungin, C. I. (1998). *Training for professionals who work with gays & lesbians in educational and workplace settings.* Washington, DC: Accelerated Development.

Bieber, I., & Wilbur, C. B. (1962). *Homosexuality: A psychoanalytic study of homosexual males.* New York: Basic Books.

Blanchard, R., Cantor, J. M., Bogaert, A. F., Breedlove, S. M., & Ellis, L. (2005). Interaction of fraternal birth order and handedness in the development of male homosexuality. *Hormones and Behavior, 49*, 405–414.

Camille, L. (2002). The impact of belonging to a high school gay/straight alliance. *The High School Journal, 85*, 13–26.

Cass, V. (1979). Homosexual identity formation: A theoretical model. *Journal of Homosexuality, 4*, 219–235.

Christensen, S., & Sorensen, L. M. (1994). Effects of a multi-factor education program on the attitude of child and youth worker students toward gays and lesbians. *Child & Youth Care Forum, 23*, 119–133.

D'Augelli, A. R., & Hershberger, S. L. (1993). Lesbian, gay, and bisexual youth in community settings: Personal challenges and mental health problems. *American Journal of Community Psychology, 21*, 421–448.

D'Augelli, A. R., Hershberger, S. L., & Pilkington, N. W. (1998). Lesbian, gay, and bisexual youth and their families: Disclosure of sexual orientation and its consequences. *American Journal of Orthopsychiatry, 68*, 372–375.

D'Augelli, A. R., Hershberger, S. L., & Pilkington, N. W. (2001). Suicidality patterns and sexual orientation-related factors among lesbian, gay, and bisexual youths. *Suicide & Life-Threatening Behavior, 31*, 250–264.

Diamond, M., & Sigmundson, H. K. (1997). Sex reassignment at birth: Long term review and clinical implications. *Archives of Pediatrics and Adolescent Medicine, 151*, 298–304.

Eliason, M. J. (1996). Working with lesbian, gay, and bisexual people reducing negative stereotypes via inservice education. *Journal of Nursing Staff Development, 12*(5), 127–132.

Equal Access Act of 1984. 20 U.S.C.A. § 4071.

Eisenberg, M. E., & Resnick, M. D. (2006). Suicidality among gay, lesbian, and bisexual youth: The role of protective factors. *Journal of Adolescent Health, 39*, 662–668.

Ernulf, K. E., Innala, S. M., & Whitam, F. L. (1989). Biological explanation, psychological explanation, and tolerance of homosexuals: A cross-analysis of beliefs and attitudes. *Psychological Reports, 65*, 1003–1010.

Espelage, D. L., Aragon, S. R., Birkett, M., & Koenig, B. W. (2008). Homophobic teasing, psychological outcomes, and sexual orientation: What influence do parents and schools have? *School Psychology Review, 37*, 202–216.

Fenaughty, J., & Harré, N. (2003). Life on the seesaw: A qualitative study of suicide resiliency factors for young gay men. *Journal of Homosexuality, 45*, 1–22.

Flores v. Morgan Unified School District, 324 F.3d 1130, 2003 U.S. App. LEXIS 6606, 2003 Cal. Daily Op. Service 3009,2003 Daily Journal DAR 3902 (9th Cir. 2003).

Ford, C. S., & Beach, F. A. (1951). *Patterns of sexual behavior.* New York: Harper and Brothers, Publishers and Paul B. Hoeber, Inc., Medical Books.

Floyd, F. J., & Stein, T. S. (2002). Sexual orientation identity formation among gay, lesbian, and bisexual youths: Multiple patterns of milestone experiences. *Journal of Research on Adolescence, 12,* 167–191.

Furnham, A., & Taylor, L. (1990). Lay theories of homosexuality: Etiology, behavior and cures. *British Journal of Social Psychology, 29,* 135–147.

Garofalo, R., Wolf, R. C., Kessel, S., Palfrey, J., & DuRant, R. H. (1998). The association between health risk behaviors and sexual orientation among a school-based sample of adolescents. *Pediatrics, 101,* 895–902.

Goodenow, C., Szalacha, L., & Westheimer, K. (2006). School support groups, other school factors, and the safety of sexual minority adolescents. *Psychology in the Schools, 43,* 573–589.

Grossman, A. H., & D'Augelli, A. R. (2006). Transgender youth: Invisible and vulnerable. *Journal of Homosexuality, 51,* 111–128.

Hamer, D. H., Hu, S., Magnuson, V. L., Hu, N., Pattatucci, A. M. L., Kruglyak, L., et al. (1993). A linkage between DNA markers on the X chromosome and male sexual orientation. *Science, 261,* 321–327.

Hendricks, M. (2000, September). Into the hands of babes. *John Hopkins Magazine.* Retrieved June 24, 2009, from http://www.jhu.edu/~jhumag/0900web/babeswb.html

Hershberger, S. L., & D'Augelli, A. R. (1995). The impact of victimization on the mental health and suicidality of lesbian, gay, and bisexual youths. *Developmental Psychology, 31,* 65–74.

Hewitt, E. C., & Moore, L. D. (2002). The role of lay theories of the etiologies of homosexuality in attitudes towards lesbians and gay men. *Journal of Lesbian Studies, 6,* 59–72.

Hu, S., Pattatucci, A. M. L., Patterson, C., Li, L., Fulker, D. W., Cherny, S. S., et al. (1995). Linkage between sexual orientation and chromosome Xq28 in males but not in females. *Nature Genetics, 11,* 248–256.

Jacob, S., & Hartshorne, T. S. (2007). *Ethics and law for school psychologists* (5th ed.). Hoboken, NJ: John Wiley & Sons.

Kinsey, A. C., Pomeroy, W. B., & Martin, C. E. (1948). *Sexual behavior in the human male.* Oxford, United Kingdom: W.B. Saunders.

Laumann, E. O., Gagnon, J. H., Michael, R. T., & Michaels, S. (1994). *The social organization of sexuality: Sexual practices in the United States.* Chicago: University of Chicago Press.

Lemoire, S. J., & Chen, C. P. (2005). Applying person-centered counseling to sexual minority adolescents. *Journal of Counseling & Development, 83,* 146–154.

LeVay, S. (1991). A difference in the hypothalamic structure between heterosexual and homosexual men. *Science, 253,* 1034–1037.

LeVay, S. (1996). *Queer science.* Cambridge, MA: The MIT Press.

Lindley, L., & Reininger, B. M. (2001). Support for instruction about homosexuality in South Carolina Public Schools. *Journal of School Health, 71,* 17–22.

Lipkin, A. (2004). *Beyond diversity day: A Q & A on gay and lesbian issues in the schools.* Lanham, MD: Rowman & Littlefield Publishers.

Lock, J. (2002). Violence and sexual minority youth. *Journal of School Violence, 1,* 77–89.

Lock, J., & Steiner, H. (1999). Gay, lesbian, and bisexual youth risks for emotional, physical, and social problems: Results from a community-based survey. *Journal of the American Academy of Child and Adolescent Psychiatry, 38,* 297–304.

Martin, A. D., & Hetrick, E. S. (1988). The stigmatization of the gay and lesbian adolescent. *Journal of Homosexuality, 15,* 163–183.

Massachusetts Department of Education. (2002, July 23). Sexual minority student data. Data presented to the GLBTQ Joint Working Group. Available from Massachusetts Department of Education.

Massachusetts Department of Education. (2006). *2005 youth risk behavior survey results: Executive summary.* Retrieved July 23, 2007, from http://www.doe. mass.edu/cnp/hprograms/yrbs/05/default.html

Meyer, L. H. (2003). Prejudice, social stress, and mental health in lesbian, gay, and bisexual populations: Conceptual issues and research evidence. *Psychological Bulletin, 129,* 674–697.

Meyer-Bahlburg, H. F. L., Ehrhardt, A. A., Rosen, L. R., Gruen, R. S., Vann, F. H., & Neuwalder, H. F. (1995). Prenatal estrogens and the development of a homosexual orientation. *Developmental Psychology, 31,* 12–21.

Michigan State Board of Education. (2006, September 12). Model anti-bullying policy adopted September 12, 2006. Retrieved June 24, 2009, from http:// www.michigan.gov/documents/mde/SBE_Model_Antibullying_Policy_ Revised_9.8_172355_7.pdf

Morris, J. A., Gobrogge, K. L., Jordan, C. L., & Breedlove, S. M. (2004). Brain aromatase: Dyed-in-the wool homosexuality. *Endocrinology, 145,* 475–477.

Murdock, T. B., & Bolch, M. B. (2005). Risk and protective factors for poor school adjustment in lesbian, gay, and bisexual (LGB) high school youth: Variable and person-centered analyses. *Psychology in the Schools, 42,* 159–172.

Nabozny v. Podlesny, 92 F.3d 446, 455–56 (7th Cir. 1996).

National Association of School Psychologists. (2008). Position statement on gay, lesbian, bisexual, transgender, and questioning (GLBTQ) youth. In A. Thomas & J. Grimes (Eds.), *Best practices in school psychology V* (Vol. 1, pp. lxxxix–xcii). Bethesda, MD: National Association of School Psychologists.

Nesmith, A., Burton, D. L., & Cosgrove, T. J. (1999). Gay, lesbian, and bisexual youth and young adults: Social support in their own words. *Journal of Homosexuality, 37*(1), 95–108.

Oswald, R. F. (2002). Resilience within the family networks of lesbians and gay men:Intentionality and redefinition. *Journal of Marriage and Family, 64,* 374–383.

Pilkington, N. W., & D'Augelli, A. R. (1995). Victimization of lesbian, gay, and bisexual youth in community settings. *Journal of Community Psychology, 23,* 33–56.

Ray, N. (2006). *Lesbian, gay, bisexual, and transgender youth: An epidemic of homelessness.* New York: National Gay and Lesbian Task Force Policy Institute and the National Coalition for the Homeless.

Remafedi, G. (1999). Sexual orientation and youth suicide [review]. *Journal of the American Medical Association, 282,* 1291–1292.

Remafedi, G., Farrow, J. A., & Deisher, R. W. (1991). Risk factors for attempted suicide in gay and bisexual youth. *Pediatrics, 87*, 869–875.

Remafedi, G., French, S., Story, M., Resnick, M. D., & Blum, R. (1998). The relationship between suicide risk and sexual orientation: Results of a population-based study. *American Journal of Public Health, 88*, 57–60.

Roger, C. (1987). The underlying theory: Drawn from experiences with individuals and groups. *Counseling and Values, 32*, 38–45.

Roselli, C. E., Larkin, K., Resko, J. A., Stellflug, J. N., & Stormshak, F. (2004). The volume of a sexually dimorphic nucleus in the ovine medial preoptic area/anterior hypothalamus varies with sexual partner preference. *Endocrinology, 145*(2), 478–483.

Rotheram-Borus, M. J., Rosario, M., Van Rossem, R., Reid, H. & Gillis, R. (1995). Prevalence, course, and predictors of multiple problem behaviors among gay and bisexual male adolescents. *Developmental Psychology, 31*, 75–85.

Russell, S. T., Seif, H., & Truong, N. L. (2001). School outcomes of sexual minority youth in the United States: Evidence from a national study. *Journal of Adolescence, 24*, 111–127.

Ryan, C., & Rivers, I. (2003). Lesbian, gay, bisexual, and transgender youth: Victimization and its correlates in the USA and UK. *Culture, Health & Sexuality, 5*, 103–119.

Savage, T. A., Prout, H. T., & Chard, K. M. (2004). School psychology and issues of sexual orientation: Attitudes, beliefs, and knowledge. *Psychology in the Schools, 41*, 201–210.

Savin-Williams, R. C. (1994). Verbal and physical abuse as stressors in the lives of lesbian, gay male, and bisexual youths: Associations with school problems, running away, substance abuse, prostitution, and suicide. *Journal of Consulting and Clinical Psychology, 62*, 261–269.

Savin-Williams, R. C. (2001). A critique of research on sexual-minority youths. *Journal of Adolescence, 24*, 5–13.

Schreier, B. A. (1995). Moving beyond tolerance: A new paradigm for programming about homophobia/biphobia and heterosexism. *Journal of College Student Development, 36*, 19–26.

Sterling v. Borough of Minersville, 232 F.3d 190, 2000 U.S. App. LEXIS 27855 (3rd Cir. 2000).

Shidlo, A., & Schroeder, M. (2002). Changing sexual orientation: A consumers' report. *Professional Psychology: Research and Practice, 33*, 249–259.

Snively, C. A. (2004). Building community-based alliances between GLBTQQA youth and adults in rural settings. In Y. C. Padilla (Ed.), *Gay and lesbian rights organizing: Community-based strategies* (pp. 99–112). Binghamton, NY: Harrington Park Press.

Swaab, D. F., & Hofman, M. A. (1990). An enlarged suprachiasmatic nucleus in homosexual men. *Brain Research, 537*, 141–148.

Theno v. Tonganoxie Unified School District, 377 F. Supp. 2d 952; 2005 U.S. Dist. LEXIS 15317 (D. Kan. 2005).

Title IX of the Education Amendments of 1972, 20 U.S.C.S. § 1681 et seq.

Troiden, R. R. (1998). Homosexual identity development. *Journal of Adolescent Health, 9*, 105–113.

Westheimer, R. K., & Lopater, S. (2005). *Human sexuality* (5th ed.). NY: Lippincott, Williams, & Wilkins.

Williams, T., Connolly, J., Pepler, D., & Craig, W. (2005). Peer victimization, social support, and psychosocial adjustment of sexual minority adolescents. *Journal of Youth and Adolescence, 34*, 471–482.

Ysseldyke, J., Burns, M., Dawson, P., Kelley, B., Morrison, D., Ortiz, S., et al. (2006). *School psychology: A blueprint for training and practice III*. Bethesda, MD: National Association of School Psychologists.

Part IV

Professional issues

13 Certification and licensure for school psychologists

Considerations and implications for education, training, and practice

Tony D. Crespi

State certification and licensure are critical credentials that grant authorization for professional practice involving mental health services. Just as a physician must possess appropriate state licensure to practice medicine, and just as teachers must acquire state certification from the state department of education to teach in the public schools, so too, school psychologists must acquire appropriate state regulatory credentials to practice school psychology with children and families in the public schools (Tharinger, Pryzwansky, & Miller, 2008). Almost uniquely, because school psychologists work within public schools, whereas clinical psychologists work outside the schools, practitioners in school psychology must acquire individual state credentialing granting authorization for professional practice in schools, through either the state department of education or other credentialing body. In addition to such state credentialing, various national certifications are available to authenticate training at the highest training standards and practitioners with appropriate doctoral degrees and post-doctoral residencies may acquire licensure from the state Department of Health Services as a licensed psychologist. Unfortunately, a growing proliferation of state and national credentials, as well as debates and confusion among doctoral and nondoctoral practitioners and organizations, has created confusion for the public, as well as for students and faculty (Hall, Wexelbaum, & Boucher, 2008). This chapter is intended to help provide clarification on the issues.

INTRODUCTION

For those interested in the professional practice of school psychology, state credentialing is a necessity for professional practice. In the United States, credentialing for school-based practice as a certified school psychologist, or in some instances as a licensed school psychologist, is granted from each individual state department of education and is necessary to practice full time in the public schools. In fact, historically, credentialing for school psychologists was first established in New York State in 1935—a decade before Connecticut first established licensure for clinical psychologists. Still, state credentialing does not fully portray the complexity of credentialing issues facing school psychologists.

For a clinical psychologist who has completed a doctorate and holds the requisite postdoctoral experience, credentialing is relatively straightforward: become a licensed psychologist through the state Department of Health Services and possibly become board certified through the American Board of Professional Psychology (ABPP). In contrast, school psychologists may acquire multiple state and national credentials and are confronted by a wide array of credentialing options and opportunities.

On a broad scheme, there are approximately 37,000 school psychologists in the United States, with approximately two thirds trained at the specialist (e.g. post-master's, 60 credit, 6th-year certificate or educational specialist) level. These individuals are typically eligible for state department of education credentialing as a certified school psychologist but not state Department of Health Services credentialing as a licensed psychologist. The former, as clarification, is a nondoctoral credential, whereas the latter requires a doctorate. Furthermore, of the approximately one third of school psychologists who do hold a doctorate, only one third—approximately—of that group hold the doctorate in psychology and are potentially eligible for credentialing as a licensed psychologist. The other two thirds hold doctoral degrees in a variety of other fields (e.g., education). Thus, the majority of school psychologists—including those trained at the nondoctoral and the doctoral levels—are not eligible for credentialing as a licensed psychologist through the state Department of Health Services, nor do they qualify for Board Certification through the American Board of Professional Psychology. For school psychologists, who largely lack doctoral training, and because those with doctorates often acquire the degrees outside areas that would qualify for licensure, the implications are profound and thought-provoking.

Because the majority of school psychologists are working within public education, for most states, this population of practitioners must seek credentialing through each individual state regulatory body. For example, in Texas, those practitioners who wish to practice psychology (regardless of specialty area) must seek licensure specific to school settings through the Texas State Board of Examiners in Psychology. In other states, the credential is through the state department of education. Those who do pursue a doctorate may acquire their advanced degrees in such school-based areas as Educational Leadership, Special Education, or Educational Psychology; whether this meets the requirement of the credentialing agency may vary by state. Educational leadership, for illustration purposes, allows an educator to acquire state department of education certification in administration and offers a school psychologist the opportunity to pursue school leadership positions, overseeing, for example, school psychological, special education, and pupil personnel services. Of note, in public education, such leadership opportunities typically require an additional state department of education credential in administration/educational leadership and can offer a lucrative and rewarding career path.

Given that only one third of school psychologists pursue doctorates, typically in areas outside psychology, it is instructive to realize that not all these school psychologists who pursue that type of doctorate realize that they are not eligible for state licensing. Most of these individuals, however, having previously completed a specialist program in school psychology, are eligible for various state and national credentials, including state department of education credentialing as a certified school psychologist, as well as national credentialing through the National School Psychology Certification Board as a nationally certified school psychologist (NCSP).

With approximately half the states willing to accept that the NCSP meets state certification standards, and with the National Association of School Psychologists serving as the largest professional group representing the specialty in the world, the credential is of note. This means that a newly minted school psychologist who completes a specialist program is eligible to become both a certified school psychologist and NCSP in those states. The NCSP is comparable to the licensed specialist in school psychology (LSSP) granted in Texas, but because of changes in the licensing law and restrictions on the use of the title psychologist, only those LSSPs who also are licensed as psychologists are allowed to use the NCSP designation.

Within this climate, school psychologists credentialed by each individual state department of education provide valuable comprehensive psychological services, often encompassing assessment and diagnosis, counseling and psychotherapy, and consultation and collaboration components. Because credentialing is intended to protect and safeguard the public from unscrupulous practitioners, credentialing remains an important gatepost for entry for professional practice. At the same time, school psychology practitioners have a much wider array of credentialing opportunities, which can create confusion. The intention of this chapter is to examine the context of credentialing issues impacting school psychology practitioners, discuss credentialing options, and provide a resource to help guide and inform beginning practitioners, senor practitioners, training faculty, and related professional colleagues. Additional information is available through the Association of State and Provincial Psychology Boards and the National Association of School Psychologists (NASP).

BACKGROUND

Prospective applicants to school psychology training programs confront an array of degree and professional credentialing options and decisions when exploring the profession and specialty of school psychology. At the present time the majority of practitioners enter nondoctoral specialist programs, which require a minimum of 3 years of full-time (or equivalent) study involving a minimum of 60 graduate credits. Two thirds of these programs are housed within a school of education, and one third are within a department of psychology, usually housed within a college of arts and sciences. Upon completion of the program of study, graduates usually acquire a master's degree (MA, MS, or MEd), as well as a specialist designation, often referred to in different ways in various parts of the country (Certificate of Advanced Graduate Study, Educational Specialist Degree, or Sixth-Year Certificate). Graduates are eligible for endorsement for state certification, and many are also eligible for national certification. These programs will typically hold state approval but may or may not hold approval/recognition from the NASP and accreditation from the National Council on Accreditation of Teacher Education Programs.

Those students interested in making application to doctoral programs must also select from an array of degree and philosophical orientations. Programs may also be housed within a school of education or college of arts and sciences, as well as within a university or a free-standing professional school of psychology. The latter are professional schools training psychologists in a model akin to professional schools training physicians or lawyers. Doctoral degree options include a PhD (doctor of philosophy), PsyD (doctor of psychology), and EdD (doctor of education). At this level, programs may or may not pursue accreditation from the American Psychological Association (APA), as well as recognition from the NASP and NCATE if they are housed in a school of education. These graduates are eligible for additional state and national designations.

For individuals who pursue a doctorate in school psychology as well as in counseling psychology, clinical psychology, or a combined program that combines two or three of these specialties, multiple credentialing options are available. Four clear credentials are possible to attain:

- Certified school psychologist (CSP)
- NCSP
- Licensed psychologist (LP)
- American Board of Professional Psychology (ABPP)

Are other options available for either those who complete a specialist program but either do not possess a doctorate or hold one outside psychology? Certainly. At the University of Hartford, for example, graduates of the NASP-approved school psychology program earn an MS degree with a major in school psychology and a specialization in clinical child counseling, as well as a sixth-year certificate in school psychology. These graduates, following completion of appropriate postdegree supervision, in addition to state and national credentialing as a certified school psychologist and

NCSP, may also become nationally certified counselors (NCCs) and licensed professional counselors (LPCs). With approximately 40,000 NCCs in the United States alone—the examination for which is used to acquire both the NCC and LPC— this credential certainly has a measure of acceptance.

In addition, such an individual who completes a specialist program, as in this illustration, and then subsequently earns a doctorate in school, counseling, or clinical psychology might hold the following:

- CSP
- LP
- LPC
- NCSP
- NCC
- ABPP

Furthermore, as noted, although a clinical psychologist in a psychiatric hospital, for example, with administrative interests might make application for an administrative position, such as director of psychological services, a certified school psychologist interested in a public school position as a director of psychological services or as director of special education would typically be required to acquire a state department of education administrative credential, a credential ordinarily requiring additional course work and training in educational leadership/educational administration and supervision. Although this credential and such opportunities do not ordinarily require a doctorate, they do require additional course work and training specific to the school setting. Clearly, such broad examples illustrate that for students and the public, the maze of credentialing options is of growing complexity.

The multiplicity of credentials available for school psychologists, then, is notable. In addition, related mental health professionals in the schools are also eligible for, and may acquire, an array of markers. A state department of education certified school counselor, for example, might be credentialed as follows: Jane L. Sincere, MA, NCC, NCSC, CCMHC, LPC (NCSC, nationally certified school counselor; CCMHC, certified clinical mental health counselor). Truly, with colleagues potentially holding multiple markers, and with so many markers available for practitioners in school psychology, there can be compelling reasons to appear equally qualified and to consider multiple markers of professionalism. However, although the reasons are compelling, the proliferation of credentials also creates confusion.

In reality, this overview, although seemingly all-encompassing, actually only portrays a sampling of the options. A school psychologist might also consider a much wider array of additional *national* credentialing options, with credentials in areas ranging from substance abuse counseling to family counseling to play therapy. Moreover, most of the associations offering such markers are licensed by individual state boards to offer such designations. At the same time, such a growing number of designations itself suggests the confusion experienced by both the public and professionals alike.

Within neuropsychology, an area of growing interest and discussion for both parents with special needs children and professionals interested in developing specialty skills, there exist a wide array of national credentialing choices.

Selective credentialing options might include the following:

- Jane Doe, PhD, ABPP, ABCN (ABCN, American Board of Clinical Neuropsychology)
- Jane Doe, PsyD, ABPN (ABPN, American Board of Professional Neuropsychology)
- John Doe, PhD, ABPdN (ABPdN, American Board of Pediatric Neuropsychology)

In a broad fashion, these credentials all require a doctorate in psychology and appropriate postdegree training and experience. Still, not all credentials in neuropsychology require this level of training. For example, although it is somewhat controversial, the American Board of School Neuropsychology awards the ABSNP diploma in school neuropsychology—a new term—to those school psychologists with specialist training and supervision. Notably, this stands as an illustration of the growing multiplicity of credentials. Who gauges appropriate entry to practice in neuropsychology? Is a doctorate necessary? Many boards would suggest such training is necessary but this relatively new credential suggests a division in viewpoints. Ultimately, who is to decide? Who decides legitimacy?

Particularly problematic is that the growing number of so-called "vanity boards" (credentialing bodies that may be approved by a state but are of varying levels of value), as well as more accepted and recognized credentialing options, means that a school psychologist can accrue a vast array of designations. What markers are of value? Will the public understand distinctions among credentials?

BOARD CERTIFICATION: THE HIGHEST STANDARD FOR PRACTICE

The ABPP board certification

For those interested in the highest credentialing standards in professional psychology, it is educative to know that ABPP board certification is intended to assure the public and profession that a school psychologist possesses the education, training, and experience of a postdoctoral specialist. This requires a doctorate and/or postdoctoral preparation with 3 or more years of qualifying experience and includes appropriate credentials review and rigorous examinations and interviews.

Requirements include a doctoral degree from a program in psychology that at the time the degree was granted was accredited by the APA or Canadian Psychological Association (CPA) or was listed in the publication *Doctoral Psychology Programs Meeting Designation Criteria* (http://www. nationalregister.org/index.html). Applicants credentialed by the National Register of Health Service Providers in Psychology or the Canadian Register of Health Service Providers in Psychology qualify.

Applicants must possess licensure or certification at the independent practice level. (Limited exceptions exist for doctoral preparation prior to 1983, and allowances are included for formal retraining). Furthermore, the applicant must have completed a 1-year (or 2-half-year) internship of at least 1,500 hr. In addition, at least 1 year of supervised experience as a licensed/certified psychologist is necessary. Two letters of endorsement must be sent with the application from psychologists attesting to the applicant's practice as a school psychologist and professional. An endorsement from an ABPP Diplomate or APA Fellow is welcomed.

The examination process is comprehensive and includes the following areas: (a) assessment and intervention, (b) science base and application, (c) ethics and legal foundations, (d) professional identification, and (e) consultation and supervision.

In a specific way, the process includes three phases: (a) Stage I involves initial application and review; (b) Stage II involves preparation of two practice samples, meeting board standards, and a professional statement; and (c) Stage III involves a rigorous oral examination by an examination committee of three board-certified specialists in school psychology. The examination is intended to examine competencies and skills within the specialty and appropriately explores ethical, legal, and professional components related to the specialty. In general, successful attainment of board certification is considered the highest standard for professional practice. Still, although board certification is considered the highest marker of excellence, it is also notable to recognize the fact that few school practitioners will qualify for the credential, and few (if any) schools will provide an incentive or reward for the attainment of such a credential. Partially for such reasons, only a minority of school psychologists ever pursue this designation.

PROFESSIONAL ROLES AND FUNCTIONS

For school psychology overall, there are few differences between doctoral and nondoctoral practitioners. The three roles of (a) assessment and diagnosis, (b) counseling and psychotherapy, and (c) consultation and collaboration remain as a cornerstone or practice. Still, how and to what the degree school psychology programs emphasize different facets of these components varies greatly among training programs. Partially because of such differences, the emphasis on different practitioner credentials can also vary.

In a broad way, although specialist programs typically target broad training roles in all three domains, it is generally accepted that PhD programs will emphasize the training of graduates who will pursue at least partial components of a career involving a dedication to research and scholarship. In somewhat of a contrast, a PsyD graduate would most logically pursue a career dedicated to professional practice. Of course, interests may evolve during a career, and certainly there are PhD graduates developing practitioner-oriented careers and graduates with the PsyD developing academic, teaching, and research-oriented careers emphasizing substantial scholarship. Looking at the EdD degree, in contemporary training, the use of the EdD is of decreasing use by school psychology training programs. Today the EdD is most often held by:

1. Senior faculty trained in a different era
2. Graduates of a rare few programs still using the degree
3. Doctorates with related degrees (counselor education, family therapy, etc.)
4. Practitioners with a degree in educational leadership

Of particular consequence, those practitioners with a PhD or PsyD who may identify as a school psychologist and who may have completed a specialist program in school psychology and later earn a PhD or PsyD cannot be assumed, though, to hold that degree in school psychology. Holders of a PhD, for example, may hold the degree in such areas as clinical psychology, counseling psychology, educational psychology, or educational leadership, as well as in such areas as child and family studies, educational technology, etc. Truly, the options are limitless.

The PsyD degree provides the public with an outward marker of a doctoral degree in professional psychology, which may reduce some confusion. Most typically the degree is in established professional areas: school psychology, clinical psychology, counseling psychology, and organizational psychology. Still, a school psychologist might acquire a PsyD in clinical psychology and possess identification in both specialties.

For the most part, graduates of all school psychology training programs—at both nondoctoral and doctoral levels—are eligible for credentialing by a state department of education as a certified school psychologist, or in Texas as a licensed specialist in school psychology. The subset of those holding a doctorate in school, counseling, clinical, and combined programs may be eligible for credentialing as a licensed psychologist through either the state Board of Examiners of Psychologists or the state Department of Health. Within schools, whether there is a distinction between responsibilities for nondoctoral or doctoral level practice varies by state, district, and even school. With this in mind, it is important that individuals not assume that all graduates receive, acquire, and hold equal levels of expertise in all three training areas. Consider the following.

Counseling and psychotherapy: how many specific courses in counseling and psychotherapy were required?

Was one class in counseling all that was required? Four classes? How much clinical supervision was provided and where was the experiential training received? A graduate with two counseling classes and trained in elementary schools may not be comparable to a graduate who completes four classes and 1 year of training in a high school setting followed by an internship in a children's psychiatric unit, with time divided between a hospital-based school and the clinical department.

Can the graduate discuss differences in counseling theories and orchestrate a psychoeducational group for disruptive children? Could a practitioner counsel a child who is actively suicidal? Can a graduate select among a systems, structural, or strategic intervention for a family with an autistic child? In gauging counseling skills, the mix is truly complex. In a basic way, the amount, degree, and extend counseling skills are developed can vary greatly among programs. Not all graduates, whether trained at the specialist or doctoral level, are trained equally.

Assessment and diagnosis

Training in psychological assessment and diagnosis can also vary widely. Although most programs routinely train graduates in cognitive assessment tools, training in personality assessment can vary quite widely across programs. Still, looking at cognitive tools, can the graduate evaluate a processing deficit? Can the graduate distinguish between reading and mathematical forms of learning disabilities? What about testing memory and learning style? Content and focus can vary among programs.

Looking at personality variables, if asked to evaluate an adolescent remanded to a local juvenile justice program for dangerous behavior, would a particular program impart the tools necessary to assess and later diagnose this child? Does the program graduate teach skills necessary to distinguish between a child who demonstrates aggressive and assaultive behavior toward family members and one demonstrating such behavior toward strangers? What about fire-setting behavior? Applicants and employers need to recognize that programs vary in philosophy and that although core training may appear similar, actual acquired skill expertise can vary widely among program graduates.

Consultation and collaboration: can a particular graduate identify different consultation models?

Are overall clinical skills sufficient for excellence in consultation and collaboration? Does a program approach classroom consultation using contemporary assessment tools to assess and suggest changes in classroom behavior and curriculum? Does the program teach incorporating innovations in consultation from school psychology, organizational consultation, and systems theory? As the proliferation of knowledge in psychology evolves, it is increasingly challenging for practitioners to remain up-to-date. Similarly, not all programs teach consultation with equal rigor. The University of Maryland, for example, using the work of Dr. Sylvia Rosenfield, is well known for innovations in teaching and mentoring in this area. Unfortunately, not all programs offer equal rigor. As graduates move forward, however, reading such work can propel our work forward.

Overall, then, applicants, graduates, and faculty must all recognize that these three facets represent highly challenging knowledge and skill sets for graduates. No one student, sadly, can graduate with exemplary expertise in three areas. At best, graduation provides an entry card for professional practice. Unfortunately, the very fact that this means competence cannot be equally attained is not easily grasped and may itself lead to dangerous behavior. At the doctoral level, a postdegree residency helps ensure continuing learning. Most states also will require continuing development. Still, how competent are each of us in each skill area? My self-disclosure: I'm not competent in all areas. There—it's been said. How many graduates would say the same? More important, how many will develop plans to ensure developing skills in areas of weakness?

CONSIDERATIONS FOR CLINICAL SUPERVISION

Clinical supervision serves as a valuable continuing education tool to upgrade knowledge, enhance skills, and expand breadth and depth of expertise for school psychologists. Within graduate education and training, supervision occurs, typically, both on-site during the practica and internship and during concurrent university-based supervision components. Still, with this in mind, not all supervisors are equal and not all experiences comparable. In fact, not all supervisors hold similar credentials, and this facet alone can have implications for credentialing.

Evaluating supervisor expertise

1. Can the supervisor provide information on characteristics of the client population you may evaluate and counsel?
2. Can the supervisor refine and expand psychological assessment skills?

3. Can the supervisor refine and expand counseling and psychotherapy skills?
4. Can the supervisor refine and expand consulting and collaboration skills?
5. Can the supervisor refine multicultural awareness and competence?
6. Can the supervisor target skills for new and expanding roles and functions?
7. Can the supervisor address limitations of skills sets?
8. Can the supervisor monitor the effects of working with children?
9. Can the supervisor promote acquisition of new skills as roles change and evolve?
10. Can the supervisor upgrade ethical and legal knowledge base?

From a credentialing perspective, consider the following questions.

Evaluating supervisor credentialing

1. *Question*: Can the supervisor's credentials be used to support credentialing as a licensed professional counselor?
   Answer: In most states, supervision must be from a licensed professional counselor, licensed psychologist, or licensed clinical social worker. Most school psychologists lack such credentials. As such, supervision may need to occur postdegree.
2. *Question*: If you complete an APA-approved PhD is your internship also necessarily APA approved?
   Answer: Universities and training sites each, individually, make application for accreditation. Thus, one might complete both an APA-approved degree and internship, or complete an APA-approved degree and non-APA-approved internship, or complete a non-APA-approved degree and APA-approved internship.
3. *Question*: If my supervisor is not a licensed psychologist but is a certified school psychologist, will that be adequate for credentialing as a licensed psychologist?
   Answer: Although applicants should contact individual state licensing boards for specifics, it would generally be expected that the internship would be supervised by a licensed psychologist.
4. *Question*: Do the credentials of the supervisor actually matter from a real-world perspective?
   Answer: Supervisor credentials can vary, and this can matter if a graduate is interested in seeking supplemental credential beyond that of a certified school psychologist. Individuals interested in acquiring credentials such as that of a licensed psychologist or licensed professional counselor, for example, must meet specific state supervision hourly requirements, and supervisors also must hold specific credentials. Not all supervisors can or do meet all standards.

5. *Question*: Does NASP and APA accreditation truly matter?

   Answer: It depends! From a practical perspective, the answer depends upon individual goals and professional aspirations. Certainly, credentialing as a licensed psychologist can be expedited much more easily if one is a graduate of an APA-accredited program. In addition, certain academic sites may prefer a degree from an approved program. Similarly, NCSP certification is much easily negotiated when graduating from a NASP-approved program. In addition, portability of credentials from state to state can be more easily accomplished when graduated from programs holding certain accreditation/approval markers. On the other hand, geographic and family obligations may prevent attendance at such programs, and evolving and changing professional goals may also impact decision making. The ultimate answer is that it depends on you.

In a basic way, clinical supervision represents one of the cornerstones of practicum and internship training. Because of this, supervision is vital. Students should know, of course, that individual state standards may vary. Graduates need to thoughtfully consider long-term goals and objectives. Whatever program considered, it is best to read individual state training standards and try to select programs and supervisors that can meet those goals and objectives.

CASE ILLUSTRATION I: JOHN EAGER, MS, EDS, NCSP

Case background

John Eager applied and was accepted to an NASP-approved 66-credit school psychology program. He completed his practicum in an elementary school and his internship in a local high school with a senior school psychologist also trained at the specialist level. John received weekly individual supervision during both years. Upon graduation, John acquired his credentialing as a certified school psychologist from the state department of education and acquired his national certification as an NCSP. Almost immediately John accepted a position in a local middle school. At this point, he has made inquiry as to possible options he might explore in private practice. Do options vary geographically? Can he work privately?

Case answers

Across the United States, there are differing state legislative standards governing title and practice rights for "independent practice." In Connecticut, for example, there is legislation allowing a certified school psychologist to work within the private sector. However, the bill does not include vendorship, which would grant third-party reimbursement from insurance carriers, and it requires that practitioners work for several years in Connecticut in order to acquire the third (highest) certification in a three-tier state department of education certification system. In Texas, on the other hand, he is not able to even use his NCSP designation because of the restrictions in the licensing law on the use of the term "psychologist," and even if he were licensed as a specialist in school psychology, the law is very clear that this is applicable only in a school setting.

How should this individual proceed? The first step would likely be to contact the state school psychological association to learn about laws governing, overseeing, and/or restricting who can practice independently. Second, what are the restrictions on title use involving private practice in the interested individual state? What other options might be considered? Would this individual be eligible for other state credentials, such as that of an LPC? Although most counseling licensure boards require a degree in counseling and outline specific classes and training requirements, sometimes an individual with an applied degree, such as in school psychology, may qualify as possessing a "related degree." This credential, the LPC, may offer private practice opportunities.

In this case, then, this individual should understand that without a doctoral degree and the appropriate training he may not use the title of psychologist, nor would he qualify for credentialing as a licensed psychologist. Violations of these restrictions would customarily violate state law and can be punishable through the court system, as well as leading to decredentialing.

CASE ILLUSTRATION II: SUSAN STUDENT, PSYD, NCSP

Case background

Susan recently—4 years ago—completed her doctor of psychology degree in school psychology from an APA-approved program. She holds state department of education credentialing as a certified school psychologist, she is a nationally certified school psychologist, and during her first year of employment she completed the necessary supervision experiences to complete a postdoctoral residency in psychology that meets state Department of Health Services standards to sit for examination as a licensed psychologist. She is interested in a university teaching post but was informed that she cannot apply as she does not possess a PhD and she must first become a licensed psychologist. She has asked for guidance on her career options.

Case answers

By virtually any professional yardstick, this is a highly educated and well-credentialed individual. Although the majority of university faculty hold the PhD, there is no requirement that mandates specific degrees. In fact, a faculty member might also hold the PsyD or the EdD degree. Similarly, there is no university standard requiring that faculty be a certified school psychologist or licensed psychologist. At the same time, certain credentials and experiences may enhance an application, such as a record of scholarly publications, professional presentations, and certain applied credentials, such as state certification, state licensure, and national designations (e.g., NCSP and ABPP). In addition, certain programs may require such credentials, consistent with accreditation requirements from APA or NASP around recommended faculty credentials, whereas other programs may not. In this case, the individual may need to examine the kind of school in which she would like to teach and consider building background experiences involving scholarship and professional presentation. Universities typically weigh scholarship, teaching, and service in promotion and tenure decisions and often examine potential colleagues with these markers in hand.

CASE ILLUSTRATION III: JANE STUDENT, MS, NCSP

Case background

Jane completed a 66-credit MS program in school psychology and subsequently accepted a position as a certified school psychologist. She earned her degree from a NASP-approved program and holds the NCSP. She has worked for 10 years and is interested in becoming a supervisor of pupil services. she has asked her advisor for guidance in selecting a PhD or EdD programs in educational leadership. Given her goals, she wonders which program makes the most sense and whether she would be eligible to work as a licensed psychologist when she completes the degree. She notes that in her area directors often earn more than $100,000 a year, and she feels the degree and administrative credential can open a very lucrative career path. How should she proceed?

Case answers

In this case, this individual recognizes that a doctorate in educational leadership and credentialing in school administration can be quite lucrative. In fact, to earn a doctorate in school psychology and to subsequently earn administrative certification would entail considerably more time than only earning a doctoral degree in educational leadership. At the same time, this degree will not qualify for credentialing as a licensed psychologist. Typically, helping to point out this restriction is important. In truth, individuals simply should be informed that certain degrees and credentials can open certain career options, but not all options. This would not be degree of choice if she wished to teach school psychology. It is logical for a career in school administration.

CONSIDERATIONS AND CONCLUSIONS

In a basic way, credentialing is intended to protect the public and provide assurance of certain competencies and educational attainments (Tharinger et al., 2008). Because of the vast number of different types of designations available to school psychologists, however, as well as the heterogeneous nature of state and national regulatory credentialing, certification and licensing has assumed a growing presence and importance. In school psychology, the array of credentials offered to practitioners is of concern, as school psychologists can and often do acquire multiple markers as a routine part of professional practice.

The examples and discussion raised here underscore the developing trend toward an increasing number of credentials. Indeed, most school psychologists who are trained at the nondoctoral specialist level of training typically complete a minimum of 60 credits and are eligible to become certified School Psychologists through the state department of education and nationally certified school psychologists through the National School Psychology Certification Board.

In addition to state and national certification, doctorates in school psychology may also become licensed psychologists through the state Department of Health Services, as well as board-certified specialists through the American Board of Professional Psychology. Although these four credentials are accepted as valuable, and even the highest markers of excellence, they are only part of the available array. Many graduates might also pursue additional accepted and respected designations that might include NCC and LPC.

With so many legitimate options, the array can be daunting. For school psychologists, state department of education and National School Psychology Certification Board credentialing provide a base vehicle to substantiate education and training experiences at the nondoctoral level, whereas at the doctoral level, state Department of Health Services licensing and ABPP Board certification offer the public and related professionals appropriate markers to substantiate specialty training at the postdoctoral level. Still, the problem of "credential creep" cannot be discounted. How will university programs maintain course loads to meet a variety of accrediting bodies? How will professionals and the public address the growing array of credentialing options? One possibility is that the school psychology community, through a variety of associations, might begin to talk about these markers in order to better address the issue. Another possibility is that associations might consider subconferences on credentialing in order to better refine and narrow specialty boards. Unfortunately, the solutions are not easy. At the same time, the vast array of options, in school psychology alone, suggests a possible area of concern. How many credentials should a graduate of a school psychology program pursue? What markers should faculty possess, model, and mentor? Truly, the array is problematic. Sometimes more is not better. Sometimes it is only more.

RESOURCES

American Board of Professional Psychology. (n.d.). *Home page.* Retrieved May 22, 2009, from http://www.abpp.org/abpp_public_about.htm
This Web site provides additional information on the ABPP and the various specialty areas in which this credential can be obtained.

Association of State and Provincial Psychology Boards. (n.d.). *Handbook of Licensing and Certification Requirements.* Retrieved May 22, 2009, from http://www.asppb.org/HandbookPublic/handbookreview.aspx
The *Handbook* includes a variety of information, including score requirements on the licensure exam, supervision required, degrees required, and so on. Each topic is available by jurisdiction (state), so students can obtain needed information on the state of interest. There is also a section on mobility of licensure.

Hall, J. E., Wexelbaum, S. F., & Boucher, A. P. (2008). Doctoral student awareness of licensure, credentialing, and professional organizations in psychology: The 2005 National Register International Survey. *Training and Education in Professional Psychology, 1,* 38–48.
This article reports the results of a survey of doctoral students and their awareness of various credentialing requirements and processes; it also includes recommendations for training programs.

National Association of School Psychologists. (2000). *Standards for the credentialing of school psychologists.* Bethesda, MD: Author. Retrieved September 27, 2008, from http://www.nasponline.org/standards/FinalStandards.pdf
This report summarizes the standards agreed upon by the Delegate Assembly in relation to credentialing.

REFERENCES

Hall, J. E., Wexelbaum, S. F., & Boucher, A. P. (2008). Doctoral student awareness of licensure, credentialing, and professional organizations in psychology: The 2005 National Register International Survey. *Training and Education in Professional Psychology, 1,* 38–48.
Tharinger, D. J., Pryzwansky, W. B., & Miller, J. A. (2008). School psychology: A specialty of professional psychology with distinct competencies and complexities. *Professional Psychology: Research and Practice, 39,* 529–536.

14 Continuing education

Fostering lifelong learning

Julie Snyder, Ralph E. Cash, Sarah Valley-Gray, and Kristen Cunningham

INTRODUCTION

School psychologists are ethically obligated to participate in lifelong learning activities to ensure the highest standard of care for the children, families, and educators they serve (Brown, 2002). This commitment is evident in graduate training program standards, where continuing professional development is explicitly taught and modeled. As practitioners, continuing professional development is facilitated throughout one's career through professional practice societies such as the American Psychological Association (APA) and the National Association of School Psychologists (NASP). However, the onus of creating a lifelong learning path is upon the practitioner.

Continuing education, in the manner in which it is delivered today, was initiated by the American Medical Association (AMA) in the early 1900s. In 1910, the AMA released the Flexner Report on Medical Education in the United States (Kokemueller & Osguthorpe, 2007) detailing training models not only for undergraduate and postgraduate education, but also for ongoing learning activities for practicing physicians. The report emphasized the value of routine participation in state and national conferences to ensure that the most effective treatments were being utilized. Recognizing the importance of postgraduate education, the AMA formalized the term *continuing medical education* (CME) and defined the objectives, goals, and evaluation procedures for recognizing an activity as a CME unit (Dryer, 1962). Maryland initiated the first continuing education requirements for renewal of psychology licensure in 1957 (Neimeyer, Taylor, & Phillip, 2008). However, the APA and the NASP did not follow suit until the 1970s, when they devised continuing education programs. The goal was to facilitate the ease with which working professionals maintained competencies, skills, and abilities (Armistead, 2007). The APA initially focused on establishing criteria and ensuring quality programming for continuing education activities, which resulted in the development of what is today known as the Sponsor Approval System. Currently, there are approximately 750 APA-approved providers of continuing professional development for psychologists, with specific information regarding programs and providers available on the association's Web site (APA, 2006).

NASP began a voluntary continuing professional development (CPD) program in 1975 that included assessment, intervention, and program development as the primary areas of focus (Walker, 1977). In April of 2005, NASP's professional development guidelines were further defined, with the establishment of the NASP approved provider (AP) system. The AP system was developed to recognize other organizations and entities that meet NASP guidelines for the provision of professional development activities. Like those of the AMA, the purposes of APA and NASP continuing education programs are to ensure that practitioners maintain competence over time, remain current with developments in the field, expand their professional development, and provide high-quality services to the public.

Currently, 44 states require psychologists to participate in continuing professional development activities for certification or licensure renewal (Armistead, 2007). State boards of education that accept the Nationally Certified School Psychologist (NCSP) credential as a route to certification require that school psychologists meet the renewal requirements established by NASP's National School Psychology Certification Board (NSPCB). At present, the NSPCB requires the completion of 75 hr of continuing professional development activities within a 3-year period for certification renewal (Merrell, Ervin, & Gimpel, 2006). Beginning in 2010, a percentage of the 75 renewal credits must be earned in NASP- or APA-approved professional development activities. All school psychologists who are employed in school districts in states that do not recognize the NCSP as a route to certification must meet the credentialing and credential renewal requirements established by their state's department of education, board of psychology, and/or other credentialing body.

Whereas the department of education certification or licensure renewal process is typically required for school psychologists working within public school systems, the board of psychology's process has generally been instituted for school psychologists working across various settings, including private practice and, occasionally, within school systems. Although the APA provides recommendations for continuing education through its Model Act for the State Licensure of Psychologists (1987), it looks to individual states to specify the number of hours required for licensure renewal. Although the number of continuing education hours required for licensure renewal varies from state to state, most psychology licensing boards require the completion of between 20 and 40 hr every 2 years (Sharkin & Plageman, 2003).

A wide variety of continuing professional development activities are available in most states, and practitioners may attend workshops on a diversity of topics; however, many state licensing/certification boards require credentialed professionals to participate in training in specified areas such as ethics or domestic violence (Armistead, 2007). Continuing education presentations are routinely offered by university training programs, private organizations, national and state professional associations, and state agencies. Furthermore, many states also allow for some credits to be obtained through course instruction, presentation or publication of papers, attendance at board of psychology meetings, and home study (Sharkin & Plageman, 2003).

Although involvement in continuing education activities is typically required for credential renewal, it is also an ethical responsibility for school psychologists to participate in ongoing learning regardless of state requirements. Ethical codes of both APA and NASP state that psychologists need to participate in ongoing activities in order to develop and to maintain their competency (APA, 2002; NASP, 2000a). The ethical codes help to ensure that psychologists maintain current working knowledge to enhance their functioning.

The importance of continuing education cannot be overemphasized. Failure to incorporate lifelong learning into everyday practice may also result in professional skills that become obsolete (Armistead, 2007). Dublin (1972) identified the half-life of professional competence of a psychologist as 10–12 years. Hynd, Pielstick, and Schakel (1981) maintained that because of the rapidly changing nature of the field of school psychology, practitioners can lose approximately half of their competence in 3–5 years. The rapidly increasing growth of scientific knowledge renders that half-life even shorter (Vandecreek, Knapp, & Brace, 1990). Failure to engage in lifelong learning can result in an inability to integrate new and effective techniques, interventions, and assessments into practice. As a result, the needs of the populations served by these professionals may suffer or be left unmet.

Although there is general agreement regarding the importance of lifelong learning, the task of training professionals for an ever-evolving skill set is complex. Ysseldyke et al. (2006) argue that most practitioners reach the "expert" level of competence in one domain of school psychology after approximately 5–10 years of practice and with consistent participation in continuing professional development activities. To achieve this goal, the importance of lifelong learning must be firmly established early in graduate training, with a focus on learning how to learn. That is, trainees should come to understand the importance of grasping and applying knowledge, not only during formalized training but throughout their career (Knoff, Curtis, & Batsche, 1997).

LITERATURE REVIEW

Although participation in continuing education activities is recognized by both APA and NASP as a key component in the lifelong professional development of the competent professional, evidence regarding the effectiveness of existing delivery systems is nonexistent. As Vandecreek et al. (1990) highlighted, there are four ways to categorize research within this area.

These studies include those that evaluate participant satisfaction, knowledge acquisition, and skill development and implementation, and overall impact of the knowledge and skills on the quality of services delivered. In addition, there have been a few studies that have been conducted that focused upon factors associated with the selection of continuing education activities. Sharkin and Plageman (2003) surveyed a group of Pennsylvania psychologists to determine their attendance patterns and attitudes regarding mandatory continuing education (CE) participation. These researchers reported that 65% of psychologists surveyed did not attend CE workshops for the sole purpose of obtaining required continuing education credit. Rather, professional skill development served as the primary motivation for engaging in lifelong learning. Furthermore, approximately 50% of the psychologists who responded to the survey reported that they sometimes attended continuing education activities even after they had met the credit requirements for renewal of their license, thus suggesting some intrinsic interest in continuing professional development. When questioned whether the skills learned during CE programs could be applied in their practice, more than half of the respondents reported frequently implementing newly learned skills following program participation; however, fewer than half reported that participation in continuing education activities increased their effectiveness as practitioners. In sum, these psychologists participated in continuing education courses to improve their skill level, although many did not report that their skills were actually enhanced (Sharkin & Plageman).

Other research has focused upon the developmental nature of lifelong learning over the course of one's career. Guest (2000) collected descriptive data from 25 school psychologists to determine the types of challenges faced throughout one's career and how these challenges could be linked developmentally to increase knowledge, proficiency, and confidence. Findings suggested that novice school psychologists commonly experience difficulties with time management, consultation skills, communication with other team members, and completion of task-specific assignments. These novice practitioners identified consulting with other school psychologists and seeking out mentoring as an effective means for increasing their skill set; however, school psychologists in all stages of their career further reported that participation in continuing education activities such as workshops, in-service trainings, and attendance at local and national conferences also contributed to their professional development (Guest). The specific topics addressed during these activities, however, were not discussed.

Fowler and Harrison (2001) surveyed 235 school psychologists to determine their professional development needs for future continuing education planning. Results indicated that the respondents were actively engaged in continuing professional development activities and demonstrated a genuine interest in integrating these activities into their practice. This group frequented workshops and in-service trainings, as well as engaged in self-study projects. When questioned regarding specific continuing professional development needs, respondents indicated a desire to participate in activities that would serve to improve their effectiveness at implementing interventions in the areas of consultation, emotional/personality assessment, and implementing social skills programming. Fowler and Harrison concluded that learning is maximized when skills are applicable to both individual interests and the demands of the workplace.

These conclusions are consistent with the major assumption found in the adult education literature. That is, engaging individuals in meaningful and relevant learning experiences is an important component of continuing professional development. For adults, learning appears to be much more productive, useful, and meaningful if viewed as a progressive, developmental process, rather than a reproductive process of memorizing and storing information for future use. Reconstructive learning, or the process of constructing and reconstructing meaning for one to change and to evolve as a person, should be at the core of adult education (Taylor, Marienau, & Fiddler, 2000). These researchers also argued that learning for the sole purpose of acquiring new information results in limited application of skills in the workplace and failure to challenge existing knowledge and beliefs. Reconstructive educational tactics, in contrast, encourage adult learners to draw upon their past experiences, to reflect on the usefulness of past techniques and newly presented skills, and to integrate both past and present information to arrive at a more meaningful understanding of the material.

Although there are a variety of CE programming formats available that will be discussed below, there are serious concerns that the most common form of delivery of CE workshops, the lecture format, is not effective in evoking significant changes in skill acquisition and performance (Guskey, 2000; Herschell, McNeil, & McNeil, 2004). In fact, physicians are moving beyond this traditional format of continuing education delivery to providing opportunities for hands-on practice enhancement, such as case discussions, role plays, and both live and virtual patients. These approaches allow the practitioner to link previous knowledge to practice for the purpose of reconstructive learning (Davis et al., 1999). Although psychology has lagged behind its medical colleagues in this regard, there has been some movement in this direction through offering peer learning groups as a follow-up to skills presented in CE programs (Wilkerson & Irby, 1998).

A variety of APA- and NASP-affiliated continuing education activities involve adult learners in opportunities for the development of lifelong learning. APA and NASP provide psychologists continuing professional development through their annual conventions at the international, national, state, and local levels. These opportunities provide not only for formal learning activities but also for informal opportunities to establish and to re-establish relationships with peers for ongoing consultation and mentoring. Similarly, university training programs frequently have continuing education offerings that are open not only to the faculty and staff but also to the community at large. Establishing relationships with local university training programs allows for continued professional development, as well as opportunities for mentoring and supervising students or teaching courses, each of which offers opportunities for professional development.

Technological advancements have also resulted in the creation of many avenues for continuous professional development. Journals and evidence-based Web sites are excellent resources for obtaining data-based information electronically to ensure that practice is guided by science. Such resources also provide quick and efficient ways to engage in lifelong learning, while also serving to link research and data-based decision making. Evidence-based Web sites are excellent for obtaining data-based information to inform practice. Examples of these Web sites and search engines include Trip Database (http://www.tripdatabase.com), SUMSearch (http://sumsearch.uthscsa.edu), The Cochrane Collection (http://www.cochrane.org), The Campbell Collaboration (http://www.campbellcollaboration.org), and Clinical Evidence (http://clinicalevidence.bmj.com/ceweb/index.jsp). Professionals may also choose to download continuing education podcasts to play at their leisure. Moreover, Internet-based resources, such as professional mailing lists, provide school psychologists with the opportunity to communicate with local or national colleagues regarding practice issues. These mailing lists may serve as general communication vehicles, or they may focus on a specific area of practice or type of client (Armistead, 2007). Caution is warranted regarding the accuracy of information provided on mailing lists, as a multitude of opinions are offered, sometimes without empirical support.

Formal, professional study groups may be established on the basis of the needs and interests of practitioners. The format of these groups involves members' selecting publications based upon topics of interest and convening periodically to discuss the applicability of these readings to practice (Armistead, 2007). These groups can be useful at the local level, where real- time issues are addressed; however, they can also serve to engage national conversation by involving professional association groups (e.g., the International School Psychology Association, NASP, APA, and state associations) to dialogue with study groups or special interest groups within these associations. Activities such as these enable practitioners to identify mentors with specific areas of expertise who can serve to facilitate lifelong learning.

Independent study programs are offered in a number of different formats and enable practitioners to engage in learning activities that best fit their individual needs and schedules. For example, professionals may choose to participate in the APA Online Academy, text-based home-study programs, or the DVD Series program. These programs require participants to view multimedia presentations, to read selected APA publications, or to watch DVDs demonstrating theories and techniques. Mastery of information is assessed through test questions on the material. Division 16 (School Psychology) of the APA produces the Conversation Series, videotaped discussions on current professional topics in the field of school psychology. Study guides accompany the tapes to enhance self-study and to meet CPD requirements. In addition, the National Register of Health Service Providers in Psychology provides free APA-approved continuing education to registrants in the form of training modules and a series of articles covering evidence-based practices. NASP's Professional Growth Committee also offers continuing professional development modules on a variety of relevant topics. Following the completion of the module and the passing of a quiz, psychologists receive self-study credits for their participation. The modules help to meet the NASP-approved CPD requirements for NCSP renewal, and all self-study activities can be documented with the NCSP documentation form that can be downloaded from the NASP Web site. Likewise, professionals may also participate in workshops, teaching, research publications, supervisory roles, or program planning and evaluation, or they may take leadership in professional organizations to assist in continuing their professional development as suggested by NASP.

Many argue that the routine format of traditional continuing education activities provides limited opportunities for practitioners to learn how to implement these interventions (Herschell et al., 2004). In an effort more effectively to disseminate empirically supported treatments effectively during continuing education activities, Calhoun et al. (1998) suggested extending the length of workshops, assessing for skill acquisition, continuing utilization of treatments through routine observation and follow-up, and increasing the level of supervision. Establishing peer learning groups following CE trainings can provide professionals with the opportunity to continue receiving professional development credits while simultaneously allowing for mentoring surrounding the implementation of newly learned techniques and interventions (Wilkerson & Irby, 1998).

In summary, lifelong learning is critical to effective practice. Most psychologists select CE programming on the basis of professional interest and to ensure compliance with requirements for licensure and certification renewal. In general, the literature on continuing education is limited, with the few studies that exist focusing on selection and motivation for continuing professional development. There are no studies documenting effective means of implementing lifelong learning for the practicing professional. Directors of CE programs should consider developing methods not only for presenting information but also for ensuring that information presented is linked to behavioral change.

TRAINING FOR PROFESSIONAL ROLES AND FUNCTION

The lifelong process of acquiring professional capabilities begins and is formally instilled during graduate training. Graduate education programs in school psychology typically adhere to training guidelines developed by

NASP and APA and are reflected in state credentialing requirements to ensure that students possess foundational skills that can be strengthened and expanded throughout their careers. It is the metacognitive skill of learning how to learn that is at the core of graduate training and facilitates the maintenance of competent and ethical practice. The APA *Guidelines and Principles for Accreditation of Programs in Professional Psychology* (APA, 2007) require that doctoral level programs provide psychology trainees with a curriculum that allows for the development of competency in five broad areas. These areas are (a) scientific psychology, (b) theoretical foundations, (c) psychological assessment and intervention, (d) cultural/individual diversity, and (e) lifelong learning/professional problem solving. Programs have flexibility in how they deliver courses in each of these areas. However, evidence of effective outcomes is required for maintaining accreditation.

The NASP *Standards for Training and Field Placement Programs in School Psychology* (2000b) specify that school psychology programs must ensure that students receive broad-based training in the theories, models, research, and techniques associated with the fields of both education and psychology. Eleven domains of competency must be incorporated into course work and training requirements. These domains are (a) data-based decision-making and accountability; (b) consultation and collaboration; (c) effective instruction and development of cognitive/academic skills; (d) socialization and development of life skills; (e) student diversity in development and learning; (f) school and school system organization, policy development, and climate; (g) prevention, crisis intervention, and mental health; (h) home/school/community collaboration; (i) research and program evaluation; (j) school psychology practice and development; and (k) information technology. It is important to note that at the time of this writing, the NASP *Standards* are currently under revision and will be released in 2010.

Another document published by NASP, *School Psychology: A Blueprint for Training and Practice III* (Ysseldyke et al., 2006) was developed to clarify and to promote the need for continuous advancement in training and practice. More specifically, this document provides guidance for lifelong learning and continuous professional development. The assumption that underlies the model for *Blueprint III* is that competence in school psychology emerges developmentally over the course of one's career. Upon completion of graduate studies, school psychologists are expected to demonstrate a novice level of competency, and over time, practitioners should move from novice to competent in all domains while becoming and remaining experts in the domains essential to their practice (Ysseldyke et al.). The eight competencies outlined in *Blueprint III*, which are organized under two broader categories (foundational and functional), are defined as separate skill and knowledge sets. Nonetheless, they are an interwoven group of professional competencies that require fluent application and integration in practice.

The four foundational competencies include interpersonal characteristics, as well as the skills acquired during academic and field-based experiences. The first of the foundational competencies is interpersonal and collaborative skills, which involves advanced listening and communication skills to provide information effectively to diverse audiences. Furthermore, school psychologists should recognize the importance of collaboration and problem-solving processes in addressing the needs and concerns of school systems, students, and families.

Diversity awareness and sensitive service delivery, the second foundational competency, emphasizes the importance of remaining cognizant of the diversity represented within a school system and how diversity impacts daily educational and interpersonal activities and interventions. The authors of *Blueprint III* encouraged school psychologists to examine their own understanding of cultural diversity and to identify biases that may negatively affect their ability to communicate, to observe, and to intervene with specific groups or individuals (Ysseldyke et al., 2006).

The third foundational competency is technological applications. Competency in utilizing technological resources, (e.g., Internet-based searches and computer programs) is essential to the effective and timely provision of school psychological services. *Blueprint III* also explains the importance of facilitating the use of assistive technology for students with diverse learning needs. The possible negative consequences associated with technology are also addressed, as school psychologists must recognize the potential dangers associated with threats to student confidentiality, student access to the Internet, and overuse of technological resources for communication that may preclude or severely limit face-to-face interaction.

Professional, legal, ethical, and social responsibility, the fourth foundational competency, enables school psychologists to practice in a legal and ethical manner. School psychologists must also expand upon their current knowledge and skills by participating in continuing education activities as a matter of ethical functioning. Moreover, it is imperative that those providing any psychological services recognize the limits of their competency and seek out consultation, collaboration, supervision, or additional training as necessary.

The four functional competencies included in *Blueprint III* describe the "processes and contexts" (Ysseldyke et al., 2006, p. 15) of the daily roles and functions of school psychologists. The first of these competencies, data-based decision making and accountability, emphasizes that school psychologists must possess advanced problem-solving skills for the purposes of evaluating student progress and outcomes and selecting appropriate curricula and interventions. Although the utilization of data-gathering to determine and to address the needs of students remains important, school psychologists must also seek out training in areas such as research methods and program evaluation to assist in improving their school systems and classroom environments. *Blueprint III* also describes the need for competency in many areas of assessment, while understanding that the purpose of assessment is to guide prevention and intervention activities.

Systems-based service delivery, the second functional competency, is based on the premise that school psychologists must understand and intervene with the systems that directly influence students' educational performance, as well as their emotional and behavioral functioning. School psychologists are encouraged to take leadership roles within school systems in providing mechanisms to ensure safety, to promote feelings of togetherness and belonging, to emphasize the link between home and school, and to strengthen the crucial role parents play in the education of their children. Ongoing professional training ensures that a school psychologist's skills are current and that he or she can respond to systemic as well as individual needs.

The third functional competency is enhancing the development of cognitive and academic skills. School psychologists are advised to assist in developing challenging, yet reasonable, academic goals for all students. School psychologists should be knowledgeable and skilled in the implementation of evidence-based instructional strategies so that they can assist teachers and other staff in the selection of alternative learning strategies for individual students. Moreover, they should be prepared to assist school personnel in linking research to practice to ensure that students are receiving the most up-to-date and best suited instructional methods and interventions.

Enhancing the development of wellness, social skills, mental health, and life competencies is the final functional competency. The authors of *Blueprint III* emphasized the importance of recognizing the role that physical, social, and emotional well-being plays in a student's educational success. School psychologists are charged with being continuously aware of students' needs that are not specifically academic and to develop prevention and intervention programs that target both physical and mental health. The authors of *Blueprint III* also recognized the importance of training school psychologists in crisis prevention and response to ensure that they are able to prepare for potential disasters, to help avoid them whenever possible, and to seek out resources and to provide effective and beneficial services to students, families, and school personnel in the aftermath of a crisis.

The ongoing demographic and cultural changes within our society, as well as the dynamic research developments in the field, require that school psychologists focus on their continuing professional development to remain responsive to the children, families, and educators whom they serve. The *Blueprint III* provides guidelines for practitioners to assess their own competencies and to determine which skills require further development. Monitoring what areas of development require further training and supervision is imperative throughout one's career.

PEDAGOGICAL/SUPERVISORY ISSUES

The strength of an individual's commitment to continuing education and lifelong learning ultimately determines his or her professional effectiveness. Consultation with peers and mentors is essential throughout one's career. School psychology faculty members teach students not only the content and skills of the specialty, but also the process of becoming a professional. Thus, not only classroom instruction but also the supervision and mentoring provided by faculty serve as a model for students to develop lifelong learning as an integral part of their professional careers.

As students graduate and venture out professionally, colleagues frequently serve as mentors and consultants. This may occur formally, through weekly, structured supervision, or informally, through case consultation. School counselors have developed models of formal peer supervision that are incorporated into the daily routines of both new and seasoned practitioners and that can be easily adapted to the needs of school psychologists (Remley, Benshoff, & Mowbray, 1987; Borders, 1991; Benshoff & Paisley, 1996).

One example of a combined consultation, mentoring experience, and supervision for the practitioner is the case conference model developed by the school psychologists in Hillsborough County Public Schools in Florida (T. Schatzberg, 2007, personal communication). Leaders of the case conference model have used this procedure to review challenging cases, to promote consultation among school psychologists, to support professional growth, and to provide mentoring and supervision services to beginning professionals in the field. A presenter is selected prior to the conference and is asked to provide participants with information pertaining to a specific case with which he or she needs assistance (e.g., determining assessment procedures or specific interventions). Following the presentation, a panel of preselected individuals deemed experts on the topic, as well as a number of outside consultants, are invited to address the presenter's questions and to provide recommendations. Audience members ask their own questions after the presenter's concerns are thoroughly addressed. Following the formal processes, all participants are invited to join in a discussion about the case to facilitate and to model the importance of mentoring to lifelong learning.

CASE ILLUSTRATION/EXEMPLAR

Although there are various supervisory and mentoring experiences that may be effective, the following illustrate a supervision training model that could be implemented within the context of a school psychology graduate program and provide examples that are useful for practitioners to instill lifelong learning. During graduate training, the collaborative hierarchical intensive programmatic supervision (CHIPS) model is especially effective and can serve as a framework for demonstrating the importance of collaboration and consultation.

As part of the applied professional practice requirements of school psychology graduate programs, students must successfully complete several practica and the capstone internship experience. These experiences allow the students to bridge the gap between theoretical foundations and applied professional practice under close supervision. The goal of the field-based phase of training is to provide supervised experiences that will enhance the development of the students' knowledge and skills as they become school psychologists.

The format of the CHIPS supervision training model provides students with an opportunity to apply specific techniques of assessment and intervention under close faculty supervision. In this model, faculty supervisors are assisted in the supervisory process by advanced (typically doctoral level) students, predoctoral interns, and postdoctoral residents, each of whom employs consultative, monitoring, and supervisory roles consistent with his or her level of training and experience. The purpose of this model is to improve the critical skills necessary for professional practice for practicum students, as well as providing a model for practicing consultation and supervision that can be utilized throughout one's career.

Within this hierarchical model of supervision, specialist students, doctoral students, predoctoral interns, and postdoctoral psychology residents may provide direct supervision to trainees commensurate with their levels of training and experience. Although the program director or designated faculty member serves as the primary supervisor, postdoctoral residents are given considerable leadership and responsibility in providing both individual and group supervision to doctoral and specialist level students. The experience of the entry level specialist and doctoral student enrolled in the practicum is enhanced by individualized mentoring by upper level doctoral level students, who can focus on the basic skills of test administration, scoring, and interpretation of results. Furthermore, specialist level students may be afforded the opportunity to mentor other specialist students in earlier stages of their training by allowing the less advanced students to shadow and to critique their activities. Students, interns, and residents, with the informed consent of clients, have the opportunity to work collaboratively on cases, at times working side by side in administering components of the assessment battery. Note that in this context, the term *clients* is used to refer only to individuals who are legally able to give informed consent. The CHIPS model is especially useful when examinees are difficult to assess, either because of their behavior or because of the complex demands of the assessment itself. The provision of live supervision helps to promote this model. Similarly, videotape of the assessment and intervention process, with the written consent of the clients, allows for additional supervision and self-reflection.

Although consultation, supervision, and mentoring experiences occur throughout graduate training, they should also be an integral part of one's entire career. Certainly, traditional definitions of supervision recognize this developmental process as essential for students and newly credentialed professionals; however, experienced practitioners also need assistance with complex professional and ethical issues, handling challenging cases, remaining current with new techniques, and, importantly, preventing professional burnout (Borders, 1991; Grant & Schofield, 2007). Oftentimes, geographic and administrative barriers interfere with opportunities for ongoing consultation. Supervision as lifelong learning is possible through the establishment of peer supervision groups as described in detail above through both live meetings and Web-based interaction. Although these groups are frequently established informally, a more formal mentoring program within school districts potentially could contribute in important ways to the professional development of both beginning and seasoned school psychologists (Guest, 2000). In fact, the CHIPS model described above can serve as a model for sharing the expertise of well-established professionals who have experience in the field with the recency of knowledge of new graduates. Similarly, studies examining the effectiveness of peer supervision for school counselors find that those who engage in this process report a number of benefits, including remaining cognizant of their own skill levels and abilities, reducing the tendency to depend on the advice of practitioners who have been working in the field for many years, and increasing self-confidence (Agnew, Vaught, Getz, & Fortune, 2000; Benshoff & Paisley, 1996).

Students enrolled in school psychology graduate programs must be mentored into the importance of lifelong learning and continuing professional development during graduate training so that the process will continue throughout their careers. In an effort to ensure that school psychology students understand the lifelong learning process, the principles of *Blueprint III* as described in detail above can be utilized. Graduate training programs may choose to require the development of a continuous professional improvement plan (CPIP) beginning with the 1st year of studies and in each subsequent year of training, with the ultimate goal of continuing this process over the course of one's profession. School district administrators may choose to implement such a process as a mechanism to encourage lifelong learning and to provide

The purpose of the CPIP is to assist students in understanding the NASP *Blueprint III* as it relates to their continuing professional development. *Blueprint III* describes eight key domains of professional functioning. As part of the CPIP, students should describe and understand each domain and list a number of lifelong learning activities that are specific, appropriate for the domain, and not a required part of their school psychology training curriculum (e.g., taking a course required in the curriculum or reading a book that has already been assigned for a class). Enrolling in an elective course within the school psychology training program, reading a relevant journal article or book that has not been assigned, and attending specific presentations at conferences or continuing education workshops would be examples of lifelong learning activities, and each should be demonstrably linked to at least one of the *Blueprint III* domains. Students are required to list at least five lifelong learning activities for each *Blueprint III* domain. A scoring rubric can be utilized to evaluate students' skills in planning comprehensive continuing professional development and to score the appropriateness and effective description of specific responses.

Following the development of the CPIP, students should be encouraged to make every effort to participate in at least some of the activities listed within their plan. During an annual review of their progress in the program, students should provide faculty members and supervisors with a detailed explanation of how they have worked to expand their knowledge base and to promote their continuing professional development utilizing the designed CPIP. In addition, they should be required to update the CPIP annually to ensure that it is timely and sufficiently comprehensive. Students could easily include these activities in their portfolio to demonstrate that they fully grasp how to formulate specific strategies for continuous improvement throughout their careers. Practitioners could similarly review the plan with their administrator to determine ways in which the district could support their continued professional development.

SUMMARY AND CONCLUSIONS

The emphasis placed upon continuing education and lifelong learning within the helping professions began with medical education. The medical profession recognized the need to incorporate professional development activities into graduate and postgraduate education beginning in 1910, but it was not until the 1970s that both the APA and the NASP began to formalize continuing education programs. Today, however, graduate training and professional practice is characterized by the commitment of both APA and NASP to continuing education activities. In fact, continuing education is also a formal component of the school psychology licensure or certification renewal process.

Although APA and NASP provide opportunities to participate in a wide variety of continuing education activities, such as attending workshops, seminars, and university training sessions, there are other options, such as study groups, reading/listening to online offerings, and demonstrating knowledge via Web-based exams to accommodate work schedules; however, the characteristics and training experiences of individuals most likely to engage in lifelong learning, the circumstances that produce greatest behavior change, and the most effective way of delivering continuing education still require much research to improve the efficacy of lifelong learning. This research should include determination of how best to present materials during a continuing education program to ensure that knowledge is retained and skills are translated into practice. Research using simulated patients/clients and taking advantage of technology to determine practice change, maintenance of practice change, and the extent of the change may also be beneficial in answering questions regarding the overall effectiveness of continuing professional development activities.

It is imperative to recognize that the template for participation in life-long learning activities begins to be developed during one's graduate training years. Both the NASP *Standards for Training and Field Placement Programs in School Psychology* (NASP, 2000) and the APA *Guidelines and Principles for Accreditation of Programs in Professional Psychology* (APA, 2007) require that trainees obtain competencies in a number of different areas, some of which are assessment, intervention, cultural diversity, technology, consultation, and research and program evaluation. NASP also expects both graduate trainees and practitioners to learn, to develop, and to enhance their competencies over time; this expectation is addressed in both the *Standards* and *Blueprint III*. *Blueprint III* provides a framework for assisting school psychologists in assessing their own competencies. Professionals must independently determine when their skills are less developed or need to be enhanced and how to go about honing these skills to remain up-to-date with new methods of service delivery and evidence-based interventions. School psychologists agree that lifelong learning and professional development activities that are meaningfully integrated into their daily practice enable them to be the best prepared to serve the needs of children and families over the course of their careers.

RESOURCES

American Psychological Association. (1987). *Model act for state licensure.* Washington, DC: Author.

American Psychological Association. (2002). *Ethical principles of psychologists and code of conduct.* Washington, DC: Author.

Armistead, L. D. (2007). Best practices in continuing professional development for school psychologists. In A. Thomas & J. Grimes (Eds.), *Best Practices in school psychology V* (pp. 1975–1990). Bethesda, MD: National Association of School Psychologists.
Armistead explains the importance of psychologists maintaining their level of competency through continuing education activities. He suggests following the National Association of School Psychologists guidelines for practitioners and continuing education providers for establishing a plan for lifelong learning.

Brown, M. (2002). Best practices in professional development. In A. Thomas & J. Grimes (Eds.), *Best practices in school psychology IV* (pp. 183–194). Bethesda, MD: National Association of School Psychologists.

Brown explains the importance of continuing professional development due to rapid changes in the field of psychology. In order to be most effective, he suggests that continuing professional development activities should follow a four-step process of (a) setting the context and identifying needs, (b) prioritizing needs, (c) selecting and implementing developmental activities, and (d) evaluating and documenting activities.

Sharkin, B. S., & Plageman, P. M. (2003). What do psychologists think about mandatory continuing education? A survey of Pennsylvania practitioners. *Professional Psychology: Research and Practice, 34*(3), 318–323.

The authors surveyed Pennsylvania practitioners on their views of continuing education requirements. The results indicated that Pennsylvania practitioners prefer to have mandatory requirements for continuing education and do not choose continuing education programs simply for the sole purpose of earning credits. Instead, they choose the programs on the basis of their interest in the topic.

REFERENCES

Agnew, T., Vaught, C. C., Getz, H. G., & Fortune, J. (2000). Peer group clinical supervisor program fosters confidence and professionalism. *Professional School Counseling, 4*(1), 6–12.

American Psychological Association. (2006). *Continuing education sponsor approval system: Policies and procedures manual.* Washington, DC: Author.

American Psychological Association. (2007). *Guidelines and principles for accreditation of programs in professional psychology.* Washington, DC: Author.

Armistead, L. D. (2007). Best practices in continuing professional development for school psychologists. In A. Thomas & J. Grimes (Eds.), *Best practices in school psychology V* (pp. 1975–1990). Bethesda, MD: National Association of School Psychologists.

Benshoff, J. M., & Paisley, P. O. (1996). The structured peer consultation model for school counselors. *Journal of Counseling & Development, 74*(3), 314–318.

Borders, L. D. (1991). A systematic approach to peer group supervision. *Journal of Counseling & Development, 69*(3), 248–252.

Brown, M. (2002). Best practices in professional development. In A. Thomas & J. Grimes (Eds.), *Best practices in school psychology IV* (pp. 183–194). Bethesda, MD: National Association of School Psychologists.

Calhoun, K. S., Moras, P. A., Pilkonis, L. P., & Rehm, L. P. (1998). Empirically supported treatments: Implications for training. *Journal of Consulting and Clinical Psychology, 66*(1), 151–162.

Davis, D., Thomson O'Brien, M. A., Freemantle, N., Wolf, F. M., Mazmanian, P., & Taylor- Vaisy, A. (1999). Impact of formal continuing medical education: Do conferences, rounds, and other traditional continuing education activities change physician behavior or health care outcomes? *Journal of the American Medical Association, 282*(9), 867–874.

Dryer, B. V. (1962). Lifetime learning for physicians: Principles, practices, and proposals. *Journal of Education, 37* (89).

Dublin, S. S. (1972). Obsolescence or lifelong education: A choice for the professional. *American Psychologist, 27*(5), 486–498.

Gillam, S. L., & Crutchfield, L. B. (2001). Collaborative group supervision of practicum students and interns. *Clinical Supervisor, 20*(1), 49–60.

Guest, K. E. (2000). Career development of school psychologists. *Journal of School Psychology, 38*(3), 237–257.

Grant, J., & Schofield, M. (2007). Career-long supervision: Patterns and perspectives. *Counseling & Psychotherapy Research, 7(1),* 3–11.

Guskey, T. R. (2000). *Evaluating professional development.* Thousand Oaks, CA: Corwin Press.

Hale, J. B. (2008, March 31). *Response to intervention: Guidelines for parents and practitioners.* Retrieved April 15, 2008, from http://www.wrightslaw.com/idea/art/rti.hale.htm

Herschell, A. D., McNeil, C. B., & McNeil, D. W. (2004). Clinical child psychology's progress in disseminating empirically supported treatments. *Clinical Psychology: Science and Practice, 11*(3), 267–288.

Hynd, G. W., Pielstick, N. L., & Schakel, J. A. (1981). Continuing professional development in school psychology: Present status-future directions. *School Psychology Review, 10*(4), 480–486.

Knoff, H. M., Curtis, M. J., & Batsche, G. M. (1997). The future of school psychology: Perspectives on effective training. *School Psychology Review, 26*(1), 93–103.

Kokemueller, P. K., & Osguthorpe, J. D. (2007). Trends and developments in continuing medical education. *Otolaryngolic Clinics of North America, 40,* 1331–1345.

Merrell, K. W., Ervin, K. A., & Gimpel, G. (2006). *School psychology for the 21st century: Foundations and practices.* New York: The Guilford Press.

National Association of School Psychologists (2000a). *Professional Conduct Manual.* Bethesda, MD: Author.

National Association of School Psychologists. (2000b). *Standards for training and field placement programs in school psychology.* Bethesda, MD: Author.

Neimeyer, G. J., Taylor, J. M., & Phillip, D. (2008). *Continuing education in psychology: Perceptions, preferences and practices among mandated and non-mandated psychologists.* Unpublished manuscript.

Remley, T. P., Benshoff, J. M., & Mowbray, C. A. (1987). A proposed model for peer supervision. *Counselor Education and Supervision, 27*(1), 53–60.

Sharkin, B. S., & Plageman, P. M. (2003). What do psychologists think about mandatory continuing education? A survey of Pennsylvania practitioners. *Professional Psychology: Research and Practice, 34*(3), 318–323.

Taylor, K., Marienau, C., & Fiddler, M. (2000). *Developing adult learners: Strategies for teachers and trainees.* San Francisco, CA: Josey-Bass, Inc.

Vandecreek, L., Knapp, S., & Brace, K. (1990). Mandatory continuing education for licensed psychologists: Its rationale and current implementation. *Professional Psychology: Research and Practice, 21*(2), 135–140.

Walker, N. W. (1977), The NASP program for continuing professional development. *School Psychology Digest, 6,* 70–83.

Wilkerson, L., & Irby, D. M. (1998). Strategies for improving teaching practices: A comprehensive approach to faculty development. *Academic Medicine, 73*(4), 387–396.

Ysseldyke, J., Burns, M., Dawson, P., Kelley, B., Morrison, D., Ortiz, S., et al. (2006). *School psychology: A blueprint for training and practice III.* Bethesda, MD: National Association of School Psychologists.

15 Collaboration in school-based crisis intervention

Stephen E. Brock, Elise L. Martinez, LLecenia Navarro, and Evelyn Teran

It has been estimated that just over 25% of children and adolescents in the general population are exposed to an extreme traumatic stressor at some point during their young lives (Costello, Erkanli, Fairbank, & Angold, 2002). When this high incidence of traumatic stressors is combined with the fact that the school psychologist's role is influenced by responding to the environmental demands that children face (Swerdlik & French, 2000), it is not surprising to find that the provision of school crisis intervention services has come to be viewed as an expected and important school psychological practice (Brock, Sandoval, & Lewis, 2001; Watkins, Crosby, & Pearson, 2001).

Similarly, the descriptions of Domains of School Psychology Training and Practice provided by the National Association of School Psychologists (2000) identify crisis intervention as a core competency where at least entry-levels skills are required for school psychology candidates to begin professional practice. Specifically, Domain 2.7 of the Training Standards, titled Prevention, Crisis Intervention, and Mental Health, states: "School psychologists have knowledge of human development and psychopathology and of associated biological, cultural, and social influences on human behavior. *School psychologists provide or contribute to prevention and intervention programs* [italics added] that promote the mental health and physical wellbeing of students" (p. 16). The expanded discussion of this domain further states: "School psychologists have knowledge of crisis intervention and collaborate with school personnel, parents, and the community in the aftermath of crises (e.g., suicide, death, natural disasters, murder, bombs or bomb threats, extraordinary violence, sexual harassment, etc.)" (p. 30).

Trends in training programs for school psychology professional practice show an increase in crisis intervention training and preparation course work requirements. Despite this trend, crisis intervention skill development is underdeveloped compared with more traditional school psychological skills such as assessment. Although crisis training standards have called for the development of crisis intervention skill at the preservice level, course work uniquely geared toward crisis intervention are minimal. For example,

Allen et al. (2002), from a national sample of 276 school psychologists who were a part of the 1999 Nationally Certified School Psychologists database (81% return rate) reported that on average, school psychologists judged their preservice preparation for dealing with crisis situations was less than adequate and that they felt professionally unprepared.

The primary purpose of this chapter is to provide trainers with effective pedagogical practices to aid in crisis intervention instruction. To orient the reader to school crisis intervention, this chapter begins with an overview of the broader multidisciplinary school crisis response and discusses the empirical foundations for the practice of crisis intervention. Next, a summary of the current status of crisis intervention knowledge within the profession is presented. Finally, the chapter offers the authors' views on how to best prepare preservice school psychologists for crisis intervention work. Examples of some of the specific activities that we believe are important to crisis intervention professional development are provided.

THE MULTIDISCIPLINARY SCHOOL CRISIS RESPONSE

It is important to acknowledge at the outset that school crisis intervention is but one part of a multidisciplinary school crisis team. Preservice school psychologists need to be informed that to fill their crisis intervention role they should be surrounded by such a team. A detailed discussion of this topic is offered in Brock, Nickerson, Reeves, and Jimerson (2008).

For the purposes of this chapter, it is important to acknowledge that the National Incident Management System (NIMS; U.S. Department of Homeland Security, 2004) provides a standard framework for the comprehensive school crisis team. Homeland Security Presidential Directive 5, Management of Domestic Incidents, signed in 2003, has required since 2005 that all federal agencies and departments adopt the NIMS, including the basic tenets of its Incident Command System (ICS), to receive federal assistance (e.g., grants, contracts). Given that collaboration with community agencies is essential to school crisis intervention, being a part of larger school crisis teams that makes use of the NIMS and its ICS will help school psychologists speak the same language as crisis responders from a wide variety of other agencies.

The ICS has five major functions (or sections): command, operations, intelligence. logistics, and finance. The command section includes the incident commander (IC) and, if necessary, a crisis leadership team that may include a public information officer, safety officer, mental health officer, and agency liaison officer. As the title implies, the IC coordinates the response to crises. In schools, the IC is typically a school or district administrator.

The operations section includes a variety of coordinators and specialists, each of whom is responsible for addressing immediate crisis response needs. This is the section from which crisis intervention services are offered and within which the school psychologist is found. Other operations section activities include those that address the reduction of immediate hazards, saving lives and property, establishing situational control, and restoring normal operations.

The intelligence section includes crisis team members who are responsible for collecting, evaluating, and disseminating incident situation intelligence to the IC. The activities of this section include preparing status reports, maintaining status of resources assigned to an incident, and developing/documenting the plan, including incident objectives and strategies.

The logistics section includes crisis team members who are responsible for obtaining all the resources needed to respond to a crisis event. Examples of the resources this section is responsible for include personnel, equipment/supplies, and transportation. When a school psychologist performing crisis intervention services needs something, he or she will obtain it from the logistics section. This section also works with the intelligence section personnel so as to identify resources needed to address future challenges.

Finally, the finance section includes crisis team members who are responsible for maintaining all expense records. It is important to acknowledge that not all crisis situations will require this section. However, when the crisis response requires financial and other administrative support services (e.g., payroll, claims, and reimbursements), it is activated. Such expense records are especially important if it is anticipated that federal or state funding will at some point be requested.

A BRIEF REVIEW OF THE CRISIS INTERVENTION LITERATURE

The following questions help to organize the salient literature for teaching crisis intervention: (a) What are the circumstances that may require the provision of crisis intervention services? (b) What are the consequences of such crisis events? (c) What is the range of crisis interventions currently considered to be effective school-based responses to youth who have been exposed to a traumatic stressor?

The characteristics of crises

According to the *DSM-IV-TR*, a traumatic stressor (or crisis event) may involve directly experiencing, witnessing, or learning about a traumatic event. The types of events that may generate traumatic stress involve actual or threatened death, serious injury, and/or other perceived threats to one's physical integrity (American Psychiatric Association, 2000). Additional characteristics that define a crisis are (a) the event is viewed by the individual as extremely negative, (b) the event is judged to be unpredictable and uncontrollable, and (c) the event is accompanied by feelings of depersonalization

(Brock et al., 2001). Critical incidents consistent with these characteristics include severe illness and/or injury, violent and/or unexpected death, threatened death and/or injury, acts of war and/or terrorism, natural disasters, and human-made/industrial disasters (Brock, 2002a; Brock & Jimerson, 2004a).

When considering the professional preparation of school psychologists, it is important to ensure that they are aware of the fact that some of these critical incidents are more traumatic then others, and as such will likely require variability in the level of crisis intervention assistance. For example, school psychologists need to recognize the fact that human-caused crisis events (as compared with most natural disasters) involving aggressive violence and resulting in fatalities represent what is arguably the most traumatic type of crisis (Brock, 2002b).

The consequences of crises

It is important to acknowledge that although a crisis event is a necessary condition, by itself it is not sufficient to generate traumatic stress and the need for crisis intervention assistance. For a critical incident to generate traumatic stress, the event must have been viewed by the individual as threatening and/or as having generated apparently unsolvable problems. Acute distress is among the more common consequences of exposure to a crisis event. Such distress is often characterized by emotional (e.g., shock, anger), cognitive (e.g., impaired concentration and memory, confusion, distortion), physical (e.g., fatigue, insomnia, sleep disturbance), and interpersonal/behavioral (e.g., alienation, social withdrawal, school impairment, tantrums) reactions. Youths who exhibit these signs may benefit from some form of crisis intervention (Brock & Jimerson, 2004b), where treatment is tailored to the specific child's or adolescent's psychological needs and adjustments are made as recovery progresses (Myer & Conte, 2006). A small portion of the individuals exposed to a crisis event will develop crisis reactions that may be beyond the typical school psychologist's training and could require referral to other mental health professionals. Such reactions include acute distress and panic, severe dissociation, intrusive, hyperarousal, anxiety, depression, and psychotic symptoms. These more severe consequences include posttraumatic stress disorder (Brock & Jimerson, 2004b). In addition, maladaptive coping behaviors (e.g., substance abuse, suicidal or homicidal ideation) are consequences of crisis event exposure that signal the need for relatively immediate and intensive crisis intervention assistance (Brock & Jimerson, 2004a).

The basic fact that a traumatic stressor can have *an* effect is viewed as being universal, cutting across age groups, countries, and cultures. However, normative cultural experiences and expectations can influence an individual's perceptions and reactions to a traumatic stressor (Dykeman,

2005; Sullivan, Harris, Collado, & Chen, 2006). For example, in the dominant African American culture, coping is often viewed as an act of will that is controlled by the individual, and failure to cope is associated with weakness. In the dominant Asian American culture, feelings and/or problems are often not expressed to save face. In both instances, crises can cause feelings of shame, which can affect crisis reactions (Sullivan et al., p. 989). Furthermore, culture influences the types of events that appear to be threatening in the first place and how individuals assign meaning to it, as well as how individuals or communities express traumatic reactions and how the traumatized individuals or communities view and judge their own responses (Tramonte, 1999). Given these cultural variables, when considering the professional preparation of school psychologists, it is also important to ensure that they consider the impact culture has on crisis reactions. Children from various cultures may not clearly show symptoms of acute stress, thus increasing the possibility their reactions are overlooked by caregivers. In addition, certain cultures, specifically oppressed minority groups, are reluctant to trust Western psychological practices. Minority groups may prefer a religious figure to intervene (Sullivan et al.). Nevertheless, school psychologists need to "become aware of their own cultural assumptions; demonstrate an ability to communicate an understanding, acceptance, and appreciation of cultural differences; and identify available resources *from the victim's culture* [italics added] to assist with crisis resolution and aftercare" (Dykeman, p. 48).

When considering the professional preparation of school psychologists, it is important to ensure that they are aware of the fact that not all individuals exposed to a traumatic stressor will be traumatized and require crisis intervention assistance and that the provision of such assistance should only be offered in response to a demonstrated need (Brock, 2002c). For example, school psychologists should be provided with training that will assist them in documenting risk for traumatic stress reactions and in the ability to assess acute distress (i.e., the ability to conduct psychological triage). The importance of ensuring the provision of such training is highlighted by the fact that just over 25% of practicing school psychologist do not use psychological triage techniques when providing crisis intervention (Nickerson & Zhe, 2004).

The response to crisis

As described by Brock (2006) and Brock and Jimerson (2004a), when responding to crisis events, the school psychologist should be prepared to offer a range of universal, selected, and target interventions. First, at the universal level, school psychologists strive to prevent psychological trauma (e.g., by minimizing exposure to stressors) and to as quickly as possible reaffirm physical health and perceptions that the school is safe and secure.

It is critical that school psychologists recognize that it is not sufficient for young people to *actually* be safe immediately following a crisis. For recovery to begin, the individual has to *believe* that the danger has passed.

Once physical and emotional safety needs have been addressed, mental health services may be implemented. The provision of these other crisis interventions requires that the school psychologist evaluate the degree of psychological injury. Psychological triage allows school psychologists to assess the emotional trauma of the student body and school staff members and to make appropriate referrals for treatment (Brock & Jimerson, 2004a). In addition to the cultural factors described above, many other factors influence the way in which a youth perceives and responds to a crisis, and it is important to note that stress reactions are individual (Brown & Rainer, 2006; Brock & Jimerson, 2004b; Brock, 2002c). Factors that influence individual reactions include crisis exposure, relationships with crisis victims, and perceived threat. The interaction of these variables can potentially increase the level of trauma experienced by an individual (Brock, 2002c; Gaffney, 2006).

Crisis exposure includes one's proximity to the crisis, as well as the duration of exposure to the crisis. Research shows that a child's physical proximity to a crisis event paired with the duration of exposure are strong predictors of acute distress. Relationship to crisis victims, or emotional proximity, also has a strong correlation to increased levels of acute stress after a crisis event. Finally, if a child or adolescent perceives the crisis event to be extremely negative and to threaten his or her safety, he or she is at an increased risk for traumatization. These risk factors are critical to assessing acute stress reactions and should be used as a guide to prioritize crisis intervention; the more risk factors a child or adolescent possesses, the higher the priority. Once risk assessment is complete and individuals are identified as at risk, there are several strategies that can be useful to help students cope with crisis (Brock, 2006).

For individuals judged to be at low risk for psychological traumatization, the reestablishment of naturally occurring social support systems (e.g., parents, teachers, friends) may be the only "intervention" that is needed, and as indicated might be offered as a universal crisis intervention (Brock & Jimerson, 2004a; Dykeman, 2005; Gard & Ruzek, 2006). As the risk of psychological injury is judged to be greater, intervention options (which might be considered universal or selected interventions) expand to include psychological education.

Once social supports have been reestablished, school psychologists can begin psychological education with the individuals who were identified as being at risk for psychological injury. The goals of psychological education is to dispel rumors, normalize and understand crisis reactions, develop adaptive coping mechanisms, and learn how and where to receive additional services if needed (Brock & Jimerson, 2004a; Gard & Ruzek, 2006). Caregiver training is also a component of psychological education, with the emphasis placed on "caregiver knowledge" to help them effectively support their children.

When the risk of psychological injury is judged to be high and/or the individual actually begins to demonstrate symptoms of posttraumatic stress, the provision of immediate and direct crisis intervention or "psychological first aid" assistance is indicated. These interventions will involve the crisis intervener working directly with the individual in crisis and can involve the taking of actions on the crisis victim's behalf. They can include referrals for psychotherapeutic treatments. In particular, in regards to the psychotherapeutic treatment options, these responses can be classified as targeted interventions and are typically made available to only a minority of trauma-exposed students and school staff members. In other words, following most traumatic events, it can be expected that most individuals will recover with relatively limited support services. For those who need more intense assistance with adaptive coping, psychological intervention will become necessary.

When considering the professional preparation of school psychologists, it is important to ensure that they are aware that when it comes to the provision of crisis intervention assistance, one size does not fit all. Although some individuals will require highly directive and sophisticated mental health interventions, others will require little if any direct support from the school psychologist. Thus, practicing school psychologists must be able to match the appropriate intervention with the needs of the individual crisis victim.

TRAINING FOR PROFESSIONAL ROLES AND FUNCTION

In this section, we will discuss the preparation, experiences, and practices of school psychologists regarding the provision of school crisis intervention. In doing so we will illustrate how the crisis intervention theory and research discussed above is currently being integrated within professional practice. This discussion will also further identify areas of needed preservice training.

Preservice preparation for school crisis intervention

Survey research presented above, conducted by Allen et al. (2002), examined school psychologists crisis intervention training. This study's sample included 276 participants (81% return rate) who were part of the 1999 Nationally Certified School Psychologist database. Regarding university training for crisis intervention, results revealed that 37% of those surveyed reported having received some training in, or having had some experience with, crisis intervention during their graduate training, and 23% received academic course work specifically addressing school crisis intervention.

However, only 5% reported having taken a class specifically devoted to crisis intervention. On average, respondents reported that as a result of this preservice training, they were less than adequately prepared to deal with crisis situations, with only 2% reporting to be "well" or "very well" prepared to deal with school crises.

A significant factor in respondents' self-reports of readiness to provide crisis intervention following preservice training may have been the fact that only 30% reported having had experienced school crisis intervention during their practicum or internship. This result points to one of the more significant challenges for preservice crisis intervention training, which is that there are typically limited opportunities to practice crisis intervention skills before beginning independent school psychology practice (Allen et al., 2002).

Allen et al. (2002) also gave respondents the opportunity to rank order topics that they thought should be emphasized during preservice graduate school training. The topic that was most frequently ranked number one was suicide, followed by school crisis plans, violence/aggression, and grief and death. This result provides guidance to school psychology trainers when developing crisis intervention courses.

Crisis intervention experiences and practices of in-service school psychologists

Nickerson and Zhe (2004) surveyed a random sample of 197 (45% return rate) members of the National Association of School Psychologists. Emphasizing the need for crisis intervention training, results revealed that more than half of the respondents reported direct experience with four or more crises. The most common crises experienced were student–student physical assault, student serious illness/injury, unexpected student death, and suicide attempt. Regarding crisis intervention practices, the vast majority reported providing teacher and parent consultations and direct crisis intervention following school crises. Overall, results were interpreted as suggesting that practicing school psychologists employ crisis interventions recommended by the literature.

Further analysis of Nickerson and Zhe's (2004) survey results reveals areas that should be addressed by graduate preservice training. Although there is no doubt that there are instances where professional mental health services are needed, there is consensus that such should not be a universal crisis intervention strategy (National Institute of Mental Health, 2002). Thus, these data might be interpreted as suggesting that at the preservice level, training should include guidance that recovery from crisis exposure is the norm and that mental health referrals should be offered only when indicated. Nickerson and Zhe's results also revealed that 28% of respondents did not endorse psychological triage as a crisis intervention strategy. This suggests that for a significant percentage of school psychologists, the provision of specific crisis interventions is not based on assessment of individual risk for psychological injury. Thus, these data might be interpreted as suggesting that at the preservice level, training should include guidance that specific crisis interventions should be offered only in response to demonstrated need (McNally, Bryant, & Ehlers, 2003) and that specific risk factors for psychological injury should be identified (Brock, 2006).

PEDAGOGICAL AND SUPERVISORY ISSUES

We view school psychology training programs as providing a foundation to build upon rather than the "end-all be-all." For preservice school psychologists to fully grasp the complexity of a crisis event, they cannot just read about it, they must in some way experience crises and practice crisis intervention skills. However, given that crisis events cannot be planned for within a school psychology training program, university-based instruction should strive to offer hands-on activities that simulate crises to the greatest extent possible. The following discussion shares some of the instructional activities that the authors have found to be helpful in training preservice school psychologists to provide school-based crisis intervention.

Field observations and/or interview

One of the first recommended activities is to observe a crisis intervention team in action and/or to talk to a practicing school psychologist about his or her role in responding to the aftermath of a crisis event. This can often be done within the context of fieldwork placements. From school psychology student observations and/or interviews a brief paper should be written, within which the essential elements of the school psychologist's role are discussed. These papers can be used by the instructor as stimuli for seminar discussion topics. Because it is often not feasible to directly observe a school crisis response (as mentioned above, these events are not predictable), for grading purposes providing a paper based only on an interview of a practicing school psychologist should be considered sufficient.

Review written crisis intervention plans

Another initial training experience for the preservice school psychologist is to review sample school crisis response and/or intervention protocols. One way to structure such review is to ask school psychology students to obtain copies of the protocols being used in their fieldwork settings (this can be made a part of the field-observation/interview activity described above), identify the key elements of these plans, and make note of the degree to which these elements are supported by best practices. Chapters written by Brock and Davis (2008); and Brock et al. (2008) might be used to provide such best practice guidance. Plan reviews could then be used to write papers, which in turn can be used to further stimulate classroom discussion about the school psychologist's role in the provision of school crisis intervention. It is important to note, however, that because there are still many schools that do not have formal written crisis response protocols, the instructor will want to have a collection of sample plans available to give to individuals who report they have been unable to get a plan to review. An Internet search for "school crisis intervention plan" will typically yield a variety of such documents.

Psychological triage practice

From lectures addressing the range of crisis interventions that should be employed following school-associated crises (e.g., Brock & Davis, 2008) and examination of the factors associated with individual vulnerability for traumatic stress reactions (e.g., Brock, 2002c), it should be emphasized that when it comes to crisis intervention, one size does not fit all. Although some crisis victims will require relatively intense school crisis intervention assistance, other crisis exposed youth will require very little professional support to recover. Thus, training preservice school psychologists to provide crisis intervention should involve ensuring that they understand that the provision of specific crisis intervention services must be matched to individual crisis intervention needs. To this end, we feel it essential to provide them with opportunities to practice psychological triage.

To provide preservice school psychologists with the opportunity to develop and practice psychological triage skills, we recommend offering small group discussion of school crisis situations designed to stimulate discussion of initial risk screening, followed by brief individually written papers that summarize the results of small group discussions. Adapted from materials first developed by Brock et al. (2001), the use of Training Exemplar A should involve first asking the school psychology students to discuss the crisis intervention situation example, estimate the potential of the given event to generate psychological injury, and then answer questions about who in the given situation would be at greatest risk for psychological injury and who would be at least risk for such traumatization.

Crisis intervention scripts

Although preservice school psychologists cannot be guaranteed opportunities to practice crisis intervention skills within the context of an actual school crisis response, they will always have the opportunity to imagine how they might be used. One way for school psychology students to reflect on how their developing crisis intervention knowledge might translate into practice is to write crisis intervention scripts. These scripts allow students to demonstrate their knowledge of what should be said during a psychological first aid intervention. Our experiences suggest that two types of scripts may need to be written. The first script should address a crisis event that, while generating coping challenges, does not generate suicidal ideation. The second script should illustrate the special form of psychological first aid necessitated when a child or adolescent *does* have suicidal ideation. The need for this second type of training activity is emphasized by Allen et al. (2002). Their survey results found the topic of suicide to be ranked as the number one preservice crisis intervention training need.

As discussed by Slaikeu (1990) and Brock et al. (2001), the essential elements of an immediate individual psychological first aid intervention are as follows: (a) making psychological contact through demonstrations of empathy, warmth, and respect; (b) exploring dimensions of the crisis problem by facilitating discussion of the event and the immediate coping challenges the child is facing; (c) examining possible solutions by asking about coping attempts already made, identifying additional coping strategies, and, if needed, providing the child with specific strategies to enhance coping; (d) providing assistance in taking concrete action by helping the child to developing a concrete plan that will facilitate a return to precrisis functioning levels; and (e) follow-up, which involves discussing ways in which the psychologist will contact the child to ensure the plan has been helpful. Training Exemplar B provides a sample of such a script that can be used to illustrate and structure this activity.

The second type of psychological first aid script that our experience has found to be important is one that includes suicide risk assessment. As discussed by Ramsay, Tanney, Lang, and Kinzel (2004) and elaborated upon by Brock, Sandoval, and Hart (2006), the essential elements of a psychological first aid intervention for these students are as follows: (a) engage with the person at risk of suicide by discussing the student's feelings and the events that may have caused the onset of such thoughts; (b) explicitly identify suicidal ideation by asking whether the student is contemplating suicide; (c) inquire about the reasons for suicidal ideation, which involves asking how the student has come to believe that suicide is the only way to cope with his or her feelings; (d) assess the degree of suicide risk by examining whether the student has a plan, whether the student has the means to carry out the plan, how soon the student wants to carry out the plan, any previous mental health issues, and resources available to the student; and (e) take action to reduce suicide risk by calling the appropriate professionals (e.g., community mental health, police, parents) to assist with services needed (cf. Gard & Ruzek, 2006; Lieberman & Davis, 2002). Training Exemplar B also provides a sample of such a script that can be used to illustrate and structure this activity.

Role plays

Following readings (e.g., Brock & Davis, 2008; Brock & Jimerson, 2004b; Brock et al., 2008) and discussions addressing the full range of crisis response and intervention activities and completion of the scripts described above, school psychology students will be ready to engage in crisis response and intervention role plays. These activities are typically more difficult than scripts because they are interactive and responses are spontaneous; students involved in role plays cannot always prepare for what will happen. Due in part to their unpredictability, role plays can begin to approximate crisis situations. Role plays can be used to simulate the response to a crisis event of the multidisciplinary crisis team, as well as providing further opportunities to practice the elements of psychological first aid.

As specified by the U.S. Department of Homeland Security's (2004) NIMS and its Incident Command System (ICS), and discussed at the beginning of this chapter, school crisis team roles should include an incident commander and operations, intelligence, logistics, and finance section chiefs (cf. Brock & Poland, 2002). To role play the multidisciplinary crisis team response, students are first directed to form groups, with each group member being randomly assigned to a specific ICS function. Then, the team is given a crisis situation and 15 minutes to discuss a hypothetical crisis response. After this brief preparation period, the group is asked to role play an initial crisis response team planning meeting. To successfully complete this role play, each student will have to be knowledgeable of the different roles and responsibilities of each crisis team position, because they will not know which member they will be role playing. After the activity is completed, students can reflect in a whole-class discussion on the difficulties and challenges of the role play and evaluate the crisis team's response. Training Exemplar C provides a sample of the handout that can be used to structure this role-play activity. In addition, while one group is participating in a role play, the rest of the class will be observing this team, and from their observations students can be asked to write short papers that examine the strengths and the weaknesses of the team's role play. Through these papers, students will demonstrate their understanding of the essential elements of the school crisis response. Exemplar C also provides a sample of a handout that can be used to structure such a paper.

To role play individual psychological first aid, students are first directed to form pairs, with each individual being randomly assigned to the role of either crisis intervener or person in crisis. Then pairs are given 5 minutes to develop a hypothetical crisis situation. It is important that pairs not be given to long to "script" their role play so as to better ensure that it retains an element of spontaneity. After this brief preparation period, and after joining with another pair (to form a group of at least four), each pair is asked to role play an immediate psychological first aid response. To successfully complete this role play and illustrate the essential elements of psychological first aid, both students will have to be knowledgeable of this intervention. While these role plays are being conducted, the other two students will be observing the role play, and from their observations, they will complete separate psychological first aid observation forms. Training Exemplar C also provides a sample of this observation form. Through the completion of these forms, students will not only further demonstrate their understanding of psychological first aid, but they will also be giving their classmates feedback about their first aid skills.

Collaboration institute

Consistent with crisis team role plays, an interdisciplinary collaboration institute can be organized to practice working with the different professionals on a comprehensive multidisciplinary school crisis team. Students from a teacher education department, counselor education department, school administration program, school nursing program, and school psychology program can come together to role play how they would work together to implement a crisis plan. Groups could be formed with students from each department in each group. The role play would be similar to that described above, with a crisis scenario presented to the groups and 15 minutes devoted to role play. This activity may be difficult to organize, as the availability of each department may be limited and training programs differ across disciplines, which could mean that crisis intervention may not be included in training.

Mental health community service volunteer

Students may also benefit from direct exposure to crisis intervention agencies; however, such an activity may not be feasible for all training programs. Nevertheless, it may be an option for some students to volunteer for a community-based agency that specializes in crisis intervention. Students would be expected to shadow the professionals involved in the agency to see first hand the dynamics of crisis intervention. Class time could be allocated to debriefing these community service activities (e.g., Allen, Jerome, White, Pope, & Malinka, 2001).

Resource file

Community resources can be very beneficial for those impacted by a crisis event. In some instances, trauma may be beyond the scope of a school psychologists training, and a referral to an outside agency will be warranted. School psychologists should be knowledgeable of the mental health resources available in their community and have these resources available for families if needed. Students can develop a resource file that includes the mental health services offered in their community. Not only will students compile these resources for future use, but this activity will also aid them in understanding how to research their community, what services are offered, and fees involved with these services. Trainees could burn the resources onto a CD and provide copies for their classmates.

TRAINING EXEMPLARS

In the pages that follow, we provide more specific and detailed examples of some of the materials that we have found to be helpful in training preservice school psychologists to fill their roles on a school crisis team. For additional information on their use, refer to the prior section, which addressed pedagogical and supervisory issues.

Psychological triage practice

Following discussion of the risk factors associated with the psychological trauma that can be secondary to crisis event exposure, a psychological triage practice activity can be used to simulate and practice the process of initial risk screening. This activity begins with an evaluation of the traumatic event itself. Such an evaluation is designed to determine the event's potential to generate psychological injury. Although not helpful in identifying individuals at risk for psychological trauma, it does help to emphasize the important point that some crises are more traumatic than are others. Next, from a consideration of crisis event facts, the activity requires students to practice making crisis intervention treatment priority decisions. A sample of a worksheet that can be used to guide this activity is provided in Figure 15.1.

Sample psychological first aid scripts

Following use of course readings (e.g., Brock et al., 2001; Slaikeu, 1990) and in-class discussions/lectures, school psychology students can be asked to write a script that demonstrates their understanding of the essential elements of a psychological first aid response. Figure 15.2 provides a sample script, which offers an example of what is to be produced by school psychology students. In this example, the crisis intervention begins with an intermediate-grade student, Chris, crying in a corner of a schoolyard, just out of view of the playground. Two days earlier, Chris had witnessed a schoolyard shooting.

In addition, following use of course readings that focus on the topic of suicide (e.g., Brock, Jimerson, Lieberman, & Sharp, 2004; Brock et al., 2006; Davis & Brock, 2002) and in-class discussions/lectures, school psychology students can be asked to write a script that demonstrates their understanding of the essential elements of a first aid response to youth who

Crisis Situation 1: A pair of students from a neighboring school, in response to the belief that they had been bullied by a student at your high school, has come on campus. A fight breaks out in the student parking lot between the pair and the student's friends. A 15-year-old student is hospitalized with a stab wound, and another one of your students is killed by a gunshot wound to the head. The principal was in the immediate area and tried to intervene; he was hospitalized with serious stab wounds and is not expected to live.

Level of response required:

No Response	Site-Level Response	District-Level Response	Regional-Level Response

Justification: _____
_____
_____

Crisis intervention treatment priorities:

Which students and/or staff members will need to be seen immediately?
_____

Justification: _____
_____
_____

Which students and/or staff members will need to be seen as soon as possible, but not right away? _____
_____

Justification: _____
_____
_____

Which students and/or staff may not need to be provided crisis intervention at all? _____
_____

Justification: _____
_____
_____

Figure 15.1 Sample psychological triage practice activity worksheet used to provide school psychology students with opportunity to practice initial psychological trauma risk screenings. (Adapted from Brock, S. E., Sandoval, J., & Lewis, S. [2001]. *Preparing for crises in the schools: A manual for building school crisis response teams* [2nd ed.]. New York: Wiley.).

Making psychological contact

Counselor:	Hi. I'm Mr. Sanchez. What's your name?
Chris:	Chris.
Counselor:	Hello Chris. You look sad; can you tell me what's wrong?
Chris:	(Through tears Chris says) I'm scared.
Counselor:	I think I know why, but could you tell me why you're scared?
Chris:	I'm afraid of being shot.
Counselor:	It is frightening to be shot at. (The counselor places an arm around Chris's shoulder.) I understand why you are crying. Would it be OK if we talked? I would like to help.
Chris:	(Chris stops crying and looks at the counselor.) OK.

Exploring dimensions of the problem

Counselor:	Do you think you could tell me about what happened to you the other day?
Chris:	Yes. I was standing right over there. (Chris looks around the corner and points to the kickball field.) I was waiting my turn when the shooting started. At first I didn't know what was happening. Then I saw all the kids screaming and falling to the ground. My friend Sam was bleeding from the foot. (Chris begins to cry again.)
Counselor:	That was real scary. You know you're not alone. A lot of kids feel the same way you do. Before now, have you told anyone about being afraid to go out to play?
Chris:	No.
Counselor:	Are their people who you can talk to?
Chris:	Yes. I would like to talk to Sam.
Counselor:	Is there anyone else who might be able to help you not be scared of the playground?
Chris:	My mom, my teacher, my other friends—(pause)—and you? (Chris looks up at the counselor as the crying begins to subside again.)
Counselor:	Yes, I think I can help. Before the shooting, what was the playground like for you?
Chris:	Fun. I was great at kickball. My friends and I would always play right there. (Chris again looks around the corner and points to the kickball field.)
Counselor:	Where are your friends now?

Figure 15.2 (Continued)

| Chris: | Right there. (Chris points to a group of eight children playing kickball field.) Except Sam. Sam's at home. Sam's foot was bleeding. I miss Sam. Sam is my best friend. Can I talk to Sam? |

Examining possible solutions

Counselor:	We can look into talking to Sam after recess. But for now what can we do about your recess time. What have you done so far about being scared to play?
Chris:	I hid here or in the restroom. Once I stayed in class with my teacher.
Counselor:	Look out on the playground and tell me what you see.
Chris:	(Chris looks around the corner and at the playground.) Kids are playing.
Counselor:	Are they having fun?
Chris:	Yes. (A tentative smile briefly flashes across Chris's face.)
Counselor:	Who are those people over there and there? (The counselor points in the direction of the two police officers that have been temporarily assigned to the school after the shooting.)
Chris:	Policemen.
Counselor:	I think that it is safe to go out on the playground today. And your friends look like they can still have fun playing kickball. Do you think that anyone will hurt you on the playground today?
Chris:	No.

Assisting in taking concrete action

Counselor:	So if it's safe and still fun, why not try going out and playing again?
Chris:	But I'm still scared. (Chris's eyes become teary.)
Counselor:	OK. Let's see what we can do to help you not be scared. What if your friends helped you? What if I stayed on the playground and watched you?
Chris:	That might help. (Chris's tears subside.)
Counselor:	I'll go talk to your friends and see what I can do about getting them to include you in their kickball game. (The counselor approaches Chris's friends and explains the problem to them. They readily agree to invite Chris to play. On member of the group walks over to Chris and says ...)

Figure 15.2 (Continued)

Friend:	Chris, kickball is still fun. Will you please come and play with us?
Chris:	OK. (The friend puts an arm on Chris's shoulder and begins to walk toward the playground.)

Follow-Up

Counselor:	Before you go, Chris, can you give me your last name and your classroom? I'd like to be able to check up on you to make sure you are OK.
Chris:	Sure. My last name is Smith, and I'm in Mrs. Wong's classroom.
Counselor:	I'll be standing right over there. (The counselor points to an area just off the playground within view of the kickball field.) I'll be there during the rest of today's recess. When the bell rings in a few minutes come over and see me and we can look into how Sam is doing.
Chris:	OK. (Chris has stopped crying and is smiling as s/he walks with the group of friends out onto the playground.)

Figure 15.2 Sample psychological first aid script used to provide school psychology students with an example of what they are to generate in order to document their understanding of the essential elements of psychological first aid. (Adapted from Brock, S. E., Sandoval, J., & Lewis, S. [2001]. *Preparing for crises in the schools: A manual for building school crisis response teams* [2nd ed.]. New York: Wiley.).

present as being at risk for suicidal ideation and behavior. Figure 15.3 provides a sample script, which offers an example of what is to be produced by school psychology students. In this example, the suicide intervention involves working with a 16-year-old student, Sam, who is at high risk of engaging in a suicidal behavior. Sam's girlfriend had recently killed herself after Sam broke up with her. Sam cut school yesterday, and the crisis intervener knows that he has been drinking heavily since his girlfriend's death. It is the start of school; Sam is in attendance and sober at the time the crisis intervener meets with him.

Crisis response and intervention role plays

Following use of course readings (e.g., Brock et al., 2008) and in-class discussions/lectures, school psychology students can be asked to role play the multidisciplinary school crisis team's response to a crisis

Engage with the person at risk of suicide

Psychologist:	Hello, Sam. I want you to know how sorry I am for your loss. How are you doing?
Sam:	OK, I guess. I just can't seem to stop thinking about Susan killing herself.
Psychologist:	I understand it must be real painful to lose someone you care about. Can you tell me some more about your feelings?
Sam:	I just can't help thinking that if it wasn't for me, Susan will still be alive right now. I just can't live with the guilt.
Psychologist:	So not only are you dealing with the sudden death of Susan, but you are also feeling real guilty?
Sam:	Yes. (Sam begins to cry.)

Identify suicidal ideation

Psychologist:	You know Sam, sometimes when people have experienced a sudden loss and feel as you do, they think of suicide. Is this something you have thought about?
Sam:	(Sam stops crying, pauses, and tentatively says) Yes.

Inquire about the reasons for suicidal thinking

Psychologist:	I think I understand, but can you tell me some more about what it is that has led you to think about suicide?
Sam:	I just can't live with this guilt. Everyone is looking at me. They know that I had broken up with Susan. No one, except you, will talk to me. I'm sure everyone hates me and wishes I were dead. I might as well do them a favor.
Psychologist:	So then you are really feeling alone right now. You are thinking that you are being blamed for Susan's death.
Sam:	You got that right. (Sam's tears have now turned to some anger.) I'll show them.

Figure 15.3 Sample psychological first aid script used to provide school psychology students with an example of what they are generate in order to document their understanding of the essential elements of a psychological first aid intervention that includes suicide risk. (Adapted from a model of risk assessment in Ramsay, R. F., Tanney, B. L., Lang, W. A., & Kinzel, T. [2004]. Suicide intervention handbook [10th ed.]. Calgary, Alberta, Canada: LivingWorks.)

Psychologist:	What do you mean "I'll show them"?
Sam:	If I kill myself, they won't have me to kick around any more!

(I have identified that Sam is feeling very guilty about Susan's death and feels isolated and alone. He is also feeling that everyone is blaming him for Susan's death [which may or may not be true]. I know that he has thoughts of suicide, but I need to assess his risk of engaging in such behavior.)

Assess the degree of suicide risk

Psychologist:	Sam, you mentioned that you think suicide is a way to cope with the feelings and problems generated by Susan's death. Do you have a plan? How would you go about killing yourself?
Sam:	Yes, I could do it with my car.
Psychologist:	Have you thought about when you would do it?
Sam:	Yes, I was planning to get drunk and drive off the bridge tonight.
Psychologist:	So the pain feels so intense you are thinking of crashing your car off the bridge tonight.
Sam:	Yes.
Psychologist:	Have you ever tried to talk to anyone about this pain before?
Sam:	I was thinking about going to my old therapist, but I don't even know if she is still around. It has been over a year since I last saw her.
Psychologist:	What were you seeing the therapist for?
Sam:	Depression.
Psychologist:	Sam, have you ever tried anything like this before?
Sam:	No.
Psychologist:	Is there anyone you can talk to about this? Anyone who you think could help you solve these problems?
Sam:	No. (Sam slumps into his chair. The anger has dissolved, and he again begins to sob.)

(Sam has a plan, he has the means to carry it out, and he has a pretty immediate time frame for engaging in suicidal behavior. He is in intense emotional pain and feeling extreme guilt. While he has no prior suicidal behavior himself, the fact that Susan has modeled it as a problem-solving strategy places him at increased risk. Finally, I have learned that Sam is unable to identify any resources that can move him from a suicide orientation and that he has a history of depression. I determine that his risk for suicide is high.)

Figure 15.3 (Continued)

Take action to reduce the suicide risk

Psychologist: Sam, I know it hurts a lot right now and it seems like there is no way out, but I believe that I can help you, if you let me.

Sam: What can you do? (A hint of anger returns to Sam's voice.) I'm ready to leave now.

(Sam gets up and leaves the office. After giving the secretary a signal that I need assistance, I follow Sam to the parking lot.)

Psychologist: Sam, we need to get some help right now. How would you like to proceed?

Sam: I'm done with all of this.

Psychologist: OK, Sam, I understand. You see no hope. But I do. You need to come with me right now. (My voice is compassionate, but firm.)

(This intervention needs to be very direct. The secretary has alerted the principal of my need for assistance. He is standing by on the edge of the parking lot. If need be, he could immediately contact the police for assistance. As it turns out, Sam responds to my very direct and firm approach. He cooperates with me and his parents, who take him to the crisis intervention clinic at the local mental health facility.)

Figure 15.3 (Continued)

situation. Figure 15.4 provides a handout that can be used to stimulate what can be described as a tabletop school crisis response drill. In addition, from school psychology student observations of other teams' crisis response role plays, they can be asked to write short papers that identify the strengths and weaknesses of the other team's role play. Through these papers, the preservice school psychologist further demonstrates his or her understanding of the essential elements of the school crisis response. Figure 15.5 provides an outline of the observation papers for the crisis response role play.

Following course readings (e.g., Brock et al., 2001) and in-class discussions/lectures, school psychology students can also be asked to role play the individual psychological first aid response. In addition, the observations provided by classmates can serve to further reinforce understanding of the essential elements of psychological first aid and can also be used to give feedback to role players regarding their crisis intervention skills. Figure 15.6 provides a form that can be used to structure role play observations.

Crisis Situation 1: A freak tornado has occurred on a very rainy Friday afternoon. This unusually powerful storm hit just as the primary-grade students were sitting down to lunch in the cafeteria. The force of the storm has blown the roof off of the building and caused significant property damage to the school. Emergency response personnel have already responded and transported 13 students to five different regional hospitals. Your crisis response team is sitting down to plan the next intervention steps. The meeting begins with the principal informing the team that as far as he knows, three students were killed and several appeared to be seriously injured. News of this freak storm is all over the airwaves, and large numbers of media personnel and parents are arriving on the scene. Both groups are very demanding of news of what has happened. In particular, parents want to retrieve their children and take them home immediately. They are, in fact, becoming very agitated. Some of the children are very frightened and are becoming hysterical.

What is your immediate crisis response? _____

_____

_____

_____

What are some of your thoughts regarding the immediate and long-term crisis intervention plan?

_____

_____

_____

If you require additional factual information about the crisis event, you may obtain it from the instructor.

Crisis Situation 2: A car crash has occurred in front of a high school on a Tuesday morning. This crash does not appear to be an accident. The parent of a child who had recently been suspended from school (and who was very angry at the school) has driven her car into a crowd of students as school was about to start. This mother also has a history of mental illness. Emergency response personnel have already responded and transported 10 students to three different regional hospitals. Your crisis response team is sitting down to plan the next intervention steps.

Figure 15.4 Handout used to stimulate a school crisis team role play.

The meeting begins with the principal informing the team that as far as he knows, one student was killed and several appeared to be seriously injured. As news of the crash spreads throughout the community, large numbers of media personnel and parents are arriving on the scene. Both groups are very demanding of news of what has happened. In particular, parents want to retrieve their children and take them home immediately. They are, in fact, becoming very agitated.

What is your immediate crisis response? _____
_____
_____
_____

What are some of your thoughts regarding the immediate and long-term crisis intervention plan? _____
_____
_____
_____

If you require additional factual information about the crisis event, you may obtain it from the instructor.

Figure 15.4 (Continued)

From your observations of other teams' crisis response role plays, write a short paper (no more than 4 double-spaced pages) that identifies the strengths and the weaknesses of the team's role play. Through these papers you demonstrate your understanding of the essential elements of the school crisis response.

1. Identify the setting within which the role play was supposed to have been conducted.
2. Describe the crisis situation being addressed by the crisis response team.
3. What were the major challenges presented by the crisis scenario?
4. What were the strengths of the role-played crisis response?
5. What were the weaknesses of the role-played crisis response?

Figure 15.5 Crisis response role-play observation paper outline.

Role Players:_____ Observer: _____

Crisis situation

_____

_____

Make psychological contact

Empathy _____
Respect _____
Warmth _____

Explore dimensions of the problem

Apparently unsolvable problem(s) _____
Immediate issues _____
Future concerns _____

Examine possible solutions

ASK: Coping attempts already made _____
FACILITATE: Identify additional coping strategies _____
PROPOSE: Direct to specific coping strategies _____

Take concrete action

Level of lethality _____
        Facilitative actions _____
        Direction actions _____

Follow-up

Identifying information _____
Follow-up procedures _____
Contract for recontact _____

Figure 15.6 Psychological first aid observation coding sheet.

RESOURCES

    1. *Diversity and crisis intervention.* This interaction between a cri-
sis event and culture is a critical topic to explore when considering
the provision of school crisis intervention services. To facilitate the

Table 15.1 Selected References Addressing the Issues of Culture, Crisis, and Intervention

---

Choi, H., Meininger, J. C., & Roberts, R. E. (2006). Ethnic differences in adolescents' mental distress, social distress, and resources. *Adolescence, 41*, 263–283.

Daniel, J. H., Roysircar, G., Abeles, N., & Boyd, C. (2004). Individual and cultural-diversity competency: Focus on the therapist. *Journal of Clinical Psychology, 60*, 755–770.

Dixon, J. C. (2006). The ties that bind and those that don't: Toward reconciling group threat and contact theories of prejudice. *Social Forces, 84*, 2180–2204.

Dunbar, E. (2001). Counseling practices to ameliorate the effects of discrimination and hate events: Toward a systematic approach to assessment and intervention. *The Counseling Psychologist, 29*, 281–307.

Fuertes, J. N., Mueller, L. N., Chauhan, R. V., Walker, J. A., & Ladany, N. (2002). An investigation of European American therapists' approach to counseling African American clients. *The Counseling Psychologist, 30*, 763–788.

Moodley, R. (2005). Outside race, inside gender: A good enough "holding environment" in counseling and psychotherapy. *Counseling Psychology Quarterly, 18*, 319–328.

Querimit, D. S., & Conner, L. C. (2003). Empowerment psychotherapy with adolescent females of color. *Journal of Clinical Psychology, 59*, 1215–1224.

Sue, D. W., & Sue, D. (2003). *Counseling the culturally diverse* (4th ed.). New York: Wiley.

---

examination of this topic the references provided in Table 15.1 are provided.

2. *NASP PREPaRE Crisis Prevention and Intervention Workshops.* Written by and for school-based mental health professionals, *PREPaRE* is an evidence-based school crisis prevention, preparedness, intervention, and recovery curriculum designed to provide educators with training on how to best fill the roles and responsibilities generated by their membership on school crisis teams. It includes two separate workshops:

   a. *Workshop 1. Crisis Prevention and Preparedness: The Comprehensive School Crisis Team.* This one-day workshop provides school-based mental health professionals and other educators with an understanding of the comprehensive school crisis team and their role on these teams.

   b. *Workshop 2. Crisis Intervention and Recovery: The Roles of School-Based Mental Health Professionals.* This two-day workshop provides school-based mental health professionals with the knowledge needed to meet the needs of students and staff following a school associated crisis event.

3. *Best Practices in School Crisis and Intervention* (Brock, Lazarus, & Jimerson, 2002). This edited volume provides a comprehensive review of the topics of crisis prevention and intervention. It includes specific chapters that address specific crisis situations.

REFERENCES

Allen, M., Jerome, A., White, A., Marston, S., Lamb, S., Pope, D., et al. (2002). The preparation of school psychologists for crisis intervention. *Psychology in the Schools, 39*, 427–439.

Allen, M., Jerome, A., White, A., Pope, D., & Malinka, A. (2001). Effective university training for school crisis intervention. *The Trainers Forum, 21*(2), 1–3, 7–9.

American Psychiatric Association. (2000). *Diagnostic and statistical manual of mental disorders* (4th ed., text revision). Washington, DC: Author.

Brock, S. E. (2002a). Crisis theory: A foundation for the comprehensive crisis prevention and intervention team. In S. E. Brock, P. J. Lazarus, & S. R. Jimerson (Eds.), *Best practices in school crisis prevention and intervention* (pp. 5–17). Bethesda, MD: National Association of School Psychologists.

Brock, S. E. (2002b). Estimating the appropriate crisis response. In S. E. Brock, P. J. Lazarus, & S. R. Jimerson (Eds.), *Best practices in school crisis prevention and intervention* (pp. 355–365). Bethesda, MD: National Association of School Psychologists.

Brock, S. E. (2002c). Identifying individuals at risk for psychological trauma. In S. E. Brock, P. J. Lazarus, & S. R. Jimerson (Eds.), *Best practices in school crisis prevention and intervention* (pp. 367–384). Bethesda, MD: National Association of School Psychologists.

Brock, S. E. (2006). *Crisis intervention and recovery: The roles of school-based mental health professionals.* (Available from National Association of School Psychologists, 4340 East-West Highway, Suite 402, Bethesda, MD 20814.)

Brock, S. E., & Davis, J. (2008). Best practices in school crisis intervention. In A. Thomas & J. Grimes (Eds.), *Best practices in school psychology* (Vol. 3, pp. 781–798). Bethesda, MD: National Association of School Psychologists.

Brock, S. E., & Jimerson, S. R. (2004a). Characteristics and consequences of crisis events: A primer for the school psychologist. In E. R Berler, Jr. (Ed.), *Handbook of school violence* (pp. 273–332). Binghamton, NY: Haworth Press.

Brock, S. E., & Jimerson, S. R. (2004b). School crisis interventions: Strategies for addressing the consequences of crisis events. In E. R. Berler, Jr. (Ed.), *Handbook of school violence* (pp. 273–332). Binghamton, NY: Haworth Press.

Brock, S. E., Jimerson, S. R., Lieberman, R., & Sharp, E. (2004). Preventing suicide: Information for caregivers and educators. In A. S. Canter, L. Z. Paige, M. E. Roth, I. Romero, & S. A. Carroll (Eds.), *Helping children at home and school II: Handouts for families and educators* (pp. S9: 33–35). Bethesda, MD: National Association of School Psychologists.

Brock, S. E., Lazarus, P. J., & Jimerson, S. R. (Eds.). (2002). *Best practices in school crisis and intervention.* Bethesda, MD: National Association of School Psychologists.

Brock, S. E., Nickerson, A. B., Reeves, M. A., & Jimerson, S. R. (2008). Best practices for school psychologists as members of crisis teams: The PREPaRE model. In A. Thomas & J. Grimes (Eds.), *Best practices in school psychology*

(Vol. 4, pp. 1487–1504). Bethesda, MD: National Association of School Psychologists.

Brock, S. E., & Poland, S. (2002). School crisis preparedness. In S. E. Brock, P. J. Lazarus, & S. R. Jimerson (Eds.). *Best practices in school crisis prevention and intervention* (pp. 273–288). Bethesda, MD: National Association of School Psychology.

Brock, S. E., Sandoval, J., & Hart, S. R. (2006). Suicidal ideation and behaviors. In G. Bear & K. Minke (Eds.), *Children's needs III: Understanding and addressing the developmental needs of children* (pp. 187–197). Bethesda, MD: National Association of School Psychologists.

Brock, S. E., Sandoval, J., & Lewis, S. (2001). *Preparing for crises in the schools: A manual for building school crisis response teams* (2nd ed.). New York: Wiley.

Brown, F., & Rainer, J. (2006). Too much to bear: An introduction to crisis intervention and therapy. *Journal of Clinical Psychology: In Session, 62,* 953–957.

Costello, E. J., Erkanli, A., Fairbank, J. A., & Angold, A. (2002). The prevalence of potentially traumatic events in childhood and adolescence. *Journal of Traumatic Stress, 15,* 99–112.

Davis, J. M., & Brock, S. E. (2002). Suicide. In J. Sandoval (Ed.), *Handbook of crisis counseling, intervention and prevention in the schools* (2nd ed., pp. 273–299). Hillsdale, NJ: Lawrence Erlbaum Associates.

Dykeman, B. (2005). Cultural implications of crisis intervention. *Journal of Instructional Psychology, 32,* 45–48.

Gaffney, D. (2006). The aftermath of disaster: Children in crisis. *Journal of Clinical Psychology: In Session, 62,* 1001–1016.

Gard, B., & Ruzek, J. (2006). Community mental health response to crisis. *Journal of Clinical Psychology: In Session, 62,* 1029–1041.

Lieberman, R., & Davis, J. (2002). Suicide intervention. In S. E. Brock, P. J. Lazarus, & S. R. Jimerson (Eds.), *Best practices in school crisis prevention and intervention* (pp. 531–532). Bethesda, MD: National Association of School Psychologists.

McNally, R. J., Bryant, R. A., & Ehlers, A. (2003). Does early psychological intervention promote recovery from posttraumatic stress? *Psychological Sciences in the Public Interest, 4,* 45–80.

Myer, R., & Conte, C., (2006). Assessment for crisis intervention. *Journal of Clinical Psychology: In Session, 62,* 959–970.

National Association of School Psychologists. (2000). *Standards for training and field placement programs in school psychology.* Bethesda, MD: Author.

National Institute of Mental Health. (2002). *Mental health and mass violence: Evidence-based early psychological intervention for victims/survivors of mass violence. A workshop to reach consensus on best practices.* Washington, DC: U.S. Government Printing Office.

Nickerson, A. B., & Zhe, E. J. (2004). Crisis prevention and intervention: A survey of school psychologists. *Psychology in the Schools, 41,* 777–788.

Ramsay, R. F., Tanney, B. L., Lang, W. A., & Kinzel, T. (2004). *Suicide intervention handbook* (10th ed.). Calgary, AB: LivingWorks.

Slaikeu, K. A. (1990). *Crisis intervention: A handbook for practice and research* (2nd ed.). Needham Heights, MA: Allyn & Bacon.

Sullivan, M., Harris, E., Collado, C., & Chen, T. (2006). Noways tired: Perspectives of clinicians of color on culturally competent crisis intervention. *Journal of Clinical Psychology: In Session, 62,* 987–999.

Swerdlik, M., & French, J. (2000). School psychology training for the 21st century: Challenges and opportunities. *School Psychology Review, 29,* 577–588.

Tramonte, M. R. (1999, April). *School psychology in the new millennium: Constructing and implementing a blueprint for intervening in crisis involving disasters and/or violence.* Paper presented at the Annual Convention of the National Association of School Psychologists, Las Vegas, NV.

Watkins, M. W., Crosby, E. G., & Pearson, J. L. (2001). Role of the school psychologist: Perceptions of school staff. *School Psychology International, 22,* 64–73.

U.S. Department of Homeland Security. (2004, March). *National incident management system.* Retrieved September 9, 2005, from http://www.fema.gov/pdf/nims/nims_doc_full.pdf

16 Community collaboration and university-based clinics in school psychology

Edward M. Levinson, Lynanne Black, Mary Ann Rafoth, and Jaime E. Slonim

INTRODUCTION

Practica and school-based experiences are important components of any school psychology training program. Although there are many ways to provide applied clinical experiences, one way is to establish university-based clinics where graduate students can practice clinical skills while being closely supervised by a faculty member. The university-based clinic can provide a myriad of additional benefits to the community. For example, universities can offer free or low-cost clinic services to community members who are in need of psychological evaluations and/or interventions at a reduced rate. Also, individuals who do not have health insurance will be able to take advantage of these clinics. Furthermore, university clinics can provide school-aged children services for issues that cannot be addressed during the school day or when parents prefer assistance that is independent from the school system. University clinic referrals are welcome from the parent, child, local school system personnel (e.g., school psychologist, counselor, or child's teacher), community agencies, or physician.

The organization, administration, supervision, funding, and advertising requirements will vary from university to university; however, the benefits of establishing a university-based clinic in collaboration with the community out weigh all "administrivia." The purpose of this chapter is to discuss the benefits of university-based clinics for the university and for the community. As such, this chapter will (a) review the literature on existing university-based clinics and their common characteristics, (b) discuss issues associated with the development of successful university-based clinics, (c) examine the benefits that university-based clinics provide to communities, (d) examine what benefits university-based clinics derive from their communities, (e) discuss methods by which universities can build bridges with their communities, (f) discuss training and supervision issues within the context of a university-based clinic, and (g) discuss the university-based clinic at Indiana University of Pennsylvania as a case example for highlighting the critical issues associated with successful clinic–community collaboration.

LITERATURE REVIEW

Lightner Witmer is credited with the development of the first university-based psychology clinic in America. His clinic was founded in 1896 at the University of Pennsylvania, and it was not unlike that of other clinics in that it pursued a tripartite mission involving training, research, and service delivery (Association of Directors of Psychology Training Clinics, 2006). Today, clinics have clear mission statements that are heavily rooted in the priorities and goals of the particular clinic, and one goal is usually to provide training for graduate level psychology students while offering a service to the community at large. Over the past two decades, university-based psychology clinics have increased in popularity, and several descriptions of clinics can be found in the literature.

COMMON CHARACTERISTICS

A review of existing university-based clinics clearly suggests a number of characteristics that most share. University-based clinics are usually located on the campus of the university. The clinics serve as a training center for university graduate students and, at the same time, provide a needed community service. The staff usually comprises graduate students in the counseling, clinical, and/or school psychology programs and is always supervised by credentialed (e.g., licensed and/or certified) psychologists. The licensed professionals may be faculty members from the university, practicing professionals from the community, or a combination thereof. Most clinics attempt to provide graduate students with exposure to a broad range of pathologies that require a variety of interventions, all the while providing students with supervision by professionals with different supervisory styles (Ebata, 1996). Such clinics provide training opportunities for interns, research opportunities for psychologists, fees for the university, and specialty services to meet the needs of university students as well as the needs of children and adults in the community at large (Benson & Hughes, 1985).

The majority of referrals come from physicians, parents, and school personnel. Referrals are typically linked to the geographic area that is in close proximity to the university and are most often for school-age children with home- or school-related problems (Murrell, Steel, Gaston, & Proudfoot, 2002). Issues such as difficulty in adjustment, behavioral problems, academic subject weaknesses, and a need for special education or gifted evaluations are some of the reasons the community makes use of a university-based clinic.

The goal of most university-based clinics is to treat anyone in need of psychological services regardless of ability to pay. Fees are usually based on a sliding scale, and appointments are often available evenings and weekends to accommodate working clients and parents of clients. In addition to providing low-cost assessment, intervention, and instruction, outreach programs and workshops are often arranged by the clinic staff (Benson & Hughes, 1985).

ISSUES ASSOCIATED WITH THE DEVELOPMENT OF A SUCCESSFUL UNIVERSITY-BASED CLINIC

Walsh (2006) examined the elements necessary for a school/community program to succeed. The key elements identified to establish a successful school- and community-based clinic are as follows. First, there must be a facility where services are available on a regularly scheduled basis. The clinic must be in a proper environment that can provide a waiting room and confidential treatment rooms. Continuity is critical for the success of a program. Second, a set of key people is necessary to organize the program, set and implement clear policies, and oversee operations. Specifically, there is a need for administrative staff to keep records, collect fees, file records with insurance companies, and set appointments. There must be a set of policies and rules that are enumerated in a clinic manual that defines the program and its operation. The manual should also specify crisis care and emergency procedures. Next, a dedicated staff is necessary whose members are effective at recruiting children and youth in need of services and can contact community agency representatives to help encourage those in the community to take advantage of the various programs that are being offered. Finally, there must also be professionals who are committed to working with youth on a regular basis.

In addition to logistics, there are a number of questions about impact that must be answered when establishing a university-based clinic. If the clinic space is provided by the university, how do the policies of the institution affect the operation of the clinic, what faculty and staff are available to work in the clinic, and how will the clinic operation will be funded? In 1990, President George H. W. Bush signed the National Service Act providing funding for community service programs in colleges (Frumkin & Imber, 2004). Universities that have the physical space, faculty members, and support staff necessary to organize and operate a university-based clinic can potentially receive funding for establishing one. The allocation and/or creation of clinical space by the university, assignment of clinical supervision as part of a faculty member's load, assignment of a clinical director who receives workload compensation, assignment of graduate assistants to assist in clinic operation, availability of clerical staff, and the maintenance of an up-to-date assessment and intervention resource library by the college or university are all critical and costly features associated with university-based clinics.

Another important issue confronting those developing university-based clinics is the extent to which the clinic will interact with the local school system in that both may be providing many of the same services. Although the clinic is likely to act independently from the school system, at times there will be a need to coordinate services. There cannot be any discrimination based on religion, race, age, sex, sexual orientation, class, gender, color, handicap, or national origin (Benson & Hughes, 1985). The needs of the community must be continually reviewed to make certain that the clinic is addressing these needs. The availability of the university-based clinic should be publicized in the community, and the community agencies that send referrals should be kept informed of the workings of the clinic.

Since the clinic offers professional training experiences to students engaged in practicum experiences, there must be a predetermined method of resolving problems between trainees and supervisors. There must also be a policy outlining the proper protocol for addressing ethical violations. In order to protect the welfare of clients, major ethical violations are often grounds for the removal of the student trainee from the program (Association of Directors of Psychology Training Clinics, 2006).

ADVANTAGES OF UNIVERSITY-BASED CLINICS FOR THE COMMUNITY

There are a number of advantages that university-based clinics provide to their local communities. These include, among others, the ability to offer services to community members who cannot afford to pay for the services and the opportunity to provide evaluation services and interventions that the local schools and community agencies may not be able to offer (Ebata, 1996). In addition, the university-based clinic can provide some relief to overburdened public agencies and school systems by offering services that they are ill-equipped to provide or unable to provide because of limited funding (Groark & McCall, 1996).

According to the National Association of School Psychologists (NASP), there are an increasing number of urban schools where the majority population is composed of minority students (Ysseldyke et al., 1997). Many minority students in urban schools do not have access to mental health services through health care benefits (Ysseldyke et al.), and many of these school systems are overloaded with students in need of services (Ysseldyke et al.). Similarly, immigrant populations, which include a large undocumented population, tend to hold jobs that do not provide health insurance benefits. The only medical services that are often received are those for a physical illness in a hospital emergency room where no one can be turned away because of inability to pay (Ysseldyke et al.). Psychological services, including evaluations and interventions, are a luxury that the uninsured and underinsured cannot afford. As such, university-based clinics can be a valuable resource for the community, especially for children from poor families.

Community agencies are often overburdened. Collaboration between community professionals and university-based clinics can free community staff resources for other tasks while providing graduate students with the opportunity to become part of the community at large. As a consequence, the community may be able to allocate more money to other items in its budget if the need to pay for psychological services is reduced because the university is working in collaboration with the community to provide such services (Benson & Hughes, 1985; Ebata, 1996). By serving members of the community while working in a university-based clinic, graduate students become familiar with the milieu of the community. Wherever the new school psychologist practices, the experience of working within the context of a community is likely to provide the professional a broader view of the opportunities and complexities faced by any school district in any community.

BENEFITS DERIVED BY UNIVERSITY-BASED CLINICS FROM COMMUNITY COLLABORATION

The clinic receives a number of benefits from community collaboration. Generally, these revolve around training, research, funding, and public relations. A university-based clinic derives its referrals from the community, which enables graduate students to experience real children with real problems. Moreover, it affords graduate students the opportunity to work with a wide range of children and their families and experience a variety of academic and mental health issues. As such, the clinic provides an authentic experience to trainees.

Community collaboration also affords faculty members working in university-based clinics the opportunity to design and plan research projects consistent with community needs and their professional interests. In many cases, these projects can be collaboratively planned and implemented with community agency personnel. Moreover, such collaborative projects may be eligible for local, state, or federal grant monies, in which case the work may generate additional finances and/or resources for the university. In addition, although university clinics are not likely to be big money earners, the fees associated with the services the clinic provides may be enough to support additional graduate assistant positions in the department, purchase additional course-related materials, or provide seed money for research by faculty.

Lastly, that clinics are able to provide high-quality services at low cost to those in the community is likely to positively impact the impression that those in the community have of the university and its faculty. Similarly, giving back to the community is consistent with professional ethics codes and serves as a model for trainees.

BUILDING BRIDGES WITH THE COMMUNITY

Relationships often exist between school psychology training programs and local school districts for practicum purposes, although students also can be provided with these experiences through school psychology clinics. Practica occurring within both local school districts and school psychology clinics can be mutually beneficial to students and districts. School psychology clinics, however, present unique opportunities to bond with the local community and offer an array of services beyond the characteristic psychoeducational assessment.

In order for school psychology clinics to be viewed by the local community as a viable option for seeking help, strong relationships must exist between the two entities. Directors of school psychology clinics, along with faculty in the department, must seek out members of the community to create and sustain these relationships. Consequently, faculty will be able to build bridges between the local community and the university. One important way for faculty members to achieve this goal is to be visible in the community. They need to demonstrate to community members they are committed to becoming active members of that community. They also need to show that they are invested in the well-being of the community members and the continued growth of the community itself. There are several ways faculty members can exhibit their dedication to the community, such as living in the community and/or surrounding area, raising a family there, sending their children to local schools, and participating in local organizations, committees, and/or governing bodies.

Another important way for school psychology clinics and department faculty to build bridges with the community is to offer their services to its members. School psychology faculty, as well as school psychology graduate students, can provide an assortment of services to the schools in the community at no charge, on a sliding scale, or for a reduced rate. Thus, the relationship becomes a mutually beneficial one. School psychology faculty can serve as consultants to local school districts and other educational institutions to facilitate the education of their students. Also, many school psychology faculty are able to obtain grants to provide supplementary programs within community schools that may not otherwise have been available. In addition, school psychology clinics typically provide services to children, families, schools, and community agencies and therefore can act as a liaison for all interested parties. As such, they continue to build connections within the community and establish their role as collaborating organizations. Furthermore, school psychology students can provide consultation, assessment, prevention, and intervention services to these same school districts, although they do require on-site supervision for this to occur.

A third way that school psychology clinics can bridge the gap between the community and the university is by providing supplementary help to school psychologists in local school districts. These district psychologists often are burdened by considerable workloads, and the schools may not have enough psychologists to meet the needs of their students. For many districts, having collaborative relationships with school psychology clinics can help to lessen the psychologists' workload. Moreover, if the clinic works jointly with the school districts to provide assessment information that is useful for them, the relationship can be strengthened even more. School psychology clinics also have the capability of allowing students to engage in other types of job-related activities, such as short-term student counseling, short-term family counseling, and intervention implementation, due to the close supervision they provide. School psychologists within school districts often do not have the time, nor are they compensated for performing these activities outside the school day. Therefore, school psychology clinics serve as a valuable agency to which school districts can feel comfortable referring their families.

ISSUES IN TRAINING AND SUPERVISION

The NASP and the American Psychological Association (APA) recognize the need for supervision by credentialed (e.g., licensed and/or certified) practitioners for all students of school psychology. Numerous professional organizations have developed standards that guide training in various areas of psychology, and these standards must be considered when operating university-based clinics. For example, in school psychology, NASP has developed standards for the provision of school psychological services and standards for training and field placement programs in school psychology that university-based clinics must adhere to when they are used as training grounds for school psychology graduate students in NASP-approved programs (Thomas & Grimes, 2002). Many NASP standards address training and supervision issues relevant to university-based clinics and emphasize the importance of community collaboration. Standards highlight the various ways university-based clinics might provide services that would benefit the community and afford graduate students needed training. For example, the guidelines state that school psychologists are responsible for presenting and disseminating information on their services to the community at large (NASP, Practice Guideline 2.3, 2002) as a regular part of training experiences for students attending NASP approved programs—the university clinic experience clearly provides this opportunity. Furthermore, the school psychologist needs to act as a liaison between schools and community agencies (NASP, Practice Guideline 8.4, 2002) in order to create linkages between schools, community agencies, and families with the goal of addressing the needs of all parties involved—university-based clinics provide this learning experience in a concrete manner. Lastly, school psychological and mental health services must be seamless in order for clients to benefit from the greatest possible support (NASP, Unit Guideline 1.3, 2002)—university clinics can serve as a model for seamless service delivery.

The Association of Directors of Psychology Training Clinics (ADPTC), in its revised manual dated August 2006, has enumerated a list of training and supervision guidelines that should be addressed in the operation of university-based clinics. These guidelines state that under the leadership of the director, every clinic should develop policies to ensure that the clinic provides high-quality supervision. Clinics are encouraged to implement an individual training/supervision plan to guide clinic training for each student, and initial plans should be based on some assessment of the student's competencies at the beginning of his or her clinic experience. The plans should be developed jointly by the supervisor and student and should specify learning goals. It is recommended that training plans be developed at the beginning of the clinic experience, reviewed at predesignated points during the clinic experience, and discussed at the conclusion of the clinic experience in order to assess progress and identify areas in need of additional training. The training plans can be used as both an evaluation tool to gauge student progress and for guidance in regard to appropriate caseload assignment to trainees.

Moreover, the ADPTC (2006) maintains that the supervisor has four responsibilities. The first responsibility is to provide leadership. The supervisor must be educated in the field and must be capable of working with supervisees to teach them how best to put their knowledge to practical use. According to the ADPTC standards, a supervisor must be licensed or certified in the area that he or she is to supervise. Furthermore, the supervisor's performance must be reevaluated on a timely basis, and this evaluation should include feedback from the trainees. The second responsibility is to enhance supervisees' functioning by guiding them in a continuing and ongoing program of learning. This learning is not only of novel methods but should incorporate attitudes, skills, compassion, and professionalism. The third responsibility is to encourage self-supervision. As supervisees become more experienced school psychologists, it should become second nature to analyze their own performance and to initiate changes as necessary. Self-supervision can be accomplished via use of such techniques as taping sessions and analyzing them, and obtaining evaluations from clients and other professionals with whom they are working. Feedback from clients, their family members, and teachers can help a school psychologist self-evaluate. The fourth and perhaps most critical responsibility is to guard the welfare of clients. The supervisor is legally responsible for all the actions of the supervisees. It is the supervisor's job to remain cognizant of all the legal and ethical issues as they relate to the practice of school psychology. The ethical principles for a supervisor include guarding the welfare of the client, providing the correct services, maintaining a professional relationship, and recognizing the responsibility to the community and to society (Jacob-Timm, 1998, as cited in Harvey & Struzziero, 2000). It is also the responsibility of the supervisor to ensure that all supervisees are practicing ethically.

As such, the ADPTC (2006) guidelines described above suggest the following:

1. Supervisors should be licensed, certified, or otherwise qualified to practice in areas of work that they supervise.
2. Supervisors and trainees should adhere to the ethical standards of professional organizations such as NASP and APA.
3. Policies should be in place to ensure that supervisors are competent to provide supervision in the activities they are expected to supervise and be qualified to provide supervision based upon their education, training, and experience.
4. Supervisors are encouraged to use written supervision contracts that specify learning objectives appropriate for each trainee.
5. Supervisors should ensure that clinic policies are followed and that case assignment, type of treatment, and the amount of supervision a trainee receives are appropriate for that student's developmental level of competence.
6. Clinics should have a written policy regarding documentation of supervision, and records of supervision activities should be maintained for each supervisor and trainee.
7. Clinics should have written policies regarding how trainees are evaluated over the course of their training.
8. Supervisor performance should be evaluated on a regular basis and should include feedback from trainees (usually through standardized supervision/supervisor evaluation forms) and peer/director input.

Finally, the supervisor must also have training in working with diverse cultural populations. Minority students can be found in the majority of schools across the United States. There may be a clash between behaviors that are culturally acceptable and behaviors that are deemed acceptable in our schools. It is therefore paramount for the supervising school psychologist to be familiar with the population with whom he or she is working. Knowledge and respect are necessary for a professional to be able to work with a culture other than his or her own (Harvey & Struzziero, 2000). Best practice mandates that the needs of the client always be put first. In order to ensure that the client's needs are properly addressed, the supervisor must deliberately discuss minority issues and allow for role playing and brainstorming as to how best to handle situations that may arise when working with clients from diverse backgrounds (Harvey & Struzziero, 2000). The school psychology supervisor must help supervisees explore their attitudes toward diverse student populations.

CASE ILLUSTRATION

In this section, we discuss the university clinic operated by the Department of Educational and School Psychology at Indiana University of Pennsylvania (IUP) as a means of highlighting the issues discussed above and other critical issues associated with successful clinic–community collaboration. In particular, we discuss community-based initiatives that the Child Study Center (CSC) has undertaken and the kinds of services the CSC provides to both the university and the community. We then discuss supervision within the context of the CSC. We begin with a brief description of the CSC, its facilities, and its organization.

Description

The CSC at IUP is housed in the College of Education and Educational Technology. The CSC is the oldest and longest running center in the university's history. The primary purpose of the CSC is to serve as a training facility for school psychology graduate students, as well as to serve the university community and the community at large. Traditionally, on-site services include psychoeducational evaluations, consultation with parents and educational personnel, behavioral assessment and intervention, brief counseling for children and families, and so on. All services are provided for a nominal fee, but a sliding scale and fee waiver are also available.

Two graduate assistants handle the administrative aspects of the clinic and consult the director, a certified school psychologist, when needed. Graduate assistantships are funded by the School of Graduate Studies and Research at IUP. The College of Education and Educational Technology (the college in which the CSC is housed) allows for a three-credit-hour release from teaching and a small summer stipend for the center director. The CSC's test, assessment, and intervention library is supported through student instructional fees. Installation of its state-of-the-art Landro digital audio and video equipment, designed to assist in the supervision and training of students, was supported by a $70,000 university grant paid for by student technology fees and awarded to the Department of Educational and School Psychology. The clinic furniture and lobby area are jointly provided/supported by the department and the college. Although the Director manages the administration of the clinic, faculty supervisors (including the director) are assigned to supervise specialist level school psychology students who register for the on-site clinical practicum as a course. Each class section is limited to seven practicum students per supervisor. Doctoral level students who are already certified school psychologists register for clinical practicum in the CSC as well and receive experience as supervisors in training. They, in consultation with faculty supervisors, provide direct supervision to specialist level students.

Clinic services are offered year-round, although the bulk of referrals are accepted during the spring and summer. Referrals come from school personnel, parents, community agency representatives, and university employees. Clients are seen on Fridays, Saturdays, and weekday evenings during the spring; and day and evening hours are available Monday through Thursday during the summer. The CSC has three testing rooms outfitted with furniture, cameras, microphones, and a call system. An observation room, into which video and audio from the testing rooms is routed, is equipped with LCD televisions, computers with hard drives, digital video recorders, DVD player/recorders, and VCRs. This equipment, built around the Landro system developed by Iris Technologies and in use at a number of clinics around the country, allows for all sessions to be viewed live and/or recorded and edited by a supervisor. The benefits of using this system for supervision are discussed below.

Community-based initiatives

Although the majority of CSC referrals are handled on campus, a goal of the CSC has always been to branch out into the community and to provide services to clients where they live as opposed to requiring them to travel to the university. Community-based initiatives can bridge the clinic experience with more traditional practicum experiences located in the community settings. To accomplish this goal, the CSC has required student clinicians completing cases in the clinic to also provide services to students in a local school district. The CSC director has made contact with local school districts and surrounding communities seeking opportunities to collaborate. Each CSC clinician placed in these school districts is assigned both a faculty supervisor and a site supervisor from the school district. The school district recruits students with academic, behavioral, and/or psychological needs and assigns a case to each clinician. As part of the clinic experience, the student clinician spends half a day per week at the school district to develop an intervention to address the needs of the referred student and either implements the intervention or consults with a teacher who implements the intervention. Supervision duties are shared by the clinic and site supervisors, and communication between the supervisors occurs on a regular basis. Reports are written by the clinicians and include the assessment, intervention design, data gathered, results, and recommendations. Copies of the report are provided to the faculty supervisor as part of class requirements, as well as to the site supervisor for the referred student's file.

In another community-based initiative, the CSC provides mental health consultation services to the Indiana County Head Start (ICHS) through a contract between the CSC and ICHS. In this case, the director serves as the mental health consultant for four Head Start centers in the community, where responsibilities include providing 10 hr of on-site service each month from September to May. As a result of this relationship, graduate students in the school psychology program have also had practicum opportunities with the preschool population as part of their work in the CSC. CSC student clinicians have been placed in classrooms at the various Head Start centers to consult with teachers, devise classroom management strategies, informally assess students, and devise individual student interventions. Referrals to the CSC, particularly of preschool children, have increased because of its affiliation with ICHS.

A third community-based initiative is currently in its beginning stages among the CSC, Early Head Start, and the Armstrong/Indiana Intermediate Unit's Family Literacy program. Through this arrangement, CSC student clinicians will provide consultation, literacy education, and assessment services to the parents participating in the program, as well as offering tutoring, individualized interventions, and assessment services to the children in the program (ranging in age from birth to 18 years).

Community-based initiatives have rounded out the clinic experience for students and in many cases brought preventative school psychology services to individuals who otherwise might not have been able to receive them. Likewise, the CSC has been able to expand the types of training experiences graduate students in the school psychology program obtain during their time at IUP. The direct and indirect alliances with local schools and community agencies have provided graduate students with truly unique experiences.

Of note, the CSC has developed collaborative relationships within the university community as well. Most remarkable among these is the collaboration between the CSC and the Advising and Testing Center on IUP's campus. Those who seek services through the Advising and Testing Center are college-age IUP students who may need an evaluation to determine whether a disability is present or may already have a documented disability and are requesting accommodations and supports in the classroom. This collaboration affords CSC clinicians the unique experience of working with traditional, as well as nontraditional, college students (18 years of age and above).

Supervision

The academic/clinical instruction in the CSC is nontraditional and skill-based; thus, student learning is heavily dependent upon adequate faculty supervision and feedback. Faculty who supervise in clinic are all certified school psychologists (or the applicable credential; see Chapter 13, this volume) and two are licensed psychologists as well. When children and families come to the CSC to receive services, adequate supervision is easily facilitated.

As described previously, the CSC is outfitted with the most up-to-date digital video and audio equipment available. The improved digital technology allows for more effective faculty supervision and feedback, which ultimately improves student learning. Using a Landro system, all sessions from all treatment rooms can be viewed live simultaneously or recorded to a hard drive or DVD. Supervisors can then provide clinicians with feedback by editing the recording by adding text and/or audio voiceover at any point. Edited recordings can be saved to a hard drive or burned to DVD for clinicians to review. Similarly, clinicians can edit these digital recordings and respond to their supervisor's comments. Use of this digital technology also permits CSC clinicians to examine and self-assess their own performances through watching and analyzing video recordings of their sessions. Following this, clinicians speak one-to-one with their faculty supervisor for further instructional supervision. Sessions, live or recorded, can be streamed to a large classroom and used by faculty for instructional purposes or for providing group supervision and feedback. Recorded sessions can also be streamed over a secure Internet site if necessary. Students can use the Landro to develop a series of audio/video clips that demonstrate proficiency in various NASP and/or APA standards to include in their electronic portfolios.

Clinicians are provided with formative feedback throughout their handling of a case, and with summative feedback in writing via use of a case evaluation form following their completion of a case. Supervisors are provided with feedback from their supervisees in several ways. First, their supervisees complete a written narrative summarizing the supervisor's strengths and needs. Second, clinicians who are enrolled in a course as part of the CSC experience complete a formal student evaluation of the instructor (supervisor) as part of IUP's faculty evaluation process. In addition, feedback is sought from CSC clients via a consumer satisfaction survey.

Partly because of the CSC's digital supervision capability, the department was approved by the Pennsylvania Department of Education (PDE) to offer the Supervisor of School Psychological Services Certificate to our graduate students. This certificate allows students to serve as supervisors of pupil service workers in Pennsylvania. Only a few sites across the commonwealth have been approved to offer this certificate by PDE. As such, the CSC provides in-service practicing school psychologists across the state, as well as our own doctoral students, the opportunity to acquire this certificate and improve their supervisory skills using the CSC's state-of-the-art equipment.

SUMMARY AND CONCLUSION

Although university-based clinics require significant resources (e.g., facilities, staff, and organizational support) there are multiple benefits to faculty, students, the university and broad community. Of great importance is the direct and indirect support to overburdened public agencies and school systems. Students engaged in graduate training where university-based clinics are available have the opportunity to provide psychological services in a unique setting where there are multiple supervisors providing tailored experience, graduated training activities, and personal professional support. Although we recognize that there is a lack of systematic evaluations of how these clinics are organized, funded, and staffed and how they interact with the community, we also view this as an opportunity for future study. In fact, documenting community impact of school psychology training would be welcomed by national accreditation agencies on all sides. Finally, it is important to note that there is limited evidence that a single training model is better than others. In fact, Benson and Hughes (1985) found that clinics use a variety of different models and practices.

RESOURCES

Hatcher, R. L. & Lassiter, K. D. (2007). Initial training in professional psychology: The Practicum Competencies Outline. *Training and Education in Professional Psychology, 1,* 49–63.

This article focuses on guidelines to measure the competency of both supervisors and supervisees. The author pays special attention to the ethical, legal, contextual, and practice issues that need to be addressed when setting standards to ensure that the standards meet the recommendations for best practices in the field.

A guide to building research partnerships with community-based clinicians. (n.d.). From the Series CTSI Guides to Community-Engaged Research. Retrieved February 13, 2008, from http://ctsi.ucsf.edu/documents/CCGuideforResearchers.pdf

This article provides guidelines for establishing research partnerships with community-based clinicians, but the guidelines put forth are useful in establishing a university-based school psychology clinic. Issues addressed include implementation, staffing, supervision, and funding.

REFERENCES

Association of Directors of Psychology Training Clinics. (2006). *Guidelines for psychology training clinics.* Retrieved February 2, 2008, from http://www.adptc. org/orb/page/guidelines/

Benson, A. J., & Hughes, J. (1985). Perceptions of role definition processes in school psychology: A national survey. *School Psychology Review, 14,* 64–74.

Ebata, A. T. (1996). Making university-community collaborations work: Challenges for institutions and individuals. *Journal of Research on Adolescence, 6,* 71–79.

Frumkin, P., & Imber, J. (Eds.). (2004). *In search of the nonprofit sector.* New Brunswick, NJ: Transaction Publishers.

Groark, C. J., & McCall, R. B. (1996). Building successful university-community human service agency collaborations. In C. B. Fisher, J. P. Murray, & I. E. Sigel (Eds.), *Applied developmental science: Graduate training for diverse disciplines and educational settings* (pp. 237–353). Norwood, NJ: Ablex.

Harvey, V., & Struzziero, J. (2000). *Effective supervision in school psychology*. Bethesda, MD: National Association of School Psychologists.

Murrell, E., Steel, Z., Gaston, J. & Proudfoot, H. (2002). Training the clinical psychologist: Profile of a university-based clinic. *Australian Psychologist, 37*(2), 123–128.

National Association of School Psychologists. (2002). Position statement on supervision in school psychology. In A. Thomas & J. Grimes (Eds.), *Best practices in school psychology IV*. Washington, DC: Author.

Thomas, A. and Grimes, J. (Eds.). (2002). *Best practices in school psychology IV*. Bethesda, MD: National Association of School Psychologists.

Ysseldyke, J. E., Dawson, P., Lehr, C., Reschly, D., Reynolds, M., & Telzrow, C. (1997). *School psychology: A blueprint for training and practice II*. Bethesda, MD: National Association of School Psychologists.

Walsh, D. (2006). Best practices in university-community partnerships: Lessons learned from a physical-activity-based program. *The Journal of Physical Education, Recreation, & Dance, 77*(4), 45–56.

Part V

Into the future

17 Creating congruent change
Linking research to practice

Tammy L. Hughes, Judith Kaufman, and Sally A. Hoover

The accountability movement, including legislation such as No Child Left Behind (NCLB), has brought into focus a clear call for all school practices to show that decisions are data driven. School-based accountability is meant to influence the decisions that impact the overall school system, the classroom, and educational practices aimed at the individual. Although this mandate has arguably caused school systems to be better equipped to demonstrate that the reading curriculum they selected, for example, has an evidence base, the ecosystem that is a school building does not easily lend itself to simple selections of evidence-based practices that sum to a total data-driven experience for children.

Although it is newly packaged, what constitutes evidence is a foundational argument that psychologists have long debated. In previous iterations, the field has debated the usefulness of findings that are based on group level comparisons as contrasted with individual needs. The nostalgic will recall debates over the importance of qualitative descriptions versus quantitative scores (Hunt, 1946; Groth-Marnat, 2000) and clinical versus statistical data (Ægisdóttir, Spengler, & White, 2006; Meehl, 1954) for decision making. In psychology, these debates remain unresolved and continue to influence how all assessment data (e.g., normative vs. curriculum-based assessment; manualized vs. tailored treatments) are used. Now that this debate has reached (almost) all aspects of school practice, school psychologists have the opportunity to lead school teams in how to balance evidence from the literature with pragmatic realities. We have the opportunity to describe the usefulness of the scientific method as it applies to real-life practice, explain not only true score variance but also the error that is included in a total score from which decisions are made, and how cultural differences impact how we determine the usefulness (validity) of the findings within groups. Although school psychologists are prepared for addressing the nuances of these tasks, a major challenge that we face is how the field can present considered opinions where formative data are available to an audience that demands summative conclusions. In this chapter, we will address the relevant literature around evidence-based practices, including the research-into-practice gap and how training programs, along with field-based trainers, can prepare school psychology students for translating scientific practice for public consumption. We provide a case example in which a district's commitment to evidence-based practices is successful and yet experiences challenges. Recommendations for creating congruent change for authentic decision making for the purpose of accountability in schools is provided.

ACCOUNTABILITY MOVEMENT: DATA-DRIVEN DECISIONS

Accountability is the watchword of the moment, in politics and in life (Ramírez, 2008). For school systems, the NCLB education act generated the principle of holding schools accountable for student learning outcomes. NCLB has imposed accountability for *all* student learning, particularly those who are poor and of minority status, who seemingly have been ill served by the education system. Statistics reported by the U.S. Department of Education (2003) show that nearly 70% of inner-city fourth graders are unable to read on a basic level, and high school seniors trail Third World countries in math skills. School dropout rate for minority youngsters is close to 50%, with large gaps in achievement between Caucasian and minority students, thus raising questions of educational equity and highlighting the need for NCLB. Although there is no universal standard to which school systems are held (each state may determine its own definition of proficiency), the expectation is to close achievement gaps by evaluating each student on the state's standard and then providing sanctions for schools that do not show improvements. In this way, NCLB was meant to affirm a national commitment to combat the educational disparities that were apparent in children from different states and from impoverished backgrounds (e.g., socioeconomic distress, limited access to health care, and limited access to affordable housing).

Although the spirit of accountability movement has much support, critics of NCLB note that there are problems with the assumptions underpinning the act. For example, it is well documented that school failure has multiple causal antecedents that are not only proximal to the school experience (Keiffer, 2008; Shumm, 2001). Many note that some disparities may be too large to overcome with curriculum-only remediation (Rothstein, 2004; Teale, Paciga, & Hoffman, 2007). Others indicate that it is not the school's responsibility to fix society's ills and thus the target for accountability is either misplaced or focused too narrowly. NCLB assumes that all children learn and will demonstrate progress in the same manner (Wenning, Herdman, Smith, McMahon, & Washington, 2003). Finally, NCLB is being used as a high-stakes assessment on curriculum, instruction, and school experience (e.g., Meier & Wood, 2004).

Despite these critiques, there is some agreement that demographics do not determine destiny (*US News and World Report*, 2008), and although better social policies are essential, there is evidence to indicate that schooling can make a difference irrespective of challenges (such as economic, health care, and housing challenges) (Rutter, 1982). In fact, there are many examples of superior public schools educating children and overcoming societal risk factors (Heacox, 1991; Levine, 1996; Shumm, 2001; among others). These successes mirror in important ways the intent of NCLB.

The NCLB model is meant to go beyond the simple assessment of performance and achievement and incorporate a best practices understanding of schooling in the context of individual students, functioning in a classroom with curriculum (that may or may not be adequate), and the influence of policy decisions occurring on a school-wide basis. This is evidenced by the mandate to provide an integrated system of reporting on a state level. School systems have the responsibility to use sound theory (psychological and learning) and research findings to design and develop school systems that are informed by and provide a data-driven foundation for policy decisions (Felner, Seitsinger, Brand, Burns, & Bolton, 2008).

In terms of school psychology, the intent of NCLB clearly aligns with the goals of the 2002 Futures Conference, where the community came together to articulate the importance of multiple systems and prevention in solving the big problems that schools face (Shapiro, 2006). That is, across the academic and social development domains, school psychologists have led efforts to respond to the needs of children prior to the need for specialized individual education programs in an effort to prevent, mitigate, and reverse impaired development (Felner et al., 2008). The response to intervention (RTI) movement is one important example of how school psychology has led the way for helping schools to demonstrate that their instruction is not contributing to a child's learning difficulties. In this way, trends in school psychology provide a model of congruence between research and practice to more effectively meet the federal mandate of NCLB; however, we recognize that at present there are significant challenges.

RESEARCH-INTO-PRACTICE GAP

The research-into-practice gap has long been acknowledged by school psychologists (Auster, Feeney-Kettler, & Kratochwill, 2006; Kratochwill & Stoiber, 2000). The assumption that clinical trial findings can be similarly applied to the school setting has been seriously challenged for years (e.g., Goldfried & Wolfe, 1996; Hunsley, 2007; Kratochwill & Stoiber, 2000; Ringeisen, Henderson, & Hoagwood, 2003). However, even as there has been successful movement to bridge the research-into-practice gap by embracing the contextual factors of the school system in research applications (cf. Kratochwill & Stoiber, 2000; Ringeisen et al., 2003), researchers also face the reality that the differences (e.g., socioeconomic status, culture, norms) that comprise our school systems are significant enough to impact the systems' selection of an evidence-based practice, as well as conclusions that we can draw from findings (Shapiro, 2006). That is, although there may be an evidence base for a particular intervention, the nature of the school, classroom, or child may dissuade its use. Also, even after the selection of an intervention, the unique characteristics of a setting can impact the desired outcome. When this happens, it becomes unclear whether the adjustments needed for success in the current setting meaningfully alter the intervention to a degree that no longer matches the original evidence base for the practice (Hunsley, 2007; Ringeisen et al., 2003).

Committed to bridging the research-into-practice gap, researchers have attempted to detail and quantify the essential ingredients for a successful intervention in the school setting. Starting with the premise that school psychologist would use the problem solving process known for its usefulness across individual and systems level consultation, Kratochwill and Stoiber (2000) highlighted the need to understand the interdisciplinary nature of the school context. They argue that by understanding the variety of perspectives in the system, there is a better chance for appropriate implementation of evidence-based interventions (EBIs). In 2003, DuPaul noted the need for school psychologists' to provide communications to concerned stakeholders to increase the designation of resources for implementing EBIs. In 2006, Shapiro expanded criteria for traversing the research gap to include (a) understanding the school context, (b) having a defined conceptual model, (c) acknowledging practical considerations such as building a staff's capacity to use research-based systems, and (d) collaborating with state and local institutions, including higher education, as essential to develop the leadership and vision required for real and sustained change. Upon review, most of the current EBI research fits into at least some portion of this model.

Graczyk, Domitrovich, Small, and Zins (2006) described three phases needed for implementing EBIs in schools. The first is the adoption phase, when a problem or opportunities for improvement has been identified and EBIs are under consideration. Second, the implementation phase is where the intervention is conducted to prevent or ameliorate an existing problem, or improve specific skills and competencies. The final phase is designing supports needed for sustaining an innovation is accepted as useful. As noted by those seeking to bridge the research-into-practice gap, systemic factors in the educational settings influence all three of these phases and are therefore important to consider when implementing EBIs in school. As these researchers point out, success is dependent on a comprehensive coordinated effort, but also on the availability of EBI practices for the presenting problem. Kratochwill and Stoiber (2000) suggest that video, manuals, and computer programs are best for disseminating EBI information to school personnel.

Now that a substantive literature base is available for review and rationale for evaluating data (cf. efficacy vs. effectiveness; Hunsely, 2007), the field of school psychology is poised to lead school districts in considering the relevant variables useful to show the adequate yearly progress (AYP) required by NCLB. We have not only made conclusions about what is an EBI but also embrace a dynamic understanding about the usefulness of establishing practice guidelines (White & Kratochwill, 2005). Indeed, the field of school psychology is prepared to contribute much.

An area that is yet underdeveloped is the translation of EBIs for public consumption. At present, teachers, parents, and the public are prepared for finite lists of adequate and inadequate strategies. We have yet to translate how psychology can solve academic and social problems in a manner that allows for nuance but resonates with the public.

TRANSLATING SCIENTIFIC FINDINGS FOR PUBLIC CONSUMPTION

Our next big challenge is to move beyond translating bench science into practice or policy to also addressing public concerns without losing the nuances of the science. Indeed, public messaging is about simplicity, sound bites, and branding, whereas school psychologists indulge in the caveats required by scientific thinking. The accountability movement and NCLB present a conundrum where the long-held traditions of children attending a local public school with certified teachers from a 3–5-year teacher training program are in jeopardy of disappearing. The shortage of highly quali-fied teachers has resulted in alternative and emergency certifications for school staff (e.g., teachers and administrators). Programs such as Teach for America provide alternative routes to teacher certification that are coupled with the simple message that educational inequity is our nation's greatest injustice. This is the type of message that connects with the public. There is no comparable message for public school certification programs.

Since the practices brought to the table by school psychologists (e.g., EBIs) are a value added to school systems, it is time to address the public. School psychologists are in a unique position to work with districts in pro-moting the services they are providing for the children in their communi-ties. District scorecards (usually based on state standards) and child find activities are common outcomes used to communicate district successes. However, local and national messages are also needed to address the big questions the public has about their children. Imagine: "Questions about your child's academic and social development? Ask your school psycholo-gist—every school has one!"

TEACHING SCHOOL PSYCHOLOGISTS: CREATING CONGRUENT CHANGE

Preparing graduate students for the changing dynamics of the school system is a challenge for training programs. The increased emphasis on evidenced-based practice and data-driven decision making requires practicing school psychologists not only to be educated consumers of research but also to engage in action research (Whitehead & McNiff, 2006) in their work environment. Pragmatic questions emerge regularly in the school setting, where intuitive conclusions rather than data-driven decisions are generated (Knoff, 2003). Typically, there are large quantities of archival data in school districts that can potentially answer important practice and implementation questions that could, ultimately, have positive fiscal implications. School psychologists are often asked to make decisions about intervention programs and allocation of resources. Although not all school psychologists have engaged in an independent research projects (e.g., a dissertation), all have relationships with graduate programs (at least their degree granting institution). Research opportunities are a natural collaborative link creating congruity between the university and field-based practices. There are mutual gains from such interaction, whereby students and faculty may evolve important research questions where local schools and systems may have groups of participants supporting their school system (e.g., NCLB requirements such as AYP). School-based practices can be enhanced through the provision of applied research opportunities, with an ongoing feedback loop. The field of school psychology is filled with examples of collaborative research that has generated quality enhancement and benefited the lives of children. For example, the work of Blom-Hoffman promoting physical activity and healthy eating in urban schools in Boston, evaluation of positive behavior support at Centennial School in collaboration with Lehigh University, the impact of Rosenfield and Gravois on instructional consultation in Maryland, and California College Preparatory Academy (a charter school partnership involving University of California-Berkeley and Aspire Public Schools), among others. School psychology graduate students need to be able to articulate how university and field-based trainers can work together to create congruent change. For example:

- Opportunities for collaboration between school districts and universities bring a host of opportunities (e.g., staff; access to resources, such as library and statistical packages for preparing data; and contact with university resources, such as the grants offices).
- Partnerships can document school-based intervention successes and needs (e.g., data-based decision making; NCLB).
- District faculty provide opportunities for real-time (action-based research) experiences that can be informal or active instructors in applied research courses in the public schools.
- University faculty and students (practicum and internship) can provide state-of-the-art in-service training for the district.
- Collaborative relationships can include access to discounted graduate courses, annual workshops on an annual basis, and continuing education experiences.

- Joint district and university faculty can present in town hall meetings to talk about successes, opportunities, current happenings, and the reciprocal education process.

Research is a natural opportunity to link universities, schools, and communities, whether formally or informally.

CASE ILLUSTRATION

In order to foster a culture of best practices that support an emerging RTI model, a district's two elementary schools created grade-level data review teams. This structure was created by the school psychologists, along with the counselors and building principals, with the aim of developing strategic thinking about the curricular needs of students. Rather than thinking about one student at a time, the data review teams were to examine broad curricular practices across a grade level as the first step. Any student needs that remained after curricular practices were examined and adjustments were made would then be considered appropriate for more individualized interventions. The ability to create data review teams with a focus broader than the individual student comes on the heels of prior years' efforts. By way of background, the district began moving toward an RTI approach 3 years ago, with each successive year bringing new adjustments and changes in implementation. To arrive at the current state of creating data teams, other essential elements of infrastructure had been developed over time. For example, the school psychologists conducted building-wide training in the RTI model, initially as it related to specific learning disability identification and then again as it became a general education initiative. Under the psychologists' leadership, the district had also instituted universal screening for reading and math, three times yearly, in grades K–2 using a mixed battery of norm-referenced and curriculum-based assessment (CBA) materials. Although the district has long had its own normative base for reading fluencies and comprehension from CBA assessments (since 1998), math was added as another essential element of the infrastructure. As a subset of the movement toward an RTI model, universal screening had its own set of changes and adjustments over the years. Initially, broad teams of teachers (Title I, gifted support teachers, counselors, kindergarten teachers, teaching interns, psychology interns, and psychologists) fanned out across the grade levels and conducted paper-and-pencil assessments with each student. Counselors and psychologists collated data, built a database, and subsequently shared data with teachers. This time-consuming, labor-intensive process has now given way to a more elegant and streamlined online application, with instantaneous results available to the teachers.

Armed with a better process and tool for assessment and with the administrative support of principals and counselors teaming with school psychologists, building level intervention teams began to work in a tiered system. This was a departure from the traditional model of child study and brought different roles and requirements for team members. Most notably, the requirement for repeated assessment and data collection was a logistical issue that was best addressed by the building principals as they helped to deploy building resources differently. By examining everything from the use of paraprofessionals to office clerical support to the availability of special teachers, the principals found ways to help with coverage and deployment that helped the classroom teachers to gather necessary data.

The desire and the necessity to move toward data review teams arose from recognizing inefficiencies and lingering traditional thinking in the existing model. Over time, working in the new tiered model began to reveal problems that signaled that more training and support were needed. The focus on individual students as the first line of thinking and intervening was preventing the requisite focus on curriculum-wide issues. That there might be a need for different instructional practices, modified delivery, or different student groupings was not being consistently recognized or endorsed. The team was attempting to model a new way of thinking with a broader, curricular focus, but the traditional mindset that was exclusively student focused was proving hard to change. Furthering the thinking that needs may permeate a grade level and thus require changes to instructional practices and be beyond an individual student was going to take an additional element of involvement and ownership.

The task of the newly formed data review teams, operational for the 2008–2009 school year, is to review existing data at a grade level and a class level to find common themes around which to make improvements in curricular practices. If, for example, persuasive writing was weak across the grade, then individual student intervention was not called for. The data reviewed included the district's yearly standardized achievement testing, yearly state testing, the three-times-per-year universal screening results, quarterly local assessments that show progress toward state standards as well as curriculum measurements that accompany both the reading and math series, and teacher-created assessments. In an effort to signal the importance of digging through data, building principals worked diligently to create blocks of time for each grade level. The buildings share substitute coverage in order to allow for an hour and a half for each grade level, each quarter, for thorough review. The team is composed of the entire grade level, the building counselor and principal, a special educator, reading specialist, and the district psychologist. During the meeting, data are combed for class and grade averages, rankings of students, outliers, and comparisons across data sources, and the school psychologist leads discussion about data differences and gives interpretative cautions. These meetings offer a rich opportunity for learning about data and the vocabulary of data, explaining data to teachers, and ultimately using it to guide instructional improvements. The teams have only recently gotten under way with their actual mission, but the process has begun to yield small pockets of success with both broader thinking, as well as concrete outcomes. While reviewing existing data for their kindergarten students, the teachers discovered that phonemic awareness was generally strong but that the developing association to letters was not. The team concluded that existing instructional practices in phonemic awareness did not need revision but that the formation of an "Alphabet Club" would be an appropriate way to target the identified weakness. The students have specific instructional activities around sound-symbol association, plus the fun status of belonging to club just for them. In the fifth-grade team review, teachers saw concerns with reading comprehension with small segment of students across the grade. Concerned that fluency may be an issue, the teachers gathered additional CBA data for words correct per minute. Compared with the general class average, their concerns proved right. As an outcome, they elected to improve fluency as means to better comprehension. Instructional practices for this small group centered on speed building, adequate decoding skills, and word knowledge as a requisite to higher comprehension skills.

As teams move forward during the course of the year, it is expected that better ways of conducting this process will come into focus and that yet again next year, there will be necessary adjustments and changes in implementation. This should be an expected norm in districts as they lay down sound infrastructure to support RTI. As a general education initiative, RTI is a significant cultural change in buildings, and for some, it radically alters teaching as they have known it. The need for ongoing support as staff are guided through and ultimately begin contributing to this necessary culture shift cannot be underestimated.

CONCLUSIONS

The case example provides a road map for implementing an RTI model over the course of several years. This required not only strategic planning but also the leadership of the school psychologist within the school team. It is easy to note the opportunities for university and field-based collaboration around data planning, collection, and evaluation. In this case, the school district routinely trains practicum and internship school psychology students, providing real-time implementation experiences for the students. Not only are the traditional roles of the school psychologists highlighted for students (e.g., assessment and evaluation), but the consultation services required to help get all parts (e.g., teachers, administrators) of the system up to speed are highlighted as well. In this case, university and field-based trainers presented at national conferences and in publications together, highlighting their collaborative relationship.

RESOURCES

Hamilton, L. S., Stecher, B. M., Marsh, J. A., Sloan McCombs, J., Robyn, A., Russel, J. L., Naftel, S., & Barney, H. (2007). *How educators in three states are responding to standards-based accountability under No Child Left Behind.* Santa Monica, CA: Rand Corporation.
The monograph presents the interim findings from California, Georgia, and Pennsylvania.

REFERENCES

Ægisdóttir, S., Spengler, P. M., & White, M. J. (2006). Should I pack my umbrella? Clinical versus statistical prediction of mental health *Counseling Psychologist, 34*, 410–419.

Auster, E. R., Feeney-Kettler, K. A., & Kratochwill, T. R. (2006). Conjoint behavioral consultation: Application to the school-based treatment of anxiety disorders. *Education and Treatment of Children, 29*, 243–256.

DuPaul, G. J. (2003). Commentary: Bridging the gap between research and practice. *School Psychology Review, 32*, 178–180.

Felner, R. D., Seitsinger, A. S., Brand, S., Burns, A., & Bolton, N. (2008). Creating a statewide educational data system for accountability and improvement: A comprehensive information and assessment system for making evidence-based change at school, district, and policy levels [Special issue]. *Psychology in the Schools, 45*, 235–256.

Goldfried, M. R., & Wolfe, B. E. (1996). Psychotherapy practice and research: Repairing a strained alliance. *American Psychologist, 51*, 1007–1016.

Groth-Marnat, G. (2000). Visions of clinical assessment: Then, now and a brief history of the future. *Journal of Clinical Psychology, 56*, 349–365.

Graczyk, P. A., Domitrovich, C. E., Small, M., & Zins, J. E. (2006). Serving all children: An implementation model framework. *School Psychology Review, 35*, 266–274.

Heacox, A. (1991). *Up from underachievements: How teachers, students, and parents can work together to promote student success.* Minneapolis, MN: Free Spirit Publishing.

Hunsley, J. (2007). Addressing key challenges in evidence-based practice in psychology. *Professional Psychology: Research and Practice, 39*, 113–121.

Hunt, W. A. (1946). The future of diagnostic testing in clinical psychology. *Journal of Clinical Psychology, 2*, 311–317.

Keiffer, M. J. (2008). Catching up or falling behind? Initial English proficiency, concentrated poverty, and the reading growth of language minority learners in the United States. *Journal of Educational Psychology, 100*, 851–868.

Kratochwill, T. R., & Stoiber, K. C. (2000). Empirically supported interventions and school psychology: Conceptual and practice issues—Part II. *School Psychology Quarterly, 15*, 233–253.

Knoff, H. M. (2003). *The Assessment of Child and Adolescent Personality.* New York: Guilford Press.

Levine, M. (1996). *Keeping a head in school: A student's book about learning abilities and learning disorders.* Cambridge, MA: Educators Publishing Service, Inc.

Meehl, P. A. (1954). *Clinical versus statistical prediction: A theoretical analysis and a review of the evidence.* Minneapolis, MN: University of Minnesota.

Meier, D., & Wood, G. (2004). *Many children left behind: How the No Child Left Behind Act is damaging our children and our schools.* Boston: Beacon Press.

Ramírez, E. (2008). End-of-course exams catching on. *US News and World Report.* Retrieved August 16, 2008 from http://www.usnews.com/blogs/on-education/2008/08/15/end-of-course-exams-catching-on.html

Rothstein, R. (2004). The achievement gap: A broader picture. *Educational Leadership, 62*, 40–43.

Ringeisen, H., Henderson, K., & Hoagwood, K. (2003). Context matters: Schools and the "Research to Practice Gap" in children's mental health. *School Psychology Review, 32*, 153–168.

Rutter, M. (1982). Epidemiological-longitudinal approaches to the study of development. In W. A. Collins (Ed.), *The concept of development: Minnesota symposia on child psychology*, pp. 105–144. Hillsdale, NJ: Lawrence Erlbaum Associates.

Shapiro, E. S. (2006). Are we solving the big problems? *School Psychology Review, 35*, 260–265.

Shumm, J. S. (2001). *School power: Strategies for succeeding in school.* Minneapolis, MN: Free Spirit Publishing.

Teale, W. H., Paciga, K. A., & Hoffman, J. L. (2007). Beginning reading instruction in urban schools: The curriculum gap ensures a continuing achievement gap. *Reading Teacher, 61*, 344–348.

U.S. Department of Education. (2003). *No Child Left Behind Act of 2001.* Retrieved August 3, 2009, from http://www.ed.gov/policy/elsec/leg/esea02/107-110.pdf

Wenning, R., Herdman, P. A., Smith, N., McMahon, N., & Washington, K. (2003). *No Child Left Behind: Testing, reporting and accountability.* (ERIC Document Reproduction Service No. ED480994)

White, J. L., & Kratochwill, T. R. (2005). Practice guidelines in school psychology: Issues and directions for evidence-based interventions in practice and training. *Journal of School Psychology, 43*, 99–115.

Whitehead, J. & McNiff, J. (2006). *Action research living theory.* London: Sage.

18 Envisioning the future

Looking into the crystal ball

Tammy L. Hughes, Judith Kaufman,
Tony D. Crespi, Cynthia A. Riccio,
and Enedina García-Vázquez

A preoccupation with the future not only prevents us from seeing the present as it is, but often prompts us to rearrange the past.

Eric Hoffer (p. 45, 1998)

INTRODUCTION

The profession of school psychology began as a school-based endeavor to address the complex needs of children (see Chapter 2, Volume I). University training programs have the responsibility and challenge of ensuring minimal competency in assessment, intervention, consultation and prevention, couched in an understanding of physiological, social, affective, and cognitive bases of behavior. The understanding of ecological factors and the development of cultural competence are additional foundational constructs trainers need to transmit to graduate students.

Graduates of school psychology training programs need to be able to address the special needs of children with a range of problems, including, for example, those with chronic illness (see Chapter 17, Volume I), those involved with juvenile justice (see Chapter 15, this volume), and those with emotional and behavioral difficulties (see Chapter 16, this volume). There is a growing awareness of the possibility that children and families may be victims of sudden trauma (e.g., natural disaster, terrorism, or violence) and that these experiences potentially impact the social–emotional life experiences of the child within both the family and school environments.

Across the myriad conferences, articles, discussions at professional meetings of the specialty definition of school psychology, discussions of credentials (see Chapter 4, Volume I; Chapter 13, this volume), and articles about the future of school psychology (see Chapter 1, this volume), ultimately, the role of the school psychologist continues to be three-pronged—assessment, direct intervention, and indirect intervention or consultation. The challenge comes in how different models define and redefine these components in response to our changing times.

The practice of psychology in the schools has always been, and likely always will be, influenced by sociocultural, legal, and political forces within psychology and education. These forces include educational legislation, such as Individuals With Disabilities Education Act (IDEA) and No Child Left Behind, and the definitions of accepted psychological practices (e.g., evidence-based practices in the delivery of academic, mental, and public health) that are provided by a host of learned societies, as well as legal influences, such as case law on issues of discrimination and separation of church and state. The changing demographics of the United States indicate the need for sensitivity to cultural differences that impact the delivery of training. Issues of cultural competency are reflected in almost all chapters in these two volumes; there is a particular focus in Chapter 8 of Volume I and Chapter 7 in this volume. Moreover, with the new millennium, technology has not only provided a more efficient means of gathering information and communicating but has brought ethical concerns and potential risks for children that did not previously exist. Taken together, these changes and challenges underscore the need for greater collaboration among schools, communities, and families, as well as across with professionals with various types of expertise.

Regardless of the focus of service delivery, or the population of concern, synergy across educational programming and mental health services is becoming more critical in our changing times. Social emotional status and achievement are intricately linked, and school psychologists are in a unique position to help school personnel in the development of school-wide or classroom-based prevention programming (Forman & Burke, 2008; McKevitt & Braaksma, 2008). Increased emphasis on wellness and characteristics associated with resiliency are taking center stage at professional conferences and in the research literature (Masten & Curtis, 2000; Sharkey, You, & Schnoebelen, 2008). Rather than only evaluating functioning in the current educational setting, the focus is shifting to the longer term outcome of children and youth, necessitating more research related to transitions (e.g., across developmental tasks and from school to work), particularly for students with special needs. As IDEA promoted the development of transition plans and the Americans With Disabilities Act provides for accommodations in the workplace, knowledge of these issues become essential (Smith & Lauritzen, 1992–1993). These added dimensions to the practice and training of future school psychologists are recent considerations, and their integration challenges an already extensive curriculum. The credential for school psychologists was initially a master's level degree (30–36 credits), but in most states is now a master's plus (60 or more credits), specialist level certificate (e.g., EdS, CAGS), with some specialist programs requiring as much as 84 credits (see Chapter 3, this volume). There are those who believe that all training in school psychology should be at a doctoral level and some who question whether many of the current specialist training programs already meet the standards of the professional practice doctorate, commensurate with other professional practice fields (Council of Graduate Schools, 2007), regardless of the label of their current degree. Needless to say, these proposals have generated discussions on many levels, and the outcome will continue to have implications for future credentialing (see Chapter 13, this volume).

Supervision provides the bridge between education and practice, as well as between the university and the field. Field-based trainers are vital to the training enterprise and play an important role in transmitting the professional values of the field in the applied setting. Informally regarded by many as the finishing school for training, the process of supervision requires close examination (see Chapter 2, this volume). Although supervision has been a consideration throughout the history of school psychology, it has not been the focus of systematic study as it has in the clinical and counseling specialty areas. However, recently, considerable attention has been paid to the inclusion of supervision courses in the curriculum, the training and credentialing of supervisors, and evaluating best practices models of supervision. Furthermore, the efficacy of technology in the supervisory process is being evaluated as well. Part II of this volume provides an in-depth review of supervisory practices at different levels of training (for the practicum level, see Chapter 3, this volume; for the internship level, see Chapter 4, this volume) and in pediatric hospital settings (see Chapter 5, this volume). Hatzichristou and her associates provide a transnational perspective on supervision at various levels, directly addressing the commonalities of practice across cultures (Chapter 6, this volume). There is no question, as all of the authors concluded, about the need to continue to articulate goals for supervision, clarify competencies for both the supervisor and supervisee, and engage in research to generate guidelines for evidence-based practice. Furthermore, there is a clear need to investigate the best methods for providing ongoing education, nurturance, and support for the field-based supervisor in order for students to receive collaborative and congruent education and training.

Just as students are challenged when in transition from school to the "real world" of work, so too are our graduate students challenged when moving from the relatively protected environment of our training programs to the reality of the field and professional practice. This volume, in its attempt to bridge the training and practice gap, targets several critical areas and highlights challenging issues. Preparing students to deal with diverse populations is a fundamental component of contemporary training programs, and Lopez and Rogers (Chapter 7, this volume) provide a model for university and field collaboration. Among the diversity issues that provide a challenge to school psychologists is effectively addressing the needs of students who are gay, lesbian, bisexual, transgender, and questioning. It is well known that such youth are overrepresented in the populations of adolescents who attempt or complete suicide (McWhirter, McWhirter, McWhirter, & McWhirter, 2004). Jacob, Drevon, Abbuh, and Taton (Chapter 12, this volume) articulated an excellent approach for providing knowledge to both our students and the field in supporting those students who may be experiencing difficulty with gender preferences. Harassment is another critical issue that our students and the children they serve may experience. Kaufman and Hughes (Chapter 10, this volume) focus on facing harassment issues and provide preventive measures for consideration.

As trainers and faculty, we are often faced with challenging students. Often these students are academically competent but emerge with interpersonal and/or personality issues when they begin engaging in practice. Dispositional and interpersonal issues are often hard to document and deal with; Theodore, Hughes, and Kaufman (Chapter 11, this volume) discussed how to build a professional reputation from a curricular standpoint aimed at the needs of all students; Cruise and Swerdlick (Chapter 8, this volume) addressed policies and procedures for those students who remain challenging despite adequate training, support, and intervention from the faculty and field.

Professional issues are in the forefront of our practice, and the fourth section of this volume has taken on the challenge of finding opportunities to collaborate with field-based practice in a number of significant areas, including crisis response (see Chapter 15, this volume) and university-based clinics that service community needs (see Chapter 16, this volume). As the demand for school psychological services continues to grow at a rate that outpaces the number of practitioners available, there is a real need to not only define minimum standards for entry into the school system but also to clarify the defining characteristics of the school psychology profession. Determining the need for congruence in training is critical for the next generation of school psychologists and in maintaining the unique value of our profession (see Chapter 13, this volume).

LOOKING INTO THE CRYSTAL BALL

Imagine giving every faculty member and every practicing school psychologist a crystal ball and asking them to predict the future. Would there be consensus or chaos? We would suspect predictions would be triadic, emphasizing administrative directions, the content and practice of training, and a consideration of a new worldview encompassing social justice and mindfulness.

Whether considering the changes in demographics, change in nature of problems presented in the schools and community, or the change in focus from solely looking at intervention to addressing intervention and prevention, the one constant is the importance of continuing education for both university and field-based supervisors (see Chapter 14, this volume). Our professional leaderships organizations (e.g., National Association of School Psychologists [NASP] and American Psychological Association [APA]), as well as the our most recent school psychology summit, the 2002 Futures Conference (Dawson et al., 2004; Ehrhardt-Padgett et al., 2003), each provide a set of themes regarding the skills needed for the future direction of school psychology practice. Certainly, some combination of these areas will likely continue in to the future; however, the knowledge base within an area can be expected to change over time; thus, a commitment to lifelong learning is essential.

University faculty, as well as those involved in field supervision, need to be engaged in professional development activities—not only as providers but also as recipients. Furthermore, field supervisors, particularly those involved in internship activities, have a responsibility to promote professional development of the interns they supervise—training needs to be a component of all practica and internship experiences. Creating congruent change in the field, along with the ongoing professional development of the student and field and university trainer, is a task that requires the cultivation of relationships and sustained focus in the delivery of professional practice (see Chapter 17, this volume). Armistead (2008) recommended the use of online study groups, chat rooms, and peer mentoring to foster continued collegial communication and support.

Advocacy has long been a cornerstone of school psychology practice in shaping the educational environment to meet the social and academic development of children. We are now at a point where these same advocacy skills are needed to help shape the future of school psychology. Authors in both volumes have reflected on the importance of addressing educational and psychological legislation that impacts the profession. School psychologists, as a coalition, need to become increasingly proactive in helping to shape legislation, rather than our profession being shaped by it. Participation on school district boards; standing for office in local, regional, and even national elections; facilitating grassroots movements; or actively supporting a proeducation/children candidate can have a real impact on the direction of our profession, ultimately supporting the positive growth and development of the children we serve.

The way we view behavior and our worldview about human interaction are undergoing a real and radical change. In the past 5 years, there has been an increased emphasis in the literature on positive psychology (Huebner & Gilman, 2003) and on building resiliency in children and adolescents, emphasizing prevention and emotional well-being in contrast to the old test-and-place practice. School psychologists are becoming vocal about issues surrounding social justice (Shriberg, 2008). Embracing these and new perspectives are essential to our future work when balanced by understanding our history, engaging in self-reflection and practicing self-care our work at the university and in the field will help to ensure the next generation of effective professionals.

CONCLUSION

It is critical to remember that our training programs today shape tomorrow's practice, and as we saw in Hoffer's sage advice, the preoccupation with the future may have us lose sight of what we are currently doing and the long-term impact it may have. How many of us have had that wonderful experience of a former student returning or writing and telling us, "Whenever I (see a child, talk with parents, do an assessment), you are sitting on my shoulder!" We often do not recognize the long-lasting impact we have and therefore we must be cognizant of our current methods and practices and their implications. We will always have our traditions and our standardized tests and our compliance paperwork; however, our practices will broaden, the populations we serve will become more challenging, and our perspectives will be modified and changed.

The skill sets needed in today's society, with increased diversity, increasing problematic behaviors, and the infusion of technology into all aspects of the development of children call on trainers (university and field-based) to go beyond the mandate that is inherent in the credentialing systems for the individual (licensure or certification) or institutions (e.g., NASP, National Council for Accreditation of Teacher Education (NCATE), Teacher Education Accreditation Council (TEAC), and APA) to forge relationships that can build and shape the future of school psychology practice. It is incumbent upon training programs to instill in students and the professionals they partner with in the field the notion that what makes up today's competency is, in fact, a moving target. However, that movement is what allows for the development of promising practices, emergent practices, and the new ideas that come from both the university and the field. The best way to continue to focus on bridging the research-into-practice gap is to foster collaborative partnerships with school districts and related settings to ensure that what is working in these settings is documented and disseminated in the research literature. It is essential for our students to adopt professional attitudes toward participating in ongoing learning and embracing change.

RESOURCES

Shriberg, D. (Ed.). Special topic: Promoting social justice [Special issue]. (2008). *School Psychology Review, 37*(4), 451–486.
This issue highlights the importance of social justice as part of the training and practice of the school psychologists.

REFERENCES

Council of Graduate Schools. (2007). *Task force report on the professional doctorate*. Washington, DC: Author.

Dawson, M., Cummings, J. A., Harrison, P. L., Short, R. J., Gorin, S., & Palomares, R. (2004). The 2002 multisite conference on the future of school psychology: Next steps. *School Psychology Review, 33*(1), 15–125.

Ehrhardt-Padgett, G. N., Hatzichritstou, C., Kitson, J., & Myers, J. (2003). Awakening to a new dawn: Perspectives on the future of school psychology. *School Psychology Quarterly, 18*, 483–496.

Forman, S. G., & Burke, C. R. (2008). Best practices in selecting and implementing evidence-based school interventions. In A. Thomas & J. Grimes (Eds.), *Best practices in school psychology V* (Vol. 3, pp. 799–812). Bethesda, MD: National Association of School Psychologists.

Hoffer, E. (1998). *The passionate state of mind and other aphorisms.* New York: Buccaneer Books.

Huebner, E. S. & Gilman, R. (2003). Toward a focus on positive psychology in school psychology. *The School Psychology Quarterly, 18*, 2, 99–102.

Masten, A. S., & Curtis, W. J. (2000). Integrating competence and psychopathology: Pathways toward a comprehensive science of adaption in development. *Development and Psychopathology, 12*, 529–550.

McKevitt, B. C., & Braaksma, A. D. (2008). Best practices in developing a positive behavior support system at the school level. In A. Thomas & J. Grimes (Eds.), *Best practices in school psychology V* (Vol. 3, pp. 735–749). Bethesda, MD: National Association of School Psychologists.

McWhirter, J. J., McWhirter, B. T., McWhirter, E. H., & McWhirter, R. J. (2004). *At-risk youth* (3rd ed.). Pacific Grove, CA: Brooks/Cole.

Sharkey, J. D., You, S., & Schnoebelen, K. (2008). Relations among school assets, individual resilience, and student engagement for youth grouped by level of family functioning. *Psychology in the Schools, 45*, 402–418.

Shriberg, D. (Ed.). Special topic: Promoting social justice [Special issue]. (2008). *School Psychology Review, 37*(4), 451–486.

Smith, P. M. & Lauritzen, A. M. (1992–1993). Claiming the promise: Parents and ADA. *Impact, 5,* 4, 16.

Index

A

AAUW, see American Association of University Women (AAUW)

ABPP, see American Board of Professional Psychology (ABPP)

ABPP Board certification, 234–235, 243

ABSNP, see American Board of School Neuropsychology (ABSNP)

Accountability movement, 310–311

Acculturation model for ethical competence, 154

Action letters, 141–142

Acute distress, 266, 267

Administrative supervision, 20, 27

ADPTC, see Association of Directors of Psychology Training Clinics (ADPTC)

"Alphabet Club," 317

Alternative school psychological services, data-based model of, 93–94

AMA, see American Medical Association (AMA)

American Association of School Administrators survey, 170

American Association of University Women (AAUW), 172, 197

American Board of Professional Psychology (ABPP), 230, 232, 234–235, 243

American Board of School Neuropsychology (ABSNP), 234

American Medical Association (AMA), 245, 246

American Psychological Association (APA), 3, 4, 5, 10, 11, 24, 61, 112, 113, 118, 119, 130, 153, 156, 160, 163, 189, 206, 232, 235, 245, 249, 258, 297, 325, 326
  accreditation standards, 112
  Ethical Principles of Psychologists and Code of Conduct (2002), 161
  Guidelines and Principles for Accreditation of Programs in Professional Psychology, 37, 129, 252, 259
  Guidelines for Accreditation (2005), 29
  Practice Directorate's Office of Policy and Advocacy, 5

American Psychological Association Task Force on the Assessment of Competency in Professional Psychology, 58, 129

Americans With Disabilities Act, 190, 199, 322

APA, see American Psychological Association (APA)

APA Model Licensure Act, 12

APA Online Academy, 250

APPIC, see Association of Psychology Postdoctoral and Internship Centers (APPIC)

Area of concentration model, 92

Armstrong/Indiana Intermediate Unit's Family Literacy program, 302

Assessing Student and Supervisee
   Performance, 130–131
Association of Directors of Psychology
   Training Clinics (ADPTC),
   298
   guidelines for supervisors, 299
   responsibilities of supervisors,
      298–299
Association of Directors of Psychology
   Training Clinics Practicum
   Competencies Workgroup, 43
Association of Postdoctoral and
   Internship Centers, 23
Association of Psychology Postdoctoral
   and Internship Centers
   (APPIC), 64
Association of State and Provincial
   Psychology Boards, 231

B

Behavioral supervision, 92
Board Certification through the
   American Board of
   Professional Psychology, 230
Boulder conference, 39
Boulder model, 9
Bush, George H. W., 293

C

The Campbell Collaboration, 250
Canadian Psychological Association
   (CPA), 235
Canadian Register of Health Service
   Providers in Psychology, 235
Carnegie Foundation on the
   Advancement of Teaching, 9
Carnegie Project on the Education
   Doctorate (CPED), 9
CBA, see Curriculum-based assessment
   (CBA)
Center for Research and Practice in
   School Psychology (CRPSP),
   93, 94, 96, 97, 98, 99, 100,
   102
Central Michigan University (CMU),
   217

Certification and licensure for school
   psychologist, 229, 243, 324
ABPP board certification, 234–235
case studies
   Eager, John, MS, EDS, NCSP,
      240–241
   Jane, MS, NCSP, 242
   Susan, PSYD, NCSP, 241–242
clinical supervision, considerations
   for
   supervisor credentialing,
      evaluating, 239–240
   supervisor expertise, evaluating,
      238–239
credentialing school psychologists,
   229–231
doctoral and nondoctoral
   practitioners, roles of
   assessment and diagnosis, 235,
      237
   consultation and collaboration,
      235, 238
   counseling and psychotherapy,
      235, 237
   doctoral programs, 232
   multiplicity of credentials, 233
   national credentialing options,
      233–234
   nondoctoral specialist programs,
      232
Certified school psychologist (CSP),
   232
Child Study Center (CSC), 300
   community-based initiatives,
      301–302
   description, 300–301
   supervision, 302–303
Children's Online Privacy Protection
   Act (COPPA), 161, 162, 163
CHIPS, see Collaborative hierarchical
   intensive programmatic
   supervision (CHIPS)
Civil Rights Act (1964), 171
Client-centered supervision, 92
Clinical Evidence, 250
Clinical supervision, considerations for
   supervisor credentialing, evaluating,
      239–240

supervisor expertise, evaluating,
238–239
CME, see Continuing medical
education (CME)
CMU, see Central Michigan University
(CMU)
The Cochrane Collection, 250
Collaborative competency-based
training, 40–41, 48–49
Collaborative hierarchical intensive
programmatic supervision
(CHIPS), 255–257
Collaborative partnerships in
multicultural training,
115–117
barriers to collaboration, 116–117
benefits of collaboration, 116
Collaborative supervision of internship,
55, 69, 323
case study, 67–68
internship training and practices,
63–67
literature review, 56–57
supporting an intern with a
problem, 67
training for professional roles and
functions, 57–58
types of supervision, 58–63
Collaborative supervision practices,
114
College of Education and Educational
Technology, 300
Committee on Preschool Special
Education (CPSE), 78
Committee on Special Education
(CSE), 78
Community-based initiatives, 301–302
Community-based service learning
programs, 114–115
Community collaboration and
university-based clinics, 295
Competence, defining, 131–134
Competencies Conference: Future
Directions in Education and
Credentialing in Professional
Psychology, 58, 129
Competency Benchmarks Work Group,
56, 58

Competency problems, 132
best practices in evaluating trainee
with, 134–136
personal therapy as remediation for,
132–133
programs for, 133
levels of professional, 140
Competency-based model training,
39–40, 49
Competency-based school psychology
practica, 37, 49–51, 323
collaborative competency-based
training, 40–41
professional competencies, 42–48
completion of work, 47–48
consultation and collaboration,
43–44
data-based decision making and
accountability, 43
dissemination of information, 48
effective instruction and
development of cognitive/
academic skills, 44
home/school/community
collaboration, 46
information technology, 47–48
prevention, crisis intervention
and mental health, 45–46
professional conduct, 48
research and program
evaluation, 46–47
school and systems organization,
45
school psychology practice and
development, 47
socialization and development of
life skills, 44–45
student diversity in development
and learning, 45
supervision in competency-based
model, 41–42
training programs, illustration of,
38–40
Congruent changes in school
psychology, 309, 325
accountability movement, 310–311
case illustration, 315–317
research-into-practice gap, 311–313

scientific findings for public
consumption, 313
teaching school psychologists,
313–315
Contemporary issues in supervision,
19, 323
cultural competence, fostering,
25–26
group versus individual supervision,
23–24
land mines in supervision, 28–32
emotional encounters, 30–31
feedbacks, 29
supervising supervisors, 27–28
supervision as lifelong learning,
26–27
transtheoretical and developmental
of supervision, 20–23
Continuing education, school
psychologist, 245, 259
case study, 255–258
collaborative hierarchical
intensive programmatic
supervision (CHIPS) model,
255–257
continuous professional
improvement plan (CPIP),
257–258
education programs, 245–246
importance of, 247
literature review, 247–251
pedagogical supervisory issues, 255
professional development needs for,
248–249
professional study groups, 250
programming formats, variety,
249–250
psychologists response for, 248
training for professional roles and
functions, 251–254
domains of competency, 252
foundational competencies,
252–253
functional competencies, 253–254
workshops, 249
Continuing medical education (CME),
245
Continuing professional development
(CPD), 246

Continuous professional improvement
plan (CPIP), 257–258
Contra-power harassment, 178
COPPA, see Children's Online Privacy
Protection Act (COPPA)
Council of Directors of School
Psychology Programs, 4
CPA, see Canadian Psychological
Association (CPA)
CPD, see Continuing professional
development (CPD)
CPED, see Carnegie Project on the
Education Doctorate (CPED)
CPIP, see Continuous professional
improvement plan (CPIP)
CPSE, see Committee on Preschool
Special Education (CPSE)
Credentialing school psychologists,
229–230, 322
Crisis intervention literature, 265
characteristic of crisis, 265–266
consequences of crisis, 266–267
responses to crisis, 267–269
Crisis response and intervention role
plays, 280, 283–286
CRPSP, see Center for Research and
Practice in School Psychology
(CRPSP)
CSC, see Child Study Center (CSC)
CSE, see Committee on Special
Education (CSE)
CSP, see Certified school psychologist
(CSP)
Cultural competence for supervisors,
25–26
Curriculum-based assessment (CBA),
315, 317

D

"Data-based problem solver" model,
39
*Davis v. Monroe County Board of
Education*, 172
Developmental supervision, 92
Disability
harassment in school, 174–175
as social phenomenon, 81
case examples

observing harassment, 179–180
    victim of harassment, 180
disability harassment in school,
    174–175
GLBT harassment in school, 174
harassment within school context,
    171–172
peer harassment in school, 172–173
prevention
    harassment and gender
        orientation in school, 177
    sexual and gender harassment in
        school, 175–177
racial and ethnic discrimination in
    school, 175
teaching students to negotiate
    difficult dialogues, 177–179
Discovery-oriented approach to
    supervision process, 22–23
Discrimination and harassment,
    169–170, 181, 323–324
Division of School Psychology
    (Division 16) of the American
    Psychological Association
    (APA), 3, 4
Division of School Psychology of
    the Hellenic Psychological
    Society, 101
Doctor of occupational therapy, 12
Doctor of physical therapy
    (DPT), 12
*Doctoral Psychology Programs
    Meeting Designation Criteria*,
    235
Doctorate in nursing, 12
Domains of School Psychology
    Training and Practice, 263
DPT, see Doctor of physical therapy
    (DPT)
DSM-IV-TR, 265
Due process rights, 146–147

E

Early Head Start program, 302
EdD degree, 236
EEOC, see Equal Employment
    Opportunity Commission
    (EEOC)

Emotional encounters in supervision,
    30–31
Envisioning future, 321–326
Equal Access Act (1984), 216
Equal Employment Opportunity
    Commission (EEOC), 171
Ethical and legal challenges, 153
    case study, 161–164
        accepting responsibility for
            decisions, 164
        alternative decisions for issues,
            163–164
        consulting ethical and legal
            guidelines for issues, 161
        describing parameters of
            situation, 161
        ethical–legal issues, defining,
            161
        evaluating rights and
            responsibilities of affected
            parties, 161–163
    decision-making model in, 157–158
    graduate course in, 158
    negotiating frequent changes in
        code of ethics, 160–161
    practitioner competencies in,
        154–156
    supervisory issues and, 158–159
    training school psychologist in,
        156–157, 159
    types of, 153–154
Ethical decision-making models,
    157–158
Ethical dilemmas in professional
    practice, 153–154
Ethical transgressions, 154
Ethics
    definition, 79
    professionalism and, 189–190
Ethics training in pediatric
    rehabilitation setting, 79–80
Evidence-based interventions, 90,
    312–313

F

Family Educational Rights and Privacy
    Act, 145
Federal statutory law, 216

Feedbacks in supervision, 29–30
Femininity, 206
Field supervisions, 5–7, 8, 27, 29, 40, 325
Field-based training, 111, 195, 196
Flexner Report on Medical Education in the United States, 245
Formative evaluations, 137
Foundational skills, 131
Functional skills, 131
Futures Conference (2002), 10, 100, 311, 325

G

Gay, lesbian, bisexual, or transgender (GLBT), 205
　harassment in school, 174, 208, 209
　preventive measures of harassment, 177
Gay, lesbian, bisexual, or transgender and questioning youth (GLBTQ), 205, 206
　advocating for school polices to protect GLBTQ students, 216–217
　family discords faced by, 209
　health problems in, 208
　literature review, 206–210
　misperceptions regarding homosexuality and transgenderism, 212–213
　providing support and counseling to GLBTQ students, 213–215
　school- and community-based GLBTQ youth support groups, 216
　school support groups for, 210
　STRUTS program, 217–218, 219
　substance use among, 208
　training school psychologist to handle issues of, 210–213
　working with families of GLBTQ students, 215
Gay–straight alliance (GSA), 210, 216
Gebser v. Lago Vista Independent School District, 171–172
Gender identity, 206–207

GLBT, see Gay, lesbian, bisexual, or transgender (GLBT)
GLBTQ, see Gay, lesbian, bisexual, or transgender and questioning youth (GLBTQ)
Goldblum, Peter, 177
Graduate Program of School Psychology, 92, 101, 102
Greek educational system, school psychology in, 92–93
Group versus individual supervision, 23–24, 41–42
GSA, see Gay–straight alliance (GSA)
Guidelines on Discrimination Because of Sex, 171
"Guidelines on Multicultural Education, Training, Research, Practice, and Organizational Change for Psychologists," 112

H

Harassment, 169
　contra-power, 178
　disability, 174–175
　GLBT, 174
　peer, 172–173
　sexual, 169, 170, 171–172
　within school context, 171–172
Higher Education Act, 8
Hillsborough County Public Schools in Florida, 255
Homeland Security Presidential Directive 5, 264
Homosexuality and transgenderism, misperceptions regarding, 212–213
Hostile environment sexual harassment, 171

I

ICHS, see Indiana County Head Start (ICHS)
ICS, see Incident Command System (ICS)
IDEA, see Individuals with Disabilities Education Act (IDEA)

IDM, see Integrated Developmental
Model (IDM)
Incident Command System (ICS), 274
command section, 264
finance section, 265
intelligence section, 265
logistics section, 265
operations section, 264–265
Indiana County Head Start (ICHS),
301, 302
Indiana University of Pennsylvania
(IUP), 300
Individual versus group supervision,
23–24, 41–42
Individuals with Disabilities Education
Act (IDEA), 59, 190, 322
Integrated Developmental Model
(IDM), 22
Integration or infusion model, 92
Interdisciplinary model, 92
Interdisciplinary work, training
implications for, 10
International School Psychology
Association, 98, 99
International School Psychology
Association Colloquium
(2005), 100
Interns
case study, 67–68
model for knowledge
transformation, 66–67
role as consultants, 66
supporting intern with a problem,
67
training activities for, 64–65
Internship supervision, 61–62
Interorganizational Committee (IOC),
4–5
Invitational Conference on the
Future of School Psychology,
97, 99
Iris Technologies, 301
IUP, see Indiana University of
Pennsylvania (IUP)

L

Landro system, 301, 303
LEA supervision, 59–60

Licensed professional counselors
(LPC), 233
Licensed psychologist (LP), 232
Licensed specialist in school
psychology (LSSP), 231
Line supervision, 58–59
Local education agency supervisor, 55
Louisiana School Psychological
Association, 64
Louisiana School Psychology
Internship Consortium, 56,
63
Louisiana State University Health
Sciences Center, 63
LP, see Licensed psychologist (LP)
LPC, see Licensed professional
counselors (LPC)
LSSP, see Licensed specialist in school
psychology (LSSP)

M

Management of Domestic Incidents,
264
Masculinity, 206
Massachusetts Department of
Education, 207
*The Meritor Savings Bank FSB v.
Vinson Supreme Court*, 171
Misperceptions regarding
homosexuality and
transgenderism, 212–213
Model Act for the State Licensure
of Psychologists (1987), 246
Multicultural competence and
diversity, 124, 323
bilingual and community issues,
cases involving, 123
collaborative partnerships in,
115–117
collaborative supervision practices,
114
community-based service learning
programs, 114–115
gender-related issues, cases
involving, 122–123
literature review, 113–114
professional development schools
(PDSs), 114

reasons for developing cross-cultural competence, 111–112
research gap, techniques to address, 117–118
supervision issues, 118–122
Multicultural supervision
advantages of, 120–121
challenges of, 121–122
definition, 120
Multilevel university-based ethics training, 158
Multitrait evaluations, 138

N

Nabozny v. Podlesny, 216–217
NASP, see National Association of School Psychologists (NASP)
National Association of School Psychologists (NASP), 3, 4, 5, 12, 19, 101, 112, 113,118, 119, 120, 129, 130, 153, 156, 159, 160, 170, 189, 206, 231, 232, 245, 249, 258, 263, 294, 297, 325, 326
approved provider (AP) system, 246
Ethical and Professional Practices Committee, 161
Guidelines for the Provision of School Psychological Services, 118
Principles for Professional Ethics (2000), 161
Professional Conduct Manual, 130
Professional Growth Committee, 251
Standard IV: Performance-Based Program Assessment and Accountability, 130
Standards for Training and Field Placement Programs in School Psychology, 37, 129, 252, 259
National Center for Educational Statistics, 169–170
National Center for Educational Statistics to the Integrated Postsecondary Education Data System, 12

Nationally certified counselors (NCC), 233
National Certified School Psychologist (NCSP), 231, 232, 233, 246, 251
National Council for Accreditation of Teacher Education (NCATE), 326
National Council on Accreditation of Teacher Education Programs, 232
National Incident Management System (NIMS), 264, 274
National Matching Service, 64
National Register of Health Service Providers in Psychology, 235, 251
National School Psychology Certification Board (NSCPB), 231, 243, 246
National Service Act, 293
NCATE, see National Council for Accreditation of Teacher Education (NCATE)
NCC, see Nationally certified counselors (NCC)
NCSP, see National Certified School Psychologist (NCSP)
Neurocognitive domains, 76
Neuropsychological testing supervision, 74–77
NIMS, see National Incident Management System (NIMS)
No Child Left Behind Act, 190, 309, 310, 311, 313, 322
NSPCB, see National School Psychology Certification Board (NSCPB)

O

"The Olympic Spirit Through Children's Voice," 98
Olympic values and ideals, 98–99

P

Parents, Friends, and Families of Lesbians and Gays (PFLAG), 215

PDS, see Professional development
  schools (PDS)
Pediatric hospitals, supervising
  school psychology interns in,
  71, 323
  aims of supervision, 72
  conflicts among clients, families
    and staff (case study), 84–85
  consultation with parents and
    medical personnel (case
    study), 82–83
  consultation with staff and families,
    77–79
  dangerousness and confidentiality
    issues (case study), 83–84
  diversity, culture and worldview in,
    80–82
  ethics training, 79–80
  evaluations conducted on pediatric
    patients, 75–76
  neuropsychological testing
    supervision, 74–77
  psychotherapy supervision,
    72–74
Pediatric psychologist
  case studies illustrating work of,
    82–85
    conflicts among clients, families
      and staff, 84–85
    consultation with parents and
      medical personnel, 82–83
    dangerousness and
      confidentiality issues, 83–84
  consultation liaison role of, 78–79
Peer harassment, 172–173
Peer supervision, 62–63
Pennsylvania Department of Education
  (PDE), 8, 303
Personal psychotherapy for
  remediation plan, 144–145
PFLAG, see Parents, Friends, and
  Families of Lesbians and Gays
  (PFLAG)
Planned Experience Competencies
  Evaluation forms, 48
*Position Statement on Supervision in
  School Psychology*, 118
PPD, see Professional practice
  doctorate (PPD)
Practice doctorate in nursing, 12

Preinternship practicum training, 38,
  48–49
Principle D—Justice, 119
Problematic behaviors, 129–131, 149
  action letters, 141–142
  assessment methodology, 138–140
  best practices for evaluating trainee
    with, 134–136
  competence, defining, 131–134
  due process rights, 146–147
  evaluation policies and procedures,
    137
  identifying, 140–141
  outcomes of remediation plans,
    145–146
  philosophy of evaluation, 137
  psychotherapy as remediation,
    144–145
  remediation plans, 142–144
  skills assessment, 138
  trainee assessment, phase model of,
    147–148
Professional competencies, 42–48
  completion of work, 47–48
  consultation and collaboration,
    43–44
  data-based decision making and
    accountability, 43
  dissemination of information, 48
  effective instruction and
    development of cognitive/
    academic skills, 44
  home/school/community
    collaboration, 46
  information technology, 47–48
  prevention, crisis intervention and
    mental health, 45–46
  professional conduct, 48
  research and program evaluation,
    46–47
  school and systems organization,
    45
  school psychology practice and
    development, 47
  socialization and development of
    life skills, 44–45
  student diversity in development
    and learning, 45
Professional development schools
  (PDS), 114

Professional identity, developing, 185, 201; see also Professionalism
  case study, 199–200
  characteristics of professionalism, 191
  current legislation, 190–191
  difficult student, challenges of, 198–199
  ethics and professionalism, 189–190
  female student challenges, 197–198
  literature review, 186–189
  pedagogical and supervisory issues, 195–197
  professional reputation, building, 194–195
  professionals culture, 191–194
Professional practice doctorate (PPD), 9, 12, 13
Professional reputation, building, 194–195
Professional supervision, 20, 27, 60–61
Professionalism
  characteristics of, 191
  competencies associated with, 187, 188
  cultural differences and, 193
  definition, 186
  dressings and, 192
  ethics and, 189–190
  personal attributes, 187–188
  trust and, 189
  values of, 188
  writing reports and, 193
Program for the Promotion of Mental Health and Learning, 95–96
Program for the Promotion of School Community Well-Being, 96
Psychodynamic supervision, 92
Psychological education, 268–269
Psychological first aid intervention, elements of, 273
Psychological first aid observation coding sheet, 286
Psychological triage practice, 276, 277
Psychotherapy supervision, 72–74

Q

Quid pro quo sexual harassment, 171

R

Racial and ethnic discrimination in school, 175
Remediation plans, 142–144
  personal psychotherapy as component of, 144–145
  outcomes of, 145–146
Research-into-practice gap, 311–312
Response to intervention (RTI) movement, 311, 315, 317
Role plays, 273–275
Rosenfield, Sylvia, 238

S

Sample Program Policies and Procedures Related to Stages of Assessment Process, 148
Sample Program Policy Listing of Relevant Professional Skills, 139
Sample psychological first aid scripts, 276–280, 281–283
Schemas, 74
School psychologists
  crisis intervention experiences of in-service, 270–271
  crisis intervention training, 269–270
  demand for evolution of, 9
  instructional activities for training preservice, 271
    collaboration institute, 275
    crisis intervention scripts, 272–273
    field observations and/or interview, 271
    mental health community service volunteer, 275
    psychological triage practice, 272
    resource file, 275–276
    review written crisis intervention plans, 271–272

role plays, 273–275
training programs, 3–5
School psychology
 challenges in profession of, 90
 clinics, 296
 current trends of, 90
 theoretical approaches in, 90–91
*School Psychology: A Blueprint for
  Training and Practice III*, 38,
  39, 113, 156, 219, 252, 257,
  258, 259
 foundation competencies, 252, 253
 functional competencies, 253, 254
School psychology interns, 71
 challenges faced by, 77, 79
 countertransference reactions, 74
 role as consultants, 77–79
 supervision of, 76–77
 test batteries and, 75
 transference reactions, 73–74
School Psychology Program Student
  Evaluation Form, 135–136
School Psychology Review, 57
School Psychology Specialty Council, 4
School Psychology Synarchy, see
  School Psychology Specialty
  Council
School psychology training, 3–4
 current trends in, 10–11
 new directions of, 11–13
 programs, 5–9, 149
School-based crisis intervention,
  collaboration in, 263, 324
 crisis intervention literature, 265
 characteristic of crisis, 265–266
 consequences of crisis, 266–267
 responses to crisis, 267–269
 multidisciplinary school crisis
   response, 264–265
 pedagogical and supervisory issues,
   271
  collaboration institute, 275
  crisis intervention scripts,
    272–273
  field observations and/or
    interview, 271
  mental health community service
    volunteer, 275
  psychological triage practice, 272

resource file, 275–276
review written crisis intervention
  plans, 271–272
role plays, 273–275
training examples, 27
 crisis response and intervention
   role plays, 280, 283–286
 psychological triage practice,
   276, 277
 sample psychological first aid
   scripts, 276–280, 281–283
training for professional roles and
  functions, 269
 crisis intervention experiences
   and practices, 270–271
 preservice preparation for school
   crisis intervention, 269–270
Scientific findings for public
  consumption, 313
Self-managed model of supervision, 26
Separate course model, 92
Service learning, 114, 115
Sexual behavior, 206
Sexual harassment, 169, 170
 hostile environment, 171
 quid pro quo, 171
 preventive measures, 175–177
Sexual orientation, 206, 207
Social and Emotional Learning
  program, 100–101
Sponsor Approval System, 245
Stage model for ethical competence,
  154–155
"Stand and deliver" education
  modalities, 7
*Standards for Training and Field
  Placement Programs in
  School Psychology*, 112
Strengthening Teen Resilience Under
  Tough Situations (STRUTS),
  217–218, 219
STRUTS, see Strengthening Teen
  Resilience Under Tough
  Situations (STRUTS)
Suicide risk assessment, 273, 280,
  281–283
Summative evaluations, 137
Summit on the Future of Psychology
  Practice, 10

SUMSearch, 250
Supervision
    administrative, 20
    advantages of multicultural,
        120–121
    behavioral, 92
    challenges of multicultural,
        121–122
    client-centered, 92
    in competency-based model,
        41–42
    contemporary issues in, see
        Contemporary issues in
        supervision
    definition, 19, 55
    developmental, 92
    general framework for, 118–119
    goal of, 56, 72
    internship, 61–62
    LEA, 59–60
    line, 58–59
    multicultural approach to,
        119–120
    neuropsychological testing, 74–77
    peer, 62–63
    professional, 20, 60–61
    psychodynamic, 92
    psychotherapy, 72–74
    types of, 58–63
    university, 62
Supervision of Psychotherapists, 23
Supervisors
    criteria for choosing, 195
    qualities of effective, 27
    relationship with supervisee, 30–31
"Supervisory pool" concept, 26

T

TEAC, see Teacher Education
        Accreditation Council
        (TEAC)
Teach for America, 313
Teacher Education Accreditation
        Council (TEAC), 326
"Tender Tiny Wing," 102
Texas State Board of Examiners in
        Psychology, 230
Thayer Conference (1954), 11, 57

Title IX of the Education Amendments
        of 1972, 171, 217
Trainee assessment, phase model of,
        147–148
Trainers of School Psychologists, 4
Transgender, 207
Translational research, 7–8
Transtheoretical model of supervision,
        20–22
Traumatic stressor, 263, 265, 266, 267
Trip Database, 250

U

University and school partnership,
        promoting, 89, 103–104,
        323
    alternative school psychological
        services, data-based model of,
        93–94
    community outreach, provision
        of alternative service in
        community, 101–102
    alumni network, 102
    crisis seminars, 101–102
    open seminars, 101
    publications, 102
    social activities in prevention
        programs, 102
    current trends of school psychology,
        90
    development of prevention
        programs in school
        community, 95–99
    awareness building on issues of
        diversity, 98
    crisis intervention in school
        community, 98
    cross-cultural program for
        building awareness on
        Olympic ideals, 98–99
    evolution process an level of
        intervention, 96–98
    Program for the Promotion of
        Mental Health and Learning,
        95–96
    psychoeducational interventions
        for children with emotional
        disabilities, 99

future of school psychology
   and alternative school
   psychological services,
   99–101
  elementary teachers, 100–101
  graduate students of school
   psychology, 100
  Greek educational system, school
   psychology in, 92–93
  models of training and supervision,
   91–92
  projects for, 95–102
  theoretical approaches in school
   psychology, 90–91
University-based clinics, 291, 304,
  324
  advantages for community,
   294–295
  benefits from community
   collaboration, 295
  building bridges with community,
   296–297
  case illustrations, 300–303
  characteristics of, 292–293
  Child Study Center (CSC), 300
   community-based initiatives,
    301–302
   description, 300–301
   supervision, 302–303
  issues associated with
   developmental of, 293–294

literature review, 292
  training and supervision, issues in,
   297–299
University faculty, 5–7, 8, 40, 325
University of Athens, 92, 93, 94, 98,
  99, 100, 101, 102
University of Hartford, 232–233
University of Maryland, 238
University supervision, 42, 62
U.S. Department of Education, 8,
  310
U.S. Department of Education's
  National Center for
  Education Statistics, 111
U.S. Department of Homeland
  Security, 274

V

Vail Conference, 9

W

Witmer, Lightner, 292
Women
  challenges faced by female students,
   197–198
  in profession of education,
   169–170
Worldviews, 81